Early Modern Skepticism and the
Origins of Toleration

D1526182

APPLICATIONS OF POLITICAL THEORY

Series Editors: Harvey Mansfield, Harvard University, and Daniel J. Mahoney, Assumption College

This series encourages analysis of the applications of political theory to various domains of thought and action. Such analysis will include works on political thought and literature, statesmanship, American political thought, and contemporary political theory. The editors also anticipate and welcome examinations of the place of religion in public life and commentary on classic works of political philosophy.

Early Modern Skepticism and the Origins of Toleration
    edited by Alan Levine

Machiavelli's Romans: Liberty and Greatness in the Discourses on Livy
    by J. Patrick Coby (forthcoming)

Well-Ordered License: On the Unity of Machiavelli's Thought
    by Markus Fischer (forthcoming)

Privilege and Liberty
    by Aurel Kolnai, edited by Daniel J. Mahoney (forthcoming)

Early Modern Skepticism and the Origins of Toleration

Edited by
Alan Levine

LEXINGTON BOOKS
Lanham • Boulder • New York • Oxford

LEXINGTON BOOKS

Published in the United States of America
by Lexington Books
4720 Boston Way, Lanham, Maryland 20706

12 Hid's Copse Road
Cumnor Hill, Oxford OX2 9JJ, England

British Library Cataloguing in Publication Information Available

Library of Congress Cataloging-in-Publication Data

Early modern skepticism and the origins of toleration / edited by Alan
   Levine.
      p.   cm. — (Applications of political theory)
   Includes bibliographical references and index.
   ISBN 0-7391-0023-8 (cloth : alk. paper). — ISBN 0-7391-0024-6
(pbk. : alk. paper)
   1. Religious tolerance—History. 2. Skepticism—History.
I. Levine, Alan, 1961–   . II. Series
BR1610.E27   1999
   322.44 '2 '09—dc21   98–47858
                                                              CIP

Printed in the United States of America

⊖™ The paper used in this publication meets the minimum requirements of American
National Standard for Information Sciences—Permanence of Paper for Printed Library
Materials, ANSI Z39.48–1984.

Contents

Preface

This book had its origins in my research on Montaigne. While assessing the connection between skepticism and toleration in his thought, I wanted to read secondary literature on this connection in the thought of other authors. To my surprise, little or nothing had been written explicitly on this important connection. The idea for this volume was born.

I am grateful that so many wise and learned scholars wanted to contribute to the volume, many of whom have became my friends. Several of the essays contained herein were presented at earlier conferences. Versions of chapters one, three, and ten were presented at a panel entitled "Skepticism and the Origins of Toleration" at the American Political Science Association annual meeting in Chicago, 1995. Versions of chapters one, two, four and five were presented at a panel entitled "Early Modern Skepticism and the Origins of Toleration" at the American Political Science Association annual meeting in San Francisco, September, 1996. Similarly, versions of chapters ten, eleven and twelve were presented at a conference entitled "Toleration and Skepticism in the French Enlightenment" held at American University in May, 1997. I would like to thank American University for the New Faculty Research Grant which made this latter conference possible. Versions of chapters eight and nine were presented at Yale University in 1992 as part of a Political Theory Workshop funded by the Bradley Foundation on the theme of toleration. I would like to thank Steven B. Smith for calling Shirley Letwin's paper to my attention and her family for permission to publish it posthumously. Also, several contributors served as commentators at the above mentioned panels or were in the audience when these papers were presented. This has helped give the volume its tight interconnectedness. I would like to thank all of these people for their contributions and moral support throughout the time it took to bring this book to fruition. Finally, I would like to thank Susan Reynolds for the good cheer she brought to much of the computer work and Brian Della Torre and Joselle Alexander for their work on the index.

-Alan Levine
Washington, DC
January, 1999

1

INTRODUCTION:
THE PREHISTORY OF TOLERATION AND
VARIETIES OF SKEPTICISM

Alan Levine

Toleration is one of the most attractive and widespread ideals of our day. It is a cornerstone of liberalism, a key protection for both individual citizens and minority groups, and in general is the predominant ethos of all moral civilizations in the modern world. But what is the justification for toleration? Is toleration a moral imperative based on natural or divine rights? A pragmatic way of dealing with pluralistic conflict? Or does it somehow just seems obvious? Since toleration has not been the obvious moral policy throughout most of the world in most of recorded history, nor indeed even throughout most of the world today, some more compelling justification must be offered for it. Justifying toleration is an important philosophical and political issue, because if we cannot explain *why* it is necessary and good, the institutions that uphold it cannot help but be weakened.

The problem is that while toleration has never been more widely applied than in the Western world today, the traditional grounds upon which it has been defended are becoming difficult to justify philosophically. Toleration has been traditionally justified by appeals to rights, political or metaphysical, yet many philosophers today find these arguments problematic. This book systematically examines arguments for toleration based on a largely forgotten tradition: toleration derived from skepticism. By focusing on the connection between skepticism and toleration, this book tries to bridge the gap between the political practice of and desire for toleration on the one hand and the problems of philosophically justifying it on the other. Its theme is universal, but its arguments are particularly timely today.

This book does two important new things. First, it takes a fresh look at the founding of modernity by focusing on and reappraising a strand of modern thought that has been vastly under-appreciated. A few books have focused on the role of skepticism and atheism during the time period (the Reformation to the revolutions) that this book covers, but none focuses on the link between atheism, irreligion, or skepticism *and toleration*.[1] Similarly, there are a few books on the history of toleration, but none focuses on the particularly skeptical arguments for it.[2] This book examines the link between skepticism and toleration by way of in-depth studies of several major early modern thinkers.

Second, this book explores the contemporary relevance of these skeptically-based arguments for toleration. The early moderns have much to teach us because, writing without an established tradition of toleration to which they could appeal, they were forced to think critically about the philosophical foundations of their ideas. In doing so, they made arguments that are wanting today. This book aims to learn from the early moderns and explicate their arguments in a way that reveals their relevance to contemporary debates.

Each essay in this volume asks the crucial questions about the linkage between skepticism and toleration which are all too often ignored. How can a skeptic argue for anything, let alone ethics and toleration? And since one can be skeptical of many different things and of the same thing to a different extent, each essay asks about the kinds of skeptical doubting each author discussed does. What are their ethics, and how do they argue for ethics from doubt? And, more generally, is skepticism a fruitful ground from which to argue for toleration? At the same time -- and very importantly -- this volume identifies the non-skeptical aspects and commitments of each thinker discussed. While showing the skeptical basis of each author's commitment to toleration, this volume also shows the *limits* to each author's skeptical doubting. For if one doubted everything, on what basis would morality be possible? Most of the thinkers discussed in this book worry that the doubting of accepted truths could lead to political instability or the total collapse of ethical standards. They therefore limited their skepticism, and this book explores the differing degrees and manners in which they did so. Analysis of their varying approaches to these questions reveals that just as toleration cannot be founded on pure skepticism, so all the paths which flow from skepticism do not necessarily lead to toleration.

I. Rights-Based Justifications and Their Problems

Liberalism has traditionally justified toleration not through appeals to skepticism but to rights, rights that exist outside of one's subjective self. To the extent that others possess them, rights serve as a check, a limit, on one's actions towards them. The possession of rights entitles one to a certain sphere in which one is not to be denied, repressed, or victimized by others. Thought and action within this protected sphere, no matter how objectionable, cannot legitimately be subjected to political interference and are to be tolerated by both the state and other citizens. The basis of these rights, however, is a much disputed question.

Liberal rights-based conceptions of toleration are justified by three kinds of arguments: metaphysical, prudential, and political. Toleration has until recently been justified by natural and divine right. Today, however, few if any political theorists find these metaphysical foundations credible; still, they are unwilling to abandon this key tenet of liberalism. These theorists either turn to prudentially based arguments for toleration or simply argue that we all agree that we should have it. However, each of these three kinds of justification is problematic.

The metaphysical basis of rights is difficult, if not impossible, to prove. America's *Declaration of Independence* asserts that it is "self-evident" that human beings *naturally* possess rights, and to make this argument *The Declaration* appeals to nature and nature's God. However, this claim is no longer "self-evident." The scientific and historicist revolutions of the past 150 years, signified by the names Darwin, Einstein, Hegel, Marx, Nietzsche, and Freud, have thoroughly problematized the original liberal conception of rights. Many theorists consider both God and nature to be historical constructions. Others consider appeals to God to be too divisive and controversial. In a pluralistic society, whose God justifies rights? How is God known? And by whom? Similarly, the Enlightenment idea that scientific progress would reveal a natural basis for morality now seems quaint and hopelessly naive. The progress of the natural sciences has led them to muteness on the question of human rights, not to definitive answers. Science is silent on moral issues. It thus seems that any convincing case for toleration must either refute historicism and science or avoid metaphysical justification.

Liberal thinkers have attempted to overcome the metaphysical uncertainty of rights by making both a prudential and political argument for toleration. The prudential argument for toleration is simple: prudence dictates that one restrict one's pursuit of self-interest to secure the rest of it. It admits that individuals do not have natural or divine rights but argues that one should relinquish one's right to victimize others because not to do so would risk being subject to victimization oneself. A restatement of the golden rule on prudential (not moral) grounds, it is most famously captured by Hobbes' attempt to overcome the fear and horrors of the state of nature. To secure stability, peace, and the goods that come with them, individuals, with no metaphysical pretenses, (do, have, or would) institute government and set up recognized punishments to keep citizens law-abiding.[3] The conventionally created law thus determines the "rights" that individuals will have and the extent to which toleration of others' views, property, and honors must be respected.

The contractarians who make this prudential argument tend, however, to have a narrow definition of self-interest which is not happily compatible with the contractual argument itself. If self-interest is one's only guide, and self-interest is, as they argue, understood as acquisition (of either power, glory, or property), the optimal position for a person might be for everyone else to follow the law while violating it with impunity oneself. Why shouldn't one steal or kill if one could get away with it? There is no reason not to -- except fear of external authority. Most people, according to Glaucon's challenge in Plato's *Republic,* might judge that it is better to give up the greatest good (unlimited pursuit of self-interest) in order to avoid the greatest evil (suffering at the hands of others), but this prudential (not moral) calculation might not persuade everyone, as indeed it does not persuade

Glaucon.[4] Why should the strong or powerful, who might not be overwhelmed by Hobbes' fear of violent death, tolerate others instead of repressing or inflicting cruelty on them? Why should they care about others at all? The prudential argument alone cannot answer these questions. An argument based on self-interest plays into the hands of people like Nietzsche and his followers who argue for the pursuit of one's interest unlimited by concern for others. Disparities in power -- real or perceived -- whether based on natural or social factors mitigate the effect of the prudential argument.

Moreover, the prudential argument for toleration might not only fail to persuade the strong, those who are in a position to be intolerant, but it might actually increase everyone's propensity towards harming others by emphasizing the pursuit of earthly goods. To the extent that liberalism tries to inculcate toleration by undermining people's religious convictions, it opens new avenues for victimizing others. The taming and debunking of religion is desirable to prevent such religious persecution as the horrible wars of religion that racked France in the sixteenth century and out of which the liberal tradition of toleration originally grew. But by directing people's attention to the pursuit of earthly goods, the prudential argument lifts the self-restraints that religion teaches. After all, the Ten Commandments not only privilege a particular God, but they categorically condemn murder and covetousness.

Contemporary America's two leading political theorists, John Rawls and Richard Rorty, attempt to address these issues by rejecting metaphysical justifications for toleration, but their proposed "political" solutions overly rely on habit and convention.[5] Rather than fully justify their principles, they choose to appeal to "our" contemporary political intuitions and preferences. By "our" intuitions, Rorty and Rawls refer to the beliefs of Western, democratic capitalists at the end of the twentieth century. Far from attempting to justify liberalism to outsiders or on first principles, Rorty and Rawls prefer not to take up the challenge. Content to harmonize our pre-existing opinions, they do not and cannot address the fundamental challenges that Nietzsche, for example, poses.[6] They rely instead on political traditions. Their work is compelling to the extent that one accepts their premises. They supply *political* arguments that might work in a polity where everyone shares their views (if a place without debate could be called a polity at all). However, their views are not compelling *philosophically* insofar as they do not even try to justify the presuppositions or intuitions of "our" age. Even if all citizens of late twentieth-century, Western style democracies agree with Rawls and Rorty, cultural consensus does not make a view true. But all such citizens do not agree.

Thus, there are serious problems with all three attempts -- metaphysical, prudential, and political -- to justify a rights-based argument for toleration. Exasperation with these problems, especially with metaphysics and "foundations," has made attempts to justify toleration on a skeptical basis a popular link to draw. However, it is one that is too facilely made. For example, in recent years there has been an attempt to justify toleration based on postmodern insights that take to heart a certain kind of skepticism. Postmodern thinkers who reject the existence of "objective truth" criticize the idea of "rights" as totalitarian, because to be forced to follow any "truth" is considered too restrictive, too confining, and a mere mask for political, religious, economic, or cultural domination. Nietzsche, Foucault, and other postmoderns argue against the "totalized," "dominating" visions of the past in order to liberate radically the subjectivity of the self, be it expressed by "will," "instinct," or "the body."[7] Several liberal political theorists have attempted to use this insight by arguing that if everyone were to privilege self-realization, as the postmoderns propose, we could live fruitful, flourishing, and diverse lives side by side with no one condemning or squelching anyone else's individuality. In other words, they attempt to justify liberalism and toleration based on the postmodern view of self-fashioning.[8]

Such radical subjectivity alone, however, cannot justify toleration either. If nothing is true, why shouldn't one follow one's subjective drives regardless of whether or not they hurt other people? As Dostoyevsky wrote in *The Brothers Karamazov*, "If nothing is true, everything is permitted."[9] The oft articulated liberal response to this problem is insufficient. All values and all ways of life, it is argued, should be tolerated, because if none is "right," neither is any wrong. No view, it is said, is more true, more just, or better than any other, so all should be accepted. According to this argument, moral skepticism leads to toleration. Indeed, moral skepticism is characteristic of most post-WW II attempts to justify toleration. This argument, however, cannot in principle exclude the toleration of intolerance. The views of a passionately committed intolerant person would be just as valid as the views of a tolerant person. Moral skepticism thus does not necessarily lead to toleration.

While there is no necessary connection between skepticism and toleration, part of the problem with recent attempts at justifying toleration is a lack of deep thinking on the range of possible connections between toleration and skepticism. Other recent movements in moral and political thought often try to make this connection in a historical void. It is almost as if these theoreticians had never confronted Nietzsche or believe that sincerely motivated people could never have taken the Spanish Inquisition or Nazism seriously. What Amy Gutmann has said of communitarianism ("the communitarian critics want us to live in Salem, but not to believe in witches") is even truer for contemporary "care" and "virtue" theory.[10] These movements argue for tolerance and morality by making assumptions about human behavior, past and present, that are totally devoid of historical reality and knowledge of the history of philosophy. They are skeptical of universal truth but seem to think that everyone basically thinks like them. They attempt to draw general conclusions about virtue or caring without fully exploring the ramifications of their views. These kinds of naive and historically uninformed errors must be remedied. While the connection between skepticism and toleration is *à la mode*, current inquiries too often lack breadth and depth.

By focusing only on arguments from a skeptical basis, this book shares the current emphasis on non-foundationalism, but it does so by re-examining arguments that predate the traditional foundations that are so scorned today. And many theorists, such as Rorty and Rawls, explicitly say that the traditions in which they operate emerged from the religious wars of the sixteenth century -- exactly the tradition upon which this book aims to shed light. A convincing defense of toleration must avoid both metaphysical "truth" and its opposite, complete subjectivity. It also cannot unduly appeal to the conventions, habits, or opinions of a particular place and time. The essays in this book reflect seriously on these conundrums.

To get a grasp on the slippery and potentially dangerous connection between skepticism and toleration, this book aims simultaneously to do two things. First, it aims to think through some of the most influential early modern theorists' views of skepticism and to show how they lead to different kinds and amounts of toleration. This book will not once and for all solve the problem of the nature of the connection between skepticism and toleration, but by revealing multiple possible links between these two key concepts of political philosophy, it aims to prevent simple-minded assumptions. Grasping the possibilities is the first step towards clarity. But this volume also aims to do something else: to specify and examine the other factors that make these authors' arguments work. For if skepticism does not necessarily lead to toleration, skepticism must be limited or supplemented by some other conviction, idea, or aim in order to reach a tolerant conclusion. This book aims to identify both the nature and extent of the skepticism of the authors it considers and the nature and extent of the authors' other attachments. To show the scope of the multiple possible connections between skepticism and toleration, both tasks must be done simultaneously.

II. The Pre-History of Toleration

This volume begins in the sixteenth century, when toleration emerged as an important political issue. Until then, no important philosopher had argued for toleration as a political principle. To appreciate the radical nature of this change, it is necessary to sketch briefly the ideas on toleration of some key thinkers before the sixteenth century. First, however, we must define toleration itself.

Toleration is a curious idea. Defined as an acceptance of difference, it is a cornerstone of liberal values and essential to many of the freedoms that liberal democracies cherish. Originally, and still often today, toleration implied an only grudging acceptance of these differences, a *principled* rejection of the thing to be tolerated and acceptance of it only as a *practical* expedient. Toleration was traditionally the second best policy for those who practiced it; the ideal was having things completely ordered one's own way. One might dislike, distrust, even detest some idea or practice but tolerate it because one cannot eliminate it at an acceptable price. Such was the political origin of toleration in the stalemated religious wars in France.[11]

Thus, practitioners of toleration embrace something as their own and reject the thing they tolerate. This should not be confused with an openness that is alive to the possibility that the thing in question, whether it be an idea or practice, may represent some truth or good. Openness delights in different possibilities; toleration, in the strict sense, accepts them only begrudgingly.

No philosophers in ancient Greece or Rome explicitly argued for toleration as a political principle. Instead, they possessed both a genuine openness towards other philosophers on the one hand, while at the same time denying that such openness was a sound basis on which to build a polity. These thinkers wanted to prove their views to each other, thrived on argumentation, and never persecuted those of differing opinions, but they debated which concrete view society should adopt, not that a good state should tolerate all views. They practiced toleration while denying it theoretical justification.

Plato never advocates toleration as a political principle, although there are aspects of his writing that seem to imply toleration. For example, Socrates' famous dictum that the unexamined life is not worth living seems to imply that each person should be free to examine himself as he sees fit, free from the interference of others. Thus, it is striking that such freedom exists for no one in Plato's account of the just city, except for the philosophers who reluctantly rule it. Accordingly, Plato scorns the idea of free speech. In his *Republic,* he recommends tight state control of writers, artists, and musicians, and he does not celebrate, but rather mocks, the unruliness of democracy.[12] Of course, it can be well argued that Plato and Socrates would be happiest living in the freedom provided by a democracy, because only under that regime can philosophy flourish (and without the burden of ruling).[13] Nonetheless, it is notable that this is not the regime that Plato recommends. The closest Plato, indeed any ancient, comes to advocating institutionalized free expression is the Nocturnal Council in Plato's *Laws*, where selected citizens are encouraged to state and debate their real opinions on many subjects for which the state has official, legislated answers. However, not only does this Council meet secretly at night, but its very existence is a state secret, unknown to the other citizens.[14] This limited, secret freedom is hardly an argument for toleration. It means that different views by citizens will not be tolerated in public. Plato does not advocate toleration simply, because the same freedom that enables good people to flourish enables bad ones to become worse. Justice demands not freedom but a noble lie.

Aristotle does not explicitly praise -- nor even list -- toleration as one of the virtues. As with Plato, however, there are aspects of his thought that seem conducive to toleration. His dialectical method of weighing and considering a whole array of others' opinions is the epitome of a tolerant attitude, except that he proceeds to refute (at least partially) all other views. In the *Nichomachean Ethics*, Aristotle speaks of friendship and goodwill towards others, even strangers, but he is always careful to specify that these are only to be practiced in the right way, at the right time, as the man of practical wisdom would do it.[15] Perhaps Aristotle never explicitly argues for toleration in the *Ethics*, because his conception of self-fulfillment is not subjective but based on universally true principles. One should be striving for virtue, not merely the freedom to do whatever one wants.

In Western history before the sixteenth century, however, toleration did exist as a political practice. Toleration of different religious views was a long-standing practice in ancient Rome. Conquered peoples were allowed to keep their gods and religious practices as long as they also accepted Rome's. This is how the pantheon grew and why Jews and Christians who refused the condition were persecuted. As we shall see in this volume, this tolerant policy helped shape Montaigne's and other important early modern thinkers' thoughts on the subject. As far as I know, however, no Roman philosopher advocated such a policy as part of his description of the best state. Cicero, for example, does not advocate toleration in either his *Republic* or *Laws*. And Marcus Aurelius, widely regarded as one of the most enlightened men of Roman times, actually persecuted Christians.

Before the sixteenth century, certain Christian arguments were made for a limited toleration on religious grounds. Early Christians such as Tertullian and Lactantius argued for the separation of church and state and freedom of conscience on the basis of New Testament declarations such as "Render... unto Caesar the things which are Caesar's; and unto God the things that are God's."[16] But while separate from the state, the realm of conscience was to be ruled by the Church, not left to each individual's conscience. The parable of the tares, which cautions against pulling weeds lest some of the crop be plucked too,[17] led to an argument for toleration based on human fallibility, and (following Saint Paul) was advanced by Origen and St. Cyprian. God alone, it was argued, knew what was truly in someone's heart and he would judge on judgment day. Men due to their fallibility, should not judge, let alone punish, each other on earth. A third Christian argument for toleration had to do with the nature of belief itself. Forced belief was considered to be worthless, because faith had to be embraced freely and be held sincerely for salvation to be achieved. Finally, it was argued that Christian love and charity should be directed towards the unenlightened, weak, or misguided, not violence. Coming from St. Paul, this was deemed the proper attitude towards unbelievers.[18] Readers of this volume will note how various restatements of these Christian arguments are used by early modern thinkers, either sincerely or to appeal to potential persecutors on their own terms.

But for each of these Christian arguments, there were Christian counter-arguments that carried the day. While arguing that faith cannot be forced, St. Augustine still asked "what death is worse for the soul than the freedom to err?"[19] Unfortunately, Augustine's less tolerant remark was the more influential. Throughout medieval times -- as the Arianists, Donatists, Catharists, Albigenists, Manicheans, and Hussites not to mention pagans, Jews, and Muslims discovered -- toleration was extremely limited, and Augustine was the fountainhead of arguments both for and against it. St. Aquinas agreed with Augustine that *if* bad "tares" could be known, they could be pulled, although it should be noted that he was much harsher on heretics than on those outside the faith. "To accept the faith," he argued, "is a matter of free will, but to hold it once it has been accepted, is a matter of necessity."[20] Thus, he concluded that heretics "must be compelled, even bodily, to fulfil what they have promised, and to maintain what they have once accepted."[21] And since Aquinas saw heresy as contagious, he said that a twice repentant heretic was too inconstant in faith and should be killed.[22]

The Christian humanists of the fifteenth century were the first to extend significantly the sphere of toleration beyond Christians, but they saw toleration as a means towards achieving doctrinal unity. Nicholas of Cusa, Marsilio Ficino, and Pico della Mirandola argued for toleration on the grounds that all the world's religions and great philosophies led to the same truth -- a Christian one. Arguing that each culture had something to contribute to our knowledge of truth, they each or separately were willing to tolerate Catholics, Greek Orthodox, Hussites, and even Jews, Muslims, Turks, Persians, Tartars, Hindus, and Platonists. (Erasmus used the same argument to preach reconciliation with the Protestants.) But their limit for toleration was stated by Ficino; he rejected atheism because "nothing displeases God so much as being scorned."[23] These Christian humanists might have been included in this volume because they were open to a wide array of cultures and ways of thought. In the end, though, they are not fundamentally skeptical, but rather optimistic that all cultures lead to the same truth.

Similarly, much of the toleration controversy that raged throughout the sixteenth century had a fundamentally religious character. One of the best known sixteenth century defenders of toleration who is not discussed in this volume is the French humanist, Sebastian Castellio. Castellio made direct ethical and emotional appeals for toleration by doubting the morality of persecution: "To kill a man is not to defend a doctrine. It is to kill a man;" "to force conscience is worse than to cruelly kill a man," because "I must be saved by my own faith and not by that of another."[24] While Castellio and other sixteenth century figures such as Jacobus Acontius, Martin Bucer, Jacob Sturm, Faustus Socinus, Sebastian Franck, Caspar Schwenckfeld, and Michel Servetus are important figures in the history of toleration, they also are not discussed here because their arguments are fundamentally religious, not based on skepticism.

In general, ancient and medieval philosophers did not advocate toleration because of their attachments to a notion of fixed truth, whether found in nature or revealed religion. It was only when the crisis of authority became so acute in the sixteenth century that skepticism arose as a leading philosophical stance and toleration emerged as a desirable political idea. The intellectual basis of sixteenth-century authority was undermined by numerous factors: political, economic, social, religious, and philosophical. The nascent rise of the nation-state, which was replacing the previous feudal organization, and the formation of trade-based towns and cities with their newly acquired wealth, led to shifts of power with all the attendant jockeying and uncertainties. These changes in basic social organization were intensified, even dwarfed, by the ideological breakdown which they both engendered and were further inflamed by. For example, the recovery by Europe of the ancient world through the re-entry of Greek and Roman pagan texts (due to the influx of scholars caused by the fall of Constantinople and to increased trade with the Islamic world) and the discovery of the "New World" exploded numerous intellectual assumptions. Renaissance scholars could not help but notice that both the "ancient" and "new" worlds were inhabited by seemingly healthy people (not to say profoundly wise in the case of Plato and Aristotle) despite -- perhaps even because of -- their lack of Biblical revelation. This was a problem that shook the very core of Christendom's self-understanding. Furthermore, the uncovering of natural phenomena based on scientific discoveries in the fields of astronomy, physics, and geography shook the foundations of medieval cosmology, according to which everything had its proper place in the cosmos. The challenges to one aspect of Christian cosmology, such as were posed by Copernicus and Kepler's questioning of the earth being the center of the universe or by Giordano Bruno's inferring the improbability of the Biblical account of Noah's ark because of the numerous peoples living on disparate continents, called into question the entire cosmological edifice. Not only was Christian culture called into question, but so was its very understanding of the place of human beings in the cosmos -- and the very nature of the cosmos itself. These cosmological shifts played their role in fomenting internal and external attacks on a corrupt Church, which together with the Reform movements, fostered a dramatic era of religious and political controversies. These ideas, discoveries, and actions provoked reason and tradition to be doubted in world-shattering ways, creating widespread interest in skepticism and toleration for the first time since the ancient pagan world.[25]

III. Contents of This Volume

The authors discussed in this volume express different versions of skepticism, are willing to tolerate different amounts or kinds of behavior, and introduce different mitigating or limiting factors into their calculations. Several essays in this volume address authors who make appeals of one sort or another to God, and some of the kinds of arguments discussed above will reappear. But with the notable exception of Luther and Calvin, the authors discussed in this volume derive their basic arguments for toleration on other, more skeptical grounds. Even Calvin and Luther, it will be seen, are deeply skeptical about human powers. Thus, this book examines thinkers who develop arguments for toleration independent of appeals to God or metaphysical notions of rights. As such their arguments are in tune with today. Moreover, since they do not have a practiced tradition of toleration to which they can appeal, they cannot attempt to justify toleration with philosophically unsatisfying appeals to existing tradition. Each essay in this volume examines an author's claim that it is in the reader's interest to be tolerant and adopt a political policy of toleration and explores the philosophical foundations of that author's reasoning.

Though each author discussed is skeptical in his own unique way, it will be helpful at the outset to distinguish three *kinds* of skepticism: Academic, Pyrrhonist, and fideist. Academic and Pyrrhonian skepticism are clearly defined by Sextus Empiricus, an ancient Roman, the re-publication of whose *Outlines of Pyrrhonism* in 1562 first brought these arguments into the modern world.[26] These two kinds of skepticism differ in the extent of their doubt over what can be known.[27] Academic skepticism, so-called because it originally came out of Plato's Academy (2nd and 3rd centuries B.C.), argues that no knowledge is possible. This assertion, traced back to Socrates' "I know that I know nothing," is paradoxical and problematic for a skeptic. If no knowledge is possible, how is this known? Pyrrhonian skepticism, named after Pyrrho of Elis, is more radical. It argues that we cannot know whether we can know anything or not. There is insufficient information and evidence, it argues, to determine whether any knowledge is possible. Hence, it argues that everyone should suspend judgment on all issues. If a Pyrrhonist persuades anyone of anything, he will immediately switch sides and argue the opposite, so that in the face of conflicting views, judgment will be suspended. Fideism, the third kind of skepticism, has a late medieval, early modern origin and bridges the gap between skepticism and Christianity. Fideists argue that no knowledge is possible by rational or other human means, but that truth is available to man through faith based on revelation. Thus, fideism accepts epistemological critiques of human reason and the human senses but maintains that knowledge is available to man through divine grace.[28] These three kinds of skepticism, Academic, Pyrrhonist, and fideist, will be carefully distinguished in the essays contained in this volume.

The essays are listed chronologically, but the issues raised do not unfold so neatly. For example, theological issues are highlighted by Luther, Calvin, Spinoza, Descartes, and Bayle, while Montaigne's arguments might most logically be placed with Montesquieu, Voltaire, or Diderot. Several authors assert that toleration is needed because diversity and a pluralism of views are inevitable among human beings, and almost all of the authors considered wail against the horrors of zealotry and fanaticism and decry the dangers of the human imagination run amok. Certain symbols play important recurring roles. For example, especially among the French authors, Julian the Apostate, ancient unnamed pagans, China, and Islam are frequently mentioned. Numerous other thematic interconnections are left for the reader to cull. Similarly, the influences of one author on others are numerous and complex. While some connections are specified in each article, numerous others are left for the reader to infer. In particular, the editor regrets the absence of Bodin, Hume (and the Scottish Enlightenment generally), and how the themes of the volume played out in the American and French revolutions. The influence of Bodin's *Colloquium,* however, is traced by Maryanne Cline Horowitz, and Hume is briefly discussed in Shirley Letwin's article on Hobbes.

The first two essays in this volume illustrate very different variations of the skepticism that characterized the sixteenth century's crisis. Joshua Mitchell begins the book by specifying the nature of Calvin and Luther's skepticism, while also showing the limit to their doubt: the belief that illumination by the holy spirit is necessary to overcome man's sad, earthly predicament. While the concerns of these two deeply religious thinkers are in many ways very different from our own, they radically challenge the authority of tradition in the form of the Catholic Church in favor of letting each individual attempt an unmediated relation to God. Their arguments in favor of privileging an individual's own conscience exerted considerable influence over later thinkers. Mitchell focuses on the epistemological skepticism of these two men. Human reason, they both argue, is fundamentally limited. Reason cannot answer the most important questions for human beings. This human inability to know the truth unassistedly is echoed in the title of Mitchell's essay, "Through a Glass Darkly." Nonetheless, Mitchell shows how a proper reading of their arguments leads not to the dogmatic rigidity of which Luther and Calvin are often accused, but rather how their skepticism about human abilities and their belief in the fundamental mysteries of the cosmos leads to a world view compatible with difference and novelty. This chapter shows how skepticism can be combined with toleration through religion. And while making his case, Mitchell has America's twentieth century religious fundamentalists in mind as possible beneficiaries of the argument.

Montaigne shares the epistemological skepticism of Luther and Calvin, but he radicalizes the argument, believing even that conceptions of God are human creations. He agrees that true knowledge and true faith can only come about through divine grace, but he doubts that anyone has ever been touched by such grace. In its absence, how should the rest of us live? Knowing and cultivating the self emerges as the greatest good for Montaigne, from which he articulates a conception of the self where self-interest properly understood is not only compatible with toleration, but demands it. Toleration and a private sphere of free conscience and free political judgment should be instituted in order to facilitate the most important and most real things a human being can do: self-exploration and self-creation. Montaigne, who internalized and provoked the crisis of authority in an unparalleled way, speaks to the modern reader like few others. His justification of toleration, without appealing to God or divine or natural "rights" on the one hand and without appealing to convention or habit on the other, has been influential on some of today's theorists, but his arguments offer what some of his latter-day followers do not.

Maryanne Cline Horowitz contributes the most historical essay in the collection to show how the skeptical ideas of the sixteenth century get transmitted in the first half of the seventeenth century. Focusing on important thinkers, such as Bodin, Montaigne, Charron, Naudé, Marie de Gournay, and La Mothe Le Vayer, who are usually neglected by political theorists, Horowitz shows how a group of free-thinkers emerged in France in the circle around Richelieu. This circle is so important because it represents what is perhaps Europe's first *culture* of tolerance towards diverse ideas. While select and limited, this circle of free-thinkers, or libertines as they were pejoratively called by critics implying that free-thinking and debauchery went together, struck a balance between the needs of political stability and the desire for free speech.

Amidst growing fanaticism and persecution, the iniquitous effects of religion were being tamed on other fronts as well. The next two essays in the volume show how Descartes and Spinoza combined different kinds of skepticism with different claims about nature to redefine the religious question and explore how both of their tremendously original but very different conceptions of nature led them to promote toleration. After the intellectual crises and tremendous skepticism of the sixteenth century, Descartes is often regarded as the originator of modern thought. Michael Gillespie shows how Descartes' thought emerged from doubts about the scholastic tradition. He also shows how the ground for Cartesian toleration is the establishment of a non-theological foundation for the self, which (as with Montaigne) is what Descartes is left with after his famous radical doubting. But within subjectivity, Descartes claims to find a basis for scientific certainty. Gillespie shows how Descartes' radical reconception of human life is implied in the famous *cogito ergo sum* and both how it leads to toleration and how it might be undermined. Given how nineteenth and twentieth century science has contributed to skepticism about the possibility of any moral truth, this confrontation with Descartes will prove useful to anyone who wants to combine scientific thinking with morality.

Spinoza is the first thinker to praise what was to develop into the modern liberal state, and he provides the basis for his principled defense of toleration in his *Tractatus Theologico-Politicus*. Steven B. Smith demonstrates both Spinoza's thoroughly skeptical doubting of established religion and his reinterpretation of it to advance a new secular religion of tolerance and obedience to the laws of a liberal democratic state. As much as he detests fanaticism, Spinoza considers complete skepticism to be worse than complete dogmatism. He did not think that a modern democratic state could exist without any core values, so Spinoza reconstructs religion on another criterion, a *fides universalis*, a minimal "universal faith" that he advances as a civil theology necessary for tolerant actions and civil peace. Some such core tolerant teaching about proper human action, Spinoza argues, is necessary for a tolerant liberal democracy, including the free speech and free trade that he advocates.

At this point the volume shifts locations to detail the important advance of skepticism and toleration in England. Having reached philosophical and political fruition in France and Holland, our theme truly blossoms in England via the persons of the Levellers, Thomas Hobbes, and John Locke. While some of these thinkers are usually not thought of as primarily skeptical, this volume shows the important role of skepticism in the formation of their ground-breaking arguments.

The Levellers are generally perceived as a religious movement, but Alan Houston shows how they defend religious toleration primarily on a secular basis. The Leveller defense of toleration is based on three main claims: that each individual's conscience is autonomous, that toleration leads to peace, and that men need submit only to God's, not other men's, will. These three claims, Houston demonstrates, are based on skepticism. The argument for autonomy of conscience is based on skepticism concerning revelation. The peace claim is purely secular. The submission to God argument is the only one that is overtly religious, yet it is related to the first claim by doubts over which human being, if any, possesses the proper interpretation of revelation. Houston links these three claims to a historical analysis of social norms that were opposed to monopolies, and he argues that the Levellers' message achieved a degree of resonance with Englishmen due to their situating their claims in a secular frame. But in addition to situating the Levellers in their own context, Houston argues that their claims are relevant today, shedding light on what have become false dichotomies. Careful consideration of the Levellers' framework, Houston argues, provides new insight into the relationships between conscience and peace, public and private, rights and duties, interests and virtues. Leveller arguments "make a mockery of contemporary arguments that liberal rights are inherently privatizing and atomizing."

Shirley Letwin examines the complexity and seeming contradictions of Hobbes' thought, identifying the strands that have led scholars to claim that he was "on the one hand a rancorous materialist and atheist, and on the other hand that he was hardly distinguishable from St. Thomas Aquinas." Letwin explores the combination of skepticism and faith displayed both in Hobbes' writings and his life, demonstrating how skepticism leads him to "a kind of religious tolerance," but to a tolerance that is "far removed from what goes by that name today." While Hobbes argues that the sovereign must have final say in religious and secular disputes to avoid the war of each against all, Letwin insists that Hobbes is anti-absolutist in philosophy and religion and that he "prohibits talk of absolute targets, indisputable commands or inevitabilities." This shows the affinities between Hobbes and many contemporary critics of absolute truth. But Letwin also argues that Hobbes is anti-pantheistic, including what Letwin considers to be the modern forms of pantheism: "humanism, Marxism, Jungianism, oriental mysticism, scientism, and rationalism."

Nathan Tarcov concludes the British portion of the book with a comprehensive discussion of Locke's arguments for toleration. While Locke is among the main thinkers connected with the idea of toleration, Tarcov, by drawing on the entirety of Locke's work, highlights Locke's numerous -- and sometimes contradictory -- arguments for toleration, showing how the most important of Locke's arguments do not derive from other-worldly but political reflections. By highlighting Locke's different claims, Tarcov can specify the exact kinds of skepticism that Locke employs and the political and psychological assertions that both underlie and limit his claims. Locke's toleration is not a consequence of metaphysical rights but of his desire for a liberal state, which he calls for based on his psychological and political insights into the tendencies of human reason and the human passions.

This volume closes with three essays focusing on skepticism and toleration in the French Enlightenment. The famous skeptic Pierre Bayle, who has been hallowed by Voltaire as the father of the Enlightenment, is notable as the first philosopher to assert publicly that a society of atheists can exist and prosper.

Kenneth Weinstein goes against the conventional interpretation of Bayle by placing atheism at the center of Bayle's political desires. It is only because a society of perfect atheists cannot be achieved that Bayle turns to toleration as the next best alternative. As Weinstein shows, Bayle argues against ecclesiastical sanctions as a means of civil restraint, preferring instead to rely on innately human forces of self-regulation such as the desire for honor. In order to enable a tolerant society to exist, Weinstein shows, Bayle favors the rule of "enlightened mandarins," i.e. skeptical men of letters who would use political power to secure toleration.

Arguing that for Montesquieu toleration is not a good in itself but a post-Christian strategy of bringing about civil calm, Diana Schaub shows how Montesquieu's anti-foundationalism consists less in a demolition of religious foundations than in a deliberate neglect of them. Rather than refute religion, Montesquieu tries to "seduce" people towards an earthly vision of the good (hence the importance of economics to him). Yet, Schaub notes how Montesquieu is far from a complete skeptic. Despite his famous accounts of human and cultural diversity, the "celebrated Montesquieu" does not "celebrate" diversity in itself (as multiculturalists today sometimes ask us to do), since a completely "open" attitude towards diversity cannot condemn the multiple forms of despotism, which Montesquieu insists on doing. Therefore, based on his understanding of natural right and the principles of natural and civil law, he establishes substantive yet secular grounds for judging what makes good citizens. Montesquieu turns to "intransigent moderation," not mere toleration, as the most effective foundation for civic order and justice. Montesquieu's appreciation both of what is different and universal in human beings makes him required reading for everyone interested in pluralism and diversity.

The volume concludes with a discussion of two of the greatest figures of the mature Enlightenment: Voltaire and Diderot. Between them, these two did more than anyone to popularize the Enlightenment's key concepts and bring them to a mass audience on an unprecedented scale. In order to illustrate their views, Patrick Riley contrasts their skepticism to Leibniz's "optimism," so deliciously spoofed in *Candide*. Unable to accept any religious authority, as the famous slogan "*écraser l'infâme*" ("crush the infamous [thing]") suggests, Voltaire and Diderot turn to a purely naturalized humanitarianism -- without a religious component, let alone a religious foundation. Thus, unlike Montesquieu, Voltaire and Diderot are "root and branch" revolutionaries, demanding to eradicate the past roots and all. Riley doubts the workability of their tolerant skepticisms, fearing that they are just as likely to abuse as the "infamous" institutions that they condemn. As such, Riley serves a cautionary note against the easygoing skepticisms that emerge from the Enlightenment.

As with everything in this life, this book's virtues and vices are linked. Because the volume ambitiously aims to cover three centuries of writers, space requirements necessitate that each essay be short. Because the philosophers examined in each essay differ widely on what they are skeptical of, what doctrinal attachments they maintain, and what they will tolerate, the book as a whole cannot definitively answer the questions it explores. Rather, this volume tries to explicate several powerful connections between skepticism and toleration in order to give the reader a sophisticated appreciation of the problems entailed in such a linkage -- and an array of possible answers. Moreover, just as the views of the authors vary widely, so do the methodological and philosophical approaches of the contributors. In the spirit of our theme, doctrinal unity has been sacrificed for the methods that seemed most appropriate for each author. While these factors may frustrate readers in search of *the* answer, the analyses offered by the contributors should be satisfying in themselves. Readers attracted to the subject of this work are more likely to have a skeptical disposition and thus, hopefully, will not expect more than can reasonably be offered in a volume of this nature. We ask readers to forgive the necessary gaps and omissions and will be content if, after reading the volume, readers finds themselves more tolerant than skeptical of our efforts.

NOTES:

1. The most famous book on the history of skepticism is, of course, Richard Popkin's *The History of Scepticism from Erasmus to Spinoza* (Berkeley: University of California Press, 1979). Other notable works include Hunter and Wootton, eds., *Atheism from the Reformation to the Enlightenment* (Oxford: Oxford University Press, 1992) and Popkin, ed., *Skepticism and Irreligion in the Seventeenth and Eighteenth Centuries* (Leiden: Brill, 1993). An excellent but more focused study is René Pintard, *Le Libertinage érudit dans la première moitié du xviie siècle* (Paris: Boivin, 1943). A history of the changing interpretations of early modern skepticism may be found in David Wootton, "New Histories of Atheism" in Hunter & Wootton, eds., 13-53. See also J.M. Robertson, *A History of Freethought*, 2 vols. (London: Watts, 1936), I.O. Wade, *The Clandestine Organization and Diffusion of Philosophic Ideas in France from 1700 to 1750* (Princeton: Princeton University Press, 1938), Henri Busson, *Le Rationalisme dans la littérature française de la Renaissance* (Paris: Vrin, 1957), and Alan Charles Kors, *Atheism in France, 1650-1729* (Princeton: Princeton University Press, 1990).

2. Books on the history of toleration tend to focus either on religious or secular arguments for it. The best religiously focused book is Joseph Lecler's monumental two-volume work *Toleration and the Reformation*, Westow, tr. (New York: Association Press, 1960). Short but useful is Henry Kamen, *The Rise of Toleration* (London: Weidenfeld, 1967). Intelligent discussions of the secular definition, grounds, and scope of toleration can be found in Susan Mendus, ed., *Justifying Toleration: Conceptual and Historical Perspectives* (Cambridge: Cambridge University Press, 1988), 1-19, and Susan Mendus, *Toleration and the Limits of Liberalism* (Atlantic Highlands, NJ: Humanities Press International, 1989). Recent works include David Heyd, ed., *Toleration: An Elusive Virtue* (Princeton: Princeton University Press, 1996), Michael Walzer, *On Toleration* (New Haven: Yale University Press, 1997), Cary Nederman & John Christian Laursen, eds. *Difference and Dissent: Theories of Tolerance in Medieval and Early Modern Europe* (Lanham, MD: Rowman and Littlefield, 1997), and Laursen and Nederman, eds., *Beyond the Persecuting Society: Religious Toleration Before the Enlightenment* (Philadelphia: University of Pennsylvania Press, 1998).

3. Suggested long ago by Glaucon in Plato's *Republic* (357a-362c), this argument has been made in modern times from Bodin in his *Six livres de la république* (Paris, 1576) onwards, although most famously by Hobbes, *Leviathan* (London, 1651). For a different account of the importance of this distinction between moral and prudential arguments, see John Dunn, "The Claim to Freedom of Conscience," in *From Persecution to Toleration,* Ole Grell, Jonathan Israel, Nicholas Tyacke, eds. (Oxford: Oxford University Press, 1991), 171-93. For a history of the *raison d'état* argument, see Richard Tuck, *Philosophy and Government, 1572-1651* (Cambridge: Cambridge University Press, 1993).

4. See Plato, *The Republic* (357a-362c).

5. Rawls and Rorty appeal to non-foundational justifications of liberalism. Even their titles -- "Justice as Fairness: Political not Metaphysical," *Political Liberalism*, and "The Priority of Democracy to Philosophy" -- make this clear.

6. Rorty says that in our society "there is no place for the questions that Nietzsche or Loyola would raise" and advocates that contemporary liberals "simply *drop* questions." He approves of Rawls' stance of not philosophically justifying first principles and rejects as crazy those thinkers with radically different views: "They are crazy because the limits of sanity are set by what *we* can take seriously. This, in turn, is determined by our upbringing,

our historical situation." Richard Rorty, "The Priority of Democracy to Philosophy" in *The Virginia Statute for Religious Freedom*, Merrill Peterson, ed. (Cambridge: Cambridge University Press, 1988), 266, 267 & 268. See also 271. Similarly, Rawls dismisses thinkers with radically different perspectives: "Although to subordinate all our aims to one end does not strictly speaking violate the principles of rational choice... it still strikes us as irrational, or more likely as mad." John Rawls, *A Theory of Justice* (Cambridge: Harvard University Press, 1971), 553-4.

7. Nietzsche's emphasis on the sub-rational, psycho-physical, instinctive will to power is well known. For Foucault, "it is always the body that is at issue." "The soul is the prison of the body" and "we are invited to free it" (*Discipline and Punish*, Sheridan, tr. (New York: Vintage, 1979), 25 & 30, respectively). For Foucault's account of his own similarity to Nietzsche, see "Nietzsche, Genealogy, History" in *The Foucault Reader*, Rabinow, ed. (New York: Pantheon, 1984), especially, 83 & 87-90. However, I believe that Foucault misses the key difference between himself and Nietzsche. Foucault's attacks on all existing power/knowledge complexes and his calls for self-liberation parallel Nietzsche's account of the liberation of free spirits, but not the Nietzsche who longs for a new horizon or the coming of the *übermensch*.

8. For example, in *Contingency, Irony, and Solidarity* (Cambridge: Cambridge University Press, 1989), 65, Richard Rorty argues that "The compromise advocated in this book amounts to saying: *Privatize* the Nietzschean-Sartrean-Foucauldian attempt at authenticity and purity, in order to prevent yourself from slipping into a political attitude which will lead you to think that there is some social goal more important than avoiding cruelty," where avoiding cruelty is Rorty's definition of a liberal. See also Mark Warren, *Nietzsche and Political Thought* (Cambridge: MIT Press, 1988). Rorty and Warren do not say that postmodern thinkers prefer liberalism, but that liberalism can be justified, perhaps even more consistently, on postmodern principles -- regardless of the political preferences originally attached to them.

9. Fyodor Dostoyevsky, "The Grand Inquisitor" in *The Brothers Karamazov*. Also stated by Nietzsche, *On the Genealogy of Morals*, Walter Kaufmann, tr. (New York: Vintage, 1967): III.24, 150.

10. Amy Gutmann, "Communitarian Critics of Liberalism" in *Philosophy and Public Affairs*: 14 (summer 1985): 319. I cite Gutmann's critique without accepting her defense of liberalism as sufficient. As an example of care theory, see Nel Noddings, *Caring* (Berkeley: University of California Press, 1984). Rosemarie Tong, *Feminine and Feminist Ethics* (Belmont, CA: Wadsworth, 1993) explores ways that Noddings' argument is naive. My thanks to Daryl Koehn for these references.

11. Lecler, *Toleration and the Reformation*, Vol. II, Bk. VI; Henry Kamen, *The Rise of Toleration*, 129-45.

12. Plato, *Republic*, 376c-417b and 555b-563e.

13. Plato, *Republic* (557c-558a).

14. Plato, *The Laws*, see Books X & XII. For different statements on the composition of the Nocturnal Council, see 951d-e, 961a-c, & 964b.

15. See, for example, Aristotle's account of the unnamed virtue resembling sociability (*Nichomachean Ethics* 1126b11-1127a14), how even mundane associations are based on friendship rather than tolerance (*Ethics* 1161b11-16), and his account of goodwill (*Ethics* 1166b29-1167a20).

16. Matthew 22:21. Translations from the King James version. For background and the influence of Lactantius and Tertullian, see Lecler, I:32-64.

17. Matthew 13:24-30, 36-43.

18. Ephesians 4:15.

19. Augustine, *Ad Donatistas*, 10. On faith not being forced, see *Joannem*, xxvi, n. 2.

20. Thomas Aquinas, *Summa Theologica*, II, II, q. 10, art. 8, ad. 2.

21. Thomas Aquinas, *Summa Theologica*, II, II, q. 10, art. 8, c.

22. Lecler, I:88.

23. Ficino, "Of the Christian Religion," ch. 4, cited in Lecler, I:111.

24. Cited in Roland Bainton, "Sebastian Castellio and the Toleration Controversies of the Sixteenth Century" in the collection *Persecution and Liberty* (New York: Century, 1931), 183-209. On the toleration controversies in general, a concise account is J.W. Allen, *A History of Political Thought in the Sixteenth Century* (London: Methuen, 1928), 73-102.

25. For fuller accounts of the crises that led the old truths to be doubted, see Popkin, *The History of Scepticism from Erasmus to Spinoza*, ch.1, as well as his essay "The Skeptical Origins of the Modern Problem of Knowledge" in *Perception and Personal Identity*, Norman Care & Robert Grimm, eds. (Cleveland: Case Western, 1969), 3-24.

26. Charles Schmitt's excellent studies detail the little that was known about skepticism prior to Stephanus' (Henri Estienne's) publishing of Sextus Empiricus. See his *Cicero Scepticus* (The Hague: Nijhoff, 1972), *Studies in Renaissance Philosophy and Science* (London: Variorum reprints, 1981), and *Reappraisals in Renaissance Thought* (London: Variorum reprints, 1989).

27. Both Academic and Pyrrhonian skepticism are opposed to "dogmatism," the view that knowledge on some subject can be known. Dogmatism in this sense does not have the negative connotation that the word has today, although the negative connotation will emerge from the skeptical critiques that are elaborated in this volume.

28. The word fideism was coined in the nineteenth century and represents a widely held scholarly view describing skepticism in the early modern period.

2

THROUGH A GLASS DARKLY: LUTHER, CALVIN, AND THE LIMITS OF REASON

Joshua Mitchell

For now we see through a glass, darkly; but then face to face: now I know
in part, but then shall I know even as also I am known.[1]

Skepticism about the capacity of human reason to arrive at certainty is not a
recent discovery, nor does reason's finitude provide an assurance that tolerance
will be placed on firm foundation. The very limit of reason may, after all, occasion
confusion of the sort that resolves itself through isolation or violence. Withdrawal[2]
and "the fury of destruction,"[3] like toleration, are also strategies of facing (or
defacing) "the other." However much an awareness of reason's limitation may be
written into the human constitution, or is earnestly taught, either or both of these
furnish little assurance that human beings will tolerate each other. The uncertainty
of reason may, in equal measure, beget tolerance and intolerance.

The ambivalent linkage between the uncertainty of reason and toleration is not
the only difficulty to be confronted here in this brief study of Luther and Calvin.
Beyond this, there is the precarious task of demonstrating the connection between
thought and action, between whatever internal intellectual or textual coherence a
tract or book may possess and its historical repercussions. This latter difficulty,
Tocqueville suggested, was a task peculiarly set before historians in ages of
democracy. In ages of aristocracy, on the other hand:

> the attention of historians is constantly drawn to individuals [and] the connection
> of events escapes them, or rather they do not believe in such a connection. It
> seems to them that the thread of history is being constantly broken as a man
> crosses its path.[4]

Historians in ages of aristocracy, he says, were unconcerned to point out the causal
ramifications of an idea; that is a project for historians in democratic ages--should
they, perhaps erroneously, believe in the power of ideas at all![5]

In this study, needless to say, ideas are taken to matter. Yet, in the light of
these early observations, the task of investigating the modern rudiments of
toleration by considering the thought of Luther and Calvin is an oddly incongruous

one: perhaps the most salient problem of contemporary democracy (that of toleration) is brought into focus by relying on a mode of investigation of the sort found in ages of aristocracy--a mode which is skeptical of the prospect of revealing the origins of an unfolding idea whose efflorescence may be more fully witnessed in later thinkers or institutions.

In this study I will not adopt the strategy of historians in ages of democracy; I make no causal claims to the effect that either Luther or Calvin were instrumental in establishing or in opposing toleration. Rather, my task will be to explore the parameters of their thought on the limits of reason, with a view to establishing: (1) their respective understandings of the relationship between the orders of reality, which understanding limited the claims that reason was able to make--contra the Roman Catholic Church; and (2) the possible, and equivocal, trajectories such thinking may map out with respect to toleration. My intention is not to be exhaustive, only to offer further provocations to thinking about what toleration may mean--if anything--in the context of the thought of two prominent Reformation figures.

1. Luther: the Center is Christ

> Jesus said, "I am the true vine, and my father is the vinegrower. He removes every branch in me that bears no fruit. Every branch that bears fruit he prunes to make more fruit. . . . Just as the branch cannot bear fruit by itself unless it abides in the vine, neither can you unless you abide in me. I am the vine, you are the branches. Those who abide in me and I in them bear much fruit, because apart from me you can do nothing."[6]

The self is nothing without God. This stumbling block to contemporary sensibilities is the point of departure for all of Luther's thought. Augustine, of course, had expressed a kindred sentiment.[7] There was, however, a difference.[8] With Luther, the *person* of God without which we are nothing is decidedly Christ.[9] Unlike Augustine (arguably), Luther was a "Second Moment Trinitarian." His thoughts about all things carnal (which includes reason) and Holy always return to Christ.

In order to speak to the question of toleration and the limits of reason in Luther's thought, therefore, it will be necessary to elaborate his understanding of the centrality of Christ, and the crisis of faith which he thought the Roman Church had in large measure brought to pass.

Simply put, the Roman Church had not understood justification, and had itself lapsed into the easy temptation of believing that justification before God was achieved by virtue of the active righteousness of works, rather than by the passive righteousness of faith. Understood in terms of the biblical narrative, the problem was that the Roman Church understood justification in terms more in accord with the Old Testament rather than the New; that is, through the Law that commanded good works, rather than through faith.

Because Christians *now* lived in the post-Incarnation epoch, in the age of faith, it was incumbent upon them not to the seek justification on the basis of the active righteousness of works, nor to think that Christ will "appear" anywhere else but in the abyss of powerlessness--about which more shortly--when "the world," along with the faculty of reason that comprehends it, has been utterly condemned by the realization of the depth of human sinfulness.

The Catholic analogical vision of reality did not, in Luther's view, adequately reflect the situation of the post-Incarnation epoch, in large part because it sought to link faith to reason rather than to the corruption of the will brought on, again, by sin.

Notwithstanding his suspicions about the active righteousness of works set forth in the Old Testament, however, it should be noted that Luther also insisted that the Old Law is necessary, paradoxically, so that Christians can get *beyond* it. The instability of this formulation cannot be underestimated, and accounts, in some measure, for his ambivalence toward the Jews. Christians must get beyond the Law to attain salvation, but to get beyond it they have to go *through* it. The sense of liberation, of freedom, made possible by this going-through-and-beyond in Luther's writings is unmistakable; yet Christian freedom was to be juxtaposed to the existing political power that had received divine sanction from the Old Testament,[10] and which cannot be superseded until Christ comes again in glory. Luther whole-heartedly rejected antinomianism,[11] a fact which in no small measure accounts for his rather stark thinking about the Peasant Revolt. Men are, because of sin, beasts; political power is, therefore, necessary. Faith may set men free, but so long as sin among the Godless and 'remnants of sin'[12] among the repentant remain, coercion will be required.

Comprehending God's creation and its relationship to its Creator in an analogical fashion, as did the Roman Church, made it possible to argue that the higher must rule over the lower orders--that the higher orders completed the lower orders by pointing beyond them to something that fully discloses their purpose and nature.[13] Luther certainly agreed with the claim that the spiritual realm was higher than the carnal, but in his view the *way* this was understood by the Roman Church was faulty. Because of its over-zealous attempt to reconcile faith with reason, the Roman Church failed to understand the substance of the spiritual domain, the centrality of grace in the economy of salvation, and the stark alternatives with which sinners were confronted: to be Christ or Satan's own. The Roman Church, he thought, had abused reason and obscured faith.

When I was young I was learned, especially before I came to the study of theology. At that time I dealt with allegories, tropologies, and analogies and nothing but clever tricks with them. . . . I know [now] that they're nothing but rubbish. Now I've let them go, and this is my last and best art, to translate the Scriptures in their plain sense. The literal sense does it--in it there's life, comfort, power, instruction, and skill. The other is tomfoolery, however brilliant the impression it makes.[14]

Christ, not reason, is salvific. "Under the papacy I was exposed to every error. The reason is that I had no faith. Faith is, as it were, the center of the circle. If anybody strays from the center, it is impossible for him to have a circle around him, and he must blunder. The center is Christ."[15] Labyrinthian philosophical investigations undertaken by the theologians of the Roman Church not only distorted the problem of sin (and the nature of the atonement offered through Christ), but were evidence of it.[16]

Contrary to the demarcations of analogical reasoning, Luther argued that there are *only two* realms, carnal and spiritual; and that the carnal realm, "the world," is steeped in sin.[17] Moreover, the relationship between the two realms, with important qualifications, maps onto the relationship between the two Testaments.

Luther's recurrence to biblical history and his rejection of analogy led him to a subtle, insightful, and (perhaps ultimately) unstable way of thinking through the manner in which the New Testament supersedes the Old--and by extension, the manner in which the spiritual is related to the carnal domain. In his view, the relationship between the two was such that the message of the Old (the need to perform works and obey the Law), though important, was--if not properly understood--a threat to the life of faith made possible through Christ and the Gospel message that is fully revealed in the New Testament. Although the New Testament fulfills the Old,[18] it does so by virtue of what can, again, with important qualifications, be called a discontinuity with the Old. No analogical relationship obtains. Here the superiority of the New Testament, of the spiritual realm to which it testifies, is comprehended in a manner quite different than had the Roman Church--which, in effect, had poured new wine into old bottles.[19]

For the spiritual, passive, realm to come to presence, the Christian must overcome the temptation to remain imprisoned within the carnal, active, realm. Adjudging the spiritual realm in terms of the carnal is tantamount to construing the meaning of Christ in terms of the Law. Like the resident aliens who inhabit the cave in Plato's *Republic*,[20] Christians must be vigilant that they not construe the world above in terms of their habitual world below. In the midst of the confusion below, where the soul is enthralled by the enticements of works, by "the world," teachers of righteousness use the *words* but are not able to grasp the thing itself because "they cling only to the righteousness of the Law."[21]

The sophistry about which Plato worried is transposed here into a Christian key. Christ, who brought the message of faith, is interpreted in terms of the Law; His message, consequently, is subverted, misunderstood, violated.

To avoid this confusion the two realms must be separated and "kept within their limits"[22]--an extraordinarily difficult task because in the final analysis only spirit can know the basis of its *difference* from the carnal realm![23]

The propensity to subvert the (spiritual) truth of Christ is not to be underestimated.[24] Because of their weakness, which, ironically, stems from a belief in their own powers of accomplishment, Christians easily fall into the "slavery of works." Far easier it is to imagine that righteousness is attained through prescribed works which they comprehend with their own limited reason than to attain a righteousness beyond designated activities or prohibitions.

> But such is human weakness and misery that in the terrors of conscience and the danger of death we look at nothing except our own works, our worthiness, and the law. When the law shows us our sin, our past life immediately comes to our mind. Then the sinner, in his great anguish of mind, groans and says to himself: 'Oh, how damnably I have lived! If only I could live longer! Then I would amend my life.' Thus human reason cannot refrain from looking at active righteousness, that is, its own righteousness; nor can it shift its gaze to passive, that is, Christian righteousness.[25]

The slavery of works does not, however, appease, but rather generates a melancholy and troubled conscience, from which fallible reason finds no escape.

It was Luther's view, in fact, that melancholy was brought on by the devil, and that the harder one tried to overcome it through good works the more it obtruded. "A Christian should and must be a cheerful person. If he isn't, the devil is tempting him,"[26] he says. God is joy, not melancholy.[27]

The troubled and melancholy conscience, then, cannot be appeased by good works or by the law.[28] It must find its respite in the interiority, as it were, of faith.

In Hegel's estimation this insight was a portentous one which signaled a grasping of the truth of Christianity of which the Roman Church had not achieved. Above all, what was necessary was that "a brokenness of the heart [be] experienced, and that Divine Grace [enter] into the heart thus broken."[29] Said otherwise, Christians must accept the radicality of sin and their inability to achieve salvation without God's gift of His son--the one sufficient Mediator. In the language of the biblical narrative, what is necessary is that Christians reenact Christ's suffering, fall into the abyss of wretchedness, into "Hell," as Christ did when He died to "the world"--by which is meant the everydayness with which souls are preoccupied in their efforts to be *actively* righteous. This (external) world, again, Christians must die to. In Luther's words, "It is evident that no external thing has any influence in producing Christian righteousness or freedom, or in producing unrighteousness or servitude. . . . None of these things touch either the freedom or servitude of the soul."[30]

The faith that produces such righteousness and quells the troubled conscience comes only when the word of God is *heard*; that is to say, when, in Luther's words, Christ is "for you and me," when He is "effectual in us."[31] The Christ who is encountered as an *object* of knowledge can be of no assistance; this is not the Christ of faith. The chasm between knowing *about* Christ and *knowing* Christ is immense. Faith *is* only underneath the everydayness of factual history and inauthenticity--if I may invoke somewhat Heideggerian language.

The Christ who is "for us" is encountered only when Christians turn away from works; or more correctly, when, in attempting to obey the commandments of God regarding works, they realize that they *cannot* accomplish what He wills.[32] In this abyss of despair the interiority, as it were, of the spiritual realm comes to presence for the Christian. Only at this point does the second portion of the Scripture speak: the promise of the Gospel. In this abyss the Christian is "truly humbled and reduced to nothing in his own eyes,"[33] and dwells far from works and commandments, from the trappings of worldly, physical, power.[34] Here, humbled by the Law, realizing that "he cannot find any means to be delivered from his sin by his own strength,"[35] and that the world--the whole of the carnal realm--is guilty before God, the Christian experiences utter powerlessness.

This *experience* is the precondition for the "appearance" of Christ for the despairing soul; an appearance which occurs only when the Christian is in another "world," far from disputes about works. *Only then* "[do we hear] the Gospel . . . that Christ died for us."[36] *This* Gospel can only be grasped *"with other eyes [than] carnal reason doth [have]."*[37] Again, in terms of the biblical narrative, before Christians may come unto the Spirit they must, like Christ, experience the abandonment of God that is confirmed in the call, "My God, my God, why hast thou forsaken me?"[38] In this depth of abandonment Christ appears.

For Luther, when, in abandonment, Christ appears, He "swallows up" sin.[39] Sin here is abrogated, taken in by the Byss of Christ,[40] who is the Ground beneath that abyss which utter self-condemnation occasions. In this abrogation, powerlessness is linked through Christ's own suffering with the omnipotence of God; a Divine configuration which gives rise to the great paradox of Christian faith: "power is made perfect in weakness."[41] Through a marriage with Christ[42] the weakness of the bride is taken in in its entirety by the bridegroom. The perfection of the bridegroom (Christ), who fought a "mighty duel" and conquered both hell and death, is, through faith in this moment of powerlessness, given over to the Christian.[43] In weakness and powerlessness the sin which utterly condemns the Christian is swallowed up by God the Son; and this act of Christ's taking sin in upon Himself imputes a penultimate perfection back to the Christian in virtue of his marriage with Him.[44] Here the Christian reenacts the drama of suffering (sin) and descent into hell (the abyss) which Christ endured and overcame; and, through a marriage with Christ, overcomes them through Him.

* * *

In light of the preceding remarks about Christian faith, and for the purpose of considering the respect in which Luther's thoughts about Christ and derivative matters may contribute to toleration, it is necessary here to briefly develop his thinking about the Christian's relationship to history--that is to say, to God's inscrutable, yet providential, plan. I return to this issue, at a more general level, in the concluding section.

To begin with, the yawning abyss into which the sinner must fall is *concealed* to him who would insist upon his radical freedom, and, consequently, to him who would oppose the providential designs of God in history. Freedom, so understood, forecloses faith: the central theme of what is perhaps Luther's most important work: "The Bondage of the Will." "No man's plans have ever been straightforwardly realized . . . for everyone things have turned out differently from what he thought they would."[45] The unforeseen, which no rational plan can plan against: this is confirmation of the weakness of human understanding, and evidence of God's will working through all apparent contingency, at times with and at times without the will of His servants.

Christians do participate freely in this providential design, not by *creating* history, but by (freely) yielding to God's will or (freely) resisting it. The task of the Christian living in historical existence is not to discover God's immutable will, to transpose it (say, into a doctrine of progress), or to create history, but rather to partake in the spiritual domain that suffering in historical existence portends. Not the actual movement *of* history, but the pilgrim's faith *in* history is the Christian's charge. Historical contingency can be an occasion through which the luminousness of faith arises, but mere mortals cannot reign over such contingencies. Attempting to do so confirms the *superbia* of reason, the machinations of which are sterile next to the fecundity of God.[46] Christians are given the Word of God, with its promises of salvation through Christ, not the freedom to create history. "It is our business, however, to pay attention to the Word and leave that inscrutable will alone, for we must be guided by that Word, and not by that inscrutable will."[47]

In freely resisting the will of God; in proceeding with mortal plans irrespective of ample evidence that they have been confuted by the movement of events, faith is foreclosed and the will is "hardened." "[T]hey become all the more averse and are made much worse when their aversion is resisted and thwarted. So it was when God proposed to wrest ungodly Pharaoh's tyranny from him."[48]

The movement away from, or against, the course of history preordained by God, who "keeps on presenting and obtruding His words and works from without,"[49] *increases* the opposition of the will that purports to be sufficient unto itself, the consequence of which is that this will that will not submit "cannot help [but hate] what is opposed to [it] and [trust further its] own strength."[50] And, because the inscrutable Will of God *is good*, persistent opposition to that Will increasingly takes on the character of evil. "[F]ree choice can do nothing but evil . . . and when confronted with a good that is contrary to it, can only become worse."[51]

The future is, as it were, a *Holzwege*, a woodpath into the darkness undiscernible to human reason.[52] Without a willingness to reverentially obey the inscrutable will working through history, the finite human will "absolutizes" itself, conceives of itself as sufficient unto itself, and opposes what it encounters with a ferocity proportional to the magnitude of the opposition it receives from God. Like earthly kings, this sinful will seeks to prevail by confronting power *with* power. Foreclosed in this confrontation is the abyss of powerlessness that is unconcealed with the self-confession that the will cannot, of its own accord, will to do good. Pelagianism, ancient or modern, confronted centuries before by Augustine,[53] obstructs the entrance to the abyss and forecloses the possibility of Christian faith. Through such faith, the contingencies of the world can be endured, if not celebrated. Through prayer and attentive faith the Christian glorifies the mysterious providence of God.

* * *

There are certain implications for temporal government that Luther drew from the inability of the carnal realm to comprehend the spiritual realm, that "secret, hidden, spiritual matter,"[54] which must be alluded to here, in part to understand his divergences with Calvin.

To begin with, physical power, the very medium of politics, cannot in principle, and ought not in practice, be used to dissuade the believer. Heresy can never be prevented by force.[55] Worldly government extends to life and property, but over the soul it holds no sway. Belief and unbelief are matters of conscience, not power.[56] The carnal and the spiritual realms have been so confused, however, that bishops rule over cities while lords rule over the souls.[57] "[W]here the spiritual government alone prevails over land and people, there wickedness is given free reign and the door is opened for all manner of rascality, for the world as a whole cannot receive or comprehend it."[58]

And elsewhere,

> I say therefore that since the temporal power is ordained of God to punish the wicked and to protect the good, it should be left free to perform its office, in the whole body of Christendom without restriction and without respect to persons, whether it affects pope, bishops, priests, monks, nuns or anyone else.[59]

Luther's understanding of the relationship between the two Testaments is clearly in evidence in his thinking about the two kinds of government. Where earthly kingship was authorized by God in the Old Testament, and given to the children of this world that there may be order, it is *not* abolished by Christ. It still applies for the unrighteous. The fulfillment that Christ offers pertains to Christians only. The sword remains--necessary for the unrighteous and justified by "divine right."[60] God the Father authorizes rule over the unrighteous with unwavering severity; God the Son rules the righteous in love.

The two realms are separable, yet related, as God the Son is dialectically related to God the Father. The Son fulfills the rule of the Father, He does not overturn it.

The work of temporal authorities is one thing; that of the spiritual kingdom, another. By leaving temporal authorities free to take care of their affairs, obstacles to salvation are removed; by insisting that the Church have no say in secular matters, the work of this world is left to those most able and authorized to perform it. Separate the two realms and both operate without doing violence to the other.

With regard to spiritual government, Luther's understanding was stark yet simple: Christians may be distinguished from one another on the basis of the work they do, but this difference is almost superficial. It is merely conventional. There is no spiritual superiority of the priest over the farmer.[61] That the priest may possess certain capabilities (even virtues) that the farmer lacks does not make the one more important, dignified, or worthy of respect than the other. Christian righteousness *levels all difference*. The eyes of the spiritual government don't look at capability, virtue, or station. In *this* kingdom all are equal. The essential difference in the Christian kingdom is not *among* Christians, but *between* Christ and *all* Christians.[62] *Lateral* relationships between persons (*coram hominibus*) are subservient and secondary to the *vertical* relationship between Christ and the Christian (*coram Deo*). No hierarchical social order meant to portend the analogical relationship between the orders of reality can convey the truth of this direct relationship between Christians and God, through His Son.

With regard to temporal government, his hopes were, perhaps unrealistically, no less informed by the centrality of Christ than were his thoughts on spiritual government. To princes who wished to rely on their own power his warnings were clear: "We must not start something by trusting in great power or human reason, even if all the power in the world were ours. For God cannot and will not suffer a good work to begin by relying upon one's own power and reason."[63] The power to be used *in* the world to oppose the forces of injustice must come from beyond it. Defense against "the rapacious wolves who come dressed in sheep's clothing"[64] requires that they be lambs possessed of God's strength.

In domestic affairs, as well, there is need of God's assistance. The Christian prince must act in a manner befitting both an earthly king and a Christian subject of the spiritual government above.[65] This is not to say that the prince is to deny himself the exercise of power; rather, that the *use* to which such power is put is informed by the prince's experience *as a Christian*. He is not powerless toward his subjects, but the abyss of powerlessness he experiences *as* a Christian discloses his true relationship with his subjects and, presumably, the boundaries beyond which the use of his power cannot transgress.

Regarding the laws which the Christian prince may institute, Luther insists that the *right* of making law is justified by the Word of God; the *content* of such laws, however, is not to be found in Scripture itself. The laws, simply put, cannot be bound if they are to emanate from God. To bind them is to ossify and harden them and to misconstrue their Source, which cannot be bound. "I know of no law to prescribe for a prince, but will simply instruct him what the *attitude of his heart and mind ought to be* with respect to all laws . . . so that if he governs himself thereby, God will surely grant him the power to carry out all laws . . . in a proper and Godly way."[66] The laws of the Christian prince are not simply his own. They issue from his person but "are occasioned by God acting through him. A prince should in his heart empty himself of his power and authority, and take unto himself the needs of his subjects, dealing with them as though they were his own needs. For this is what Christ did for us; and these are the proper works of Christian love."[67]

The *derivative* quality of sociality cannot be overlooked, though this is not at all to dismiss it as insignificant. Christian righteousness is a matter between the Christian and God; yet as a consequence *of* this relationship, of this marriage with Christ, the foundation of sociality is revealed. Christians cannot have a genuine affiliation with others without the assistance of Christ. Only through a marriage between the Christian and Christ can this happen. The obligations between Christians derive from the relationship between each individual Christian and Christ.[68]

Here as elsewhere in Luther's thought, Christ--not the Commandments[69]--is the center. Through a marriage with Christ that excludes all others, the Christian, prince or otherwise, is able to (indeed must) include all others; the pattern established by the bridegroom (Christ) is reproduced in the bride's (the Christian's) relationship to all others. "As our heavenly Father has in Christ freely come to our aid, we also ought freely to help our neighbor through our body and works, and each should become as it were a Christ to the other that we may be Christs to one another and Christ may be the same in all, that is, that we may be truly Christian."[70] The marriage with Christ provides the basis for the twin orientation that the Christian must have: on the one hand, toward the Divine; on the other hand, toward all others. By "reduc[ing] himself to nothing in his own eyes"[71] the Christian, in that mystery of abandonment and Divine love, discovers the basis of relationships with others. "A Christian lives not in himself, but in Christ and his neighbor . . . he lives in Christ through faith, in his neighbor through love. By faith he is caught up beyond himself unto God. By love he descends beneath himself unto his neighbor."[72] Here, finally, the meaning of the paradox Luther cites at the outset of "The Freedom of a Christian" is clarified. "A Christian is a perfectly free lord of all, subject to none. A Christian is a perfectly dutiful servant to all, subject to all."[73] Through Christ, Christians partake in the Divine ground of their freedom from, and supersession over, the carnal realm; they attain a freedom from all *things*; that is, everything carnal. In reproducing the pattern established by Christ, they, like Him, become a servant to all.

* * *

At the outset I mentioned that, for Luther, the two alternatives are either to be Christ's own or Satan's own. I will conclude these remarks on Luther by alerting the reader to how his thinking about reason is informed by these two alternatives.

To begin with, Luther would be perplexed by the three prevailing dichotomies (ancient virtue vs. modern self-interest; aristocratic glory vs. modern self-interest; or medieval religion vs. modern enlightenment) invoked by political theorists in order to situate and assess the modern political project. Theologically, the error in each case is not simply the belief that mankind can do without God, but the belief that Evil no longer exists--or if it does, that it can be eliminated by some human institutional contrivance. Evil is supra-human; only God can save us from it. Thus, when Luther reviles "the world," it is not because he hated the body, as, say, Nietzsche--that innocent child of the Enlightenment--would have it. Matters of the body were not Luther's concern; the devil was. "The world is like a drunken peasant. If you lift him into the saddle on one side, he will fall off on the other side. One can't help him, no matter how one tries. *He wants to be the devil's*."[74] Looking to the world for spiritual sustenance, tempting as it was, offered the Christian no prospect of keeping the devil at bay; only Christ could do that. Without Christ at the center, the devil takes command of the soul, and the faculty of reason, in turn, serves him.

> Reason that is under the devil's control is harmful, and the more clever and successful it is, the more harm it does.... On the other hand, when illuminated by the Holy Spirit, reason helps to interpret the Holy Scriptures. . . . So reason, when illuminated [by the Spirit], helps faith by reflecting on [the Word], but reason without faith isn't and can't be helpful.[75]

The deficiencies of reason, then, will always be recompensed by the Divine, whether it be Satan or Christ! For reason not to go astray, Christ must be in possession of the soul. (Not only is reason at stake, of course, but also the very possibility of living with others in Christian love.)

Notwithstanding the vehemence of his attacks against the Roman Church, Luther himself occasionally worried that his 'foothold on faith' had slipped out from under him, and that his teaching was the work of Satan. His solace, his assurance that his reason had not gone astray, however, was Christ.

> Satan often said to me, 'What if your teaching by which you've overthrown the pope, the mass, and the monks should be false?' He often assailed me in such a way as to make me break out in sweat. Finally I answered, 'Go and speak with my God, who commanded us to listen to this Christ.' Christ must do everything. Accordingly we wish to be Christians and leave it to Christ to answer for this.[76]

Through Christ, once fallen faculties are not perfected; they are, however, guided and illuminated enough so that Christians may discern their duties toward their neighbor and glorify God. Pilate's mocking question, "What is truth?",[77] meant to suggest that human reason discerns only the relativity of all things moral, receives its corrective only by the Divine irruption of the God the Son. On this basis, and no other, can there be that mysterious unity of the different professed by the Gospel.[78] Whatever tolerance there may be must arise through it. Carnal nature, without the supplement of the Spirit, yields only faction and discord. Quoting Paul, Calvin would later say: "For our God is not author of division, but of peace."[79] Luther agrees.

2. Calvin: the Gifts of the Spirit

For Luther, faith consolidates around Christ. For Calvin, Christ, too, is the center; yet the burden of Calvin's theology concerns what emanates *from* that center and into the world, through the workings of the Holy Spirit.[80]

This is not to say that Luther was unconcerned with how Christian faith displays itself in the world, or with the workings of the Holy Spirit. Rather, with Luther, the crucial problem around which his Christo-centric theology revolves is that of *justification*. This led him to emphasize the passivity before God the Son which faith entailed, to the detriment, perhaps, of a fully developed understanding of the relationship of such faith to the workings of temporal government. As we saw earlier, Luther's advice to princes evinces precious little certainty about how to advance the glory of God in history, of the sort we find in greater measure in the thought of Calvin.

Calvin, while in agreement with Luther about this passivity whereby man is humbled and faith secured, was, to invoke a useful short-hand, more of a "Third Moment Trinitarian." He sought to understand the *sanctification* brought by the Holy Spirit, and the evidence that weak human reason may find for such sanctification in fallen historical existence.

To begin with, Calvin, like Luther, found no great solace in reason's ability to comprehend God or His creation. Above all, for Calvin, what man can know of God's glory comes from his recognition of his utter dependence on Him. Relying upon reason blinds man to this recognition of utter dependence. "For what is more consonant with faith than to recognize that we are naked of all virtue, in order to be clothed by God? That we are empty of all good, to be filled by Him."[81] True, man is granted glimpses of God's glory in His creation,[82] but these are fleeting and unsustainable. The bond between God and man has been broken by human sin, and the faculty of reason cannot reestablish it. What alone *can* reestablish the bond is faith in Christ through the Holy Spirit. Spirit yields truth--not custom or tradition, as the Roman Church had argued. "[I]n the Kingdom of God his eternal truth must alone be listened to and observed, a truth that cannot be dictated to by length of time, by long-standing custom, or by the conspiracy of men."[83]

To be sure, this derogation of custom and tradition could, and did,[84] have revolutionary implications; yet conjoined with this understanding of the one sufficient ground of truth in the Spirit was an acknowledgement by Calvin that the political order *as it now stood* was also part of God's providential plan, and so could not be overturned lightly. Here, as elsewhere in his thought, there is an extraordinary tension, whose root derives from the mysterious paradox that the world is, on the one hand, darkened by sin and by the works of Satan and, on the other, the unfolding of the glory of God in history, in which most participate by opposing His will in darkness. Through the efficient--and in spite of the deficient[85]--will of man, God's glory is realized in history.

> [In times of old], because [men] had refused to obey [God's] truth and had extinguished His light, He allowed their blinded senses to be both deluded by foolish lies and plunged into profound darkness, so that no form of the true church remained. Meanwhile, he preserved his own children from extinction, though they are scattered and hidden in the midst of these errors and darkness.[86]

I shall return to this image of the Holy remnant shortly. In order to understand why God's people will always be a remnant, however, we must first further explore the perversity of man--that is, the extent to which he is turned in upon himself, closed off from God by his sinfulness, and worships the fancies of his own imagination.

The problem with which Calvin was concerned has been eloquently treated in the late 20th century by Levinas,[87] whose distinction between *totality* and *Infinity* is eminently helpful here. Obvious differences aside,[88] they are in accord that *the problem of man's existence is the problem of totality*.[89] Merely consult Calvin on total depravity for confirmation.[90]

Being so cut off does not, however, stop man from *trying* to make the ascent--as Hobbes so eloquently pointed out in the 17th century.[91] Calvin, as I say, well understood the problem.

> For each man's mind is like a labyrinth, so that it is no wonder that individual nations were drawn aside into various falsehoods; and not only this--but individual men, almost, had their own gods. For as rashness and superficiality are joined with ignorance and darkness, *scarcely a single person has ever been found who did not fashion for himself an idol or specter in place of God.*[92]

And further on: "Yet hence it appears that if men were taught *only by nature*, they would hold to nothing certain or solid or clear-cut, but would be so tied to confused principles as to worship an unknown god."[93] Man longs to understand the Infinite, yet, unassisted by God Himself, man creates a totality, a mere projection of God from man himself.[94] Feuerbach was right[95]--unless there is a God who, by grace, gives Himself to man so that the unyielding totality projected by man is shattered through an irruption of the Infinite into time, as Calvin argued was the case.

By nature, or rather by fallen nature,[96] then, human reason creates a god in its own image. Man worships himself unless God comes to the rescue. He ought, therefore, "to seek [his] conviction in a higher place than human reasons, judgments, or conjectures, that is, in the secret testimony of the Spirit."[97]

The locus of God's revelation of Himself to man was, of course, the Word. The Word of God corrects for man's idolatrous tendencies; about this Calvin was certain. This led him, as I mentioned at the outset, to oppose the Roman Church's purported authority to *interpret* God's Word. As he put it: "God alone is a fit witness of Himself in his Word."[98] That is, "Scripture will ultimately suffice for a saving knowledge of God only when its certainty is founded upon the inward persuasion of the Holy Spirit."[99] Less well known, however, is that this position led him also to oppose the Eastern Church, for which iconography was integral to its practice.

The problem of image vs. substance can already be found in Plato's *Republic*, when Glaucon wonders why the fathers have given the sons of Athens only the appearance of justice. "No one has ever provided proof that [justice] is the greatest good and [injustice] the greatest of evils. Why do all of you not do this from the beginning and convince us from our youth up?"[100] The task posed for Socrates is, therefore, to move beyond the image of justice to justice itself--a massive and perhaps insurmountable problem in light of the human tendency to be drawn to and charmed by the images that the poets convey.[101] Here, too, to invoke Levinas' distinction anew, man's tendency is to create a totality that stands in for the Infinite (Good). Only the philosopher is immune from the totality to which imagery always attests.

> But in the highest subdivision [of knowledge] the soul makes no use of images. It also begins with assumptions and hypotheses but rises to a level where it relies exclusively on forms, a level of intellection that is free from all hypothetical thinking.[102]

Calvin's rejection of iconography is akin to Plato's wariness about the poets. Resorting to iconography, Calvin says, is a corruption that arises when the Church is unable to hear the Word of God; the Eastern Church turned to images when the reality of God had been lost.[103] The Roman Church succumbed to constructing totalities in one way; the Eastern Church, in another. The Spirit alone is evidence of the Infinite breaking in, and is, therefore, man's only guide in this world where corrupt reason is turned in upon itself. The Word of God is man's salutary and corrective guide--which the Spirit alone can confirm *is* God's Word.

* * *

In this light, the problems of man's historical existence--from petty pride and the lack of personal charity to more grand scale violence--stem not from revealed religion, but rather from its absence, from the *closure* of man to God and to the unbounded expression of man's sinful nature without Divine corrective.

> If God has willed this treasure of understanding [of His Word] to be hidden from His children, it is no wonder or absurdity that the multitude of men are so ignorant and stupid. . . . Whenever, then, the fewness of believers disturbs us, let the converse come to mind, that only those to whom it is given can comprehend the mysteries of God.[104]

Because most men will never receive the gift of the Spirit and so believe, the true Church will always be a remnant among the ungodly.

Tempting as it may be, however, to see in this thought a bald confirmation of the perennial need in human affairs to manufacture an enemy,[105] Calvin was led toward it because of the gravity of the epistemological dilemma that we have outlined above. It is because of the limit of reason and the tendency of reason to manufacture gods in man's own fanciful image--in short, the totality that reason generates--that led Calvin to a radical understanding of man's dependence upon God's free gift as the only way out of the prison of sin.

The paradox, of course, was that this understanding of absolute mortal dependency upon God contained both the aspect of judgment *before* God, and confidence that through the Holy Spirit the work *of* God was being done by the true remnant of the Church. Through the Spirit, the Christian "takes care to advance [God's] glory," Calvin says.[106] The believer, inspired by the Spirit, *can* know of his election and sanctification. The true Christian is both humble *and* certain, sinner thirsting in the waterless pit[107] *and* quenched by the Holy Spirit. The confirmation that through the center that is Christ the sinner is saved, is the emanation from that center which is the work of the Holy Spirit in those who are sanctified.

The excess to which this understanding is prone is easily seen. Indeed, when Hobbes claims that "vain esteem" is the wellspring of human misery,[108] he has in mind, among others, those who purport to be possessed by the Spirit. Calvin knew of the problem: "How much the ignorance of this principle [that God does not indiscriminately adopt all into the hope of salvation but gives to some what he denies to others], how much it takes away from true humility, is well known."[109]

Calvin was not, however, daunted by this difficulty. The pridefulness of man certainly laid open the possibility of corruptions of understanding and action of the most horrendous sort, yet *without* sin (and the Law that identifies it) there is no possibility of man's recognition of his *dependency* upon God--an understanding that is captured in St. Paul's succinct observation: "Moreover the law entered, that offenses might abound. But where sin abounded, grace did much more abound: That as sin hath reigned unto death, even so might grace reign through righteousness unto eternal life by Jesus Christ our Lord."[110]

Sin moves man toward transgression; but such transgression, properly understood, moves God toward man through grace. This paradox is written into fallen, human, existence. Man descends beneath the beasts *and* ascends above the angels; both propositions are true.

It would be a stretch, of course, to suggest that through sin man achieves his dignity in creation; there is, however, a kernel of truth in this claim. If by dignity we mean that a creature performs the purpose for which it was created, then it can be said that through sin man comes to know that his purpose is to glorify God. The sinfulness of man is, thus, a necessary but not sufficient occasion for the glorification of God by man in the world.

Having said this about the risk, as it were, of pride which Calvin (contra Hobbes) knew had to be taken, he was of the mind that God's providential ordering of the world provided the wherewithal to redress the excesses of pride. (In this respect Calvin had a confidence about the stability of temporal order that Hobbes could not have had.) Ready at hand are helps upon which sinful man can depend. God watches out for man, and provides what he needs.[111] "God's providence does not always meet us in its naked form, but God in a sense clothes it with the means employed."[112]

The first of these was, of course, the Word of God. While Calvin did believe, like Luther, that salvation is not achieved *by* works sanctioned through the Law; he did believe, unlike Luther, that *once sanctified*, those works performed that were specified by the Word had as their object the glorification of God, and so were part of the Christian life. The theological distinction upon which this significant difference hinges is the well-known "third use of the Law," of which Calvin makes extensive use, and Luther little. "The third and principal use, which pertains more closely to the proper use of the law, finds its place among believers *in whose hearts the Spirit of God already lives and reigns.*"[113] Through the third use of the Law, Christians find the guidance they need to do the work of God; through it, they are "drawn back from the slippery path of transgression."[114] "Here is the best instrument for them to learn more thoroughly each day the nature of the Lord's will to which they aspire, and to confirm in them the understanding of it."[115]

Calvin's measured confidence[116] in the ability of the Christian to do God's work finds no analog in Luther, to be sure; yet in his defense, Calvin was not haunted by the sort of melancholy to which Luther's "Table Talk" amply attests.[117] Whether Luther would have responded by suggesting that the proof that such melancholy *was*, in fact, lurking under the surface of the worldly activity Calvin endorsed is an open question. However one sides on the matter, it is nevertheless clear that for Calvin the Word of God does provide help for the Christian ever in danger of falling back into sin, and of losing the quiet of conscience.

Beyond the Word, there is, as well, the institution of government that God has ordained. In this regard, Calvin and Luther differ somewhat. Where Calvin may be characterized as a covenantal theologian, Luther is much more of a dispensational theologian. Both argue that temporal power derives its authority from the Old Testament; for Calvin, however, the Old Testament covenant is crucial for understanding a *Christian* polity. Oddly consonant with Hobbes, Calvin claims that Christ restored rather than abrogated the Law.[118] Luther, whose theology rests upon the Law-Gospel distinction, did not understand the meaning of Christ's fulfillment of the Law[119] in this way, and would have wondered, again, whether Calvin had failed to understand the distinction and relationship between the Law and faith, between political power and spiritual power.

Calvin does, of course, acknowledge that there are two types of government: "[W]hoever knows how to distinguish between body and soul, between the present fleeting life and that future eternal life, will without difficulty know that Christ's spiritual Kingdom and the civil jurisdiction are things completely distinct."[120] Yet here, as with so much of Calvin's thought, there are nuances that modify the stark distinctions of the sort with which Luther might have happily rested. In Calvin's view, the pilgrimage below requires the help of civil government,[121] which itself is authorized by God. The pridefulness of man, the self-referential judgments which prolong corruption and sloth in the name of freedom,[122] receive their corrective by the *extant* institutions of government. In passages that foreshadow the claims Hobbes would make a century later, Calvin argues that obedience to the sovereign power is obedience to God Himself.[123] Here, as in Calvin's understanding of the importance of the Word for sinful, fallen, man, there are helps ready at hand which guide man to glorify God and to attenuate man's sinfulness. God is transcendent, and cannot be understood by any ascent that mortal man may make relying upon his own corrupted faculties; nevertheless, God has given man certain gifts which may serve as correctives and guides. That they are indeed Divine gifts is confirmed by the very sinfulness of man.

3. Conclusion

Is there "toleration" in the thought of Luther and Calvin, the most prominent of the Reformers? If we mean by this a wariness about the tendency of reason and human judgment to absolutize itself, then certainly the answer is "yes." Yet Luther and Calvin did not move in the direction they did in order to sanctify human skepticism, and so, perhaps toleration; but rather to revitalize Christianity against those who they thought had placed mortal reason in the way of salvation and the glory of God. Their assault against mortal reason was meant to remind Christians that they are nothing without God.

How difficult this thought is to comprehend through the lens of the enlightened eye can be seen when we consider the assumption upon which much conventional thinking about toleration today rests.

In its contemporary usage, toleration generally supposes an intact self whose "values" ought to be respected by virtue of the fact that the self from which they emanate is worthy of respect. For Luther and Calvin, in contradistinction, God alone is the measure, and the self becomes what it truly is by virtue of glorifying God. Calvin well expressed the epistemological corollary to this understanding at the outset of the *Institutes*: "[M]an never achieves a clear knowledge of himself unless he has first looked upon God's face, and then descends from contemplating Him to scrutinize himself."[124] How far this is from contemporary attempts to generate a doctrine of toleration out of an understanding of the limits of reason and the dignity of each and every autonomous soul ought to be clear. The thought of Luther and Calvin "maps" onto the debate about toleration only marginally. The skepticism of later thinkers about reason's grasp bears only a rough resemblance to what is found in Luther and Calvin.

Indeed, the best way to characterize the relationship may be to say that the "skepticism" of those early Reformers was a parallel evolutionary development having morphological similarities, but genetic divergences.

The matter cannot be left at that, however. I have already made some mention of Luther's understanding of God's providential history as a way to comprehend the mystery of faith and the problem of sin. Calvin, too, moves in this direction. Disregarding the question of whether they thought of the matter in terms of this, their thinking raises issues of historical contingency--in short, *novelty*--which ought to be at the heart of any doctrine of toleration. True, for neither of them are *all* things possible; nevertheless, God's plan, though beyond the understanding of human reason, does not give rise to the "terror of history."[125] Novel historical events ordained by the God "who laid the foundations of the Earth"[126] await all who are born before God the Son comes again in glory. Until then, Christians "walk by faith, not by sight."[127] All historical contingencies--indeed, *every* manifestation of evil--point beyond themselves toward the glory of God that is as yet unseen by the eye of reason. (Worth considering is whether such contingencies can be long borne without faith of this sort.[128])

Until then, as well, as the Parable of the Wheat and the Tares suggests,[129] no good of the world is unambiguously so; evil--the tares--will be present, until the End, until the harvest. It cannot be eradicated by mortal effort.

This is a lesson not easily learned by the intolerant man, for whom the ambiguity of all temporal goods seems anathema to well-ordered living. The intolerant man is, above all, impatient with ambiguity, with *difference*; waiting "until justice be turned into judgment,"[130] is not endured, for he, not God, is the harvester. Both Luther and Calvin were attuned to this fact, as it were, of providential history, though Calvin--again foreshadowing Hobbes--was most explicit in his exposition of it.

> [L]ook around and glance at the world as a whole, or at least cast your sight upon regions farther off, [and you will see that] divine providence has wisely arranged that various countries should be ruled by various kinds of government. For as elements cohere only in unequal proportions, so countries are best held together according to their own particular inequality.[131]

There are differences, in other words, that will only be surmounted at the end of history. To attempt to overcome them at any moment before the End Time is to supplant God's mysterious unity with a brittle man-made unity--a tendency Tocqueville thought peculiarly in evidence, ironically, among democratic peoples ostensibly most committed to freedom.[132]

Luther and Calvin, with their insistence that Christ be the center, would, I suspect, appear to be intolerant today, at least to the ecumenically minded; yet the irony is that the inscrutable mystery of God's providential history to which they recurred in order to comprehend the meaning of that center provides a Divine authorization, as it were, for difference, for the ambiguity of goodness in the world, and for patient endurance. "For now we see through a glass, darkly; but then face to face: know I know in part, but then shall I know even as also I am known."[133] To be sure, this countenance is counterpoised by the demands of righteousness, whether it be passive (Luther) or active (Calvin); for both thinkers, however, such righteousness, properly understood, was imputed by God, not bestowed on man by man himself. Nature cannot grace itself. While *Christians* in the Reformation may have unwittingly done this, *Reformation* Christianity urgently warns against it.

This is not to say, of course, that difference and ambiguity were *embraced* by Luther and Calvin; such things abided in historical existence, as Augustine had pointed out long before, as tests of faith.[134] Both would be overcome by God, moreover, at the End of Time. Difference is subsumed by identity--not through the vagaries of human agency, as the post-modern critique of much modern thought would have it, but rather by the inscrutable Will of God.

As we move into the 21st century it is worth pondering whether in the age of democracy the predominant disposition that animates the very real need for toleration is linked to the only apparent need to overcome difference, as Tocqueville argued.

As conditions grow more equal, each individual becomes more like his fellows, weaker, and smaller, and the habit grows of ceasing to think about the citizens and considering only the people. Individuals are forgotten, and the species alone counts. At such times the human mind seeks to embrace a multitude of different objects at once, and it constantly strives to link up a variety of consequences with a single cause. *The concept of unity becomes an obsession.*[135]

In a democracy, envy drives citizens to look to the one *visible power* of the state for universal rules by which all must live.[136] In the name of equality, difference is obliterated.

Theologically, the issue associated with this tendency is easy to discern: in such an impulse man takes upon himself the task of bringing about the unity which is not his to achieve, as the story of the Tower of Babel indicates.[137]

In this light, while conditions of democracy are peculiarly suited to be an occasion for aspiring to build a Tower of Babel in the way, say, that conditions of aristocracy are not, the root of the aspiration for a false universalism that breeds intolerance is theological, not political or historical.

Should this be the case, we will be required to turn to a consideration of theology in order adequately to understand intolerance. Whether the thinking of Luther and Calvin can be of some assistance to citizens who live in this age of democracy in which centripetal forces of "unification" grow ever stronger remains an open question. What they can at least provide is an understanding that the problems of this and all other ages cannot be disentangled from questions about God.[138]

NOTES:

1. I Cor. 13:12.

2. This was Tocqueville's worry. In the face of overwhelming uncertainty, he thought democratic citizens would withdraw into themselves and abdicate their freedom to a tyrant who settles everything in the material world in order to compensate for the disarray in the world of ideas. Because he thought Christian religion provided an antidote to this debilitating uncertainty, Tocqueville was able to say: "If [a man] has no faith he must obey, and if he is free he must believe." (Alexis de Tocqueville, *Democracy in America*, J. Mayer ed. [New York: Harper and Row, 1969], Vol. II, Part I, Ch. 5, 444).

3. See G.W.F. Hegel, *Phenomenology of Spirit*, A.V. Miller trans. (Oxford: Oxford University Press, 1977), §589, 359.

4. Tocqueville, *Democracy in America*, Vol. II, Part I, Ch. 20, 495.

5. Again, Tocqueville is helpful here. Consider his observation: "No longer do ideas, but interests only, form the links between men [in ages of democracy], and it would seem that human opinions were no more than a sort of mental dust open to the wind on every side and unable to come together and take shape" (*Democracy in America*, Vol. II, Part I, Ch. 1, 433).

6. John 15:1-2, 4-5.

7. Only God is able to say, "I AM THAT I AM" (Exodus 3:14); all other beings *are* only inasmuch as they participate in God. See St. Augustine, *Confessions*, Henry Chadwick trans., (New York: Oxford University Press, 1991), Bk. I, Ch. ii, 4: "Without you, whatever exists would not exist."

See also St. Augustine, *City of God*, in *The Fathers of the Church*, Roy Joseph Deferrari ed. (New York: The Fathers of the Church, Inc., 1950), Vol. 7, Bk. XIV, Ch. 28, 410: "worldly society has flowered from a selfish love which dared to despise even God, whereas the communion of saints is rooted in the love of God that is ready to trample on self. In a word, this latter relies on the Lord, whereas the other boasts that it can get along by itself." Throughout this paper I will first cite the more authoritative Deferrari edition (as *City of God* in *Writings*), and subsequently cite the page or pages to which it corresponds in the more readily available Henry Bettenson translation (New York: Penguin Books, 1972) as (*CG*)--in the case of the passage above: (*CG*, 593).

8. For some informative yet critical remarks by Luther about Augustine see Martin Luther, "Table Talk," in *Luther's Works*, Helmut T. Lehmann ed., (Philadelphia: Fortress Press, 1967), Vol. 54, No. 347, 49-50.

9. See Luther, "Table Talk," in *Works*, Vol. 54, No. 1543, 155: "One shouldn't think of any other God than Christ; whoever doesn't speak through the mouth of Christ is not God."

10. Hence the apparent incongruity of his earnest defense of the freedom of a Christian (see Martin Luther, "The Freedom of a Christian," in *Luther's Works*, Vol. 31, 333-377) and his repudiation of the peasant's cause against the political status quo in the War of 1525. See Martin Luther, "Against the Robbing and Murdering Hordes of Peasants," in *Luther's Works*, Vol. 46, 49-55. Notwithstanding this tract, his sympathies were generally with the poor. See Martin Luther, "Treatise on Good Works," in *Luther's Works*, Vol. 44, 51.

11. See Luther, "Table Talk," in *Works*, Vol. 54, No. 3554, 233: "For anybody who abolishes the teaching of the law in a political context abolishes government and domestic life, and anybody who abolishes the law in an ecclesiastical context ceases to

have knowledge of sin."

12. See Romans 7:23 ("I see another law in my members, warring against the law of my mind, and bringing me into captivity to the law of sin which is in my members.")

13. The resonances with Aristotle cannot be overlooked here. See Aristotle, *The Politics*, Ernest Baker, trans. (Oxford: Oxford University Press, 1958), 1252a: "all associations aim at some good; and we may also hold that the particular association which is the most sovereign of all, and includes all the rest, will pursue this aim the most, and will thus be directed to the most sovereign of all goods. This most sovereign and inclusive association is the polis." See also Aristotle, *Nicomachean Ethics*, Martin Oswald, trans. (New York: Macmillan, 1986), 1094b: "since [the science of politics] uses the rest of the sciences . . . its end seems to embrace the ends of the other sciences. Thus it follows that the end of politics is the good of man."

Luther has great contempt for Aristotle. See, for example, Martin Luther, "To the Christian Nobility of the German Nation Concerning the Reform of the Christian Estate," in *Luther's Works*, Vol. 44, 201: "this dead heathen [Aristotle] has conquered, obstructed, and almost succeeded in suppressing the books of the living God. I can only believe that the devil has introduced this study."

14. Luther, "Table Talk," in *Works*, Vol. 54, No. 5285, 406. See also Martin Luther, "Lectures on Isaiah," in *Luther's Works*, Vol. 16, 327: "faith must be built on the basis of history, and we ought to stay with it alone and not so easily slip into allegories."

15. Luther, "Table Talk," in *Works*, Vol. 54, No. 327, 45.

16. See B.A. Gerrish, *Grace and Reason, A Study in the Theology of Luther* (Oxford: Clarendon Press, 1962), 127-36, for an excellent treatment of Luther's divergences from Aquinas.

17. Luther, "Freedom," in *Works*, Vol. 31, 344. Cf. II Cor. 4:16; Gal. 5:17. Cf. Paul Ricoeur, *The Symbolism of Evil* (Boston: Beacon Press, 1967), 331-36. In St. Paul there is almost an equivalence between the notion of the exile of the soul and the carnal realm; a theme, Ricoeur notes, Luther also draws upon. Calvin would subsequently also develop this notion of exile.

18. See Matt. 5:17 ("Think not that I have come to destroy the law, or the prophets: I have come not to destroy, but to fulfill").

19. Matt. 9:17; Mark 2:22; Luke 5:37.

20. See Plato, *Republic*, G.M.A. Grube trans. (Indianapolis, IN: Hackett Publishing Co., 1992), Bk. VII, 514a-517a.

21. Martin Luther, "Lectures on Galatians," in *Luther's Works*, Vol. 26, 9, *passim*.

22. Luther, "Lectures on Galatians," in *Works*, Vol. 26, 7. See also Ibid., 8: "between the active righteousness of the law and the passive righteousness of Christ, there is no middle ground."

23. See Luther, "Table Talk," in *Works*, Vol. 54, No. 1234, 127: "There's no man living on earth who knows how to distinguish between the law and the gospel. We may think we understand it when we are listening to a sermon, but we're far from it. Only the Holy Spirit knows this."

24. Cf. John 1:5 ("And the light shineth in darkness; and the darkness comprehended it not").

25. Luther, "Lectures on Galatians," in *Works*, Vol. 26, 5 (emphasis added). Here Luther worries about the reluctance of human beings to break out of the safe world of Law, within which the charge of righteousness falls squarely upon humankind. See Thomas M. McDonough, *The Law and the Gospel in Luther* (Oxford: Oxford University Press, 1963), 30: "for Luther, the human will is somehow curved in on itself... and bent

ineluctably on earthly goods. This is the concupiscence or carnality that Luther identifies with sin." Human reason, too, is corrupted by sin, as we shall further discover in our discussion of Calvin.

Cf. Martin Heidegger's essay, "The Essence of Truth," (in *Martin Heidegger: Basic Writings* [New York: Harper & Row, 1977], 134). Heidegger there suggests that 'filling up the world' intimates a hiding from Being. Luther has the same insight, *viz.*, that the terror of conscience, the terror of looking below the everyday world of works, leads Christians to "look at nothing except . . . works." See also Jean-Jacques Rousseau, *Emile*, Allan Bloom trans. (New York: Basic Books, 1979), Bk. IV, 229-30.

26. Luther, "Table Talk," in *Works*, Vol. 54, No. 522, 96.

27. Consider Luther's advice to young people: "If you are sad, seek whatever relief you can. I absolve you of all pastimes through which you seek recreation, except such as are manifest sins, no matter whether they are eating, drinking, dancing, gaming, or anything else" (Luther, "Table Talk," in *Works*, Vol. 54, No. 461, 76).

28. Luther, "Lectures on Galatians," in *Works*, Vol. 26, 5.

29. G.W.F. Hegel, *Philosophy of History* (New York: Dover, 1956), Part IV, Sec. III, Ch. I, 424.

30. Luther, "Freedom," in *Works*, Vol. 31, 344-45.

31. Luther, "Freedom," in *Works*, Vol. 31, 357.

32. Here the flesh acts in the service of the spirit; the Old in the service of the New. The Old is thus annulled yet preserved in the New. See Luther, "Lectures on Galatians," in *Works*, Vol. 27, 87: "a Christian struggles with sin continually, and yet in his struggle he does not surrender but obtains victory."

33. Luther, "Freedom," in *Works*, Vol. 31, 348.

34. See Luther, "Table Talk," in *Works*, Vol. 54, No. 1385, 146: "Christ governs his kingdom in a remarkable way. He hides himself so that none of his power may be seen, and yet he confounds kings and emperors."

35. Luther, "Lectures on Galatians," in *Works*, Vol. 26, 131. See also Luther, "Freedom," in *Works*, Vol. 31, 346-47: "[The moment you begin to have faith] you learn that all things in you are altogether blameworthy, sinful, and damnable."

36. Luther, "Lectures on Galatians," in *Works*, Vol. 26, 234 (emphasis added).

37. Luther, "Lectures on Galatians," in *Works*, Vol. 27, 86 (emphasis added). Cf. I Cor. 2:9. Gerrish notes that Luther accorded reason its place in matters pertaining to the "world," but insisted that "reason stumbles at the doctrine of the Incarnation, . . . not because reason refuses to believe in God, but rather [because] it does not understand who God is; consequently it invents a God after its own fancy" (*Grace and Reason*, 14). As Hobbes (and even Rousseau, in *Emile* [Bk. IV, 255, *passim*]) would later argue, reason concludes *that* there is a God (*quod sit Deus*), but not *what* God is (*quid sit Deus*). In insisting that reason cannot comprehend the mystery of faith, the labor of reason is directed entirely and with legitimacy toward the "world," Gerrish suggests. Luther's insistence that reason cannot understand salvation frees reason from a burden it is not capable of bearing.

Tocqueville remarks about the peculiar way in which Christian faith and reason can work together and, in fact, argues that, unlike Islam, Christianity and enlightenment are not contradictory impulses precisely because Christian faith demands that reason defer *only in matters of salvation* (see *Democracy in America*, Vol. II, Part I, Ch. 5, 445).

38. Matt. 27:46, Mark 15:34. From Psalm 22:1.

39. Luther, "Freedom," in *Works*, Vol. 31, 357.

40. Byss: the alpha privative of abyss; it is the bottom underneath the apparently bottomless. The term is first used by Jacob Boehme (1575-1624), a Lutheran mystic. More recently, Tillich's theology is predicated on the experience of the abyss and of the Byss beneath it. See Paul Tillich, *The Courage to Be* (New Haven: Yale University Press, 1951).

41. Luther, "Freedom," in *Works*, Vol. 31, 355. Cf. II Cor. 12:9.

42. This metaphor is found in both the Old Testament (Ps. 19:5) and New (Rev. 19:7-9). The marriage spoken of there was interpreted by the Church fathers to be the marriage between Christ and the Church, *not* between Christ and the Christian--Luther's interpretation. Cf. Mark 2:19; John 3:29.

43. Luther, "Freedom," in *Works*, Vol. 31, 352.

44. In the Divine-Human equation, then, human beings are the passive, feminine principle, while God (the Son) is masculine. This is further confirmed by Luther's insistence that Christian righteousness is *passive* righteousness, not active. Cf. Rom. 7:2-4. Calvin's theology does not emphasize the passive aspect of Christian righteousness.

45. Martin Luther, "The Bondage of the Will," in *Luther's Works*, Vol. 33, 41.

46. Cf. Tocqueville, *Democracy in America*, Appendix I, Y, 734-35.

47. Luther, "Bondage," in *Works*, Vol. 33, 140.

48. Luther, "Bondage," in *Works*, Vol. 33, 177. Cf. Rom. 9:17-23.

49. Luther, "Bondage," in *Works*, Vol. 33, 179.

50. Luther, "Bondage," in *Works*, Vol. 33, 179.

51. Luther, "Bondage," in *Works*, Vol. 33, 180.

52. For a brief discussion of Heidegger's *Holzwege*, see David Farrell Krell's "General Introduction: 'The Question of Being,'" in *Martin Heidegger: Basic Writings* (New York: Harper & Row, 1977), 34-35. Heeding Heidegger's caution that "often it seems as though one [woodpath] were identical with another [while in fact it is not]" (Ibid., 34), there is, nevertheless, something to be said about the resemblance between Luther's way and Heidegger's. Heidegger notes that "[theology] is slowly beginning to understand once more Luther's insight that the 'foundation' on which its system of dogma rests has not arisen from an inquiry in which faith is primary, and that conceptually this 'foundation' is not only inadequate for the problematic of theology, but conceals and distorts it" (Martin Heidegger, *Being and Time*, John Macquarrie and Edward Robinson trans. [New York: Harper and Row, 1962], Introduction I, §3, 30).

53. Pelagius' doctrine that human beings have free will was condemned at the Councils of Carthage in 416 and 418 upon the insistence of Augustine. Pelagius held that grace merely helps the Christian accomplish what is already in his own power. Neither Augustine nor Luther believed that the Christian could achieve salvation without the assistance of Christ. See Augustine, *City of God*, in *Writings*, Vol. 7, Bk. IX, Chs. 14-15, 98-101 (*CG* 359-61); Luther, "Bondage," in *Works*, Vol. 33, 107, *passim*.

54. Martin Luther, "Temporal Authority: To What Extent It Should Be Obeyed," in *Luther's Works*, Vol. 45, 108.

55. Luther, "Temporal Authority," in *Works*, Vol. 45, 114.

56. Luther, "Temporal Authority," in *Works*, Vol. 45, 108. The category of conscience is a central theological category for Calvin, but less so for Luther, in large part because, for Luther, righteousness is ever linked to Christ alone.

57. Luther, "Temporal Authority," in *Works*, Vol. 45, 109; see also Ibid., 115-16.

58. Luther, "Temporal Authority," in *Works*, Vol. 45, 92.

59. Martin Luther, "To the Christian Nobility of the German Nation Concerning the Reform of the Christian Estate," in *Luther's Works*, Vol. 44, 130.

60. Luther, "Christian Nobility," in *Works*, Vol. 44, 131-32; see also Luther, "Temporal Authority," in *Works*, Vol. 45, 87.

61. Luther, "Christian Nobility," in *Works*, Vol. 44, 129. See also Ibid., 134, where St. Peter gives the keys to the Church to all Christians; and Ibid., 168, where no one should kiss the Pope's feet.

While all Christians are equal in the eyes of God, and while the work a Christian does is a mere convention, Luther did have a contempt for those who were idle and yet reaped wealth from the work of others. That work is a mere convention does not mean that it is irrelevant. See Ibid., 190: "if a man wants to be rich, let him put his hand to the plough and seek his fortune in the land." This sentiment is not yet temporal equality, however. (Cf. Tocqueville, *Democracy in America*, Vol. II, Part I, Ch. 1, 429-33.) The injunctions of Luke 20:25 and Rom. 13:1 remain intact, as Luther points out in "Against the Robbing and Murdering Hordes," in *Luther's Works*, Vol. 46, 50, *passim*.

62. Luther, "Temporal Authority," in *Works*, Vol. 45, 117.

63. Luther, "Christian Nobility," in *Works*, Vol. 44, 125. Cf. Augustine, *Confessions*, Bk. IV, Ch. xvi, 72: "When you are our firm support, then it is firm indeed. But when our support rests on our own strength, it is infirmity."

64. Luther, "Christian Nobility," in *Works*, Vol. 44, 145. In the full passage from which this is taken, Luther clearly believes that the princes are Christian and not rapacious wolves. The prospect that the princes themselves might be the 'wolves in sheep's clothing' did not occur to him here. (Later, Locke would argue against Hobbes for making the same error about the Leviathan's relationship to the people of the commonwealth. See John Locke, *Second Treatise*, in *Two Treatises of Government*, Peter Laslett ed. [Cambridge: Cambridge University Press, 1988], Ch. VII, §93, 328.) Luther's subsequent "Temporal Authority" attempts more to carve out a domain for conscience that would be impervious to the machinations of either the Roman Church or the State.

65. Hence, Luther's claim at the beginning of "Temporal Authority" that Christian princes are incorrect in believing that because the two realms are separated they may do what they please in the earthly kingdom. See "Temporal Authority," in *Works*, Vol. 45, 83.

66. Luther, "Temporal Authority," in *Works*, Vol. 45, 119-20 (emphasis added). See also Luther H. Waring, *Political Theories of Martin Luther*, (New York: G. Putnam's Sons, 1910), 163-84. Waring's chapter, "The Objects of the State," is especially good at showing that Luther believed that Christian princes must be Christians in order that their power be used well.

67. Luther, "Temporal Authority," in *Works*, Vol. 45, 120. The difficulty faced by Luther and subsequent reformers was what to do when princes derogated their Christian charge. When princes do not treat subjects in a Christian manner, when is it acceptable to resist? See Quentin Skinner, *The Foundations of Modern Political Thought* (Cambridge: Cambridge University Press, 1980), Vol. 2, 189-238, for a discussion of the idea of the right to resist in Reformation thought. Skinner contends that "the main influence of Lutheran political theory in early modern Europe lay in the direction of encouraging and legitimating the emergence of united and absolutist monarchies" (Ibid., 113).

68. Later, Rousseau understood the utter interiority of Christian religion to mean that human beings are left "without bonds of union" (see Jean-Jacques Rousseau, *The Social Contract*, Maurice Cranston trans. [New York: Penguin Books, 1984], Bk. IV, Ch. 8, 186). Failing to grasp Luther's claim that *through Christ* the Christian discovers the

foundation of his relation with others, Rousseau calls for the inception of a civil religion to compensate for the absence of social bonds within the Christian community.

69. See Luther, "Treatise on Good Works," in *Works*, Vol. 44, 23. Cf. John 6:28-29.

70. Luther, "Freedom," in *Works*, Vol. 31, 367-68. See also Ibid., 371, where, as Christ "puts on" the Christian, so, too, the Christian must put on his neighbor.

71. Luther, "Freedom," in *Works*, Vol. 31, 348.

72. Luther, "Freedom," in *Works*, Vol. 31, 371.

73. Luther, "Freedom," in *Works*, Vol. 31, 344.

74. Luther, "Table Talk," in *Works*, Vol. 54, No. 630, 111 (emphasis added).

75. Luther, "Table Talk," in *Works*, Vol. 54, No. 439, 71.

76. Luther, "Table Talk," in *Works*, Vol. 54, No. 1310, 134.

77. John 18:38. Consider, in this light, a conversation recorded between Luther and Melanchthon: "They spoke at length and sorrowfully about future times, when there would be many teachers. 'There will be great confusion [said Luther]. Nobody will conform with another man's opinions or submit to his authority. Everybody will want to be his own rabbi, as Osiander and Agricola do now, and the greatest offenses and divisions will arise from this" (Luther, "Table Talk," in *Works*, Vol. 54, No. 3900, 290).

78. See Gal. 4:28 ("there is neither Jew nor Greek, there is neither bond nor free, there is neither male not female: for ye are all one in Christ"). See also I John 2:9 ("He that saith he is in the light, and hateth his brother, is in darkness even until now").

79. I Cor. 14:33. See John Calvin, *Institutes of Christian Religion*. John T. McNeill ed. (Philadelphia: The Westminster Press, 1960), "Prefatory Address," §8, 30.

See also Augustine, *City of God*, in *Writings*, Vol. 7, Bk. 12, Ch. 22, 288 (*CG*, 502): "[God] created man's nature as a kind of mean between angels and beasts, so that if he submitted to his Creator . . . he should pass over into the fellowship of the angels . . . but if he used his free will in arrogance and disbelief . . . he should live like the beasts . . . and be the slave of his [own] desires."

80. See Calvin, *Institutes*, Bk. I, Ch. XIII, §18, 143: "to the Spirit is assigned the power and efficacy of [the activity of the Father and wisdom of the Son]."

81. Calvin, *Institutes*, "Prefatory Address," §2, 13.

82. See Calvin, *Institutes*, Bk. I, Chs. III-IV, 43-51; Ch. VI, §14, 68.

83. Calvin, *Institutes*, "Prefatory Address," §5, 23.

84. The writings of certain French Huguenots (see Marnay, *A Defense of Liberty Against Tyrants*); Scottish resistance leaders (see Knox, *Political Writings*); and Dutch Calvinists (see Phillip de Marnix, "Letter to William of Orange") are instructive. As William Stevenson Jr., to whom I am indebted for these references, has put it: "That Calvin sowed the seeds of later 'Calvinist' excesses is not difficult to perceive. But that his thinking was as simplistic as these later excesses implied can be flatly refuted" (*Christian Freedom in the Political Thought of John Calvin*, Part II, Ch. 3, 39 [manuscript in progress]).

85. See Augustine, *City of God*, in *Writings*, Vol. 7, Bk. XII, Ch. 7, 257 (*CG*, 479-80): "no one, therefore, need seek for an efficient cause of an evil will. Since the 'effect' is, in fact, a deficiency, the cause should be called 'deficient.' The fault of an evil will begins when one falls from Supreme Being to some being which is less than absolute." As in Plato, there is, properly speaking, no agency until the soul is rightly oriented to and by what veritably is. See Plato, *Republic*, Bk. IX, 588e-589a, where until the soul is oriented by the Good it is a multi-headed beast who only *appears* to be a unitary being, and so cannot act coherently as a *single* agent.

86. Calvin, *Institutes*, "Prefatory Address," §6, 25-26.

87. See Emmanuel Levinas, *Totality and Infinity*, Alphonso Lingis trans. (Pittsburgh: Duquesne University Press, 1969). The Introduction, written by John Wild, offers a rendition of the distinction Levinas wishes to make: "As [the author] points out, one answer [to the question of life] is given by the totalizers who are satisfied with themselves and with the systems they can organize around themselves as they already are. A very different answer is given by those who are dissatisfied, and who strive for what is other than themselves, the infinitizers, as we may call them. The former strive for order and system; the latter for freedom and creative advance."

In Tocqueville's words: "the short space of sixty years can never shut in the whole of man's imagination; the incomplete joys of this world will never satisfy his heart" (*Democracy in America*, Vol. I, Part II, Ch. 9, 296). Religion must exist in the world to answer to the hopes of a being so constituted that it is forever called beyond the world; religion violates its charge if it aligns itself with worldly power and becomes, in Levinas' idiom, a *totality*.

88. See Emmanuel Levinas, "Loving the Torah more than God," in *Difficult Freedom: Essays on Judaism*, Seán Hand trans. (London: Athlone Press, 1990), Part III, 144: "the link between God and man is not an emotional communion that takes places within the love of a God incarnate, but a spirit or intellectual [*esprits*] relationship which takes place through an education in the Torah. It is precisely a word, not incarnate, from God that ensures a living God among us."

Beyond this massive theological difference, there is the fact that Levinas argues that the Infinite is revealed through the experience of another person--a thought to which Calvin would never accede.

89. Consider Augustine's claim that the propensity to turn from God, to glory in the totality of the City of Man, is so powerful that God had to take mortal form to provide a way out for man. Were He (through the Son) *merely* human He could not have averted the temptation; had God remained God and not taken human form, He could not have mediated (Ibid., Bk. IX, Ch. 15, 99-101 [*CG*, 359-61]). He must have taken on the poison of mortal life, in order to provide the antidote to the sin that characterizes it. See Augustine, *The Trinity*, Edmund Hill trans. (New York: New City Press, 1991), Bk. IV, Ch. 4, §24, 169: "health is the opposite pole from sickness, but the cure should be half-way between the two, and unless it has some affinity with sickness it will not lead to health." Also see Ibid., Bk. VIII, Ch. 3, §7, 247: "this indeed it is useful for us to believe and to hold firm and unshaken in our hearts, that the humility thanks to which God was born of a woman, and led through such abuse at the hands of mortal men to his death, is a medicine to heal the tumor of our pride and a high sacrament to break the chains of our sin." Christ is the *pharmakon*.

In this light, consider the verses added by the early Church fathers to the Gospel of Mark (Mk. 16:8-20), notably 16:18 ("They shall take up serpents; and if they drink any deadly thing, it shall not hurt them; they shall lay hands on the sick, and they shall recover.") Mortal poisons receive their antidote through the resurrected Christ. Cf. Jacques Derrida, "Plato's Pharmacy," in *Dissemination* (Chicago: University of Chicago Press, 1981), 62-171.

90. See Calvin, *Institutes*, Bk. II, Ch. I, §9, 252-53. See also Martin Luther, "Lectures on Genesis" (in *Luther's Works*, Vol. 1, 55-68). He concludes that, "since the loss of this image [Gen. 1:26] through sin we cannot understand it to any extent" (Ibid., 61), and that, "not only have we no experience of [this likeness to God], but we continually experience the opposite; and so we hear nothing except bare words" (Ibid., 63).

91. See Thomas Hobbes, for whom the problem of human existence in history before the End Time stems from this fact. In his words, "whereupon having both eaten, [Adam and Eve] did indeed take upon them God's office, which is judicature of good and evil; *but acquired no new ability to distinguish between them aright*" (*Leviathan*, Michael Oakeshott ed. [New York: Macmillan Publishing Co., 1962], Part II, Ch. 20, 157 [emphasis added]). For Hobbes, the problem for which the Leviathan is the remedy stems from the human unwillingness to admit that the relationship really was broken off! For a consideration of Hobbes's use of the myth of Ixion to convey the same point see Joshua Mitchell, *Not By Reason Alone: Religion, History, and Identity in Early Modern Political Thought* (Chicago: University of Chicago Press, 1993), Ch. 2, 54-55.

See also St. Augustine, *The Trinity*, Edmund Hill trans. (New York: New City Press, 1991), Bk. IV, Ch. 1, §2, 153: "we were exiled from this unchanging joy, *yet not so broken and cut off from it* that we stopped seeking eternity, truth, and happiness even in this changeable time-bound situation of ours" (emphasis added).

92. Calvin, *Institutes*, Bk. I, Ch. V, §12, 64-65 (emphasis added).

93. Calvin, *Institutes*, Bk. I, Ch. V, §12, 66 (emphasis added).

94. See Levinas, *Totality and Infinity*, Sect. I, B, 7, 80: "It is not the insufficiency of the I that prevents totalization, but the Infinity of the Other."

95. See Ludwig Feuerbach, *The Essence of Christianity* (New York: Harper and Row, 1957), Ch. XXVII, 270: "we have shown that the substance and object of religion is altogether human; we have shown that divine wisdom is human wisdom; that the secret of theology is anthropology; that the absolute mind is the so-called finite subjective mind." "Love of man," he continues, "must be no derivative love; it must be original. . . . The relations of child and parent, of husband and wife, of brother and friend--in general, of man to man--in short, all the moral relations are *per se* religious" (271). Karl Barth's Introductory Essay (x-xxxii) offers the same insight that Calvin would have, *viz.*, that without God's gift of the Spirit, Feuerbach is unequivocally correct.

96. See Calvin, *Institutes*, Bk. II, Ch. I, §11, 254-55.

97. Calvin, *Institutes*, Bk. I, Ch. VII, §4, 78.

98. Calvin, *Institutes*, Bk. I, Ch. VII, §4, 79.

99. Calvin, *Institutes*, Vol. I, Ch. VIII, §13, 92. See also G.W.F. Hegel, *The Spirit of Christianity*, in *Early Theological Writings*, Richard Kroner ed. (Philadelphia: University of Pennsylvania Press, 1971), §iv, 255: "only spirit grasps and comprehends spirit."

100. Plato, *Republic*, Bk. II, 366e-367a.

101. See Plato, *Republic*, Bk. X, 601b-c: "Are not [the poets'] words *like faces* that were young but never beautiful and from which youth is not departed? . . . Consider still another proposition: the imitator, the one who creates illusions, does not understand reality but only what reality *appears* to be" (emphasis added).

102. Plato, *Republic*, Bk. VI, 510b.

103. See Calvin, *Institutes*, Vol. I, Part I, Ch. XI, §7, 107.

104. Calvin, *Institutes*, Bk. I, Ch. VII, §5, 81.

105. See, for example, Vamik D. Volkan, *The Need to Have Enemies and Allies* (London: Jason Aronson, 1988), Chs. 6-10, 82-154, for a psychological account of this perennial need. Volkan's concern is with why conflicts based upon identities constituted in and through relations with an *other* "seem to defy all concerted efforts at resolution" (Ch. 1, 6). His conclusions are coincident with Nietzsche's observations about the soul ruled by the ethic of resentment, though for Nietzsche such a soul is an historical creation, not a given datum of psychology.

106. Calvin, *Institutes*, Bk. I, Ch. II, §2, 42.

107. Zechariah 9:11.

108. Hobbes, *De Cive*, in *Man and Citizen*, Bernard Gert trans. (Gloucester, MA: Humanities Press, 1978), Ch. I, 117. See also Hobbes, *Leviathan*, Edwin Curley, ed. Indianapolis: Hackett, 1994) Part I, Ch. 8, 66: "the burden of faith is not possession, but rather obedience."

109. Calvin, *Institutes*, Bk. III, Ch. XXI, §1, 921.

110. Romans 5:20-21.

111. Cf. Luther, "Table Talk," in *Works*, Vol. 54, No. 87, 10: "It's remarkable that men should be so arrogant and secure when there are so many, indeed countless, evidences around to suggest that we ought to be humble. The hour of our death is uncertain. The grain on which we live is not in our hands. Neither the sun nor the air, on which our life depends, lies in our power, and we have no control over our sleeping and waking. I shall say nothing of spiritual things, such as private and public sins which press upon us. Yet our hearts are hard as steel and pay no attention to such evidence."

This passage suggests a greater hesitancy on Luther's behalf about the friendliness of the world, as it were. Calvin, illuminated by the Holy Spirit, does God's work; Luther, saved by Christ, seems satisfied to rest there. To move beyond is to risk falling into the "slavery of works."

112. Calvin, *Institutes*, Bk. I, Ch. XVII, §4, 216.

113. Calvin, *Institutes*, Bk. II, Ch. VII, §12, 360 (emphasis added).

114. Calvin, *Institutes*, Bk. II, Ch. VII, §12, 360-61.

115. Calvin, *Institutes*, Bk. II, Ch. VII, §12, 360.

116. It would be wrong to suggest that Calvin thought that the remnants of sin, about which Luther spoke, could ever be eradicated. He notes, for example, that faith is "tinged with doubts" and that all believers "are in perpetual conflict with their own unbelief" (*Institutes*, Bk. III, Ch. II, §17, 562). Nevertheless, Calvin has greater assurance about the ability of Christians to perform works without succumbing to active righteousness of the sort about which Luther worried. See Ibid., Bk. I, Ch. XVII, §11, 224-25, the title of which reads: "Certainty about God's providence puts joyous trust toward God in our hearts."

117. See Luther, "Table Talk," in *Works*, Vol. 54, No. 122, 15-16, *passim*.

118. See Hobbes, *Leviathan*, Part III, Ch. 41, 355: "*The end of Christ's coming was to renew the covenant of the kingdom of God, and to persuade the elect to embrace it, which was the second part of his office.* If then Christ, while he was on earth, had no kingdom in this world, to what end was his first coming? It was to restore unto God, by a new covenant, the kingdom, which being his by the old covenant, had been cut off by the rebellion of the Israelites in the election of Saul" (emphasis in original). Calvin does not go quite this far, of course. Yet he, like Hobbes, understood the error of antinomianism. See Calvin, *Institutes*, Bk. II, Ch. VIII, §§ 5-8, 371-75.

119. See note 18 Supra.

120. Calvin, *Institutes*, Bk. IV, Ch. XX, §1, 1486.

121. Calvin, *Institutes*, Bk. IV, Ch. XX, §2, 1487. Skinner's observation (see note 67 Supra) that Protestant thought abetted the concentration of State power is apropos here as well. Nevertheless, what should also be noted, in Calvin's case at any rate, is the importance of clemency (see Ibid., Bk. IV, Ch. XX, §10, 1498-99). As God's power is conjoined with His gift of grace, so, too, is the magistrate's power conjoined with his prerogative to grant clemency.

122. See Calvin, *Institutes*, Bk. IV, Ch. XX, §1, 1486: "For certain men, when they hear that the gospel promises a freedom that acknowledges no king and no magistrate among men, but looks to Christ alone, think that they cannot benefit by their freedom so long as they see any power set up over them. They therefore think that nothing will be safe unless the whole world is reshaped to a new form, where there are neither courts, nor laws, nor magistrates, nor anything which in their opinion restricts their freedom."

123. See Calvin, *Institutes*, Bk. IV, Ch. XX, §§22-27, 1510-15.

124. Calvin, *Institutes*, Bk. I, Ch. I, §2, 37.

125. See Mircea Eliade, *The Myth of the Eternal Return* (Princeton: Princeton University Press, 1954), Ch. 4, 139-62. Eliade argues that religious faith in the God of the Bible "constitutes a new formula for man's collaboration with the creation--the first, but also the only such formula accorded to him since the traditional horizon of archetypes and repetition was transgressed. Only such a freedom . . . is able to defend modern man from the terror of history--a freedom, that is, which has its source and finds its guaranty and support in God" (Ibid., 161).

See also Søren Kierkegaard, *The Sickness Unto Death*, Howard V. Hong and Adna H. Hong trans. (Princeton: Princeton University Press, 1980), Part I, C, ß, 39: "[the believer] leaves it entirely to God how he is to be helped, but he believes that for God everything is possible." That is, the believer is the person for whom the possibility of redemption from despair no longer exists by mortal effort. In this abyss, *and only here*, can there be the avowal that the radically new confirms the transcendence of God rather than the contingency of Fate. Rather than terror, the yield is a frail comfort that submits to new verities.

126. Job 38:4.

127. II Cor. 5:7.

128. See Richard Rorty, *Contingency, Irony, and Solidarity* (New York: Cambridge University Press, 1989).

129. Matt. 13: 24-30.

130. Augustine, *City of God*, in *Writings*, Vol. 6, Bk. I, Preface, 18, (*CG*, 5). The citation is from Ps. 94:15.

131. Calvin, *Institutes*, Bk. IV, Ch. XX, §8, 1494. In Hobbes's view, the problem with the Roman Church was that it claimed universal jurisdiction before the End Time. When Christ comes again in glory the Universal Church will appear, but not until then (see Hobbes, *Leviathan*, Part III, Ch. 38, 335-36; also Ibid., Ch. 41, 353). While the Reformed Church may have been correct in denying authority to the Pope, the effect of the controversy between them undermined the authority of both, for now the Word of God was in the hands of the people. "After the Bible was translated into English," Hobbes says, "every man, nay, every boy and wench, that could read English, thought they spoke with God Almighty, and understood what He said" (Hobbes, *Behemoth*, Ferdinand Tönnies ed. [Chicago: University of Chicago Press, 1990]), Dialogue I, 21). The resolution was to accord the sovereign of each nation the right to interpret Scripture; each nation, was, in effect, to have a Pope.

132. See Tocqueville, *Democracy in America*, Appendix I,Y, 734-35: "men think that the greatness of the idea of unity lies in means. God sees it in the end. It is for that reason that the idea of greatness leads to a thousand mean actions. To force all men to march in step toward the same goal--that is a human idea. To encourage endless variety of actions but to bring them about so that in a thousand different ways all tend toward the fulfillment of one design--that is a God-given idea."

133. I Cor. 13:12.

134. See Augustine, *City of God*, in *Writings*, Vol. 6, Bk. I, Ch. 8-9, 28-33 (*CG*, 13-17).

135. See Tocqueville, *Democracy in America*, Vol. II, Part I, Ch. 7, 451 (emphasis added).

136. See Tocqueville, *Democracy in America*, Vol. II, Part IV, Ch. 3, 671-74. See also Calvin, *Institutes*, Bk. I, Ch. XI, §8, 108, for the intimation that looking to the one visible power is more of a theological than political matter. In his words: "The example of the Israelites shows the origin of idolatry to be that men do not believe God is with them unless he shows himself physically present. 'We do not know,' they said, 'what has become of this Moses; make us gods who may go before us' [Ex. 32:1]."

137. See Reinhold Niebuhr, "The Tower of Babel," in *Beyond Tragedy: Essays on the Christian Interpretation of History*, (New York: Charles Scribner's Sons, 1951), 29: "[human life] touches the fringe of the eternal." The human temptation is to confuse the fringe for the center; all our efforts and understandings, consequently, are prone to be enterprises of the sort described in the story of the building of the Tower of Babel (Gen. 11:1-9).

138. See Tocqueville, *Democracy in America*, Vol. II, Part I, Ch. 5, 442-43: "There is hardly any human action, however private it may be, which does not result from some very general conception men have of God, of His relations with the human race, of the nature of their soul, and of their duties to their fellows. Nothing can prevent such ideas from being the common spring from which all else originates."

3

SKEPTICISM, SELF, AND TOLERATION IN MONTAIGNE'S POLITICAL THOUGHT[1]

Alan Levine

While toleration is usually justified as a matter of rights, political or metaphysical, the sixteenth century French philosopher Michel de Montaigne (1533-1592) argues for toleration on a non-rights basis. Instead of appealing to the "rights" of potential victims, Montaigne appeals only to the self-interest, properly understood, of an individual. His conception of self-interest is not only compatible with toleration, it demands it. Thus, understanding Montaigne's thought can lead to an alternative or supplementary justification for liberalism.[2]

Toleration as a political principle is grounded by Montaigne on a skeptical basis, but Montaigne is not (equally) skeptical of everything. Montaigne's toleration is based not on self-denial but on a certain kind of phenomenological self-knowledge (which survives his skeptical attack). Montaigne's self defers to no rights or any other factors that exist outside itself. Toleration is completely rooted in Montaigne's view of the human good as sensual self-exploration.

This paper traces the movement of Montaigne's thought from his skepticism to his recommendations for tolerant political institutions. Section one describes the motives behind Montaigne's skeptical attack. Section two systematically explains Montaigne's skepticism, showing the precise nature of his skeptical doubts and how and why he leaves universal truth behind to redefine knowledge as phenomenological knowledge of oneself. Only on this basis can he speak of knowledge at all. The third section specifies the limiting factors that a self must abide by in order to be healthy and whole. The final section shows how this conception of the self leads Montaigne to toleration and to call for the creation of a private sphere of free conscience and free political judgment.

I. The Current Human Problem
In order to understand Montaigne's skepticism, we must understand how he uses it. Montaigne does not trifle over the sweetness of honey, use skepticism to

uphold religious faith, or doubt the world in order to put it back together again, as Descartes attempts to, on firm foundations. Montaigne's skepticism arises out of human concerns and human needs.

Montaigne uses skeptical doubt to expose the groundlessness of habit and opinion. He claims that human beings are born so far from man's natural state that the world does not appear to us as it actually is. He despises the unnatural and corrupt "civilization" of which we are so proud. Everywhere one turns, one meets pomp and pretention. All people claim to be something that they are not. Princes claim grandeur; scholars claim wisdom; priests claim to know divine will; Europeans claim to be the quintessence of man.

Montaigne attacks human opinions and cultures not only in the pursuit of truth but also to overcome the anxiety and cruelty they provoke. We are taught to worry, to fear unseen things, and to desire all sorts of extraneous and questionable goods. We are led to wars, tempted to convert sinners, and forced to punish heretics. It is bad enough if the actors believe their claims to be true, but Montaigne thinks that the ambitious, including monarchs, priests, and revolutionaries, are cynical. Needing men to fight for their cause, they exploit human gullibility. Ordinary men are susceptible to these claims because of natural human weaknesses. The common inability to distinguish convention from truth, and man's unruly imagination, which can always be excited, make human beings mistake the appearance of things for the real things. Wherever anyone looks, triumphant impostors and satisfied dupes are to be found. "Any opinion is strong enough to make people espouse it at the price of life."[3]

Montaigne sets out to alert human beings to their natural tendencies and to tame the pretentious and ambitious individuals who incite the problems. "Presumption is our natural and original malady. The most vulnerable and frail of all creatures is man, and at the same time the most arrogant."[4] Montaigne attempts to put us in our proper place by attacking human pride from above and below.

Montaigne challenges most of the principle tenets of Christianity as mere opinion rooted in hubris. The epitome of human arrogance, according to Montaigne, is revealed religion, because it creates God after our own form. The greatest human hubris would be to imagine ourselves as the creator of the universe. Because our power reveals itself as unable to do anything of the sort, i.e., create new universes, I suppose no doctrine has ever maintained this. The next most hubristic notion would be that we are created in the image of the all-powerful creator, and that if we are not the creators of the universe, we are the lord and master of it on earth. Both of these notions characterize central tenets of Christianity, and both are explicitly attacked by Montaigne as the height of hubris.[5]

Just as Montaigne distances man from God, he lowers man to the animals, arguing that we are fundamentally the same as animals and that if we are different, it is only to our disadvantage. He again accuses human beings of presumption for the way we unjustly denigrate the animals. They do everything that we do, he claims, but to demean them, we assert that they act by compulsion not by choice.

We flatter ourselves that "goods acquired" make us nobler and better than them, as if it were better to have to work for things than possess them by nature.[6] God gives us life, we tell ourselves, but we give ourselves the good life, thus ennobling ourselves even more than God does.

Montaigne argues that there is but one law and one nature for all living creatures and that our difference from the animals is only one of "orders and degrees."[7] However, we generally break away from the natural order because our "freedom of imagination" deceives us and makes us unruly and licentious. "It is an advantage that is sold [to man] very dear and in which he has little cause to glory. For from it springs the principal source of the ills that oppress him: sin, disease, irresolution, confusion, despair."[8]

We are alienated from ourselves, says Montaigne, not because of the economic system or political regime; the problem is in our mind. Our imagination, a natural faculty, tempts us and leads us out of ourselves. Instead of pursuing natural desires -- eating, drinking, and sexual intercourse -- we pursue "superfluous and artificial" desires.[9] Our tendency to think about the future ruins the present. Our mind takes us away from the here and now, making us anxious and afraid about the future. "Fear, desire, hope, project us toward the future and steal from us the feeling and consideration of what is."[10] "We are never at home, we are always beyond."[11] Human beings are thus unfortunately contradictory creatures with a natural state but with a natural faculty, imagination, that naturally tends to alienate us from ourselves. Eden ends where the human faculties begin.[12]

Montaigne's analysis of this problem, however, reveals its remedy: imitate the animals. "Animals are much more self-controlled than we are, and restrain themselves with more moderation within the limits that nature has prescribed to us."[13] Montaigne, like Aristotle and unlike Hobbes, speaks of natural limits. Learning to remain within these natural limits, both in action and desire, is the key to human happiness.

> We attribute to ourselves imaginary and fanciful goods, goods future and absent, for which human capacity by itself cannot answer, or goods which we attribute to ourselves falsely through the license of our opinion, like reason, knowledge, and honor. And to them for their share we leave essential, tangible, and palpable goods: peace, repose, security, innocence, and health -- health, I say, the finest and richest present that nature can give us.[14]

Health and the other goods of the animals become the good for man. Health is mental as well as physical. Avoiding fear and anxiety is as important as avoiding pain and disease. Montaigne idealizes a sensual and robust tranquility, happily compatible with bodily pleasures, which more closely resembles the lusty, sensual tranquility recommended by Epicurus than the know-nothing tranquility of Pyrrho or the asceticism of saints. This combination of inner peace and sensual satisfaction, free of the falsities produced by unruly minds, serves as the standard throughout the *Essays*. But human beings cannot "go back" to the simplicity of the animals or of the primitive peoples around the world. The animals and simple people serve as a guidepost, but acquiring the tranquility of soul that they possess will turn out to be a most complicated and sophisticated process. Achieving what I call this "sophisticated simplicity" is Montaigne's goal for himself and his recommendation for all human beings. This image of the human good underlies his call for tolerant and moderate political institutions.

II. A Systematic Critique of Reason

How seriously are we to take Montaigne's arguments in favor of hedonism and mental tranquility? Is there nothing higher for which man should strive? If there is, Montaigne does not think human beings can know what it is. Montaigne, like the Academic skeptics of the Hellenistic era, argues that he knows he knows nothing. But if no knowledge is possible, how is this known? To understand Montaigne's skepticism and his political recommendations which follow from it, this riddle must be solved.

Montaigne is most famous for his skepticism,[15] but in an irony that would have delighted him (and supported his point about the difficulty of knowing anything outside oneself), this is also the most debated aspect of his thought among scholars. Montaigne classifies thinkers by their epistemological positions. Everyone who inquires, he says, must come to one of three positions: either we can know, we cannot know, or we cannot know whether we can know or not. These groups were called dogmatists, Academic skeptics, and Pyrrhonist skeptics, respectively.[16] At first glance, this classification seems to cover all the possibilities, except it leaves out the one that most modern scholars ascribe to Montaigne, fideism.[17] Fideists agree with the Academics that no knowledge is possible by rational or human means, but they believe that truths have been revealed to us in the form of the Bible. These truths, they claim, are the only truths available to us and can be grasped only by faith.

Montaigne, however, is not a fideist. The fact that Montaigne does not even mention this position among the epistemological possibilities alone should make one doubtful that he believes in Christian revelation. Moreover, despite numerous references to God, Montaigne never says that he *believes in* a God. To the contrary, he describes God as a human construction. We are not created in God's image, he argues, but create God in our own. Montaigne's discussion of God begins and ends with an account of His human origins. Montaigne reveals the psychological origins of the deities. We create gods to support us and calm us. Our views of God originate from "the utmost effort of our imagination toward perfection, each man amplifying the idea according to his capacity."[18] To be useful in inspiring different peoples, God has been given a body "as necessity required,"[19] and Montaigne argues that if the animals have gods, they "certainly make them like themselves, and glorify themselves as we do."[20] "In short, the construction and the destruction of the deity, and its conditions, are wrought by man, on the basis of a relationship to himself. What a pattern and what a model!"[21]

When Montaigne does venture to offer a judgment, the conception of God that he describes as the "most excusable"[22] is more Greek (philosophic not Homeric) than Jewish or Christian. Montaigne says God does not care about human beings, nor does He have anything to do with the cares that make up our lives.[23] Montaigne also questions the immortality of the soul and advises us not to concern ourselves with thoughts of an afterlife. He dismisses the Garden of Eden version of natural man,[24] the notion of a virgin birth,[25] and the possibility that God could have a human incarnation. Montaigne further argues that God cannot be understood in human terms such as justice or goodness. These are but our attempts to create God out of our concerns. Thus, even if Montaigne did believe in Christianity, unlike Thomas Jefferson, he does not tremble because he does not know that God is just.[26] Indeed, he argues that God has nothing to do with justice. Montaigne concludes his most systematic account of God by saying that "In Socrates' opinion, and in mine too, the wisest way to judge heaven is not to judge it at all."[27] Thus, at minimum, Montaigne argues that human beings can know nothing about God that has any moral or political consequences. In this world, the world of the here and now in which we live, human beings must find their own way.

Montaigne upholds religion to the extent that he does, because religion is useful. The alternative to religion is atheism, which Montaigne criticizes not because it is untrue, but because it is "not easy to establish in the human mind."[28] When atheists are about to die, he says, they panic and fearing death, "let themselves be managed by the common faith and examples."[29] Montaigne does not explicitly attack Christianity because it is the "common faith" of his time. Without it, people would have nothing. To the extent that he does, Montaigne upholds Christianity not because he thinks it true, but because from time to time, and especially when dealing with death, human beings need a crutch. Indeed, Montaigne seems to describe all religious and philosophical ideas as attempts by their authors to be useful in this way. What he says of the ancient philosophers: "some things they wrote for the needs of society, like their religions,"[30] seems just as true for Christianity, whose customs Montaigne describes as "warm[ing] the souls of the people with religious emotion very beneficial in effect."[31] And just as the ancients judged that "on that account it was reasonable that they did not want to bare popular opinions to the skin, so as not to breed disorder in people's obedience to the laws and customs of their country," so Montaigne upholds Christianity as a custom of his time and place. If he lived in a different time and place, he would have upheld its customs instead. Montaigne is not a believer -- but even if he is, it would be a belief, as noted above, without any political consequences.

Just as Montaigne is not a fideist, nor is he a Pyrrhonist.[32] Pyrrhonists are the most radical skeptics, that is to say the most doubting. They do not know whether they can know anything or not. They argue that there is insufficient evidence to determine if any knowledge is possible, and hence that one ought to suspend judgment on all questions concerning knowledge. If they convince an interlocutor of any position, they will immediately switch positions and argue the opposite, even when the subject is the possibility of knowledge. Montaigne does use Pyrrhonist arguments and the Pyrrhonist mode of procedure throughout the "Apology," and like the Pyrrhonists, Montaigne begins his analyses by noting the multiplicity of views on the subject under consideration. Unlike the Pyrrhonists, however, Montaigne focuses his inquiries on human things. Because the Pyrrhonists know nothing, no topic is inherently more important or more interesting to them than another. They will argue over the whiteness of snow or the sweetness of honey just as soon as they will argue about the nature of man. Montaigne, by contrast, focuses on human concerns. In the "Apology," for example, his longest discussions concern God, the soul, and the human body. Montaigne is not working the Pyrrhonist agenda. Instead, he uses Pyrrhonism to support his own agenda.[33] And whereas the Pyrrhonists argue that there is no way to determine which, if any, of the many chronicled views are true, and thus suspend their judgment on all things, Montaigne probes behind the multiplicity. He wants to know why there are so many different views of things, and why the same things are always being re-explained. The recurrence of certain questions and themes across cultures and across time suggests to Montaigne something important about the human condition. Montaigne looks for psychological explanations of these phenomena rather than for scientifically exact accounts of them. By learning about the human psyche, he implies, one can learn how to live.

In the end Montaigne even questions whether Pyrrhonism is liveable. He says, "it is almost incredible that it can be done."[34] Montaigne's doubts are easy to understand. Pyrrhonists live their lives by following their internal, immediate impulses and by conforming to external pressures where necessary. They eat but they never judge that it is good to satisfy their hunger pangs. They just eat. They follow the local customs, but they do not judge the possible consequences of doing so. They merely obey. What happens when impulse and custom conflict? Must not they *choose* between them? But how? Will they, like Descartes, just do what everyone else does? But is it not likely that different people will act differently? And why choose this method over others? Can they not calculate at all? But how can they avoid it? Perhaps this explains why Montaigne calls Pyrrhonism an "amusing science"[35] and summarizes its doctrine by calling it a "*fantasie.*"[36] What Montaigne finds absurd is the over-application of this "science of ignorance."[37] At one and the same time, the Pyrrhonist character is inflexible while its mode of argument is weak and spineless.[38] Pyrrhonists argue that true ignorance means "*une entiere ignorance,*" including being ignorant of oneself.[39] This is too rigid, because Montaigne thinks that at least some self-knowledge is possible. It is spineless, because it prevents them from arguing truly and consistently based on what can be known. Moreover, the Pyrrhonist call to suspend one's judgment completely is antithetical to Montaigne's approach. Montaigne strives for self-knowledge; it is the aim of his life's writing and thinking. The aim behind his *Essays* is to essay himself, to refine his judgment. He seeks to develop and refine his judgment, not to eliminate it. Montaigne is not a Pyrrhonist.

Montaigne never thematically discusses Academic skepticism, because he is an Academic skeptic. His entire book exemplifies this position. Academic skeptics argue that no knowledge is possible. But from this, they must paradoxically admit to knowing one thing, that human beings cannot possess knowledge. Although this may not seem like much, it is surprisingly troublesome for a skeptic: how does one know that one knows nothing? What kind of knowledge allows one to be certain of this? Unlike other types of knowledge, Montaigne considers knowledge of the self both possible and worthwhile. But before we examine how Montaigne tries to obtain self-knowledge, let us examine why he thinks no other types of knowledge are possible.

Montaigne makes several arguments about why he thinks no knowledge is possible. First, to buttress his claim, he argues that most philosophers thought knowledge was impossible to achieve. He argues that of all the dogmatists, that is, of all those who have claimed to possess knowledge, "most of them have put on the mask of assurance only to look better."[40] They only choose to *appear* dogmatic. Montaigne thinks that philosophers do not believe their own doctrines for several reasons. First, he claims that if one reads them carefully, one will see that they claim only to give something plausible, not true. He cites Plato and Cicero to defend this claim.[41] Second, he cannot persuade himself that such obviously intelligent people believed such questionable doctrines as Epicurus' Atoms and Plato's Ideas. But if this is the case, why did they advance such unbelievable theoretical speculations? The answer, according to Montaigne, is pedagogy -- both for individuals and for their societies. Some of the philosophers, Aristotle for example, want us to think our way through their tangles. They arrange their arguments to show us their problems, thereby forcing us to think them through. "By the variety and instability of opinions they lead us as by the hand, tacitly, to this conclusion of their inconclusiveness."[42] This is what Montaigne means when he says that Aristotle's philosophy is "in fact a Pyrrhonism in an affirmative form."[43] Writers such as Aristotle, Montaigne argues, also write this way out of a playful sense of pedagogy, to lead the readers "as by the hand, tacitly," into the pleasure of thinking. (This applies to Montaigne's writing, too. Insofar as every reader must "essay" Montaigne's essays in order to make sense of them, the reader is forced to retrace and rethink Montaigne's own thought process, which he considers to be immensely pleasurable.) A final reason philosophers wrote dogmatically was for the public benefit. "Some things they wrote for the needs of society, like their religions."[44] Thus, they teach those who look carefully to doubt by showing the limits of inquiry. For those who look less carefully, they formulate doctrines that if believed, will benefit the believers, individual and society alike. The differences in their doctrines can be explained, in part, by historical circumstances. "They did not want to bare popular opinions to the skin, so as not to breed disorder in people's obedience to the laws and customs of their country."[45] This applies to Montaigne, too.

In any case, if all philosophers agree, as Montaigne claims, that knowledge is impossible, Montaigne aims to make us all "wise at our own expense" and show us why.[46] He does this by showing that human reason and the human senses, the only two means by which human beings can obtain knowledge, are pliable and therefore cannot serve as a foundation for knowledge. If the foundation is lacking, everything else falls flat. In making these arguments, Montaigne draws heavily on the Pyrrhonist arguments of Sextus Empiricus but with one crucial difference: unlike the Pyrrhonists, Montaigne is not unsure of his critique. He asserts limits based on truth claims about the self.

Montaigne cites five factors that prevent our judgment and reasoning from being pure. The first factor is the distortion that necessarily occurs in human sense perception. As proof that we do not perceive an object's essence, Montaigne notes how the same object is perceived differently by different people and even by the same person at different times. For example, Montaigne cites wine as affecting sick and healthy people differently, and he says that wood feels different to "normal" and chapped skin.[47]

Second, Montaigne argues that "it is certain" that our body affects our judgment and all the faculties of the soul.[48] Physical things, it seems, can be known. Some bodily movements, such as diseases, fever, or a cold, are noticeable, and we can try to compensate for the way we expect them to affect our judgment. But is it possible to determine exactly how much to compensate? Other imperceptible bodily movements also affect us and dislodge reason from its natural equilibrium. Insofar as these alterations are continual, can reason ever be in its natural home?

Third, our emotions affect our reason, even more so than the body does. This is apparent to everyone. We act, react, and think differently when we are angry, afraid, jealous, or in a tranquil state of mind. And "no eminent and lusty virtue is without some unruly agitation."[49] If we always have an emotion, our reason is always disturbed. We should note, however, that both the effects of the body and the emotions are mitigated in proportion to the achievement of tranquility.

Montaigne raises two other factors that affect our reason and judgment: time and place.[50] The three factors discussed in the preceding paragraphs are caused by nature alone. Time and place, however, are caused by happenstance and human decisions. They are a testament to the power of custom more than to that of nature. Peoples and epochs have a character. They are more or less bellicose, just, temperate, and docile. Montaigne asserts that people, like animals and plants, grow differently in different physical locales and atmospheres. And because there have been so many different nations in so many different centuries, who is to say that this or that people -- or all of them -- was not mistaken?

Three internal, natural factors, perception, body, and emotion, and two outside factors, time and place, lead Montaigne to consider reason to be completely unreliable. "Reason," he says, is "that semblance of intellect that each man fabricates in himself."[51] It is bendable, stretchable, pliable, and adaptable to all biases and all measures, easily justifying conflicting sides in any case. Ask any lawyer. "All that is needed is the ability to mold it."[52]

Montaigne then proceeds to dash our last hope for knowledge by systematically criticizing the human senses.[53] He raises many problems. First, human beings may not have all the senses of nature. If we are lacking any senses, our reason and other senses cannot discover the lack. For all we know, all of mankind can be doing something very foolish for lack of some other sense. Our five senses form the limit to our faculties. Second, as we already said, our senses are inaccurate. At best, we sense partials and not essences. This is further confirmed by the many animals with particular senses that are keener than ours. Third, our mind also limits our sensory data. How often do we alter or completely miss something because our mind is occupied or looking elsewhere? Finally, different senses can give conflicting data. Something can look smooth but feel rough. To get an objective measure one would need an adjudicative instrument. To verify the instrument we would need a demonstration, but to verify the demonstration we would also need an instrument: there's the circle! Reason cannot judge because in and of itself it has no contact with outside objects. Even if our reason were completely unbiased, which it is not, the uncertainty of our senses makes everything they produce or that depends on them uncertain. Thus, no knowledge is possible.

Given Montaigne's skeptical attacks on the status of reason, revelation, and the senses, is there any criterion for judging how to live? Montaigne refuses to have his "duty" determined by an arbitrary standard such as custom, because "I cannot have my judgment so flexible."[54] "Truth must have one face, the same and universal."[55] This is surprising, because in several places throughout the "Apology"[56] and in other essays, notably in his warning to the princess,[57] Montaigne says that it is necessary to obey the law. He says this knowing full well that law, legal and customary, is "filled and soaked with twaddle and lies."[58] But while Montaigne deems custom and habit necessary for the sake of a stable *political* order, he considers following custom an unsatisfactory *moral* principle.

Following "experience" emerges as the alternative to following laws or reason. Reason misleads us more than it helps us, and law represents nothing but the "changes of passion" of the prince or people.[59] Montaigne turns to the self and its experiences, because it is the thing that we know best and to which we can have access. To paraphrase the old joke, wherever we go, there we are. We have direct, unmediated contact with ourselves at all times (unless, of course, learned opinions mediate ourselves to ourselves. But if this is so, Montaigne wants to overcome it). We have the experience of changes, aches, pains, and pleasures that seem undeniable. Every healthy person trusts his or her own faculties and judgment more than anything else. As Montaigne says, referring to the claim that snow is black because it is made of water and when water is in a deep pool it looks dark, "We are nearer to ourselves than the whiteness of snow."[60]

This experiential "knowledge" is phenomenological, not transcendent. Montaigne gives up his search for universal truths that are always and everywhere true, and instead focuses on subjective appearance, the truth as it is perceived by a particular person at a particular moment in time. It is only by changing the definition of what constitutes knowledge that Montaigne is able to look for it at all. Thus, Montaigne asserts that "we see clearly enough" that human sense perception does not receive the forms of its objects,[61] that "it is certain" that our judgment is affected by our body[62] and that "there is no doubt that judgment is biased" by emotions.[63] All of Montaigne's truth claims relate to phenomenological knowledge of the self. He shows his awareness of the subjectivity of these "facts" by quickly downgrading them from being "the truth of experience" to "the apparent facts of experience" and finally to the "more likely things."[64] But he still says "I would rather follow facts than reason"[65] because the alternatives to "experience" are worse.

Here lies Montaigne's explanation of his -- and Academic skepticism's -- paradoxical claim that he knows that he knows nothing. The two "knows" in this sentence refer to different types of knowledge. By phenomenologically knowing the inconstancy of his body and sense organs, he knows that he could never possess any transcendental truth. The statement that one knows that we can know nothing implies knowledge of the limits of human capabilities. Knowing nothing is a function of self-knowledge.

The nature of Montaigne's skepticism is thus clear: a wise individual will be fully aware of his ignorance of all transcendent matters (i.e., he will not be a fideist or a dogmatist) and understand what can be known (i.e., not a Pyrrhonist) while appreciating its merely phenomenological status.

III. Structural Limits on the Self

If phenomenological self-knowledge is all that is available to human beings, it is in this sphere that the human good must lie. For a self to be healthy and whole, it must recognize and accept its structural constraints that form the limit of health. To do this one must recognize humanity's epistemological limits (as discussed above), and accept three other limits of the human condition. A healthy self must reject the metaphysical impulse, accept death, and "go home."

1. Reject the Metaphysical Impulse. The first limit that must be accepted involves accepting the lack of metaphysical foundations for our world. Such an acquiescence is intrinsic to Montaigne's skepticism. Whether there is no God or a God that we cannot know, all living based on metaphysical speculation is unverifiable at best and harmful at worst. Montaigne describes people who seek refuge from man's metaphysical void as dangerous. "They want to get out of themselves and escape from the man. That is madness: instead of changing into angels, they change into beasts; instead of raising themselves, they lower themselves."[66] For Montaigne, this link between horrifying actions and improper appreciation of the human condition is direct: "these are two things that I have always observed to be in singular accord: supercelestial thoughts and subterranean conduct."[67]

We human beings must admit our lack of knowledge and our tendency towards presumption and vanity. The search for dignity and meaning may be a perennial human activity according to Montaigne, and he approves of this kind of searching, but he thinks that wise men discover the psychological drives underlying their vain desires, not answers that satisfy their vanity. We must accept the world as flux and flow. There is no creator to endow us with dignity or give meaning to our lives. Montaigne's account of our coming into the world resembles Heidegger's notion of "throwness." Existing is assigned to us without prior consent and it remains our job until death, the fundamental fact of life. We are "entirely destitute and void"[68] and it is the awareness of this natural state that often sends us looking for other truths. Anxiety is not our natural condition, but we grow to feel anxious over a vain concern with our emptiness and thus flee from ourselves. This leads to what Montaigne detests most: self-hatred and self-cruelty, because those who live and judge by otherworldly standards tend to reject and to despise the world that we have and the beings that we are. "The most barbarous of our maladies is to despise our being."[69] We have no knowable metaphysical purpose in life and must accept, to use the contemporary term, a lack of foundations. Nothing expects anything from us, and no demands are made on us. Yet, there is no reason to fear or despair. Life is sweet. All we have to do is be.

2. Accept Death. The second limit that must be confronted is death. By accepting that we are finite and that there is nothing after death, that it is our end (not as final cause), and by realizing that there is nothing to fear, we are free to live. Death is the moment of truth. We can go through life pretending and masquerading and fooling everyone including ourselves, but dying is a solitary, lonely act. No one can help us and we cannot fool ourselves. There is no future to be drawn into; there is only the here and now. We come face to face with our own true character. Death and truth are allies. The former reveals the latter about ourselves. Thus, death becomes the supreme moment of authenticity and freedom. It is almost to be welcomed.

By liberating us from the fear of death, Montaigne liberates us to live. As Jean Starobinski says, "death unmasked becomes death the unmasker."[70] If we are not afraid of dying, we are not afraid of living. "There is nothing evil in life for the man who has thoroughly grasped the fact that to be deprived of life is not an evil."[71] Accepting the fact of death and keeping it in full consciousness at all times is both a kind of psychological break with life and an enhancement of it. Life experienced in full consciousness of the possibility of its ending at any moment is more enjoyable, enabling us to savor every moment and every flavor as if it were the last. Paradoxically, it is only the giving up of our tenacious clinging to life that liberates us to enjoy it more.

Only after accepting death can we be truly autonomous and free. Accepting death allows us to contemplate the character with which we will approach it. This character or form, known to us in part by how we deal with the trials and tribulations of life, simultaneously affects how we deal with those trials and tribulations -- and with our happy moments. Thus, by self-consciously confronting death, we can self-consciously confront life.

3. "Go Home." In addition to accepting the fundamental limits of humanity, Montaigne thinks that to achieve self-conscious tranquility, one must, so to speak, "go home" ("*chez toi*") Just as he warns his readers against being taken outside of themselves by concerns for metaphysics or fear of death, so he harkens his readers to return to themselves. The "home" analogy is central to Montaigne's conception of the self. A normative notion of "home" allows him to reconcile the existing reality, "We are never at home, we are always beyond"[72] with the moral injunction, "You have quite enough to do at home; don't go away."[73]

> The range of our desires should be circumscribed and restrained to a narrow limit of the nearest and most contiguous good things; and moreover their course should be directed not in a straight line that ends up elsewhere, but in a circle whose two extremities by a short sweep meet and terminate in ourselves. Actions that are performed without this reflexive movement, I mean a searching and genuine reflexive movement -- the actions, for example, of the avaricious, the ambitious, and so many others who run in a straight line, whose course carries them ever forward -- are erroneous and diseased actions.[74]

And what does Montaigne find at the core of the self? We are "entirely destitute and void;"[75] "Man, in all things and throughout, is but patchwork and motley;"[76] "Life is an uneven, irregular, and multiform movement;"[77] "We are all patchwork, and so shapeless and diverse in composition that each bit, each moment, plays its own game."[78] In one sense, the emptiness that Montaigne finds "at home" is disappointing. But it is disappointing only if one expects cosmic answers. If one is less demanding, more realistic in one's expectations, one can find oneself full of never-ending delights. Montaigne constantly discusses the wonders of self-exploration and attempts to make the reader feel the joy of the activity by writing down his own self-explorations. Montaigne writes his essays in such a way that reading them is to think Montaigne's thoughts with him. One cannot help but look inward as one thinks through Montaigne's own self-questioning. Pascal testifies eloquently on this point when he says, "*Ce n'est pas dans Montaigne, mais dans moi, que je trouve tout ce que j'y vois.*"[79] Moreover, Montaigne has been exciting centuries of readers to a life of sensual self-seeking. As Nannerl Keohane says, "More than any other writer, Montaigne succeeded in making such a self-centered life attractive."[80] Montaigne's goal is to make the reader feel that what we are is enough to keep us happy and content "at home."

In short, Montaigne wants us to accept ourselves for what we are: an integral unity of body and soul. "There is nothing in us... that is purely either corporeal or spiritual;" everything is both in a "close and brotherly correspondence."[81] To sequester the body and soul, as Christians do, is "to tear apart a living man."[82] Body and soul communicate with each other, and in a well-ordered person, they harmonize and complement each other. There is but a "narrow seam" between them, "through which the experience of the one is communicated to the other."[83] They need "mutuality and reciprocity."[84] Given the dual nature and close interconnectedness of a human being, it is no wonder that Montaigne represents the good life as including the pleasures of both soul and body, and that he repeatedly warns against the extremes of neglecting either (hence the praise of the hedonistic philosophers). Not only does Montaigne praise both sources of pleasure, but he maintains that each partakes of the other, according to "the general human law" that all pleasure is "intellectually sensual, sensually intellectual."[85]

Montaigne's radical emphasis on the body is limited only by the need for mental tranquility. In agreement with Aristotle and Epicurus, Montaigne argues that feverishness and rapacious desires that dominate one's soul are unhealthy. Montaigne would reject Machiavelli's claim of the necessity for unlimited acquisition as well as the unlimitedness of Hobbes' notion that happiness is the continual satisfaction of desire after desire that ceases only in death. Many men might live this way, but Montaigne considers such a life a sign of a "sick and disordered grasp."[86] He considers unlimited desires "irresolute and uncertain" and says such a person "does not know how to keep anything or enjoy anything in the right way."[87] Montaigne rejects Hobbesian or bourgeois grasping.[88]

This limiting of and discrimination between desires is perhaps the key aspect of Montaigne's moral enterprise. One can reasonably ask how a skeptic can make such distinctions. Montaigne, however, would reverse the question. Anyone who thinks they already know what is best or how they should live is the one making a truth claim -- and an unverified one at that. Rather than precisely defining what is healthy and natural for the species as a whole or for particular individuals, Montaigne redirects the focus of inquiry to what one can confidently claim to know about oneself and one's desires. His aim is to encourage his readers to ask these questions and in asking, one is led naturally into the labyrinth that is each individual self. One is led to question one's motives and desires and thus to seeing how little one knows. One is led away from the ignorant, "diseased," and zealous pursuit of opinions and towards self-examination, self-exploration, and to further dialogue with oneself.

According to Montaigne, self-exploration is the fundamentally important and healthy occupation for a human being. Self-exploration is based on another kind of dual nature, which is captured in the following quotations. "I presented myself to myself for argument and subject."[89] "I look inside of me; I have no business but with myself; I continually observe myself, I take stock of myself, I taste myself. Others go elsewhere...as for me, I roll about in myself."[90] On the one hand, we are passive. We simply are. On the other hand, we are active and critical, aware of, yet distanced from things, including ourselves. In the former case, our body, impulses, thoughts and habits are beyond our control. They are flux and movement caused by nature or a fixed pattern caused by habit. In the latter case, we perceive and have an active, critical, probing judgment that engages and affects its objects. Only by knowing how these phenomena work in oneself can a human being have any knowledge at all. The cannibals (Montaigne's account of natural man) represent a happy combination between natural impulses and habit. We have no choice between these two. Our only choice is whether we should consciously affirm how nature and habit work in us or whether we should fight those unchosen tendencies. In either case, we make ourselves and the world more our own than do unreflective people. We are freer than they because our actions are self-consciously accepted and affirmed.

To do this requires self-consciousness and work. "Being consists in movement and action. Wherefore each man in some sort exists in his work."[91] "It takes management to enjoy life."[92] The proper work for man is to live well. This requires self-study and self-knowledge. Like Montaigne, we must make ourselves the subject of our work and reflection. We cannot know abstract truths, but we can gain knowledge of our self through our deeds, including thoughts. If we do business or something else outside of our self, with which we have no intimate care, we take our self out of itself. We do "business only for busyness."[93]

Not only can we know ourselves, but to a limited extent we can also create ourselves. The process of exploring oneself not only leads to the uncovering of a pre-existing self, but to the creation of oneself. Montaigne speaks of his *Essays* as "a book consubstantial with its author;"[94] each makes the other: "I have no more made my book than my book made me."[95] "I have had to fashion and compose myself so often to bring myself out, that the model itself has to some extent grown firm and taken shape. Painting myself for others, I have painted my inward self with colors clearer than my original ones."[96] Self-exploration not only locates and amplifies a pre-existing self, but the process changes the self that is being sought. Unlike Nietzsche, however, Montaigne does not posit self-creation to be a violent process where suffering is integral. His is a gentle one. We cannot simply will our self to be more fully or other than what we are. Changing the self comes about, paradoxically, by accepting the self and its elusiveness. The self "does not lend itself to expression in actions" or to "this airy medium of words."[97]

Language represents but a clumsy attempt at self-articulation. It is neither subtle nor flexible enough to capture human thoughts and feelings. Not only is it overly rigid and insufficiently penetrating in its descriptions, but it imprisons the self in the terms and analysis it uses and invents. Human beings use language to reveal, but it creates and conceals at the same time. Feeling, however, is a less articulate but more reliable guide than language. Because man lives in a phenomenological world, feeling serves as a conduit to life. "I shall know it well enough when I feel it."[98] "I judge myself only by actual sensation, not by reasoning."[99] This rejoins Montaigne's desire to "judge by experience" that we saw in the "Apology."[100] If human beings cannot know essences, they can feel phenomena. If they cannot know truth in the abstract, they do have the power to know truths about themselves. This is nothing to glory in, but it can and should be a never-ending source of wonder and delight. This work is never-ending and more than enough to keep one happy, healthy, and whole "at home."

IV. Toleration and the Private Sphere

Montaigne's understanding of the self leads him to toleration in a powerful three-fold manner. First, his skepticism undermines all the opinion-based convictions that lead to intolerance, since he views religious, moral, and political opinions as illusory and unreal fantasies. Second, he argues that an awareness of the very fallibility of our opinions should make us tolerant of the opinions of other selves. "At least our faulty condition should make us behave more moderately and restrainedly in our changes. We should remember, whatever we receive into our understanding, that we often receive false things there, and by these same tools that are often contradictory and deceived."[100] And finally, Montaigne's conception of the human good as the inner calm that results from self-seeking removes the allure of exploitation. Since what we find in ourselves is ignorance, we have no interest in forcing anything on another self -- and, unlike Nietzsche, the self has nothing to force.

In addition to this, Montaigne thinks that persecuting another would cause the self-aware person pain. By nature people who are healthy and whole, aware of themselves and their natural condition, and content to stay "at home," feel a mutual sympathy between all people. Others are to be tolerated instead of victimized not because they are the bearers of some abstract "right," but because awareness of one's own weakness and precariousness creates a bond, a sympathy through identification, with other selves. Anticipating Rousseau and the romantic ideals of moral sympathy, Montaigne says that the feeling of one's own weaknesses and of one's own pain and suffering makes one identify with and want to prevent it in others: "The sight of other people's anguish causes very real anguish to me."[101] Whereas Rousseau will later posit that human beings are born with these feelings of pity and compassion, Montaigne suggests that only individuals "at home" feel this way.[102] Only by straying "away from home" can one be insensitive to another's condition. A knowing self will therefore feel a strong desire for all selves to develop in their own way. One's inner feeling of weakness and one's own need for self-mastery lead one to the imperative of respect for one's fellows' self-experiments. A self-knowing man will feel horror at the thought of a self being dispossessed of itself. Toleration springs not from self-denial, but from self-knowledge.

To secure a tolerant atmosphere for individual development, Montaigne proposes creating a private sphere, a space for individual peace and self-creation. Montaigne's private sphere allows one the *possibility* of escaping from the turbulence and slavery of the political and conventional world, enabling one to live at peace with oneself, in self-dialogue, faithful to one's nature. However, Montaigne's private sphere is more limited than how we conceive of freedom of conscience today. For example, Montaigne's private sphere does not protect conscientious objection. One does not have to agree with civil authority, but civil disobedience and public protest to it are not permitted. "All deference and submission is due to [the political authority], except that of our understanding. My reason is not trained to bend and bow, it is my knees."[103] Not our minds, but the knees, our actions, can be prescribed. Thus, what is new and important in Montaigne's private sphere is the intellectual protection that it affords.

Montaigne's radically differing attitudes towards thought and deed are perhaps the most distinctive aspects of his political thought. His low opinion of the actions of most people leads him to agree with Epicurus and anticipate Hobbes in thinking that without law, human beings would devour each other like "brutish animals."[104] Law is not necessary to promote virtue, goodness, or nobility, but in the interests of stability, order, and protection. As with all human creations, it will necessarily include injustice. Trying to remove injustice from law, Montaigne says, would be like trying to cut off Hydra's head.[105] His low expectations of what can be achieved through politics makes Montaigne indifferent to regime type. He does not seem to believe that any form of government is more likely to be just than any other and never speaks of an individual's "right" to participate in the law making process. Nonetheless, he insists on a moderate government that leaves individuals' consciences alone.

The private sphere is the political institution that makes Montaigne's vision of the self and the individual good flourish. Montaigne promotes the private sphere primarily for the sake of those individuals who partake in sensual self-seeking; they are among the few who can take advantage of the liberty of philosophy, judgment, and conscience it affords. But according to Montaigne, almost everyone else benefits from a private sphere of free conscience and free judgment, too.

The state -- and therefore the rulers -- gains more control over the public when it relinquishes its claims to the private. In making this argument, Montaigne agrees with Bodin, L'Hôpital, and the other *politiques* that by shrinking the scope of its claim to power, the state can establish its control more effectively.[106] Montaigne argues that a private sphere makes the populace less likely to revolt from the state authority for two complementary reasons, both of which ring true in the American political experience. "It may be said, on the one hand, that to give factions a loose reign to entertain their own opinions is to scatter and sow division; it is almost lending a hand to augment it, there being no barrier or coercion of the laws to check or hinder its course."[107] "Complete freedom," "freedom of conscience," he argues, leads to a multiplicity of sects that divide and factionalize the population, making an organized revolt from below more difficult. To some extent, but with a different focus, this anticipates *Federalist* #10. It may be objected, as it was at the time, that such factions would turn violent and lead to civil disorder, but Montaigne is not worried. Making an argument that anticipates Tocqueville's description of the effects of religion in America, Montaigne asserts "that to give factions a loose reign to entertain their own opinions is to soften and relax them through facility and ease, and to dull the point, which is sharpened by rarity, novelty, and difficulty."[108] Toleration is originally needed because of animosity, and it mitigates the causes of animosity at the same time that it controls its effects.

Montaigne's private sphere also benefits the people because public stability enables them to live more tranquil lives. They do not need toleration to pursue the eccentricities of an inner private life, but they gain peace with the removal of contentious issues from the public arena. Agitators may still sway particular individuals or groups, but they will be less likely to kill each other over issues of conscience. More optimistically, Montaigne imagines that the multiplicity of arguments might degenerate into increasingly academic debates between intellectuals, leaving the mass of people untouched and unscathed.

The only real losers in the creation of a private sphere are the rambunctious intellectuals and zealots who, convinced of the correctness of their opinions, want to institute them and force them on everybody. These people gain the right to maintain their own personal beliefs, and perhaps babble on about them, but not to institute them. Montaigne's skepticism aims to change unruly, presumptuous intellectuals into more reflective, humble people. He gives them reasons of self-interest to moderate and change themselves, but if they do not, they must be tamed and controlled. This is the price Montaigne is happily willing to pay for the creation of a private sphere.

Two difficulties, however, exist in Montaigne's institutionalization of the private sphere. First, his theory of political obligation is tenuous. The boundary he draws between a free, private, political *judgment* and restricted public *actions* is unclear. Montaigne clearly encourages us to judge everything, and political judgment is no exception. He says "we should conform to the best rules, but not enslave ourselves to them."[109] But if we are to judge and withhold ourselves from the best laws, what more should we do with poor ones? Why not criticize, break, or change them? Montaigne is willing to obey the state except when compelled to break a higher bond: not to his opinions, but to friend, family, or to himself. The modern insistence on conscientious objection and the right to be heard publicly on every issue would, I think, strike Montaigne as vanity. If one truly knows oneself, one does not need to prove one's cleverness, seek external recognition, or worry about humbling oneself in obedience to established customs. One can be silent, one can play roles -- as long as one can "*be.*" Nonetheless, Montaigne himself publicly and aggressively published his ideas several times. He tried to change the attitudes and culture of his times through his writing. The reason to obey the law is to avoid its punishments and out of respect for the need for peace and stability. Beyond that, what one ventures by way of changing the laws is left to individual prudence. Montaigne could articulate no broader principle.

Second, because of his radical separation between the public and private spheres, Montaigne argues that role playing is both inevitable, because the human condition requires that we all play many roles, and desirable, because of the insulation it affords to the self. Viewing the world as a stage and oneself as an actor allows one to detach from one's deeds.[110] This distance allows one to keep an inner peace regardless of what happens. This understanding, especially by political actors, is essential to securing decent and moderate politics.

Montaigne knows, however, that role playing when sufficiently understood by the actor as role playing, might require wisdom, strength, and a sense of playfulness that exceeds the capacity of a typical individual. A true role player must be wise because he must see the world as it is and understand the necessity of playing roles. He must understand why roles exist, why they must be upheld, and the demands of his particular role. He must be strong because it is difficult to live such a complicated, multilayered life and strive for excellence in something that one knows is artificial. He must be playful, because he must enjoy his roles. Role playing should not be flat and serious like the life of a bureaucrat. Montaigne wants us to delight in our roles and be creative; this requires light-heartedness. While the role playing demanded by a complex society can be compatible with tranquility of mind in strong, playful individuals, one wonders whether weaker people can act successfully. Might they not take their roles too seriously and thus worry about success in them? Will this not lead to the anxiety that role playing was set up to avoid? Failure seems inevitable among ordinary people. Montaigne's solution is aristocratic. It can only be achieved by the few best people. Yet, it is only intended for a few. Montaigne accepts that most people will believe the customs into which they are born. He is addressing, rather, the more reflective people who understand the contingent nature of mores and belief.

V. Conclusion

Montaigne's toleration is not based on self-denial but on self-knowledge. He is skeptical of claims about "rights" or any truth claim about things that exist outside the self. His advocacy of toleration is rooted in his understanding of the human good as sensual self-seeking.

Montaigne provides reasons to be tolerant based on self-interest. He argues that there is no good reason for intolerance, since customs are merely human creations and opinions cannot be proven categorically. At the same time, he supplements our lack of transcendent knowledge with his concept of phenomenological knowledge to elaborate a positive vision of the self that serves as the foundation for his tolerant political principles. Two features of Montaigne's self, self-awareness and his conception of the human good as self-exploration, each promote tolerant behavior. Because self-awareness of one's own weaknesses and vulnerabilities leads us to sympathize with the suffering in other selves, one would not inflict suffering on another. Doing so would indirectly harm a self-aware person's own self. Montaigne thus emphasizes the universality and mutuality of each individual's ignorance and inabilities rather than appealing to the rights of potential victims. He also discusses a substantive human good, the pleasure derived from self-seeking, which is intellectually sensual and sensually intellectual. This good, if pursued, offers more than enough to keep one busy and content "at home."

Toleration is secured politically by creating a private sphere of free conscience and free judgment on the condition that one accept a public sphere where obedience to common norms must be observed. Less creative selves do not reap the primary benefit of the private sphere, but they benefit indirectly from the public peace it secures. Public conformity is necessary because while a stable order is necessary for the private sphere to be protected, Montaigne does not want to expose the groundlessness of authority due to a fear that an entire population will prove incapable of respecting authority without more grandiose claims. For those who can have a deeper understanding, Montaigne emphasizes an enlightened, dialogic, individual self-interest rather than calling for a right to toleration, in part because he does not conceive of such a "right" existing by nature and in part because he does not want to call for a crusade to institute them politically, because he fears that any crusade -- even one for toleration -- can be perverted and lead to horror and cruelty.

Without discussing the democratic and constitutional protections that today seem so essential to the institution of a humane society, Montaigne nonetheless articulates a powerful vision of a private life that should be politically protected by instituting a private sphere of free conscience and free political judgment. To allow individuals to blossom, Montaigne calls for the state to relinquish control over matters of conscience and judgment. Individuals must still obey the laws and conform in public, but they get to think what they want. This may seem unduly quietist -- complete acquiescence to the authorities that be -- but it is important to remember two things. First, Montaigne may not have gone as far in protecting individual liberty as we do today, but he articulated, almost for the first time, some of the key concepts of liberalism. Second, Montaigne does advocate change, but through the pen not the sword, reform not revolution. Given the outcomes of most revolutions, this is not a bad thing. Unlike a quietist, he was very active in both politics and publishing. He advised leaders of both the Catholic and Huguenot factions, negotiated peace treaties, and served as mayor of Bordeaux.[111] He also published his work several times during his own lifetime, and his writing went a long way toward fostering the moral sensibility that needs to be shared if liberal political institutions are to work. It is for this reason that Voltaire described Montesquieu as Montaigne plus institutions.[112] Given the failed attempts to export liberal institutions outside the West, we see that Montaigne's accomplishment was no small feat.

Finally, the non-transcendent nature of Montaigne's justification for toleration makes him a figure for today. Indeed, Rorty has been influenced by him through Judith Shklar, Lyotard refers to him as postmodern, and Derrida quotes him in the title of his most political essay.[113] But unlike these postmodern thinkers and unlike other non-foundational American theorists of today, Montaigne can give a reason, based on his conception of the self, why it is in an individual's self-interest to tolerate others. The postmoderns and Rorty and Rawls do not -- and perhaps cannot -- do this. Instead, they rely on the democratic values of the day, a luxury that Montaigne did not have. Montaigne's conception of the good as the inner calm and wonder that results from self-examination certainly is aristocratic. He had no illusions that his vision would be taken up on a mass scale, nor would he be surprised to see his conception overtaken by conceptions of the self that advance material pursuits and comfort, those conceptions that played such an important role in liberalism's later development. These later ideas obviously have a wider audience. Having his moral teaching be rejected by most people would not disturb Montaigne, because he did not particularly fear that political disturbances would come from the people. The masses, he thought, by and large, follow the customs and habits of the time and place in which they are born and raised. Conversely, Montaigne did fear troublesome elites, particularly intellectual elites. Intellectuals and their crazy ideas, he thought, are the source of most political turmoil. In his day, trouble was caused by the religious fanatics, Catholic and Protestant. The twentieth century has seen numerous other versions of ideologically driven politics, and Montaigne's calls for moderation and intellectual humility would have been well heeded in our own times.

Montaigne is especially timely today, both as a supplementary vision of the good life and as a way to tame rambunctious intellectuals. It is those who are dissatisfied with this world that lash out. This is not to say that injustices should not be fought. Montaigne categorically condemns the Spanish Inquisition, the murder of the Indians in the New World, slavery, and numerous other acts of cruelty and barbarism. But so much moral indignation is misplaced and leads to cruelty. Before lashing out in the world, Montaigne wants individuals truly to take stock of themselves. He wants to try to mitigate the hypocrisy and opportunism that is so rampant in politics, and he does this by offering a profound and appealing vision of human life, one that tries to get people to refocus their energies inward. Instead of acting out, he wants human beings to return "home,"at least as the basis of all further actions. His vision avoids metaphysical speculation and reliance on mere custom or habit, and it is a vision in which interest and toleration are united.

Liberal skeptics must give a reason why one should not violently inflict one's will on another. If nothing is true, why isn't everything permitted? This is the question of our age for all those disillusioned by metaphysics but desirous of moderate politics. Montaigne gives a compelling answer to this question.

NOTES:

1. For textual citations to Montaigne's *Essais* I give four numbers. The first Roman numeral joined by a period to an Arabic numeral refers to the book and essay number, respectively. (II.12 thus means book two, essay twelve.) The middle number is the page number in the French Pléiade edition, Montaigne, *Oeuvres complète*, Albert Thibaudet and Maurice Rat, eds., (Paris, 1962). The last number [in brackets] refers to the page number in Donald Frame's English translation, *The Complete Works of Montaigne* (Stanford: Stanford University Press, 1957).

2. Montaigne's "internal" justification for toleration (appealing only to one's own self-interest) must be understood in contradistinction to traditional rights-based conceptions which appeal to rights *external* to the individual.

3. I.14, 52 [35].

4. II.12, 429 [330].

5. II.12, 429-30 [331] and II.12, 427 [329].

6. II.12, 437 [337]

7. II.12, 436 [336].

8. II.12, 437 [336].

9. II.12, 450 [346].

10. I.3, 18 [8].

11. I.3, 18 [8].

12. Despite the similarity here to the Bible's Garden of Eden account of man's fall, Montaigne's own account of natural man (I.31) presents mankind as this way from the beginning without any devilish downfall. This is our natural condition to be understood and dealt with, not a "fallen" condition for which we should or could atone.

13. II.12, 450 [346].

14. II.12, 464 [357].

15. Montaigne's skepticism has been described as "the *coup de grace* to an entire intellectual world" and as "the womb of modern thought, in that it led to the attempt either to refute the new Pyrrhonism, or to find a way of living with it." Richard Popkin, *The History of Scepticism from Erasmus to Spinoza* (Berkeley: University of California Press, 1979), 54. I agree with Popkin's assessment of Montaigne's importance, but for the reasons spelled out below, not with his characterization of the nature of Montaigne's skepticism.

16. II.12, 482 [371]. These names come from Sextus Empiricus' *Outlines of Pyrrhonism*, which had its first printed edition (1562) during Montaigne's lifetime. For a fuller explanation, see the introduction to this volume.

17. Herman Janssen, Donald Frame, and Hugo Friedrich, the leading Dutch, American, and German Montaigne scholars respectively, all consider Montaigne a fideist, but for different reasons. Janssen considers Montaigne a fideist because this doctrine is "typical of [Montaigne's] whole age," whereas Friedrich states of Montaigne that "son propre fideism n'est pas plus orthodoxe" and is in fact noted by its "bizarrerie." Herman Janssen, *Montaigne Fideiste* (Utrecht: Nijmegen, 1930), 78. Hugo Friedrich, *Montaigne* (Paris: Gallimard, 1968), 109. For Frame's views, see his "What Next in Montaigne Studies" in *The French Review* 36:6 (May 1963): 577-587, *Montaigne: A Biography* (New York: Harcourt, Brace, and World, 1965), and *Montaigne's Discovery of Man: The Humanization of a Humanist* (New York: Columbia University Press, 1955).

18. II.12, 494 [381].

19. II.12, 494 [381].

20. II.12, 514 [397].

21. II.12, 512 [396].

22. II.12, 493 [380].

23. II.12, 493-517 [380-400].

24. Montaigne's account of "natural man" has nothing to do with Eden. Instead, he attributes it to the "cannibals" of the New World (see I.31).

25. II.12, 513 [397]. When Montaigne criticizes divine "cuckoldries" and virgin births, he attributes such claims to the "religion of Mohammed," but these are, of course, among the central miracles of Christianity.

26. On the significance of this point, see David Wootton, "New Histories of Atheism" in *Atheism from the Reformation to the Enlightenment*, Hunter and Wootton, eds. (Oxford: Oxford University Press, 1992), 27 and Wootton, "Unbelief in Early Modern Europe" in *History Workshop Journal* 20 (1985): 82-100.

27. II.12, 517 [400].

28. II.12, 423 [325].

29. II.12, 423 [325].

30. II.12, 492 [379].

31. II.12, 494 [381].

32. M.F. Burnyeat patronizingly "honours" Montaigne by referring to his thought as "the country gentleman's interpretation" of Pyrrhonism. Burnyeat makes Montaigne seem shallow: "One advantage of the country gentleman's interpretation is that there is no great difficulty in understanding how he can walk about his estate making arrangements for next year's crops while proclaiming himself a skeptic about space and time." M.F. Burnyeat, "The Skeptic in his place and time" in *Philosophy in History*, Rorty, Schneewind, Skinner, eds. (Cambridge: Cambridge University Press, 1984), 231. Other scholars who consider Montaigne to be a Pyrrhonist include Popkin, *The History of Scepticism from Erasmus to Spinoza*. See also the several excellent publications by Zbigniew Gierczynski.

33. Philosophers interested in the history of Pyrrhonism tend not to perceive how Montaigne uses and alters Pyrrhonism for his own purposes. See, for example, the otherwise excellent book by Julia Annas and Jonathan Barnes, *The Modes of Skepticism* (Cambridge: Cambridge University Press, 1985), 6.

34. II.29, 684 [533].

35. II.29, 683 [533].

36. II.12, 485 [374].

37. II.29, 683 [533].

38. II.12, 482-6 [372-4].

39. II.12, 482 [372].

40. II.12, 487 [375].

41. II.12, 487-9 [375 & 377].

42. II.12, 527 [408].

43. II.12, 487 [376].

44. II.12, 492 [379].

45. II.12, 492 [379].

46. II.12, 546 [423].

47. II.12, 545 [422].

48. II.12, 547 [424].

49. II.12, 550 [427].

50. II.12, 559-60 [433-4].

51. II.12, 548 [425].

52. II.12, 548 [425].

53. II.12, 571-86 [443-55].

54. II.12, 563 [437].

55. II.12, 562 [436].

56. II.12.

57. II.12, 540-42 [418-20].

58. II.12, 521 [403].

59. II.12, 563 [437].

60. II.12, 544 [421].

61. II.12, 545 [422].

62. II.12, 547 [424].

63. II.12, 547 [424].

64. II.12, 554-55 [430].

65. II.12, 554-55 [430].

66. III.13, 1096 [856].

67. III.13, 1095 [856].

68. II.8, 364 [278].

69. III.13, 1091 [852].

70. Jean Starobinski, *Montaigne in Motion* (Chicago: University of Chicago Press, 1985), 74.

71. I.20, 85 [60].

72. I.3, 18 [8].

73. III.10, 981 [767].

74. III.10, 988-89 [773].

75. II.8, 364 [278].

76. II.20, 656 [511].

77. III.3, 796 [621].

78. II.1, 321 [244].

79. This translates as: "It is not in Montaigne, but in myself, that I find all that I see there." Pascal, *Pensées*, pensée #64 in the Brunscvicg edition (Paris, 1934); #689 (according to Pascal's own text) in *Oeuvres complètes*, Louis Lafuma, ed. (Paris, 1963), 591.

80. Keohane, *Philosophy and the State in France* (Princeton: Princeton University Press, 1980), 99.

81. III.5, 871 [681] and III.13, 1094 [855] respectively.

82. III.5, 871 [681].

83. I.21, 103 [74].

84. III.5, 872 [682].

85. III.13, 1087 [850].

86. I.53, 297 [225].

87. I.53, 297 [225].

88. For a contrasting interpretation of Montaigne's view of acquisition, see David Schaefer, *The Political Philosophy of Montaigne* (Ithaca: Cornell University Press, 1990), 340-86. Schaefer argues that Montaigne is a bourgeois individualist who advocates

unlimited acquisition.

89. II.8, 364 [278].

90. II.17, 641 [499].

91. II.8, 366 [279].

92. III.13, 1092 [853].

93. III.10, 981 [767].

94. II.18, 648 [504].

95. II.18, 648 [504].

96. II.18, 647-8 [504].

97. II.7, 359 [274].

98. III.13, 1050 [821].

99. III.13, 1074 [840].

100. II.12, 546-7 [424].

101. I.21, 95 [68]. It is because of this "natural compassion" which has an "infinite power over me" that Montaigne says he is more likely to devote himself to the "little people" (III.13, 1079 [844]), that he "sympathize[s] very tenderly with the afflictions of others" (II.11, 409 [314]), that "there is nothing that tempts my tears but tears, not only real ones, but all sorts" (II.11, 409 [314]), that "the dead I hardly pity, and I should rather envy them; but I very greatly pity the dying" (II.11, 409 [314]), and why he does not mind the cannibalism of the dead so much as the torturing of the living (II.11, 409-10 [314]; I.31, 207-8 [155]; III.6, 889-90 [695]).

102. Indeed, in "Of Cruelty" (II.11), he cites the examples of several philosophers who agree with him. Montaigne's and Rousseau's notions of pity may very well have Christian roots. Rousseau, in his *Second Discourse,* ascribes it to all men in his description of the original state of nature.

103. III.8, 913 [714].

104. II.12, 541 [419].

105. II.20, 657 [511]. "The very laws of justice cannot subsist without some mixture of injustice" (II.20, 656 [511]). Montaigne carefully distinguishes between "justice in itself, natural and universal" and "that other, special, national justice constrained to the need of our governments" (III.1, 773 [604]). Montaigne never defines "justice in itself" and one can wonder whether he believes it exists. The point here, however, is that despite its admitted faults, law is necessary.

106. See Stephen Holmes, "Jean Bodin: The Paradox of Sovereignty and the Privatization of Religion" in *Nomos* XXX (1988): 5-45.

107. II.19, 654 [509].

108. II.19, 654 [509].

109. III.13, 1063 [831].

110. Skakespeare got this image from Montaigne, who in turn got it from the rich tradition of ancient Roman literature.

111. The best account of Montaigne's political involvements is Geralde Nakam, *Montaigne et son temps: Les événements et les essais; l'histoire, la vie, le livre* (Paris: A-G Nizet, 1982). Also see Arthur Armaingaud, "Etude sur Michel de Montaigne" in Armaingaud, ed., *Oeuvres complètes de Michel de Montaigne,* 12 vols. (Paris: Louis Conard, 1924-41), I:1-257; Alphonse Grun, *La vie publique de Michel de Montaigne: Etude biographique* (Paris: D'Amyot, 1855); David Maskell, "Montaigne médiateur entre Navarre et Guise" in *Bibliothèque d'humanisme et Renaissance* 41 (1979): 541-553; and, Malcolm

Smith, *Montaigne and Religious Freedom: The Dawn of Pluralism.* Étude de philologie et d'histoire, no. 45 (Geneva: Droz, 1981).

112. Voltaire, cited in Judith Shklar, *Montesquieu* (Oxford: Oxford University Press, 1987), 114.

113. Influence of Shklar's use of Montaigne may be seen in Richard Rorty, *Contingency, Irony, Solidarity* (Cambridge: Cambridge University Press, 1989), xv, 74, 89n, & 146. See also Judith Shklar, *Ordinary Vices* (Cambridge: Harvard University Press, 1984), especially ch. 1, "Putting Cruelty First," and her "The Liberalism of Fear" in *Liberalism and the Moral Life*, Nancy Rosenblum, ed. (Cambridge: Harvard University Press, 1989), 21-38; Jean-Francois Lyotard, "Answering the Question: What is Postmodern?" in *The Postmodern Condition: A Report on Knowledge*, Durand, tr. (Minneapolis: University of Minnesota Press, 1984), 81; and, Jacques Derrida, "Force de Loi: Le 'Fondement Mystique de l'Autorite'" found in French and English in *Cardozo Law Review*: 11 (5-6) July-Aug. 1990: 919-1045.

4

FRENCH FREE-THINKERS IN THE FIRST DECADES OF THE EDICT OF NANTES

Maryanne Cline Horowitz[1]

In intellectual circles of free-thinkers patronized by Cardinal Richelieu in the 1620s and 30s, continuing to some extent under Mazarin, toleration for reading and discussing alternative religious opinions and the curious world-wide diversity of religious rituals enters into stylish skeptical modes of discourse. La Mothe le Vayer's fashionable titles "De la Diversité des religions" in *Le Banquet sceptique* (1630) or *De la Vertu des païens* (1642), like Gournay's steady stream of new editions of Montaigne's *Essais*, serve as legitimate and cultured antidotes to the theological disputes among Huguenot sectarians (French upholders of the Dutch Synod of Dort of 1618 vs. French Arminians) or among Catholic adversaries (Jesuit Garasse vs. Jansenist Saint Cyran). The lands of France, lowlands, and England experience civil discord and war justified by religious ideologies. The toleration edict emerging in France in the "politique" sentiment of newly Catholic King Henry IV (1598, Edict of Nantes) is in effect an internal civic peace treaty in a land where one religious denomination no longer holds hegemony; the French Edict of Nantes ensures that the king and the established church would be Catholic, as the English Toleration Act after the Glorious Revolution ensures that the monarch would not be Catholic. The freedom of selected unconquerable dissenters to live and worship is the early modern realm of toleration in states with such established churches. Such edicts are compromises and their enforcement suffers from a fundamental ambiguity as expressed by Justus Lipsius (1547-1606) in his influential *Politicorum* of 1589.[2] On one hand, "One religion is the author of unitie; and from a confused religion there alwayes groeth dissention," and on the other hand, "what if the times be so disposed, *that a suddaine constraint will bring more damage than profit to the commonwealth? ...that it be better to differ* [defer] *the suppressing of overgrowne vices, then to make it openly knowne, that our force is too weake to checke and controll them.*"[3]

With a skeptical weighing of benefits and losses, the "politique" position replaces persecution and suppression, as well as rebellion and warfare, by carefully defined, limited toleration for the goal of civic harmony. Such edicts and revocations are not without precedent: throughout the medieval period, edicts of permission of residence to Jews (by definition not heretics in contrast to baptized individuals who deviate from the established Christian church) were regularly followed by revocations, exile, and sometimes later invitations of return. Neither Jews, nor Lutherans for that matter, receive toleration from the Edict of Nantes; in fact, Jews in France again receive an edict expulsion on April 23, 1615, and an expulsion from French colonies on Nov. 30, 1683.[4] While there were continued privileges of residence to "the Portuguese" in Bordeaux and other Jews in Metz, the French toleration of Jews as citizens awaits the disestablishment of the Church by revolutionaries and the subsequent decree of the National Assembly of Sept. 27, 1791, granting Jews citizenship in France; this enfranchisement accompanies the victories of French troops in Holland, Italy, and temporarily in Prussia. Yet in the first decades of the Edict of Nantes, free-thinkers enjoy circulating a long, difficult manuscript in which the Jew Salomon is a key speaker in a discussion set in Venice among representatives of seven religious viewpoints; the author of this *Colloquium Heptaplomores* is none other than the famous author of *The Six Books of the Republic,* Jean Bodin.

Encouraged by the revival of skeptical inquiry, the comparative study of religious beliefs and customs, travellers' and humanists' admiration of the virtue of some non-Christians, a succession of French authors--most prominently, Jean Bodin, Michel de Montaigne, Pierre Charron, Gabriel Naudé, Marie de Gournay, and François de La Mothe le Vayer--focus on the moral cultivation of *"preud'hommes"* and *"preude'femmes,"* individuals who achieve moral character and civic reponsibility. These authors tolerate their own learned consideration of diverse religious opinions and rituals, participate among friends on discussion of such topics, write about such thoughts, publish some of these thoughts, and read and collect manuscripts too radical for publication. These are all important steps that occur among an even greater audience of *"honnêtes hommes"* and *"honnêtes femmes"* in France at the close of the sixteenth and during the first half of the seventeenth century. Toleration of diversity of religious opinion is one of the fundamental foundations of the modern political principles of freedom of thought and expression, as in Article 1 of the United States Bill of Rights.[5] Despite rumors to the contrary, the historical evidence shows these free-thinkers living ritually within the confines of the established French Catholic Church, limiting their freedom of speech to private settings, and appropriately dedicating works for publication in France in awareness of state and church censorship of the press. Their skeptical and curiosity-provoking publications still have the power to create an atmosphere conducive to "nothing-human-is-foreign-to-me" discussions and to an openminded and tolerant society.

Multiple editions of Charron's *De la Sagesse* and Montaigne's *Essais,* and Bodin's diversely annotated books on historical method, on government, and on natural philosophy circulate publicly as examples and precedents for an author's toleration of freedom of thought and expression. Gabriel Naudé (1600-1653), Marie de Gournay (1565-1645), La Mothe le Vayer (1588-1672) and other "*libertins érudits*" recognize such works and write their own to contribute to a climate supportive of dialogue and tolerant inquiry. This succession of French thinkers (liberal in thought and Catholic by ritual) are in fact recognized as a school of thought by their seventeenth-century ardent Catholic critics, who name them "Libertins" in an accusation that free thinking and debauchery go together.[6] Nevertheless, these authors function in the highest circles, dedicating works to Cardinal Richelieu, receiving royal patronage, and thinking about what would benefit the welfare of the royal family and the state.

The 1620s is a particularly tumultuous decade. History books stress Cardinal Richelieu's 1627 siege of La Rochelle which takes away the fortresses that had initially protected Huguenot settlements. Less dramatic, yet equally influential is the French conflict between upholders of greater freedom of expression and advocates of stricter censorship and religious conformity--a confict of lasting importance to Protestant, Catholic, and secular communities of Europe and its colonial settlements. A cluster of intellectuals, as well as poets and dramatists, receive patronage from Cardinal Richelieu (secretary of state 1616, cardinal 1622, and chief minister to Louis XIII 1624).

In his advocacy of "raison d'état," he is supportive of intellectual successors to Montaigne and Charron who possibly deter sedition by buttressing the civic virtue of French Huguenots and Catholics upon their shared human nature, rather than upon sectarian theology. Montaigne in "On Utility and Honesty," discusses the vices repugnant to conscience that a ruler often is required to perform, and Charron less reluctantly permits royal policy to apply vices in the prudent acting for the public good.[7] From 1619-1625, there are open attacks on the *libertins érudits*, especially by Jesuit François Garasse--*La Doctrine curieuse des beaux esprits de ce temps, ou pretendus tels* (1623), *Apologie...pour son livre contre les atheists & libertins de nostre siecle* (1624) and *La Sommme Theologie des veritez capitales de la Religion Chrestienne* (1625). Nevertheless, Jansenist Saint-Cyran, supporting Richelieu in court factions, writes an effective anonymous rebuttal *Sommes des fautes et faussetez capitales contenues en la Somme théologique du père François Garasse*. The dedication to Richelieu advances his policy of balancing church and state interests and of distinguishing justice in matters of state from justice in private life and its critique of Garasse helps bring about the Sorbonne's condemnation of Garasse in 1626.[8] With the intermingling of topics in literary works, it is indeed a delicate matter to determine which writings serve the public good.

A common accusation against the French free-thinkers is that their fideism--their acceptance of Catholic doctrine on faith--and their appeal to God's grace is insincere. In his "Apology of Raimond Sebond," where he applies Sextus Empiricus to showing the limits of human reason, Montaigne's appeal at the end of the essay to divine grace has aroused a storm of controversy. Montaigne's 1580 or 1582 *Essais* applies the commonplace image of God's hand (common in Calvin as well)[9] that cannot be confused with ancient divine immanence. In 1580 Montaigne writes, "He will rise, if God by exception lends him his hand; he will rise by abandoning and renouncing his own means, and letting himself be raised and uplifted by divine grace, but not otherwise." After 1588, after reading Du Vair among others,[10] Montaigne adds "It is for our Christian faith, not for his Stoical virtue, to aspire to that divine and miraculous metamorphosis."[11]

In such an essay that maximizes its use of human reason to dispute human reason, are the closing words a lip service, as suggested most recently in Alan Levine's "Skepticism, Self, and Toleration in the Political Thought of Michel de Montaigne"? Or does the closing indicate the earnest Christian life in which ancient philosophy is allowed to play a role? For centuries, scholars have split between those who find him a religious skeptic who doubts revelation, and others who find him pious. Montaigne succeeds in communicating with a great variety of readers--Armingaud is pleased to find rationalism, doubt, and religious insincerity in Montaigne while Dréano confidently finds religiosity.[12] Italian humanists struggle with the same issues. The image of God's hand reaching out to lift humanity clearly distinguishes Montaigne from Ficino who uses the more ambiguous light imagery for the divine kindling of the sparks already making ascent. Light may be natural or divine. If divine, a light image may refer to explicitly Christian and Augustinian illumination of the Trinity or to any variety of pagan Sun-God or philosophical light imagery.[13]

An obvious Christian conclusion precedent to Montaigne is "On Immortality of the Soul" (1516) in which Pomponazzi states his Stoicizing view that "those who claim the soul is mortal seem better to save the grounds of virtue than those who claim it to be immortal. For the hope of reward and the fear of punishment seem to suggest a certain servility, which is contrary to the grounds of virtue, etc."[14] At the close he turns from natural reason to revelation where he can with certainty proclaim, "Since therefore such famous men disagree with each other, I think that this can be made certain only through God" and then he cites the New Testament and Thomas Aquinas for the soul's immortality (377-78). Pomponazzi is a precursor to Montaigne in balancing arguments pro and con immortality to show the incapacity of reason alone to build theology and in concluding with an appeal to God for the truths of faith.

From the Huguenot theorist Sebastian Castellio's *On Heretics* (*De Haereticis* 1554) Montaigne learns that no idea is so important that it is worth killing someone for it. "To kill men, we should have sharp and luminous evidence, and our life is too real and essential to vouch for these supernatural and fantastic accidents" (OC 1009, S 789). In application to contemporary trials for witchcraft, Montaigne gets his reader laughing at evidence that confessions are sometimes unreliable "for such persons have sometimes been known to accuse themselves of having killed people who were found to be alive and healthy" (OC 1009, S 789). Montaigne himself examines some witches in prison and declares with Socratic analogy "I would have prescribed them rather hellebore than hemlock" (S 790).

Montaigne does accept the evidence of experience. He personally suffers on seeing a chicken twisted at the neck in a slow death. When the censors in Rome in spring 1581 criticize his "On Cruelty" for his protest against torture in trials ("even in justice, all that goes beyond plain death seems to me pure cruelty," OC 410, S 157), he criticizes torture further in his later additions including the torturous execution he observed that week in Rome.[15] In Montaigne's bond of sympathy between himself and others, he experiences anguish in "feeling" a whip falling on another person. A major source for Montaigne's abhorrence of persecution and intolerance stems from his awareness of human credibility and his repulsion at the accompanying cruelty. He contributes to free-thinking a "humane" approach to the issue of persecution and forced conversion. That perspective influences La Mothe le Vayer in his important prince manual dedicated to Richelieu for the use of the dauphin Louis XIV: advising "maintaining edict that they have found established before their reign" and true piety and concern for peace among his people rather than extirpation of heresy.[16] Montaigne's wording in "On Cruelty" reflects Montaigne's timely reading of the 1579 French translation *Les Tyrannies et cruautez des Espagnols*,[17] and "On Cannibals" repeats Bartolomé de Las Casas' viewpoint that others will assess Christianity by how Christians treat them. To excessive inhumanity to animals, Amerindians, or neighbors who perhaps worship in a different way, Montaigne prefers the toleration of normal daily life with its pleasures and its natural pains.

Less subtle and amusing, more organized and programmatic, Pierre Charron's *De la Sagesse* reaches a much wider public than the *Essais* in the first half of the seventeenth century and thus serves as a "breviary" of free thought. In the following passage Pierre Charron (1541-1603), a Catholic priest and admirer of Montaigne, vividly expresses the war-weary mood of the "fin de la siècle" and his hopeful civic concern to build a foundation for morality independent of religion:

> Whoever is a good person by religious restraint and scruple, beware of him and do not value him: and he who has religion without virtue, I do not mean to say that he is more wicked, but he is more dangerous than he who has neither the one nor the other....I say this because people having no taste, image, or conception of virtue, except as the result and in the service of religion, and thinking that being a good man is nothing else than advancing and promoting their religion, believe that any activity whether it be treason, perfidy, sedition, rebellion, and any offense against anyone is not only allowable and permissible, under the colors of zeal and concern for religion, but moreover is praiseworthy, meritorious, and worthy of canonization.[18]

Charron, having seen what he believes to be immorality condoned by religion, searches for an independent source for ethics.[19] There is a close coincidence in timing between the preparing of the Edict of Nantes in 1598-99, which grants the Huguenots religious liberty in protected towns and estates and civil liberties throughout France, and Charron's writing of the *De la Sagesse*, February 1597 through April 1599.[20] In his avoidance of polemical attacks on Protestant beliefs and of polemical defenses of Catholic beliefs, in his exposition of the similarity of all religions, in his reliance on God's revelation and grace for right belief, in his advocacy of skepticism on metaphysical and theological questions on which there was no agreement, in his repudiation of dogmatic partisanship, and in his main purpose of founding an autonomous ethic that might be shared by all, Pierre Charron in *De la Sagesse* expresses the "politique" sentiment of the contemporaneous document *L'Edict du Roy*.[21] Charron preaches doctrinal humility and skepticism and advises that his contemporaries give their prime attention to acting in accordance with prudence, justice, courage, and temperance.

Published in 1601, Pierre Charron's *De la Sagesse* purports to teach "human wisdom." As the first edition is met by a storm of religious criticism of his intention, Charron in his revised preface published posthumously in 1604 justifies his decision to omit discussion of divine wisdom on the grounds that it is distinctly different from human wisdom, is best treated separately, and is already treated in his earlier works.[22] The contrast is striking with his 1593 and 1595 publication of a polemical tract, *Les trois veritez*, which sets out to prove that God exists, that Christianity is the true religion, and that the Catholic Church alone keeps the truth pure.[23]

One might very well ask, though, how Charron purports to teach "wisdom," because he is a skeptic, as so many of his earliest critics and recent commentators have maintained.[24] Charron's work does reflect the influence, through Montaigne especially, of Pyrrhonian and Academic skepticism, and is instrumental in its further spread; however, the major motive for Charron's advocacy of skepticism is the purpose it might achieve: mental tranquility that would allow the individual to concentrate attention on leading the good life. In fact, the liberty Charron recommends affects the will as much as the judgment. In the context of *De la Sagesse*, the purpose is to free the judgment from the lesser purpose of pursuit of truth and to free the will from the adherence to superfluous or harmful truths in order that the esprit in judgment and in will might guide one in the conduct of one's individual and public life.

Cicero had said, "the art of living is prudence." Charron considers prudence, which he defines as knowledge of what to desire and what to reject, as the guide to all the virtues, and therefore calls wisdom "*preude prudence*, a supple and strong *preud'hommie*, a well-advised probity."[25] Widely used in the sixteenth and seventeenth centuries and a goal that deters free thinkers from free behavior, *preud'homme* means, most simply, "man of integrity." When other authors consider *preude'femme*, "woman of integrity" as well, the *preud'homme* may take on a generic connotation for "good human being," with goodness adapted as Charron suggests to one's station in life.[26]

For Charron, the major characteristic of the *preud'homme* is independence from one's times, the source of which is the internal integrity of judgment and his will. Like the sage described in Epictetus's *Manual*, Charron's *preud'homme* has a noble constancy and self-sufficiency. He directs his attention to the realm of life that is within his own control.[27] In order to discover who is a true *preud'homme*, it is necessary to look within at the source and motivation of the external actions.[28] Charron's conscious indebtedness to the ancient Stoics for this doctrine is indicated by the following Senecan statement: "the doctrine of all the sages states that to live well is to live according to nature"... 'it is the same thing, to live happily and to live in accordance with nature,' understanding by nature the equity and universal reason which shines in us.[29] Thus to be virtuous one should look within to find the sure standard of natural law.

Thus despite Charron's doubts about the power of human reason, he still views reason as the standard and source of human knowledge of natural law. Freedom of the mind in judgment and in will restores human nature to its natural harmony and order. Having one's own in order, one is then in a better position to put it in harmony with the order of the universe. No longer believing all the opinions and laws of the locality, the skeptic is a "citizen of the world" and has a mind open to accept natural law. The human being, as a microcosm of the world, may also be said to contain a government. When the soul is in its natural order, the sovereign understanding rules the lower faculties by the law of nature.[30] The will submits itself to right reason for the proper ordering of the passions.[31] Thus when human nature is in its proper order, human reason is able to follow the instructions of universal reason.

Whereas in medieval writers the reference to "the law written in the heart" is usually a basis for discussion of "common notions," Charron rejects this concept for explaining human knowledge of natural law. Like the Academic skeptic Carneades in his attack on the Stoic school, and indebted to Montaigne for many of his examples, Charron compares customs from different lands and compares arguments from different so-called authorities to show that there is no notion universally accepted. Furthermore, he proclaims that because the number of fools far exceeds the number of sages, the ideas commonly held are likely to be false. But like Cicero before him, Charron's recognition of the skeptical attack does not stop him from believing that natural law is within. He argues that if the nature of humankind were ordered according to reason, then common consent would be a trustworthy guide.[32]

In satire, Charron writes, "They want one to be a good person, because there is a paradise and a hell....You guard yourself from being evil, for you do not dare, and fear to be beaten; and already in that you are evil."[33] Deleted from the second edition was the statement "you become a good person so that one pays you, and that one gives you great thanks."[34] Charron is reviving an authentically "classical" or "pagan" theory of morality. For Charron, as in Pomponazzi, virtue is its own reward.

Charron thus distinguishes moral from religious motivation. Probity, *preud'hommie*, and conscience go together as do piety, religion, and devotion. He criticizes those who are religious without being virtuous, as well as those who are virtuous while being nonbelievers. Not explicitly saying which extremes he thinks are worse, Charron says that religion without virtue is easy and common while virtue without religion is difficult and very rare. Such virtuous individuals are "powerful and generous souls."[35] Charron, in his belief that God has provided us at birth with the means to achieve the good life and in his belief that the human virtue of pagans would be lessened by initially directing it to a divine end, keeps his Christianity in a separate compartment from his ethics, and declares an ecumenical foundation for morality.

The 1601 edition of *De la Sagesse* is under attack from the moment of its publication and the 1604 edition is condemned by the Sorbonne and the Congregation of the Index. One study has tried to explain this condemnation as a product of factional politics.[36] While that may well be, it is also of great interest to know the intellectual reasons for the condemnation. We can get some insight into the reasons for this attack from Charron's attempt in the "Petit Traicté de Sagesse" to answer complaints leveled against his book. These are: endangering religious belief by advising readers to judge all things; causing Pyrrhonian incertitude by admonishing readers to free themselves from dogmatic attachments, proclaiming to teach *preud'hommie* independently of thought of reward or punishment; and stressing the sufficiency of natural law to the neglect of grace. These become stock complaints against the subsequent free-thinkers. Charron answers these complaints not by changing his views, but by justifying what he has done and claiming he has not intended these irreligious implications.[37] To appease his critics, he also makes omissions, modifications, and additions to the second edition of *De la Sagesse*.[38] However, one is struck by how small the changes are in the sensitive area of the role of grace. While in the first edition grace is not discussed at length, the discussion of it in the second edition clarifies even further the small role he attributes to it in the development of virtuous human behavior.

By stressing the independence of religion and morality, Charron makes religion subordinate to virtue. He rejects the basic religious perspective that "religion is a generality of all good and of all virtue, that all virtues are comprised in it." Instead he claims "it is in the reverse, because religion, which is posterior, is a special and particular virtue, distinct from all other virtues."[39] Justice, which requires giving to each his due, teaches obedience, service, and worship of God. True piety, as a particular part of justice, is a crowning achievement of *preud'hommie*. In Charron's view, there is a law which God has put within us from our origin. This law, which is the source of human virtue, is part of humans by creation and thus is anterior to religion.[40]

Jean Bodin (1529/30-1596) is a French thinker who contributes to historiography, jurisprudence, comparative religion, demonology, natural theology, political philosophy, and economics.[41] In the Renaissance and Reformation discussions of depravity and dignity, Bodin is one of the strongest advocates of human dignity and of the freedom of the will (both God's will and human will).[42]

Agreeing with the Stoics that sages are few, Bodin exhibits a high assessment of human potential--as in his citation of the Stoicizing and Platonizing allegorical commentaries on Genesis of Philo of Alexandria (before the codification of Rabbinic law) and of *De libero arbitrio* (Augustine's book on free will before his debate with Pelagius and before his refinement of the doctrine of original sin). To Bodin, how might a God who provided all of nature with its sources for growth and development not provide the human soul with the seeds for its flowering?

Jean Bodin's life and religion have been a matter of controversy[43] partly because his name is a common one in the historical records.[44] There is general agreement among historians that born in Angers, Bodin studied in a Carmelite house in Paris in the mid-1540s. Like Erasmus, Lèfevre d'Étaples, and Calvin, Bodin attains proficiency in the trilingual humanist curriculum of Latin, Greek, and Hebrew texts. Some contemporaries report that Bodin's mother was a Jewish refugee from Spain, and seventeenth-century readers of the *Colloquium* often identify Bodin with the position of the Jewish speaker Salomon. Nevertheless, documents published in 1933 indicate Catholic family background[45] and Bodin took an oath to Catholicism in 1562, joined the Catholic League briefly the same year as Charron, 1589, and received a Catholic burial in 1596. Already in the 1580s, Bodin's books received criticism for unorthodoxy, and several of his books appeared on the Index of Prohibited Books: *De Republica libri XVI*, 1592; *De Daemonomanie*, 1594; *Methodus*, 1596, Index of Clement VIII; *Universae naturae theatrum*, 1633.[46]

Free-thinkers highly value his secret manuscript, but Pierre Charron and the general public read some of Bodin's natural theology in the posthumous French translation of his treatise on nature and natural theology. In the *Colloquium*, the doctrine of original sin receives refutation, not only from a Jew, a Muslim, and a doubter, but also from a natural philosopher expounding principles declared in the *Theatrum*. What follows next from the natural philosophy of Toralba, which is consistent with the principles of the *Theatrum*, is an argument against the possibility of the union of the divine and human in Jesus. Toralba views God as "eternal essence, one, pure, simple, and free from all contact of bodies, of infinite goodness, wisdom and power"(325; 248). The gap between Creator and created is too great for a union of infinite immaterial divine and the finite bodily human (351; 267). Likewise Salomon borrows the same technique from Bodin's *Methodus* to suggest how religion can corrupt humankind: "All this discussion about the Fall of origin, which I think is no fall, has its beginnings in the leaders of the Christian religion ....Hence the seeds of errors began to creep far and wide through men's minds." (404-5; 306). He then refers to God ordering Noah after the flood to be good as commanding only what is possible (430; 327).

Theatrum proceeds in five books: the principles of nature, the minerals, the plants and animals, the soul, and the heavenly bodies. It appears to be designed for both erudite and popular audiences: while the margins contain numerous book references, the text is a dialogue between Theorus, an adult student who asks troubling questions, and Mystagogue, a mystical natural philosopher, who generally claims to know the answers. They expound on everything from the abundance of plants and animals to the God-given human capacity to contemplate the divine order in nature. In an overall tone of appreciation for the divine blessings of life in this world, Bodin's work proclaims human dignity in contrast to Pierre Boaistuau's frequently republished *Le théâtre du monde* (1558), which laments the misery of the human condition amid diseases and disasters.[47] Our focus will be on Book IV, On Souls, which makes this book not only a natural philosophy but a natural theology.[48]

Book IV, On Souls, is a natural theology. It challenges Bodin to support his view that truth is singular, consistent in all disciplines. Upholding the position of the Catholic Church in rejecting the doctrine of the double truth (suspected in Boethius of Dacia and Pomponazzi), Bodin in his *Theatrum* states "What is true must be the same for physicists, theologians, dialecticians, medical doctors and there cannot be more than one truth."[49] In Book IV of the *Theatrum*, in his ninth section "On intellection and on the intellect, truth, the sciences, and cognition," Bodin raises the issue of the path to knowledge by having Theorus inquire of Mystagogue his thoughts on the Aristotelian dictum "*Nihil esse in mente, quod non prius fuerit in sensu*" "Nothing is in the mind, that is not first in the senses" and the corresponding notion that the mind is a *tabula rasa*. This epistemological discussion has origins in the Stoic debates with other schools recorded in Aetius and Diogenes Laertius.[50] The issue is topical in late sixteenth-century France: Henri Estienne's publication of Sextus Empiricus in Latin in 1562 and in a complete edition of 1569 increases scholarly attention to the deceptions of the senses.[51] The issue of the path to knowledge comes under notorious discussion in relationship to natural theology in Michel de Montaigne's "Apology" *Essais*, II, 12 (1580), following his French translation of rationalist Sebond's *Theologia naturalis* (1569, rpt. 1581).[52] Already in 1581 Bodin confronts the Pyrrhonian evidence of natural sources for faulty sense knowledge: in his 1581 Preface to *Démonomanie*, he differs greatly from Montaigne in suggesting instead that there is evidence of demonic distortion of the senses.[53] Books IV and V of the *Theatrum*, likewise, testify that the human soul is the battleground between the temptations of demons and the encouragement of angels.

Nevertheless, in considering the Aristotelian dictum, both Bodin's student and teacher give examples of the senses helping one achieve understanding. Very significantly in a passage which influences Pierre Charron to be more assertive than Montaigne about how the mind has access to conscience in guiding conduct despite possible distortion in the senses, the teacher uses light and seed images to proclaim that the understanding has its own resources. Then Mystagogue proposes that God provided a seedbed in the human soul by which the soul comes to know the virtues and the sciences. Bodin uses the Stoic epistemological concept "seed"--"*semina virtutum*" in his *Epitome* and "*semina pietatis ac religionis*" in his *Oratio*. Yet, here in the *Theatrum*, the Stoic "seed" appears in the full context of garden imagery to indicate the extent of possible development of the human soul.

Bodin answers the skepticism of the New Academy by citing the founder Plato's crucial book on whether virtue can be taught or comes by nature--the *Meno*. During the dialogue by which Socrates draws out truth from Meno, a young male slave is brought as a test of how anyone may discover within the mind the fundamental principles of geometry. This dialogue is useful for it gives only the preliminary suggestion of the doctrine of reminiscence by which the mind has notions previous to birth, while exemplifying how a tutorial dialogue may bring forth principles from the mind. Particularly useful for Bodin is that Plato extrapolates from the example that "You see, he can do the same as this with all geometry and every branch of knowledge."[54] Mathematics to Bodin implies both a number mysticism of microcosm-macrocosm correspondences and an organizing principle by which a field of study approaches a science where true and false may be distinguished.[55] His works seek the kinds of principles that Meno finds. The ultimate truth, the comprehension of the divine, appears most simply and clearly to the human mind as the geometrical figure of the holy Tetragrammaton, the unutterable four consonant name YHWH; through the four-sided figure, opposition and discord are resolved in one harmony.[56]

After showing that humans have reason to a greater extent than animals, Mystagogue rhetorically asks whether the creator of nature has equipped humans even better than animals through the "seeds of the sciences and virtues"? Fougerolles, marking his addition with an asterisk, adds that light in the human mind aids in understanding; for this addition, Fougerolles cites the Vulgate Latin of Psalm 4:6 *"Signasti super nos lumen vultus tui,"* "The light of thy countenance is impressed upon us."[57] Thomas Aquinas, nominalists, and Erasmus utilize that passage as a reference to the natural light given by the divine. Like other light images it does allow a reader's Augustinian, neo-Platonic, or Lutheran interpretation as illumination, although advocates of that position in the early seventeenth century would be more likely to reject the Vulgate historical account for the prayer "Lord, lift thou up the light of thy countenance upon us."[58]

The teacher returns to the seed and light imagery to draw out an analogy from the student: the soil of the earth would not yield plants if there were not seeds hidden within and ashes would not light up if there were not sparks hidden within (478; 690). While one may not see the seeds hidden in the ground, nature is inseminated: "by the succession of time it will bear plants, according that nature has inseminated it: I leave to you to make the same judgement on the understanding of humans."[59] What might the student learn about the human understanding from that analogy? Obviously, that the human understanding would not yield growth and light if it were not provided by God who provided nature so well. Using the argument of Augustine, *On the Trinity*, Book 9 and Duns Scotus, Book I, section 3, questions 6 and 7, Bodin proclaims "all force and power of the senses depends so on the soul."[60] Thus, in the context of the dialogue, Mystagogue's stand on the special wisdom of the sages allows him to declare that the intellect can understand separate from the senses, and to put the student on the defensive by suggesting that without the soul's activity, the senses can do nothing.

In the *Colloquium*,[61] we meet the Catholic host Coroaneus who conforms to the Council of Trent, a strict Lutheran Fridericus, a moderate Calvinist Curtius, a Stoicizing Jew Salomon, a natural philosopher and advocate of natural theology Toralba, a congenial doubter and religious universalist Senamus, and a tolerant convert to Islam Octavius. Non-Christians outnumber Christians in a discussion which concludes with a criticism of religious persecution and an agreement to nourish their piety in peaceful harmony (Kuntz 471; Noack 358). While Christian Europe had produced records and literary versions of disputations intended for conversion to Christianity, never before was there such an open-ended tolerant work, in which each religionist expresses both his own theology and his points of contention with the other theologies presented. Unlike Montaigne, Bodin does not poke fun at those who attest to "seeing" witches fly or "witnessing" a werewolf transform--strange phenomena proclaimed by their contemporaries; in fact one point on which all speakers agree is that if one is on a boat in the Mediterranean during a violent storm, to rid the ship of demons one should throw any Egyptian mummy overboard!

In the conversation at the close of the dialogues, Senamus declares the minimum beliefs shared by all present necessary for religion--that God is the parent of all gods and creator of nature, and that prayer with a good heart to God will please God and lead to knowledge of true religion (465; 354-5). In the criticism there of the persecution of the Jews in Spain and Portugal emerges the notion that religious belief cannot be forced, but must stem from freedom of the will. Even stronger evidence that a skeptical mentality towards religious truth is a source for the toleration advocated in this work is the declaration of Senemus: "But I, lest I ever offend, prefer to approve all the religions of all rather than to exclude the one which is perhaps the true religion" (465; 354).

The issue of religious toleration is also discussed in Book IV, chapter 7 of Bodin's *République*. His preference in this public work is a state which maintains the "one true religion" and is not beset by religious disputation, yet his examples reflect diverse religions: rulers of the Orient, Africa, Spain, and Russia; the ancient Hebrews; and the 1555 closure of the German religious wars, which allows each prince to choose whether his people should be Catholic or Lutheran. These examples support the ruler's domination over the one religion of the state. In the situation where there is a diversity of religions or of sectarian viewpoints, Bodin advises the rulers to restrain from forcing the consciences of their subjects. Instead the examples of Emperor Theodosius and the Turkish government suggest that the good ruler lives, exemplifies, and supports the true religion, yet "permits each to live in liberty of conscience."[62]

Encouraged by Senamus' seeking a common religion, Toralba and Salomon agree with him that the oldest religion is the best, and they cite the religion of the biblical patriarchs (182-3; 1140-142). Utilizing a Stoic cluster of terms--"reason," "light," "innate," "planted"--Toralba views the law of nature commanding the worship of one God: "Indeed as I view the almost infinite variety of sects, Christians differing with Ismaelites [Muslims] and pagans differing among themselves, no standard of truth seems more certain than right reason, that is, the supreme law of nature, planted in men's minds by immortal God" (337; 257; also 185; 142). This view meets the approval of the Calvinist and the Catholic. After a debate about the doctrine of reward and punishment in an afterlife, Senamus suggests tolerance to disagreement, and Toralba concludes "is it not better to embrace that most simple and most ancient and at the same time the most true religion of nature, instilled by immortal God in the minds of each man from which there was no division (I am speaking of that religion in which Abel, Enoch, Lot, Seth, Noah, Job, Abraham, Isaac, and Jacob, heroes dearest to God, lived) than for each one to wander around uncertain?" (462; 351-2). An antidote to skepticism during doctrinal dispute is thus a minimalist shared natural theology.

A fuller discussion by Toralba, Senamus, and Salomon of this ancient religion focuses on the Decalogue, that is the Ten Commandments. Salomon suggests a correspondence between the divine laws and hidden secrets of nature, as have been revealed by Philo Hebraeus, Abraham Aben Ezra, King Solomon, and Leone Hebreus, and cites Ezra for the Decalogue as natural law (191; 147).[63] Toralba confirms that the two tablets are the law of nature, and all the commands except the resting on Sabbath are common to other nations (193; 148). He boldly declares a Pelagian view: "If true religion is contained in the pure worship of eternal God, I believe the law of nature is sufficient for man's salvation" (225; 172).

Against Curtius's citation of Paul "The law was given by Moses, but grace has been given through Jesus Christ," (410; 311) both the Jew and the Muslim argue for the benefits of obeying divinely granted law (Mosaic law or the Koran respectively) for attaining a life of virtue and a life worthy of salvation (415, 420; 315, 319). Toralba and Senamus go further into free thinking in suggesting that neither revealed law nor faith in Jesus Christ is necessary. Toralba avows the outstanding virtues of ancient philosophers, and denies they could be eternally suffering (421; 319). Salomon proclaims in an opening phrase which influences La Mothe le Vayer's book on the virtue of pagans: "What lawgiver was ever so cruel that he commanded his people to do something which was impossible?" (430; 327) Salomon on several occasions indicates God's praise for people after Adam such as Noah, Enoch, and Moses, and Toralba confirms that God provided them with "the most true religion of nature" (VI, 407). However, to Toralba's plea for that natural religion today, Salomon suggests that common folk, and even the educated, hold more constant in religion through rites and ceremonies (462-3; 352). Nevertheless there is the suggestion that all that humans need for living a good life--the natural law indicating that one should worship God and treat other human beings well--is contained in the divine law and explicitly in the divinely-revealed Decalogue. Speaking the civic religion of Bodin's *Oratio*, Senamus suggests that those most natural and worthy are religious to the gods, pious to their country, loyal to their parents, charitable to their neighbors, and kind to those in need (422; 320-321).

Copies of Bodin's *Colloquium* (with title *De rerum sublimium acranis*) become favorite outrageous reading for European free thinkers as a result of Gabriel Naudé's 1633 citation in his book which analyzes current historical and political books. In a letter to Claude Peiresc about 1630, Naudé mentions reading Bodin's manuscript that "cannot be published." In 1632 Hugo Grotius seeks out the hand-written multi-lingual manuscript "to refute it"; finding it "very worthy to be read," Grotius comments on Bodin's erudition in Latin, Greek, as well as Hebrew rabbinical literature. Naudé in his *Bibliographie politique* (1633) draws public attention to the *Colloquium*, while at the same time indicates that God would not want ever published *De rerum sublimium arcanis, Des Secrets des choses d'en hault*. Thus intriguing the reader, he links it with two other works which endanger true piety by comparing diverse religions with one another: Pierre D'Ailly's *De tribus sectis* and Cardan's *De la Subtilité*. Yet Naudé is already known for having published books reflecting his enjoyment in researching and ridiculing occult, secretive sciences, (1623 on Roicrucians, 1625 on falsely acclaimed magicians); in his *Advis* he is to advocate collecting such books if even to refute them. In fact, both Queen Christine of Sweden and Hermann Conring, friend of Leibniz, seek out the manuscript based on Naudé's suggestion. Naudé's close associate Gui Patin (1600-72) acquires a copy of the *Colloquium*, which they discuss together; Patin relates that Bodin died a Jew, and Naudé relates that Guillaume Postel shared with Bodin his papers on a conversation of four religionists in Venice.[64]

Gabriel Naudé provides learned advice for the open-minded and skeptical reading of a full range of valuable books in his *Advis pour dresser une bibliotheque* (1627, 1644), dedicated to Henri de Mesme for whom he built the Bibliotheca Memmiana. After serving Cardinals De Bagni and Barberini in Rome for twelve years, he is appointed librarian by Cardinal Richelieu just before the Cardinal dies in 1642, and serves in fact as librarian to Mazarin for the next decade, building the first French public library of 40,000 volumes. Thus, Naudé's accomplishment as a professional librarian, together with his renown as a free thinker, bring public attention to his reading recommendations.

In his *Advis*,[65] Naudé recommends that a good library should acquire the principal ancient and modern authors in every field of learning; the original texts of the major authors; best authors in each field; best commentators on ancient authors; all general or specific compilations or tractates on a subject; all critics of a particular science so that one might engage in mental facing (including skeptics Sextus Empiricus, Sánchez, and Agrippa); new scientific authors (Copernicus, Kepler, Galileo, etc.); first books on a topic rather than imitators; books on obscure topics for amusement or to refute them (pseudo-sciences included here); the Talmud and Koran, Luther and Calvin and other heretics in order to refute them. Speaking in Charron's imagery of the "*preud'homm*e" withstanding a storm, Naudé justifies reading the Talmud and Koran, which he thinks are full of blasphemies, "since they can be prejudicial only to those who, lacking the basis of right conduct, suffer themselves to be carried away by the first puff of the wind that blows" (28). Like the other free thinkers, Naudé's distinction between the many and the few sustains confidence that those raised in "*preud'hommie*" won't be led astray by inquiry into strange sets of beliefs.

To complete the library, Naudé also advises sets and collections; major authors; reference books; and books valued in one's time and place, such as history and politics in his day. He advises purchasing both old and recent books (linking "Montaigne, Charron, Verulam, along with Seneca and Plutarch" (36); small books as well as large (including Machiavelli's *Prince* and *of Epictetus Manual* (38) and minor works of major authors; important but out-of-print books no longer valued in our time; and manuscripts both of ancient authors and of recent authors yet unpublished. Directly after discussing manuscripts, he cites Bodin's *République* as one of the best known recent authors, treating a subject for the first time, and translated into several languages (44-45); the mention of Bodin may very well suggest to his friends and readers of his earlier *Bibliographie politique* that he has collected also the unpublished work of this great author which marks a first in the comparative study of religions (ms. 6564 of Président de Mesme, Fonds latin, Bibliothèque nationale).

Marie de Gournay has not previously been included in scholarship on "*libertins érudits*" but her contemporaries and later scholars view her as an important associate of Montaigne and of La Mothe le Vayer and she moves in the same circles to the extent possible for a woman intellectual. She receives the commission from Montaigne's wife to edit his posthumous edition, receives pensions and patronage, and gains specific privilege to publish the 1635 folio edition of the *Essais* dedicated to Richelieu. As the editor who keeps Montaigne's *Essais* in print until her death three years after Richelieu's and as a friend of La Mothe Le Vayer who bequeaths to him her books, she aims to be a "*preude'femme*." She persists in her scholarly work despite scurrilous attacks, especially following her 1595 preface in defense of Montaigne and her political treatise in response to the assassination of Henry IV, *Adieu de l'âme du roi de France et de Navarre à la Reine avec la défense des Pères Jésuites* (1610), followed by Courbouzon-Montgomery's *Anti-Gournay*. Even in the 1620s when Jesuit Garasse is at the height of his attack on the "pernicious" influence of Pierre Charron in particular, Gabriel Naudé, La Mothe le Vayer, and Marie de Gournay persist in their recognition of the values of their literary forbears. Marie holds meetings of literary men, including neighbor Marolles, brothers Ogier, brothers Habert, Colletet, Malleville, and La Mothe le Vayer. Marolles claims that at her house meetings began that later became the Academie Française.[66] Other evidence of her literary influence is that while debarred from official meetings of the academy, she appears in satires of the academy, such as the Comédie des Académistes.

In the 1620s at the height of the controversy on "*libertines*," Marie de Gournay publishes *L'Ombre de Mademoiselle de Gournay* (1626), her own collection of her essays, poems, and diverse works. It includes some comments on religion. In "Égalité des Hommes et des Femmes," she argues by the authority of philosophers, Fathers of the Church, and Scriptures. She points out that the Salic Law, excluding women from French kingship, was made for only military reasons. Differing from most other premodern feminists (male or female) in her concerns not only for female dignity but for opportunities for females in the social order,[67] she mentions the exclusion of women from law practice and the priesthood and understands that men have embedded prejudice against women into the political and social order through justifications based on theology. Her 1635 folio Richelieu edition of Montaigne's *Essais* is replete with names of authors quoted, French translations and notation of his Greek and Latin quotations, which invite readers to further explore ancient Epicurean, Stoic, and Skeptical philosophers.[68] Montaigne had left some of the more bold or lewd quotations in Greek or Latin, perhaps not anticipating that a lady would be the one to research and translate them for the general public. In defense of Montaigne's religion, in his revision of her 1595 preface, she adds her response to the Huguenot Baudius, who had evaluated Montaigne in his *Poemata*, 1607. Marie proclaims his reason was that the *Essays* are "*ennemyh profez des Sectes nouvelles,*" and praises Montaigne for "La Foy des simples."[69]

A companion in learned conversation with Naudé and Patin and with Marie de Gournay, La Mothe le Vayer (1588-1672) gives further evidence of a secular, natural foundation for virtue in his *La Vertu des Payens*, 1642. Yet he dedicates this book to Richelieu to please him in his current arguments with St. Cyran and the Jansensists who emphasize Augustinian original sin.[70] Notwithstanding that the virtue of pagans is of course nothing comparable to virtues of Christians, La Mothe's point is not simply the possibility of virtue among ancient philosophers and their contemporary followers but also the possibility of salvation for those of the quality of Socrates or Confucius. He relies on the respect for great ancient philosophers and awareness of the excessive Augustinian focus on original sin as taught by Protestants and Jansenists, and La Mothe takes on Augustine by the Thomist tradition of recognizing virtue in infidels (*De la Vertu*, V, 1, 3-16). He triumphantly suggests that according to Augustine following virtue for love of virtue is in fact love of God (V, I, 7). A precedent is Lipsius' hermeneutics for Christianizing Stoicism: "No one should place the End or happiness in Nature, as the Stoics do; unless by the interpretation which I gave, namely in God."[71] While this formula allows Lipsius to turn the seeking of virtue into the seeking of God, it also restores the ancient Stoic equivalency of God and nature (a problem in Bodin's natural theology and a heresy of which Vanini is accused)--Romanized and Christianized to be God's immanence or participation in nature.

In inquiring questions, La Mothe arouses the readers' concerns for a merciful divine justice when considering some descendants of Adam who did not receive revelation (V, 1, 84), namely the peoples newly discovered by Europeans, who had no opportunity to have known Christianity (86). Lest we find this viewpoint radically challenging, we must note La Mothe (and Richelieu) upstage with this publication Issac La Peyrère who differs from Jewish, Christian, and Muslim traditions in a radical theological innovation that there were men before Adam.[72] From Bordeaux, La Peyrère moves to Paris in 1640 and is among the "*libertins érudits*" and in the service of the Prince of Condé. Naudé in a letter to Cardinal Barberini of 1641 reports people trying to get the manuscript of La Peyrère's *Prae-Adamite* which was banned by Cardinal Richelieu (ultimately published in 1655 with no press name). Within that context, La Mothe le Vayer's consideration of virtue among non-Christian descendants of Adam fits well his dedication to Richelieu; "faith obliges us to believe that all humans that we find in this other hemisphere have come from Adam, and had only the same origin as us" (84).

Meanwhile like Salomon of Bodin's *Colloquium*, La Mothe asks "Also is it not the goodness of God to never oblige humans to do the impossible?" (86). Thus, La Mothe in a publication endorsed by Richelieu, asks questions hidden from the public in Bodin's unpublished Latin, Greek, and Hebrew text, and we are led to consider seriously whether natural law is sufficient for the virtue God expects of pagans of the globe, as it was for Noah who lived before the Mosaic revelation. Yet La Mothe le Vayer, dedicating to Richelieu a prince manual for the dauphin Louis XIV, becomes the tutor to Louis XIV's younger brother in 1649 and briefly also to Louis XIV before 1653.[73] His "De l'instruction de Monseigneur Le Dauphin," begins with the importance of religion, advising piety, opposing hypocrisy, and recommending as the cure to the schism besetting the French state the doctoring of piety and virtuous behavior, rather than violent remedies. He advises Louis that French kings have promised to maintain the "peace among their peoples" and to "guard the edicts that have been established before their reign."[74] La Mothe le Vayer is praised highly by his churchman son, who dedicates the *Oeuvres* of his father to Mazarin in 1653, and to King Louis XIV in 1662.

Authors receiving patronage in the circle of Cardinal Richelieu, continuing under Mazarin, do support a tolerant climate of questioning dialogue on contemporary subjects discussed among individuals of differing religious sensibilities. These authors' questions are considered by the court culture not to be as radical or threatening as the new theological dogmas current among Protestants, or the heretical statements of unfortunate Vanini burned at the stake in Toulouse in 1619, or the censorious rebuke of great French Catholic extremists; furthermore, like La Mothe and St. Cyran, Naudé is responsive to the political needs of the moment, as in writing *Considérations politiques sur les coups d'Etat*, 1639, which obliquely supports the "raison d'état" of Richelieu's Day of Dupes by analogous historical examples.[75] While La Mothe finds virtue in some pagans, neither he or other free thinkers will disassociate atheism from immorality; Vanini won't find a defender until 1582 when Bayle, questioning assumptions on cause and effect in *Reflections on the Comet*, cites Vanini's moral life as an example of Bayle's outspoken proposition that an atheist might be virtuous.

Consideration of the ties between toleration and skepticism on human capacity to know God's judgments is especially appropriate given the ecumenical impact of Vatican II in our time. The Second Vatican Council, opened by Pope John XXIII, October 1962 and completed by Pope Paul VI in December 1965, published "The Declaration on the Relationship of the Church to Non-Christian Religions," "The Declaration on Religious Freedom," and "The Decree in Ecumenism." The Synod of Bishops, called by Pope John Paul II in 1985 to reevaluate Vatican II, reaffirms the important principles of the above documents: "The Second Vatican Council affirmed that the Catholic Church denies nothing which is true and which is holy in other non-Christian religions....The Council also affirms that God does not deny the possibility of salvation to all men of good will...."[76] Pope John Paul II reaffirms the inclusive, ecumenical viewpoint in *The Splendor of Truth*.[77] La Mothe le Vayer, under Richelieu's patronage, takes up the issue of salvation or justification for people of good will or virtue. La Mothe builds upon humanist knowledge of the sources in classical, Hebrew, and Christian civilization for belief in human capacity for virtue; in arguing against Sepulveda in the tradition of Las Casas a century before, he aids ecumenical efforts for building mutual respect and community among peoples of diverse faiths and traditions.

The splitting up of church authority and the discovery of peoples of diverse moral beliefs and customs raises a question with religious, political, and social implications: Is there a sure and universal foundation for morality? This profound and practical question leads French authors living during the crises of the French Religious Wars, such as Bodin, Montaigne, and Charron to seek a source for morality that is natural to humanity. On one hand, Justus Lipsius, the most internationally influential neo-Stoic finds support for human dignity in ancient Stoicism, as he wavers between Protestantism and Catholicism to secure academic appointments; on the other hand, Jean Bodin functions in society as a Catholic, but, to a greater extent than Pico della Mirandola before him, finds support of ethical optimism within the Jewish tradition.

Bodin's *La République* links the notion of human reason to its ties with God's eternal natural law, which provides a normative guideline to the conduct of a sovereign monarch; his comparisons of the customs and institutions of different peoples influence Montaigne, Charron and subsequently the circles of "*libertins érudits*." Through his intertextual blending of Jewish, Christian, Muslim, and classical sources, Bodin contributes an important step as a model for the possibility of civilized ecumenical discussion.

Michel de Montaigne in his *Essais* is not only influenced by evidence of the relativity of values to historical cultures, but also, under the influence of Sextus Empiricus, as well as Cicero, questions whether there is a secure source outside of revelation for human knowledge and virtue. Craig Brush in his book *Montaigne and Bayle* distinguishes from the philosophical skepticism of Montaigne from religious skepticism found in Bayle.[78] Philosophical skepticism, inherited form ancient philosophers, doubts the truth-giving capacity of reason. Among philosophical skeptics, there are two schools: the Pyrrhonist asks the Academic

"How are you so sure that you do not know?" as in Montaigne's motto "Que sais-je?" That distinction is of less significance than Academic and Pyrrhonian skeptics' difference from religious skeptics who doubt the veracity of revelation and view the biblical texts as works written by humans. Such religious skepticism enters the public arena with La Peyrère's *Prae-Adamite* (1655), Hobbes' *Leviathan* (1551), Spinoza's *Éthique* in 1677, and Bishop Richard Simon's *Histoire critique de l'Ancien Testament* in 1678, and influences Pierre Bayle.

There is another form of skepticism, a mixture of philosophical and religious skepticism which questions particular alleged supernatural events, upon which both Montaigne and Naudé innovate in contention with demonologists such as Bodin. Early modern scientists find paths out of philosophical skepticism, by using the power of reason to set up repeatable experiments; in doing so they too contribute to religious skepticism as in Montaigne's increased questions about special supernatural experiences, either miraculous or demonic (ones which by empirical methods are not repeatable and testable). Montaigne is particularly effective in citing Vives' translation and commentary on Augustine's *City of God* for a theological authority that distinguishes between the miraculous events during the life of Jesus and the alleged miraculous events of one's own time. Like Augustine, Montaigne proclaims it is likelier that a man was dreaming than to believe his tale of being transformed into an animal.[79] Naudé's decision to catalogue the science of Copernicus and Galileo separately from the curious ideas of Agrippa, Lull, and magicians further works to remove much superstition and mere speculation about mysterious causes from both science and traditional religion.

Bayle's skeptical and tolerant writings and Locke's "Letter on Toleration" of 1688 follow upon their sojourn in the Lowlands (a land with Jewish as well as diverse Christian communities) coincident with the demise of the Edict of Nantes (revoked by Louis XIV Oct. 17, 1685)[80] and the emigration of French Calvinists to the Lowlands and the smuggling of such Enlightenment works back into France. Writing his *Dictionnaire historique et critique* (1697) in the aftermath of the Revocation of the Edict of Nantes, Huguenot refugee Pierre Bayle praises the succession of free thinkers who innovated in critical thinking and thus builds the bridge from the "*libertins érudits*," to the "*philosophes*" of the Enlightenment. The Second Vatican Council of the 1960s, in taking an ecumenical conclusion of mutual respect and toleration different from its Counter-Reformation predecessor the Council of Trent, renews the political relevance not only of Erasmus (whose entire works are receiving translation into English) but also of the French Catholics Bodin, Montaigne, Charron, Gournay, Naudé, and La Mothe le Vayer who rely on an education of doubt and judgment to invigorate sparks of conscience in humanity.

NOTES:

1. I would like to thank Princeton University Press for permission to intersperse in this chapter some selections from Maryanne Cline Horowitz, *Seeds of Virtue and Knowledge* (Princeton, New Jersey: Princeton University Press, 1998). The selections are mainly from the last three chapters on Bodin, Montaigne, and Charron.

2. Educated at Louvain and living through the Dutch wars against Spain, Lipsius publicly turns to Lutheranism while at the University of Jena (1572-75) and to Calvinism while at the University of Leiden (1579-91). Then as he prepares to return to Louvain, he returns to Catholicism. For the controversy during his lifetime over his religion, see Jason Saunders, *Justus Lipsius: The Philosophy of Renaissance Stoicism*, 11-14, 18-20, 31-34, 36-39, 40.

3. Richard Tuck, *Philosophy and Government* 1572-1651 (Cambridge: Cambridge University Press, 1993), 58-59 citing Lipsius, *Politicorum* (Antwerp, 1589), IV, 62, 64-65. Italicized as in Tuck.

4. Gaston Bonet-Maury, *Histoire de la liberté de conscience en France* (Paris: Félix Alcan, 1900), 42-43.

5. Dec. 15, 1791: "Article I-Congress shall make no law respecting an establishment of religion, or prohibiting the free exercise thereof; or abridging the freedom of speech or of the press; or the right of the people peacably to assemble, and to petition Government for redress of grievances."

6. A long French line of scholars has taken seriously the evidence of such authors as Garasse on alleged "atheism" and "libertinage." The controversy reached summation with Lucien Febvre, *Le problème de l'incroyance au XVIe siècle: la religion de Rabelais* (Paris, 1942), which claims that atheism was not possible in the sixteenth century. See Henri Busson's update of his 1922 book, *Les Sources et développement du rationalisme dans la littérature française de la Renaissance (1533-1601)* (Paris: J. Vrin, 1957). Scholarship set off in a new direction--recognizing Christian fideism in skeptical thinkers and not dwelling on behavior--with Richard H. Popkin, *The History of Skepticism from Erasmus to Descartes* (The Hague: Van Gorcum, 1960), as evidenced by the expanded *The History of Scepticism from Erasmus to Spinoza* (Berkeley: University of California Press, 1979).

7. William F. Church, *Richelieu and Reason of State* (Princeton, New Jersey: Princeton University Press, 1972), 72-75.

8. Church, 154-57.

9. "God's hand" is particularly prevalent in Calvin. William J. Bouwsma, *John Calvin: A Sixteenth Century Portrait* (New York: Oxford University Press, 1988), 169.

10. Michel de Montaigne, *Essais*, 2nd ed. (Bordeaux, 1582) (Cambridge, Mass.: Harvard University Press, 1969), 610: "Il s'eslevera, si Dieu luy preste la main: il s'eslevera abandonnant & renonçant a ses propres moyens & se laissant hausser & soublslever par la grace divine, main non autrement." Michel de Montaigne, *Oeuvres complètes* (Paris: Gallimard, 1962), II. 12. 587-589; *Complete Essays*, trans. Donald M. Frame (Stanford: Stanford University Press, 1965), 457.(a) "Il s'esle-vera si Dieu lui preste extraordinairement la main; il s'eslevera, abandonnant et renonçant à ses propres moyens, et se laissant hausser et soubslever par les moyens purement celestes." See notes in both texts for variants.

11. II. 11. P 589; S 610.(c) "C'est ... nostre foy Chrestienne, non à sa vertu Stoïque de pretendre à cette divine et miraculeuse metamorphose."

12. Alan Levine, article presented at American Political Science Association Meeting, Chicago, 1995. For legitimate multiple readings of Montaigne's religious sensibility, see

Maryanne C. Horowitz, "Montaigne's Doubts on the Miraculous and the Demonic in Cases of His Own Day," *Regnum, Religio, et Ratio: Essays Presented to Robert M. Kingdon*, ed. Jerome Friedman (Kirksville, Missouri: Sixteenth Century Journal Publications, 1987), 81-91.   13. See Eugene Rice on the subtlety of Ficino, *The Renaissance Idea of Wisdom* (Cambridge: Harvard University Press, 1958) 65-68, 210-211.

14. Pomponazzi, "On the Immortality of the Soul," *Renaissance Philosophy of Man*, eds. E. Cassirer, O. Kristeller, and J. H. Randall, Jr. (Chicago: University of Chicago Press, 1948), XIV-XV, 375-381.

15. Malcolm Smith, *Montaigne and the Roman Censors* (Geneva: Droz, 1981), especially ch. 6.

16. La Mothe le Vayer, Conseiller d'État, *Oeuvres* (Paris, 1669) (rprt. Dresden: Michel Groell, 1756, dedicated to Frederick, Duke of Saxony) I, l, 29-31.

17. Edition in Bibliothèque nationale.

18. Pierre Charron, *De la Sagesse*, ed. Amaury Duval, 3 vols. (Paris, 1827) II, v, 155. Unless otherwise stated, references to Charron refer by book, chapter, and page number to Duval's edition of *De la Sagesse*. Authenticity has been judged by comparison with the three early editions of *De la Sagesse*: Bordeaux: Simon Millanges, 1601; Paris: David Douceur, 1604; Paris: David Douceur, 1607. Duval's critical edition follows the tradition of the 1607 edition in that it contains smaller works of Charron along with the 1604 text of *De la Sagesse* and attempts, not altogether completely, to list all passages from the 1601 edition which were modified or omitted later.

Charron, II, v, 155: "qui est homme de bien par scrupule et bride religieuse, gardez-vous en, et ne l'estimez gueres: et qui a religion sans preud'hommie, je ne le veux pas dire plus meschant, mais bien plus dangereux que celuy qui n'a ny l'un ny l'autre.. . mais cela vient que n'ayant aucun goust ny image ou conception de preud'hommie, qu'à la suite et pour le service de la religion, et pensant qu'estre homme de bien, n'est autre chose qu'estre soigneux d'avancer et faire valoir sa religion, croyent que toute chose, quelle qu'elle soit, trahison, perfidie, sedition, rebellion et toute offense à quiconque soit, est non-seulement loisible et permise, colorée du zele et soin de religion, mais encores louable, meritoire et canonisable."

19. Joseph Le Cler, *Toleration and the Reformation*, trans. J. L. Weston, 2 vols. (New York: Association Press, 1960), II, 3-191.

20. "Lettres de Pierre Charron à Gabriel Michel de la Rochemaillet," ed. L. Auvray, *Revue d'histoire littèraire de la France*, I (1894), 318, 320.

21. King Henry IV, *Edict du Roy & Declaration sur les precedent Edicts de Pacification* (Paris?: Royal Press, 25 February 1599), Houghton Library, Harvard University.

22. J. B. Sabri ,,*De l'humanisme au rationalisme: Pierre Charron (1541-1603), l'homme, l'oeuvre, l'influence* (Paris: Felix Alcan, 1913), 53-65. Pierre Charron, "Discours Chrestien," *De la Sagesse*, ed. Duval, III, 349-58.

23. Pierre Charron, *Les Trois Veritez Contre Tous Athéés, Idolatres, Juifs, Mahumetans, Heretiques, & Schismatiques*, 2nd ed. (Bordeaux: S. Millanges, 1595); rpt. in *Oeuvres de Pierre Charron*, 1635 (Geneva: Slatkine reprint, 1970).

24. Richard Popkin, *The History of Scepticism...to Spinoza*, 57-63. On the early criticism of Father Garasse and Father Mersenne, see Jean Daniel Charron, *The Wisdom of Pierre Charron* (Chapel Hill: University of North Carolina Press, 1960), 22-30.

25. Charron, I, preface, xlviii.

26. Huguet, ed., *Dictionnaire de la langue française* (Paris: Didier, 1925-1962), VI, 177-78. Charron's book is in the tradition of educational treatises for males; he has little to

say on "preude'femme" and treats women as unequal partners in I, chs. xlviii-ix on marriage, parents and children and in III, x on flattery. See section on Marie de Gournay below.

27. *Le Manuel d'Epictète*, is available in translations by André Rivaudeau and Guillaume Du Vair, as well as incorporated in Du Vair's *De la saint philosophie*, from which Charron borrows directly.

28. Charron, II, iii, 75-81.

29. Charron, II, iii, 86-87: "la doctrine de tous les sages porte que bien vivre, c'est vivre selon nature, 'idem beatè vivere et secundùm naturam' entendant par nature l'equité et la raison universelle qui luit en nous."

30. Charron, II, ii, 55; I, ii, 14-15.

31. Charron, III, vi, vol. II, 444.

32. Charron, I, viii, 59-63; I, xv, 123, 127; II, iii, 92. Cicero, *De natura deorum* I.63; *De re publica* III.7-33.

33. Charron, II, v, 152-53: "Ils veulent que l'on soit homme de bien, à cause qu'il y a un paradis et un enfer, ...Tu te gardes d'estre meschant, car tu n'oses, et crains d'estre battu; et desja en cela es-tu meschant."

34. Charron, (1601 edition) II, v, 156-57: "tu fais l'homme de bien afin que l'on te paye, et l'on t'en dise grand mercy."

35. Charron, II, v, 150: "esprits forts et genereux."

36. Alfred Soman, "Pierre Charron: A Revaluation," *Bibliothèque d'humanisme et Renaissance*, 32 (Jan. 1970), 57-79.

37. Charron, "Petit Traicté," III, 304-13. This work was found among Charron's writings after his death.

38. "Lettres de Pierre Charron ... Gabriel Michel de la Rochemaillet," 322-25, 328.

39. Charron, II, v, 151: "Ils pensent que la religion soit une generalit, de tout bien et de toute vertu, que toutes vertus soyent comprinses en elle,...Or c'est au rebours, car la religion qui est posterieure, est une vertu speciale et particuliere, distincte de toutes les autres vertus."

40. Charron, II, iii, 101; II, v, 152.

41. The following is a brief list of Bodin's works in the chronological order of their first publication: *Oratio* (1559), *Methodus* (1566); *Response...à M. de Malestorict* (1568); *République* (1576); *Distributio* (1580); *Démonomanie* (1580); *Epitome* (1588); *Paradoxon* (1596); *Le Paradoxe* (1598); *Theatrum* (1596); manuscript "*Colloquium Heptaplomeres.*"

42. Paul Lawrence Rose reveals that Bodin's view of natural goodness is especially evident in the *Paradoxon*: see *Bodin and the Great God of Nature: The Moral and Religious Universe of a Judaiser* (Geneva: Librairie Droz, 1980). See the brief summary of Bodin as a natural theologian in Françoise Berriot, *Athéismes et athéistes au xve siècle en France*, 2 vols. (Université, de Lille: Éditions de CERF, 1984), II, 775-797.

43. Jean Bodin, *Colloquium of the Seven about Secrets of the Sublime*, ed. and trans. Marion Leathers Daniels Kuntz (Princeton, N. J.: Princeton University Press, 1975), xv-xxviii, especially notes 5-6, 25-15. Jean Bodin, *Colloquium heptaplomeres de rerum sublimium arcanis abditi*, ed. L. Noack (Schwerin, 1857). My references to *Colloquium* will be to Kuntz's translation followed by page number in Noack's Latin with Hebrew and Greek text. Jean Bodin, *Colloque entre sept scavans*, ed. François Berriot with Katherine Davies, Jean Larmat and Jacques Roger (Geneva: Librairie Droz, 1984) follows a 1923 French manuscript with variants; an international team of scholars currently is working on a critical edition. For source study, see G. Roellenbleck, *Offenbarung...und juedische Ueberlieferung bei Jean Bodin* (Gütersloh, 1964). For posthumous criticism of Bodin, see Pierre Bayle, selection from *Dictionnaire historique et critique* (1734) in Jean Bodin, *Oeuvres*, ed. and

trans. Pierre Mesnard (Paris: Presses Universitaires de France, 1951), xxiii-xxxvii, especially xxxiii; also Mesnard's "Vers un portrait de Jean Bodin," vii-xxi. I have examined aspects of the religious issue in "La religion de Bodin reconsiderée: Le Marrane comme modèle de la tolérance," *Jean Bodin: Actes du Colloque Interdisciplinaire d'Angers*, 2 vols. (Angers: Presses de l'Université d'Angers, 1985), I, 201-215, and II, 568-573, and "Judaism in Jean Bodin," *The Sixteenth Century Journal*, 13 (1982), 109-113.

44. Emile Pasquier, "La famille de Jean Bodin, *Revue d'histoire de l'église de France* 19 (1933), 457-62.

45. For example, a Jean Bodin was tried as a heretic in Paris in 1548; a Jean Bodin was noted in the marital records of Geneva in 1552.

46. For examination of documents showing the criticism that leads to book condemnation, see Berriot, "La fortune du *Colloquium heptaplomeres*," *Colloque entre sept scavants*, xviii-xxiv.

47. Pierre Boaistuau, *Le Théâtre du Monde, ou il est faict un ample discours des miseres humaines* (1558), ed. Michel Simonin (Geneva: Librairie Droz, 1981). Boaistuau takes the optimist side himself in *Bref Discours de l'excellence & dignité de l'homme* included in editions after 1562.

48. A very general overview of Book IV appears in Pierre Mesnard, "The Psychology and Pneumatology of Jean Bodin," *International Philosophical Quarterly* 2 (1962), 244-64.

49. *Theatrum*, 475; *Théâtre*, IV, 9, 686. The section "De intellectione & intellectu, vero, scientiis, cognitione," appears on 470-82; French, 678-89. The medieval scholastic phrase has origins in Aristotle, *De Anima*, 432a 5-11. See Cranefield, "On the origins of the phrase *Nihil est in intellectu quod non prius fuerit in sensu*," *Journal of the History of Medicine*, 25 (1970), 77-80.

50. Aëtius, in Joannes von Arnim, *Stoicorum veterum fragmenta* (SVF), 4 vols. (Leipzig, 1005-10), II, 83.

51. Richard H. Popkin, *The History of Scepticism...to Spinoza*, 18-65.

52. Raymond Sebond, *Theologia naturalis* (Lyon: Balsarin, 1484); *Théologie naturelle de Raymond Sebond*, trans. Montaigne (Paris: Jean Martin, 1568). See Yvonne Bellenger, Montaigne: *Une fête pour l'esprit* (Paris: Balland, 1987), 95-106, 318-19. Montaigne, *L'Apologie de Raymond Sebond*, critical edition of original text, annotated by Paul Porteau (Paris: Fernard Aubier, 1937), 244-45.

53. Jean Bodin, *De la démonomanie* (Paris: Jacques du Puys, 1581), preface. Richard H. Popkin, *The History of Scepticism ...to Spinoza* (New York: Harper & Row, 1968), 83-84.

54. *Theatrum*, V, 630. *Meno* in *Plato*, trans. W. R. M. Lamb (London: Heinemann, 1924), especially lines 70a, 81, 82-86, 89, quote 85E, 321-22. Bodin may have been influenced by any Ficino citation of Meno's rapid learning to prove that the mind is fertile with seeds; Ficino, *De Amore*, Speech VI. 12.

55. Marion L. Kuntz, "Pythagorean Cosmology and its Identification in Bodin's '*Colloquium Heptaplomeres*'," *International Congress of Neo-Latin Studies* (1976), 2, 685-796, especially 689-90, citing *Colloquium*, 372-3; 282. *Theatrum*, 143-44. *Laws*, II, which he cites in *Distributio* concerns the importance of teaching the young proper musical harmony.

56. Philippe Desan, *Naissance de la méthode* (Paris: A.-G. Nizet, 1987), 100-06. The unutterable Hebrew letters for God appear on the engraved title page of the 1596 edition; Salomon in the *Colloquium*, 372-73; Noack, 282, argues that God as a quaternity is more meaningful than God as a trinity.

57. Fougerolles, 688, explains the seeds emerging by "moyenneant la lumière qu'il leur en a communiqué par son esprit." Rose, *Bodin and the Great God of Nature*, 132-33, note

34, interprets this to transform Bodin's meaning to illuminated light. However Bodin refers
to natural light in citation of Empedocles. Likewise, Bodin in the *Epitome* utilizes "ray of
light" to indicate what God implanted in creation. Fougerolles marks his addition from
Bodin's text by an asterisk at the addition and at the marginal note; he may have been
influenced by reading the passage cited below from the *Paradoxon*. Another example is in
Theatrum (1597), 190; Fougerolles, 261, cited by Blair, in *Acta Conventus* (1991).

58. Robert A. Greene, "Whichcote, the Candle of the Lord, and Synderesis," *Journal
of the History of Ideas* 52 (1991), 632 shows Whichcote and Culverwell, 1647-48, viewing
Psalm 4:8 as "Lift thou up the light of thy countenance upon us," and utilizing instead for
the natural light Proverbs 20:27 "The spirit of the Lord is a lamp, searching out the hidden
chambers of the heart."

59. 478; 691 "...illa verò stirpes sibi à natura congenitas promet: idem quoque de
mentibus humanis relinquitur iudicandum, si vel levissimo sensuum adiumento utantur:
neque tamen ab iis scientiarum perfectionem adipiscuntur...." Note Philo's influence on
Ambrose, *Paradise*, 10, 48,11, 51 in *Hexameron, Paradise, and Cain and Abel*, trans. John
J. Savage (Washington, D.C.: Catholic University of America Press), 327, 329. Also
Ambrose's student Augustine repeats the point in *Free Choice of the Will*, in *The Teacher,
The Free Choice of the Will, Grace and Free Will*, trans. Robert Russell (Washington, D.C.:
Catholic University of America Press, 1968) 224-5: "We would be wrong to call the young
and tender sapling barren, even though it goes through several summer seasons without
bearing fruit until the proper time arrives to show its fruit. Why then, should the soul's
Creator not be praised with all due reverence if He has given the soul a kind of beginning
that enables it to mature with the fruits of wisdom and justice by its efforts and growth, and
when He has so dignified it that it is within its power to reach out for happiness, if he wills
to do so?"

60. 478-79; 691 "...cùm tamen sensuum omnium vis ac potestas ab anima dependeat...."

61. For the influence of this manuscript, see Berriot, "La fortune de *Colloquium
heptaplomere*," *Colloque*, xv-l, and Richard Popkin, "The Dispersion of Bodin's Dialogues
in England, Holland, and Germany," *Journal of the History of Ideas* 49 (1988), 157-60, and
"The Role of Jewish Anti-Christian arguments in the Rise of Scepticism," *New Perspectives
on Renaissance Thought*, ed. John Henry and Sarah Hutton, 5-8.

62. Bodin, *Six livres de la République* (1576) (Paris: Fayard, 1986), IV, 204-211,
quotation 207: "Il permit à chacun de vivre en liberté de conscience."

63. A possible source for Bodin's knowledge of Ibn Ezra is a book by a Hebraicist with
whom Bodin studied in Paris: Jean Mercier, *Aseret ha-Devarim Decalogus*, containing
commentary by Abraham ibn Ezra, Hebrew and Latin (Lyon, 1566-68). Isaac Husik,
Medieval Jewish Philosophy (New York: Macmillan, 1916) 194, confirms that Ibn Ezra
(1089-1164) holds that the Decalogue, with the exception of the seventh day of rest, consists
of laws planted by God in the minds of rational beings; that is exactly the consensus of
Bodin's seven speakers. Technically, while recognizing that the Decalogue is acknowledged
by the intelligent of all nations, Ibn Ezra does not refer to it as natural law. The first Jewish
philosopher to introduce into Hebrew the term *dath tiv ith*, "natural law" is Joseph Albo (d.
1444). Colette Sirat, 243, 383 citing Joseph Albo, *Sefer ha-Ikkarim*, trans. I. Husik
(Philadelphia: Jewish Publication Society of America, 1946) and J. Guttmann, "Towards a
Study of the Sources of the Book of Principles," *Dat u-Maddah* (Jerusalem, 1955), 169-181
(in Hebrew).

64. François Berriot, "La Fortune du *Colloquium heptaplomeres...*," *Colloque entre
Sept Scavans* (Ms. français 1923, Bibliothèque nationale) , ed. Berriot *et al.* (Geneva: Droz,
1984), XXIV-XXIX. See also Maryanne C. Horowitz, "Bodin and Judaism," *Il pensiero*

politico, 30,2 (1997).

65. Gabriel Naudé, *Advice on Establishing a Library* (Berkeley:University of California Press, 1950. Page references refer to this reprint of John Evelyn's English translation of 1661, based on the 1644 edition except for additional section on the most beautiful existing libraries. *Advis pour dresser une bibliothèque* (Leipzig: VEB, 1963), reprint of 1627 edition.

66. Boase, 51-2.

67. Constance Jordan, *Renaissance Feminism: Literary Texts and Political Models* (Ithaca: Cornell University Press, 1990), 269-70. See Maryanne C. Horowitz, "Marie de Gournay, Editor of the Essais of Michel de Montaigne: A Case-Study of a Mentor-Protegée Friendship," *Sixteenth Century Journal* 17 (1986), 271-83; Marie de Gournay, *L'Ombre de la Demoiselle de Gournay* (Paris: Jean Libert, 1626). Special collections, UCLA Libraries.

68. Montaigne, *Essais* (1635). Special Collections, UCLA Libraries.

69. A. Boase, *The Fortunes of Montaigne* (London: Methuen, 1935), 22. Gournay, "Preface," *Montaigne Studies*, II, 2 (1990), 83-84.

70. La Mothe le Vayer, *De la Vertu des Payens, Oeuvres* (1757),V, 1, Dedication III, 1. Boase, *Fortunes*, 267.

71. Lipsius, *Manuductio, ad lectorum* (IV, 617f), quoted in Saunders, 55; 69.

72. Popkin, *The History*, 216.

73. Mr. L'Abbé le Vayer, "Abregé de la vie de Monsieur de la Mothe le Vayer de l'Academie Françoise, Précepteur du Philippes de France Duc d'Anjou, & ensuite du Roi Louis XIV" *Oeuvres*, I, 1, 21, 48, 56.

74. La Mothe le Vayer, "De l'instruction de Monseigneur le Dauphin," *Oeuvres*, I, 1, quotations 30-31: "ils promettent de maintenir inviolablement la paix parmi leurs peuples" and "les contraint de faire garder des Edits qu'ils ont trouvé établis devant leur regne."

75. 1639 edition with translated citations of 1667 (New York: Verlag, 1993). Tuck, 93; Church, *Richelieu and Reason of State*, 416.

76. *New York Times* (Dec. 8, 1965), Final report, second edition, Dec. 7, 1985, trans. from Latin, 8, citing Confer NAE 2 and Confer Lumen Gentium 16.

77. (Washington, D.C.: U.S. Catholic Conference, 1993), 6-7. The church's concern is that conscience has become dislocated from the natural moral law (84-98).

78. Craig Brush, *Montaigne and Bayle: Variations on the Theme of Skepticism* (The Hague: Nijhoff, 1966).

79. Maryanne C. Horowitz, "Drogue médicinale ou vieux conte: l'histoire et la justice chez Montaigne, Bodin, et saint Augustin," *Montaigne et l'histoire*, ed. Claude G. Dubois (Bordeaux: Université de Bordeaux Press, 1991).

80. *An edict of the French King, prohibiting all publick exercise of the pretended reformed religion in his kingdom. Wherein...he recalls....the edict of King Henry the IV...given at Nantes.* Tr. out of French. (London: G. M. 1686). Clark Library, UCLA. Maryanne C. Horowitz, "Cary J. Nederman & John Christian Laursen, eds. *Difference and Dissent: Theories of Tolerance in Medieval and Early Modern Europe* and *Beyond the Persecuting Society: Religious Toleration Before the Enlightenment*," *American Political Science Review*, 92 (1998).

5

DESCARTES AND THE
QUESTION OF TOLERATION

Michael Allen Gillespie

The question of religious toleration as we understand it today arises in response to deep disagreements about religious doctrine and practice that produced the Reformation and the wars of religion in the sixteenth and seventeenth centuries. Western Christianity had been riven in important ways on many previous occasions, but these divisions were either accommodated within the Church, if this proved possible, or eliminated by force. The religious differences that arose in the sixteenth and seventeenth centuries, however, were both fundamental and ineradicable. The idea of religious toleration is an attempt to find a means not of eliminating these differences but of living with them, a means of bringing conflict to an end and establishing the grounds for the peaceful coexistence of the contending parties.

René Descartes recognized the tremendous problem that religious passions posed for his times. In his late work, *The Passions of the Soul*, he castigates

those who believe themselves devout, but are merely bigoted and superstitious. These are people who--under the pretext of frequently going to church, reciting many prayers, wearing their hair short, fasting, and giving alms--think they are absolutely perfect and imagine they are such close friends of God that they could not do anything to displease him. They suppose that anything their passion dictates is a commendable zeal, even though it sometimes dictates the greatest crimes that men can commit, such as the betrayal of cities, the killing of sovereigns, and the exterminations of whole nations for the sole reason that the citizens do not accept their opinions.[1]

For Descartes, religious intolerance was not merely the result of disagreement about religious doctrine and practice. It was rather the consequence of the broader and more profound failure of human thinking to grasp the truth about man, God, and the world. Rooted in the senses and the imagination and misguided by the passions, thinking at least since Plato had misconceived what was true and real, and this misconception had in turn disastrously distorted human arts and practices, setting men at odds with one another and leaving them to suffer from the ravages of nature. Descartes devoted his life to the development of a universal and apodictic science (*mathesis universalis*) that would reveal the truth about man, God, and nature, and thus allow human beings to develop the arts and practices necessary to master the problems that confronted them. He believed that this science would extend life, secure liberty, and promote human flourishing. Integral to its success in Descartes' view was a proper understanding of the place of religion in human life that would moderate religious antagonisms and provide the foundation for religious toleration.

The Theological-Political Context of Descartes' Project

In both his *Discourse on Method* and *Meditations*, Descartes characterized his thought as a new beginning that rejected all previous authority. The widespread acceptance of this claim has led to the view of Descartes as the father of modern philosophy. In the early years of the twentieth century, however, scholars began to call this claim into question, revealing Descartes' important debt to his medieval predecessors.[2] This claim of indebtedness, however, obscured the truly radical innovations of Cartesian thought. Thus, while admitting Descartes' debt to earlier thinkers, Martin Heidegger, for example, argued that he had initiated a fundamental turn in human thought from a way of thinking centered on God to a way of thinking centered on the human subject. This view of Descartes as a philosophical revolutionary has held great sway in the latter part of the twentieth century and forms the core of the postmodern interpretation of Descartes. In recent years, however, scholars such as Hans Blumenberg and Amos Funkenstein have argued that while Descartes' philosophical innovations were clearly revolutionary, they were answers to the fundamental problems that brought the medieval world to its end.[3] These scholars thus suggest that Descartes' thought can only be properly understood in the context of and as a response to a set of questions that arise out of the medieval world and the scholasticism that underpinned it.

Scholasticism was an attempt to reconcile Christian theology with pagan and especially Aristotelian philosophy. In its classical form, it rested on the realist belief in the extramental existence of universals. This realist ontology provided the foundation for a syllogistic logic, and together they served as the basis for the syllogistic sciences of natural theology, cosmology, and anthropology. The scholastics believed that God had created man and the world, but they argued that he had created them according to reason. As a result, humans could come to know God's will not merely through revelation but also and perhaps even more clearly through a philosophical investigation of his creation.

This scholastic synthesis depended on the complicated counterbalancing of pagan philosophy and scripture. This structure, however, was unstable, and the contradictions between the two juxtaposed elements eventually brought it down. On one hand, a more secular philosophic spirit developed that paid increasingly less attention to scripture and correspondingly greater attention to Aristotle and ancient philosophy in general. This tendency was decried by those in the Church who had long been suspicious of the influence of philosophy on Christianity and longed for a more scriptural theology. The fundamental scholastic claim that God was essentially rational increasingly seemed to them to be a denial of his divinity since it subordinated his omnipotent will to the laws of reason and the order of nature. The resulting furor led to the condemnation of Aristotelianism in 1277 and the growth of nominalism, an anti-scholastic theology, that emphasized God's radical omnipotence.[4]

Nominalism, which grew out of the thought of William of Ockham, seriously undermined scholasticism.[5] If God was truly omnipotent, the nominalists reasoned, then every being must be radically individual, created directly by God and not merely a member of a preexistent species. Nominalism in this sense rejected realism and with realism all syllogistic logic and science. Nature and reason reflect God's will but this will was seen as fundamentally and necessarily capricious. God today may save the saint and damn the sinner; but tomorrow he may do just the reverse. God can thus only be understood, if at all, through revelation, and even this source of guidance is suspect, since as Ockham repeatedly pointed out, God is no man's debtor, and is thus not bound in any way by his promises to man. The nominalist movement thus represented a decisive turn away from philosophy toward pure religious practice, exemplified perhaps most clearly by Franciscan asceticism.

The world that nominalism imagines is a fundamentally chaotic world of radically individual beings governed by a dark and unpredictable God. Such a vision of the world would have seemed unbelievable to the Christians of the twelfth and even the early thirteenth centuries, but in the aftermath of the Papal Schism, the Black Death, and the Hundred Years War, this grim vision of God became much more convincing. Because it called into question the basic doctrines and authority of the Church, nominalism was repeatedly condemned by Rome, but it was triumphant on many fronts, especially in the German universities, but also in important ways in France and England. This nominalist vision of God with its emphasis on divine power and its apparent sacrifice of divine mercy and predictability was a source of considerable insecurity in the succeeding centuries, and many of the intellectual movements of this period were attempts to deal with the problems presented by this God. This was especially true of the Reformation.

The problem of divine omnipotence was central for both Luther and Calvin. Luther's philosophical and theological training were nominalist and he characterized himself as an Ockhamist.[6] The problem around which Luther's own theological concerns turned was the uncertainty of salvation in the face of an omnipotent God. Scholastic reason had been shattered by the nominalist critique and scripture at best seemed to offer only an elusive security in the face of a capricious God. Luther discovered the solution to this problem in his belief that each of us stands in an immediate relationship to God and that through faith and direct scriptural intercourse with God, we can obtain certainty of our own salvation.[7] Thus, for Luther it is faith alone and not works that save.

This notion represented a direct assault upon the traditional doctrines, structures, and practices of the Church. In particular, it called into question the authority of the clergy because it undercut notions of hierarchy and denied the priesthood's unique ability to intercede with God. By extension, it similarly called into question the supposed divine right of kings and princes to rule over their subjects. The spread of the Reformation thus posed a real threat not only to traditional religious belief and practice but also to the patriarchal structures of authority that had existed in Europe for hundreds of years.

The initial success of Protestantism led to an internal effort to reform the Catholic Church. This Catholic Reformation, or Counter-Reformation as it is often called, had several important intellectual components. On one hand, Christian humanists such as Erasmus, often deeply influenced by the nominalist critique, adopted a skeptical attitude, jettisoning scholastic reasoning, as "higher lunacy," but also attacking the Protestant notion of inner illumination as lacking a criterion for judgment.[8] In fideistic fashion, they argued for a reliance not upon abstract arguments but upon traditional Church practice. On the other hand, the Jesuits developed a program of education based on the classical elements of scholasticism. Drawing on the fifteenth and sixteenth century revival of Aristotelianism, their intellectual project culminated in Suarez's *Metaphysical Disputations*, the definitive work of late scholasticism. This revival, however, was not a return to scholastic realism. For all his admiration of Aquinas, Suarez deploys an essentially nominalist ontology. While Aristotelianism continued to play an important role in shaping the intellectual life of Europe, it thus played a different role than it had in the medieval period.[9]

While the philosophical differences between Protestants and Catholics were profound, it was the impact of these differences on politics that led to disaster. These religious differences reinforced long-standing social and political differences, and thus gave a new vehemence to partisan passions. The horrors of this confluence of politics and religion were nowhere more evident than in France which was convulsed by eight wars of religion between 1562 and 1588. These wars were punctuated by brief periods of peace in which the crown sought to impose a doctrine of toleration to reunite or at least pacify the country. Success, however, was fleeting, for the Protestant Huguenots wanted virtual independence, while the Catholic Holy League wanted to abolish even the Huguenots' freedom of conscience. Time and again peace settlements were shattered by intrigue and assassination, including the horrible Massacre of St. Bartholomew's Day in which 20,000-30,000 Huguenots lost their lives.

These wars of religion only came to an end when Henry of Navarre, the Huguenot leader, converted to Catholicism and assumed the throne as Henry IV. His Edict of Nantes (1598) granted the Huguenots freedom of conscience but only a very limited freedom of worship. It allowed them to form a state within a state with their own fortified cities, and provided royal financial support for their pastors. While the Edict is a landmark in the history of toleration, its impact should not be overrated, for it did not change basic attitudes. It was won and maintained only by armed force. Moreover, while the Edict remained in place until 1685, its effectiveness waned dramatically after the assassination of Henry IV in 1610. The chaos of the early years of the reign of his successor Louis XIII saw the resumption of religious warfare, and fighting was brought to an end only in 1624 when Richelieu came to power. Richelieu, however, was no friend of toleration, promising the King that he would use all his power to destroy the Huguenots, break the nobles, and establish the King's absolute authority. He was as good as his word, capturing La Rochelle, the principal Huguenot city in 1627, and revoking the Huguenots' corporate independence with the Edict of Alais in 1629.

It was into this world in 1596 that Descartes was born.[10] His family was Catholic but they resided in Poitou, a Huguenot stronghold, and had close ties to Châtellerault a secure city under the Edict of Nantes. In 1606, Descartes was sent away to the Jesuit school La Flèche founded two years earlier by Henry IV. Life in the school was extremely regimented but the children were treated kindly and punishment was seldom employed.[11] Descartes learned his philosophy from Jesuit commentaries under the tutelage of François Veron who later became a thorn in the side of the Protestants and perhaps also under a nominalist teacher.[12] He was a superb student with a deep love of mathematics who was given an unusually wide latitude in his studies which included all of the traditional disciplines and works on the occult sciences as well. He participated in the memorial service when the heart of Henry IV was buried at La Flèche after his assassination in 1610, and this event apparently had a great effect on him.

After leaving La Flèche, Descartes returned to study law in Poitou which was then in virtual revolt against Louis XIII. He did not pursue a career in law, however, and instead entered the peacetime army of the Protestant Prince of the Netherlands, Maurice of Nassau in 1618. Since the Prince was France's ally against Spain, Descartes was not acting disloyally to either his country or his religion in serving Maurice.[13] He next joined the army of Maximilian I, Prince of Bavaria, who defeated the Protestants in Bohemia at the battle of White Mountain. There is no evidence that Descartes fought in the battle or that he believed in its cause. During his time in Germany, Descartes did make contact with the Rosicrucian mathematician Johannes Faulhaber and other members of this movement. The Rosicrucians were a semi-secret society, which combined an interest in science, mathematics, and the occult or hermetic sciences with a millenarian vision of spiritual renewal and education. They apparently understood themselves as a Protestant answer to the Jesuits.[14] Their movement, which was initially quite successful, dissolved after the defeat of Protestantism in Bohemia. The specter of their secret society, however, continued to excite and alarm Europe for many years thereafter.

In 1622, Descartes returned to Paris and was charged with being a Rosicrucian.

He apparently responded to this charge by appearing regularly in public to show that he was not in league with members of this sect whose members were known to live reclusive, secretive lives. Perhaps still troubled by these accusations, however, Descartes left Paris after a short time for Italy where he remained for two years. He returned to Paris in 1625 and remained there for the next three years.

Parisian intellectual life during this period was astonishingly varied. The leading spirits were the libertines.[15] These men had been dispirited by the religious fanaticism of their time and were deeply influenced by the skepticism of Montaigne and Charron, and the philosophic thought of Campanella and Galileo. Indifferent to God, they despised scholasticism, loved liberal examination, were scientifically curious, and argued for the subordination of religion.[16] Their numbers included among others Naudé, Gassendi, Vanini, Le Vayer, Elie Diodati, Jean-Louis Guez de Balzac, Théophile de Viau, and Father Claude Picot, known as the atheist priest. They were all free thinkers. The more flamboyant were given to debauchery, deism, and Machiavellianism, while the more erudite were concerned with politics, theology, science, and philosophy.[17] While their private activities were generally tolerated by the state authorities, any attempt to present their ideas publicly was harshly punished. Vanini, for example, was burnt at the stake for heresy at Toulouse in 1619. In 1623, the Parliament of Paris ordered the arrest of four libertine authors for scurrilous verse mocking religious themes. In 1624, three libertines were exiled from Paris on pain of death for trying to hold a public meeting critical of Aristotle, and in the same year, a campaign was begun against Hermeticism in general and Rosicrucianism in particular.[18]

While Descartes was acquainted with many of these men and shared some of their ideas he was not a libertine.[19] Indeed, he rejected the skepticism that was essential to their basic intellectual outlook. The famous incident by which Descartes came to public attention makes this clear. The chemist/alchemist Chandoux gave a speech at the home of the Papal nuncio Bagni attacking Aristotle and laying out his own mechanistic philosophy. He received the acclaim of everyone present except Descartes. When asked why he demurred, Descartes praised Chandoux's anti-Aristotelianism, but criticized his reliance on merely probable arguments. The company challenged him to produce something better and to their astonishment he did, apparently laying out his notion of clear and distinct ideas.[20]

Descartes' answer especially intrigued Cardinal Bérulle, an Augustinian who had founded the Oratorian teaching order in 1611 to rival the Jesuits and who was then in the process of forming the Compagnie du Saint-Sacrement, a militant secret society of Catholic laymen to fight Protestantism. Bérulle tried to recruit Descartes to the Catholic cause but the success of his efforts is uncertain. Scholars have often assumed that he convinced Descartes to take a greater interest in metaphysics and theology, becoming Descartes' spiritual mentor.[21] This view, however, is difficult to reconcile with Descartes' actions, for within weeks he left Paris for the Protestant Netherlands, henceforth taking great precautions to conceal his whereabouts, and not returning to France for 16 years. Whether he was frightened by Bérulle or simply desired to avoid becoming entangled in religious controversy, it is clear that Descartes was acutely aware of the dangers of taking an active part in the religious struggles of his time and did his best to avoid them.

Descartes' departure from Paris was not the result of any lack of desire to have an intellectual impact. In fact, we know that since his famous dream in 1619, he had sought to develop a universal science that would transform human life in a profound way, making man master and possessor of nature. In his fragmentary manuscript *Rules for the Direction of the Mind*, Descartes had tried to lay out such a science on the basis of his notion of clear and distinct ideas. During his early years in Holland, however, he began to reflect on the metaphysical and theological assumptions of his science and soon realized the great difficulties posed by the problem of divine omnipotence that the nominalists had first opened up and that was a central question for Protestant Reformers and Augustinians like Bérulle and his follower Gibieuf.[22] These reflections led Descartes to his astonishing theory of the divine creation of eternal truths, which undermined his original idea of a *mathesis universalis*. No necessity, he argued, impelled God to create the eternal truths and he could have created them other than they are.[23] The possibility of such a powerful and unpredictable God calls into question any notion of an apodictic science. Descartes consequently realized that the success of his science depended upon coming to terms with the metaphysical and theological implications of divine omnipotence. However, he was acutely aware from the fate of the libertines and from the intolerance of the times that such an investigation was fraught with danger. He thus entered onto this path only hesitatingly and with great caution. In the period between 1628 and 1633, he developed a science of nature on Copernican grounds that was generally compatible with prevailing metaphysical and theological views. This project culminated in his manuscript *The World.* As the manuscript was going to press, however, he learned of the condemnation of Galileo. He was shocked and withheld the work from publication. He later remarked in his *Discourse* that he had not seen anything objectionable in Galileo's work, and therefore concluded that his own work which also rested on a Copernican foundation might not be as innocuous as he assumed.[24] It is clear though from his letter to Mersenne that first and foremost he wanted no part of religious controversy. He may well have believed as he wrote that "he lives well who lives unseen," but he was also clearly devastated by the condemnation.[25]

The fate of Galileo convinced Descartes that his hope of developing a universal science without attending in an explicit way to the metaphysical and theological questions of his age was untenable.[26] He came to understand that the success of his scientific teaching depended not merely on its efficacy but on a demonstration that it was compatible with prevailing theological and metaphysical assumptions. Descartes' problem arose from the fact that his science was at odds with these assumptions, at least insofar as these assumptions rested upon Aristotelian physics and the Biblical account of creation. Descartes was thus driven to develop a new theological metaphysics to complement his mechanistic, Copernican physics. With the fate of the libertines and the Rosicrucians in mind, however, Descartes realized that such a metaphysics would have to appear to be compatible with orthodoxy.[27] In the development and presentation of his metaphysics, Descartes thus aimed not at a revolutionary transformation of the prevailing views but at a long-term reformation and correction of the confused and misguided ideas about man, God, and the world. Descartes was convinced that when one properly understood this relationship, religion would cease to be so socially disruptive.

Descartes' Theological Metaphysics

Metaphysics and theology in Descartes' view had hitherto rested on false judgments about man, God, and nature. Scholasticism imagined an essentially rational God who had created man and nature according to the laws of reason. Descartes recognized that this teleological view was incompatible with the idea of divine omnipotence. The eternal truths of reason did not guide God in the creation of the world.[28] Or to put the matter in other terms, for Descartes there are no final causes; nature is pure mechanism. On the basic theological point, Descartes sides with the nominalists and the more radical Protestants. The existence of such an omnipotent God, however, seems to make science impossible, since it permits only probabilistic and not apodictic reasoning. The doctrine of radical omnipotence apparently ends in irremediable skepticism. The success of Cartesian science thus depends upon the demonstration that radical omnipotence does not render nature unknowable and produce skepticism. Descartes' project from the *Discourse* on, is thus an effort to overcome skepticism.[29]

In reflecting on the uncertainty of knowledge in the *Meditations*, Descartes systematically considers all of the possible sources of deception.[30] He concludes that the idea of divine omnipotence is the supreme source of skepticism because in contrast to sense deception, and the delusions of madness and dreams, it calls into question the truths of mathematics. A malicious God or evil genius, as Descartes calls him to deflect charges of impiety, might for example make it the case that $3 + 4 = 7$. It is the goal of Descartes' metaphysics to show that this is not the case, that divine omnipotence when properly understood does not call into question the truths of mathematics. He does so by refounding knowledge on the human subject.

Descartes argues that even the most powerful and most malicious demon cannot deceive me about everything because he cannot deceive me about my existence in the moment I think it. This is the meaning of Descartes' fundamental principle, *ego cogito, ergo sum*.[31] The I as a thinking thing (*res cogitans*) thus has a certain freedom or independence that even God cannot negate. This freedom is the ground on which Descartes believes he can construct an apodictic science, the Archemedian point on which he can stand in his effort to move the world. It is not a mere freedom of thought but a freedom of the will. However powerful the deception, human beings do not have to affirm that it is the case. They can withhold their assent or will from the judgment. Thus, even if they cannot know the truth, they can at least avoid error. The independence that this free will gives us, Descartes argues, makes us like God.[32]

This new understanding of what it is to be a human being leads to a new understanding of nature and of God. Nature is henceforth understood in and through the representation of things that the I constructs out of sense impressions in the imagination. The heterogeneous nature of substantial forms, imagined by Aristotle and his scholastic followers, is thereby replaced by the notion of a homogenous matter, or more accurately, by a mathematically analyzable extension *(res extensa)*. As decisive as this new understanding of nature is for the development of science, it is Descartes' new vision of God that is more important for our purposes here.

Descartes does not proclaim the novelty of his God. Given the religious sensibilities of his time, this would certainly have led to censure. Instead, he claims that he has merely produced a new and more powerful demonstration of God's existence.[33] There is some truth in this claim, but it conceals the fact that the God whose existence Descartes demonstrates is not the traditional Christian God. As Jean-Luc Marion has pointed out, Descartes gives three different but related definitions of God. In the third *Meditation*, he is the *idea infiniti*, in the fifth *Meditation* the *ens summe perfectum*, and in the first and fourth *Replies* the *causa sui*.[34] The demonstration that God is not a deceiver follows from the demonstration of his perfection. The idea of divine perfection, however, follows from the idea we find in ourselves of perfection and our recognition that it cannot come from us because we are finite and therefore imperfect beings. The proof of God's existence in this sense rests upon the self-knowledge of the *cogito ergo sum*.

This ontological proof of God's existence is not new but its subjective presentation changes it in a fundamental way. The ontological argument was first employed by Anselm, who also argued that God was perfect because he was infinite. But for Anselm to say that God was infinite was to say that he was fundamentally mysterious, of a different order of being than the finite beings of this world. When Descartes defines divine perfection in terms of divine infinity, he does not mean to render God unintelligible but to bring him within the realm of beings that can be understood mathematically. Descartes in this way abolishes the absolute distance between God and man that characterized medieval thought.[35]

This is also apparent in Descartes' definition of God as the *causa sui*. No Christian had hitherto made such a claim. Indeed, as Jean-Luc Marion has pointed out, Descartes in this way actually reverses the traditional understanding: for the medieval world God was the source of causality while in Descartes' view he is subordinated to the concept of causality.[36] This definition of God is buttressed by the fact that God's infinity renders him incapable of reorganizing himself as a being different from other beings, since he has no limits and thus no other, no opposition to engender self-recognition. He thus cannot be a deceiver because he is not other than that which he would deceive.[37] In this manner, Descartes' God is effectively identical with the order of nature.

Finally, we see in Descartes' definition of God as the *causa sui* an acceptance of the nominalist understanding of God as essentially willful rather than rational. The infinity of divine will, however, is mirrored by the infinity of the human will, which Descartes declares is identical to the will of God. Man is thus not essentially different than God, but is distinguished only by the extent of his knowledge. In this way, man is elevated to quasi-divine status while God is lowered toward the human level.

Descartes' new understanding of God has two important consequences. First, it makes God irrelevant for the study of nature. Descartes no longer has to fear that his *mathesis universalis* will be undermined by divine omnipotence. Science can thus operate without concerning itself with divine will. Descartes' God who appears in the *Discourse* thus only sets matter in motion without completing creation in any way.[38] He is radically different than the God of *Genesis*. Indeed, Descartes himself suggests that the account of creation in *Genesis* may be merely metaphorical.[39]

Second, this new understanding of God produces a merely formalistic and thus empty or blank theology, as Marion has called it.[40] God for Descartes is a radically attenuated being that may necessarily exist but that has no character and does nothing. Descartes' proof of the existence of God is thus not a proof of the existence of God as he was traditionally understood by Christianity. The omnipotent God is excluded from the bastion of reason that Descartes establishes with his fundamental principle. God may enter into Descartes' citadel but only if he behaves rationally and leaves human beings to their own devices. In this way, Cartesian metaphysics seeks to diminish the theological stakes and thereby also creates the conditions for greater religious toleration.

Descartes is careful in this context to limit his theological claims. He writes:

> I do not wish to appear to be assuming the right to question someone else's religion, I shall simply say in this context that three different sorts of questions should be distinguished. First, some things are believed through faith alone--such as the mystery of the Incarnation, the Trinity, and the like. Secondly, other questions, while having to do with faith, can also be investigated by natural reason: among the latter, orthodox theologians usually count the question of the existence of God, and the distinction between the human soul and body. Thirdly, there are questions which have nothing to do with faith, and which are the concern solely of human reasoning, such as the problem of squaring the circle, or of making gold by the techniques of alchemy, and the like.[41]

In principle, this seems to leave revealed theology entirely untouched. Indeed, Descartes suggests in a thoroughly orthodox fashion that real theology depends on revelation alone and that no Catholic could believe that natural light is superior to light of grace.[42] He also repeatedly claims that he has no concern with that which depends on revelation alone, and that not a word in his work touches on religious controversy or the differences of religions.[43]

Descartes' protestations of innocence notwithstanding, it is clear that his understanding of the relation of revealed theology with both natural theology and philosophy imposes radical restrictions on the domain of revealed theology. Descartes argues, for example, that revealed theology cannot enter into the domain revealed by the natural light and inveighs against those who try to combine science and revelation.[44] To try to use revelation to get science in his view is to use the Bible for purposes for which it was not intended.[45] He particularly objects to "the people who confound Aristotle with the Bible and abuse the authority of the Church to vent their passions--I mean the people who had Galileo condemned."[46] He similarly ridicules his Protestant antagonist Voetius for asking whether the denial of substantial forms is compatible with scripture, pointing out that such philosophical entities were unknown to those who wrote scripture at the dictation of the Holy Ghost.[47]

While all of this would seem to leave considerable room for revealed theology to play an important role in human life, Descartes further delimits its authority with his assertion that the truths of philosophy and the truths of religion cannot contradict one another.[48] On the surface, this claim seems to be quite pious. When more closely examined, however, it becomes clear that it calls into question all of the teachings of theology that contradict the apodictic truths of Descartes' science. Descartes obviously did not point this out, but it was clear enough to many of his friends and enemies.

Descartes realized that he would not be able to conceal his true position from close scrutiny. He thus remarks to Mersenne that he fears he may have to fight a war with the Jesuits.[49] This concern was particularly pressing because he hoped that the Jesuits would adopt his work in their curriculum in place of Aristotle. He thus went to great lengths to placate them, dedicating his *Meditations* to the members of the theology faculty at the Sorbonne, and responding carefully and courteously to his inconsequential Jesuit critic, Pierre Bourdin. He even wrote to Bourdin's Jesuit superior, Father Dinet, to defend himself against Bourdin's accusations and ask for a broader review of his works, arguing that his orthodoxy was demonstrated by the numerous Protestant attacks on his work. The incident that reveals most explicitly the lengths to which Descartes was willing to go to gain the support of the Jesuits, however, was his attempt to give a philosophical explanation of the transubstantiation of the Eucharist.[50] Catholic opinion was apparently troubled by the question of whether Cartesianism could be reconciled with transubstantiation, especially because the Calvinists believed that transubstantiation could not be philosophically explained. A natural philosophy that could not explain transubstantiation thus could not make any claim to orthodoxy.[51] In the long run, however, Descartes may not have helped his cause by attempting to explain transubstantiation rather than simply asserting it to be a mystery, for it was this argument more than anything else that led to the inclusion of his works on the Index.[52]

Whatever his efforts at concealment, Descartes himself clearly recognized the real problems that a Copernican physics such as Galileo's and his own posed for religion. He remarks that if the universe is infinite, then it is difficult to believe in the prerogatives that Christianity grants to human beings, because man can no longer be imagined to be the most godlike of all creatures, residing at the center of creation.[53] God's purposes are hidden from us, Descartes argues, and it is at least possible and even probable that he has given greater gifts than even Christ [!] to other beings elsewhere in the universe.[54] This view, of course, was anathema to orthodox Christianity.

The Cartesian Argument for Toleration

Descartes delimits the traditional sphere of religious authority in substantial ways and thus also delimits the range of issues that can lead to religious conflict. However, he does not stop here. He also seeks to ameliorate conflict within that sphere by providing the grounds for toleration and a greater sense of community among people of different religions.

Descartes' argument for religious toleration needs to be understood within his general understanding of man as a free being. To be free for Descartes is to act without constraint and with true knowledge in pursuit of one's ends. Descartes' fundamental principle that establishes the foundation for certain knowledge thus also establishes the grounds for freedom of the individual will. The realization and assertion of the fundamental principle depend upon our capacity of doubt, to suspend judgment in cases of uncertainty. Doubting for Descartes is a form of willing and the ability to doubt, to not accept what is presented to one, is the primordial moment of human freedom. By suspending our judgment in all doubtful cases we can preserve ourselves from error. This negative freedom, however, produces no action, leaving us suspended in the void. Descartes in this way follows the traditional skeptical path to what was the typical skeptical conclusion. His great innovation lies in following this path of doubt one step further to a new conclusion which overturns skepticism and establishes in its place the absolute certainty of *cogito ergo sum*. This fundamental principle is in turn the foundation for a universal science which empowers man and points him toward an unlimited and Godlike freedom and power.[55]

While Descartes sees such an unlimited freedom as the long-term goal of humanity, he also recognizes that human beings have to act in the moment and that the press of events seldom allows time for reaching apodictic judgments. Even under these circumstances, however, human beings can act more or less freely. Using their natural reason, they can judge better rather than worse and attain what Descartes calls moral certainty.[56] They thus can act with greater or lesser knowledge and consequently with greater or lesser freedom. What is crucial in these circumstances is resolving on a particular course of action and following it to the end. Such resoluteness is an expression and assertion of the free will in the face of uncertainty, a denial that one is subject to fortune.[57]

The knowledge that is essential to freedom in both the realms of nature and human affairs is discursive knowledge. It is publicly available and verifiable. True knowledge is equally important to freedom in the religious realm. The great difference in religious matters is that the standards of truth for the most important points are different than those in the realm of nature. Descartes argues that in matters of faith some questions such as the existence of God and the immortality of the soul are susceptible to analysis by natural reason. On these matters it is possible to know with certainty and to act freely on the basis of a conviction that arises out of our natural light. In such cases, disputes may arise but they can always be resolved by demonstration and proof. When it comes to purely theological questions such as the trinity and the incarnation, however, natural reason tells us nothing. In these matters, we can have neither scientific nor moral certainty. Certainty in religious matters arises not through our natural light but only through the light of grace or faith. "Each believes that his religion is instituted by God himself, who does not know how to deceive; and as a result one believes that it is not possible to make a single change, without it being bad."[58] What we know in this realm, we know not as a result of discursive reasoning, but by means of an inner revelation or light. Our freedom in this realm thus depends upon being able to follow this light. Truth in matters of faith is thus fundamentally subjective, the product of a radically individual experience unavailable to anyone else. Faith thus cannot be coerced. Indeed, coercion produces only hypocrisy.[59] Religious authority that insists on conformity of conscience thus unjustly constrains individual freedom.[60] Indeed, in Descartes' view such a denial of liberty is tyrannical.[61]

While Descartes clearly supports freedom of conscience, he takes a more equivocal stance on freedom of worship, similar in many respects to that articulated in the Edict of Nantes.[62] Given the experience of his times, Descartes greatly values public peace and clearly believes that this has to be weighed in any decision about tolerating diverse religious practices. He sees most change as ill-considered and dangerous. He thus will have nothing to do with those "meddlesome and restless characters who, called neither by birth nor fortune to the management of public affairs, are yet forever thinking up some new reform."[63] Such men produce civil strife. In the provisional morality of the *Discourse*, he determines "to obey the laws and customs of my country, holding constantly to the religion in which by God's grace I had been instructed from my childhood, and governing myself in all other matters according to the most moderate and least extreme opinions."[64] While this determination at first glance appears to be a quietistic acceptance of the prevailing structures of power, it is actually somewhat more liberal than this. Descartes gives us a hint of this in his elucidation of this principle. He does not unquestioningly accept the opinions of those in power as authoritative, but chooses to live only by those opinions that are most moderate, counting "as excessive all promises by which we give up some of our freedom."[65] His decision to accept and follow the most moderate opinions is thus a decision in favor of both political and religious liberty, but it produces a practice that is quiet and intense rather than boisterous and revolutionary. Such moderation in Descartes' view is conducive to peace, and thus to the long-term success of science which alone can bring about decisive and lasting change. Religious fanaticism, by contrast, produces civil war and undermines all chances of rational reform.[66] Moreover, such fanaticism, in Descartes' view, is unChristian, for love of peace, according to Descartes is the most Christlike virtue.[67]

While Descartes recognizes the pragmatic necessity of living according to the laws and customs of the country in which he resides, he also suggests that one can choose where one wants to live. He writes to Princess Elizabeth that it is important for the individual to examine all of the mores of the place in which he lives in order to determine whether he can follow them.[68] While it may be too disruptive to insist on practicing one's religion in the midst of one's opponents, this does not mean one has to adopt their practice. One can move to a community that is either more akin to one's own or more tolerant, if one so desires.

Descartes himself made such a choice when he abandoned France for the Netherlands. He claims to have moved to the Netherlands because of his high opinion of the King and his confidence in the King's protection and government.[69] He particularly seems to have respected and enjoyed the sober and responsible liberty afford by the Dutch republic: "I know well that the citizens of these provinces passionately love liberty but I assure myself that this liberty consists in the security of the good and the innocent and not in the impunity of the malefactors. . . . I believe that the liberty of this republic consists above all in the equality of rights of all, in the incorruptible integrity of their judgments."[70] For Descartes, religious freedom, or at least freedom from religious persecution, was one of the chief attractions of Holland in contrast to France where the King obliged the people to leave decisions on religious matters to the superiors of the Church.[71] Descartes also recognized that for similar reasons the Dutch were much less hostile to Copernican science than the French and that this attitude would make both his work and the propagation of his science easier than in France.

While Descartes generally supports religious toleration, he does not believe every belief and practice should be tolerated. He calls blasphemy the most odious and punishable crime under the laws, and remarks in a similar vein that atheism is a crime that no state that prizes liberty can tolerate.[72] While both of these remarks were made in the context of his defense against charges of blasphemy and atheism and therefore cannot simply be accepted as his settled opinion, they are not mere camouflage for a secular rationalism that is antipathetic to religion or that regards religion as superstition.[73] Descartes recognizes similar limits to toleration in his answer to the question whether it is permissible to doubt God's existence. He argues that it is possible for those with true faith to doubt God's existence intellectually if they cannot demonstrate it, but that once they have grasped the demonstration, it is no longer possible to doubt or permissible to express doubts about this matter, except as a false hypothetical for purposes of refutation.[74] On similar grounds, he does not believe that polytheistic religions such as those of the

Greeks should be tolerated, since they can be shown by natural reason to be confused and misguided.[75] Among Christians, however, it is necessary to tolerate a diversity of beliefs and practices, because the differences in religious practice are philosophically indistinguishable and only subjectively justifiable. There are thus no objective grounds for calling another's beliefs or rites into question. Descartes also believes that the differences among Christians are of no great moment. Thus, he remarks that, "I respect all theologians as servants of God, even those who are of a religion different from mine, because we all adore the same God."[76] In a similar vein, he tells Princess Elizabeth that she should not take her brother's conversion to Catholicism too seriously since it matters little if one espouses the Protestant or Catholic cause.[77]

While Descartes was clearly cognizant of the necessity and benefits of toleration, he never imagined that toleration would be sufficient in itself to restrain partisan passions. This fact was driven home to him by the increasingly vigorous attacks on his work by both Catholic and Protestant theologians after the publication of his *Meditations*. Both of his chief antagonists, the Jesuit Pierre Bourdin and the orthodox Calvinist Gisbert Voetius were Aristotelians. The arguments that both presented were complex but essentially Bourdin argues that Descartes is a skeptic and Voetius that he is an atheist.[78] Bourdin's argument can be easily dismissed. He argues that Descartes only pretends to refute skepticism in order to present an argument *for* skepticism. Given the strength and importance of Descartes' argument against skepticism, however, it is difficult to take Bourdin's charges seriously. Voetius' claims are another matter.

Voetius asserts that Descartes is an atheist. This charge is more complicated than it might at first appear. In the seventeenth century, 'atheist' was a term of abuse that did not have any exact meaning. However, one meaning it did not have was the belief in no God.[79] Voetius clearly believed that atheists aimed not at showing that God did not exist but that his will did not have to be obeyed.[80] Atheism, as Voetius understands it, thus has much in common with Pelagianism. Pelagianism rests on the notion that the human will is never determined by any antecedent event or cause. This has two important theological consequences. First, human beings are not tainted by original sin, and second they can attain salvation without grace through will alone. Under these circumstances, divine law is not binding and Christ's sacrifice unnecessary. In practical terms, we can be certain of salvation if we lead a good and virtuous life. Given what Descartes has to say about human freedom, it is easy to see why one might suspect him of Pelagianism.[81] Descartes, of course, denies these charges, but he does not answer them directly or fully.[82] Still, this is a debatable issue and hardly grounds for the vicious *ad hominum* charges brought forward by Voetius. Descartes rightly sees them as an assault on his freedom of thought and conscience.[83] What was particularly telling for Descartes was the fact that these charges were leveled against him by an important public figure (Voetius was Rector of the University of Utrecht and pastor of its chief church), and that they were the basis not only for an assault on him, but also for a general prohibition against teaching Cartesian science.[84] In the most tolerant society of his time, Descartes thus found his own quite circumspect religious beliefs and his science under attack. This fact made it eminently clear to him, that mere toleration could not succeed without a reformation of the basic relationships among human beings.

A policy of toleration is difficult to sustain because toleration is essentially negative, not an action but an inaction. It always only constrains without enabling. In itself, it thus only frustrates the passions without offering them a countervailing satisfaction. Toleration thus can only be sustained in Descartes' view if it rests on and grows out of more positive human interactions. This insight, arising particularly out of his own experience of persecution, led Descartes to move beyond his earlier position with its emphasis on the radically individualist ego toward a greater concern for the intersubjective relations of human beings.[85]

In his last work, *The Passions of the Soul*, Descartes argues that the I is pulled towards and repulsed from others by its passions and desires. Human beings are attracted to those things they judge to be good for them and repulsed by those they judge to be bad.[86] From this perspective, toleration is an attempt to moderate our repulsion from and anger with religious beliefs and practices different than our own. Such moderation, however, can only be sustained in the actual world if it is underpinned by an active concern with the well-being of others. In order to feel such concern, an individual must be able to imagine that he is part of a larger whole that includes both him and those whose beliefs and practices he opposes.[87] For Descartes, the anger arising out of disagreements on the most important spiritual matters thus can only be restrained if humans are connected to one another by a deeper and more embracing love or affection.

Descartes distinguishes two different kinds of love, a concupiscent love that wants to possess that which it loves and a benevolent love that wants the well-being of that which it loves.[88] Descartes sees this second form of love as essential to human community. On its own, however, this passion may not suffice to counteract the effects of the other passions that disjoin us from our fellows. Thus, it is crucial that this passion be formed and guided by the soul. The soul can only accomplish this by resolving to follow "firm and determinate judgments bearing upon the knowledge of good and evil."[89] Without such judgments, even the strongest soul cannot control the passions, since most of the passions have already been wrongly habituated according to false judgments during the period of childhood when humans are incapable of reasoning properly.[90]

Descartes names this benevolent love guided by determinate judgments generosity. Generosity, as he understands it, combines elements of Christian charity and Aristotelian magnanimity.[91] The concept itself is a refinement of the notion of resoluteness that Descartes discussed in the provisional morality in the *Discourse*. There Descartes argued that we need to be resolute when we are uncertain which direction we should go. In so doing, we act more freely than when we vacillate and second-guess ourselves. Generosity, as Descartes explains in the *Passions*, is free will combined with such resoluteness.[92] Generosity, however, is more than this free resoluteness, for it does not operate in the dark but on the basis of a determinate judgment about the nature of good and evil. What is good for human beings is freedom; it is the source of their greatest self-esteem.[93] True human happiness thus is only possible if humans act freely, since only such freedom brings perfect contentment of mind and inner satisfaction.[94] Human beings act freely, however, only when they put aside their passions and interests in favor of those of their fellow human beings. Generosity is thus the highest human good because it considers nothing more highly than doing good to others; it is having a good will toward others, a will that desires their freedom.[95]

Generosity in Descartes' view is the basis for friendship and thus for human community. Christian fanatics lack all such generosity. In a thoroughly unChristian fashion, they violate the laws of friendship and charity, throwing society into war.[96] They are driven not by a real concern for the well-being of others but by vanity and arrogance. It was such men, Descartes believed, who had created the religious conflagration that had engulfed Europe. Their influence could only be combated indirectly by means of a new and more rational science and by fostering a spirit of generosity. Descartes believed that human beings could foster such generosity by accustoming themselves to forming certain and determinate judgments.[97] Only such judgments can provide true peace of mind rather than prejudice and fanaticism. Such generosity may not eliminate all religious antagonism, but as it gains sway toleration will become increasingly more widespread.

Conclusion

Descartes lived in an age in which partisan religious passions had propelled the peoples of Europe into internecine war. In his view, human life and freedom could only be secured by the development and deployment of a new science that would make man master and possessor of nature. This science, however, was incompatible with prevailing theological conceptions. It thus could succeed only if the sphere in which religious authority held sway could be delimited and if the conflict within this sphere could be moderated or eliminated. Descartes developed a theological metaphysics that aimed at accomplishing both of these tasks. God, as Descartes portrays him, does not intervene in the order of nature. Nature thus can be mastered by the human will through the application of science to secure human freedom and well-being. Descartes also redefines religious authority. He argues that our relationship to God depends upon grace and that it is fundamentally subjective and private. Coercion can play no role in shaping true faith. Descartes thus lays out the grounds for toleration. He further argues that toleration is essential because it is necessary to guarantee human freedom. He understands, however, that a doctrine of toleration will not be sufficient to curb partisan passions and thus articulates the grounds for reconstituting a human community that will produce affective relations to bind men together that will counteract the disaffective passions of religious fanaticism.

From his earliest years, Descartes sought to avoid becoming entangled in the religious disputes of his time. He was forced, however, to lower his oars into these dangerous waters in order to set the ship of his science in motion. From this point on, he was caught up in an almost irresistible current that bore him to the center of the maelstrom. From his almost exclusive concern with science and mathematics, he was driven first to a consideration of metaphysics and theology, and then finally to a consideration of the moral foundations of human community. The brilliant young man who wanted to live well by living unseen in the end was forced against his character and almost against his will to become the generous man he admired and praised. In an age in which active participation in public life often involved one in violence and crime and the retreat from society was effectively a submission to tyranny, Descartes sought a new path to human security and freedom. He found it in his vision of a universal science in the hands of a tolerant and generous humanity, making itself master and possessor of nature. For better and for worse, we are the heirs of this Cartesian vision.

NOTES:

1. *The Passions of the Soul, Oeuvres de Descartes*, ed. Charles Adam and Paul Tannery, 13 vols. (Paris: Vrin, 1957-68), 11:472 (hereafter cited as AT); *The Philosophical Writings of Descartes*, ed. John Cottingham, Robert Stoothoof, and Dugald Murdoch, 2 vols. (Cambridge: Cambridge University Press, 1985), 1:396 (hereafter cited as CSM). See also, Rodis-Lewis, *La Moral de Descartes* (Paris: P.U.F., 1957), 105.

2. On this point see Georg Freiherr von Hertling, "Descartes' Beziehung zur Scholastik," Kgl. Bayerishe Akad. d. Wissenschaften in München, *Sitzungsber. d. Philos.-histor. Klasse* (1897); Etienne Gilson, *La Liberté chez Descartes et la théologie* (Paris: Alcan, 1912), *Index scholastico-Cartesien* (Paris: Alcan, 1913), and especially *Études sur le rôle de la pensée médiévale dans la formation du système cartésien* (Paris: Vrin, 1930); and Alexander Koyré, *Descartes und die Scholastik* (Bonn: Cohen, 1923).

3. Hans Blumenberg, *The Legitimacy of the Modern Age*, trans. Robert W. Wallace (Cambridge: M.I.T. Press, 1983); Amos Funkenstein, *Theology and the Scientific Imagination from the Middle Ages to the Seventeenth Century* (Princeton: Princeton University Press, 1986).

4. For a general discussion of this event, see Edward Grant, "The Effect of the Condemnation of 1277," in *The Cambridge History of Later Medieval Philosophy*, ed. Norman Kretzman et al. (London: Cambridge University Press, 1982).

5. For a comprehensive discussion of Ockham and nominalism, see Jürgen Miethke, *Ockhams Weg zur Sozialphilosophie* (Berlin: de Gruyter, 1969), and Marilyn McCord Adams, *William Ockham*, 2 vols. (Notre Dame: University of Notre Dame Press, 1987).

6. On this point see Ludger Meier, "Research That Has Been Made and Is Yet to Be Made on the Ockhamism of Martin Luther at Erfuhrt," *Archivum Franciscanum Historicum* 43 (1950):56-67; Paul Vignaux, "Luther commentateur des Sentences," *Études de philosophie médievale* 21 (1935); and William Courtney, "Nominalism and Late Medieval Religion," in *The Pursuit of Holiness in Late Medieval and Renaissance Religion*, ed. Charles Trinkhaus and Heiko Oberman (Leiden: Brill, 1974), 58.

7. Martin Luther, *Three Treatises* (Philadelphia: Fortress, 1960), 274-97.

8. Cited in Bernard C. Flynn, "Descartes and the Ontology of Subjectivity," *Man and World* 16 (1983):5.

9. Ignatius Loyola had recommended that Aristotle as interpreted by Aquinas serve as the philosophical framework of his Jesuit order. While there clearly was a revival of Aquinas in the early sixteenth century and a corresponding decline in interest in scholastic critics such as Ockham and Scotus at least among the Catholic intellectuals, this new Thomism was never able to accept wholeheartedly the realism of scholasticism. Stephen Gaukroger, *Descartes: An Intellectual Biography* (Oxford: Clarendon Press, 1995), 52.

10. Gaukruger's *Descartes* is the best English language biography of Descartes.

11. Gaukroger, *Descartes*, 42. On life at La Flêche see Camille de Rochmonteix, *Un Collège de Jesuites aux XVIIe et XVIIIe siecles*, 4 vols. (Le Mans: Leguicheux, 1839).

12. Geneviève Rodis-Lewis, "Descartes aurait-il eu un professeur nominaliste?" *Archives de Philosophie* 34 (1971):37-46; and Gaukroger, *Descartes*, 54.

13. Gaukroger, *Descartes*, 65.

14. For a comprehensive discussion of the Rosicrucians, see Frances A. Yates, *The Rosicrucian Enlightenment* (London: Routledge & Kegan Paul, 1972). He portrays the Rosicrucians as an extension of the Elizabethan Renaissance. The libertine Naudé was also attracted to the mathematical and scientific side of Rosicrucianism. Ibid., 112.

15. On the libertines, see Gaukroger, *Descartes*, 135-39; and René Pintard, *Le Libertinage érudit dans la première moitié du XVIIe siècle* (Paris: Boivin, 1943).

16. Roger Lefèvre, *L'Humanisme de Descartes* (Paris: P.U.F., 1957), 188-93.

17. Gaukroger, *Descartes*, 136.

18. Gaukroger, *Descartes*, 136-37.

19. Lefèvre, *L'Humanisme*, 203.

20. Descartes to Villebressieu, summer 1631, AT, 1:213.

21. Gaukroger, *Descartes*, 186.

22. This question of divine omnipotence is related to skepticism but is not identical with it. While Gaukroger is right that Descartes was not concerned with skepticism in the traditional sense during this period, Descartes was concerned with the question of divine omnipotence that he later characterized as the supreme source of skepticism in the *Meditations*. *Descartes*, 304.

23. Descartes to Mersenne, 27 May 1630, AT, 1:151.

24. AT, 6:60; CSM, 1:142.

25. Descartes to Mersenne, end of Nov. 1633, Feb. 1634, and April 1634. AT, 1:270, 281, 285. See also Gaukroger, *Descartes*, 292.

26. Gaukroger, *Descartes*, 304.

27. Lefèvre has argued that Descartes' thought can best be understood as the encounter of the science of mechanism with scholasticism and with the conflict of religious libertinism and religious apologetics. *L'Humanisme*, 187.

28. Descartes to Mersenne, 6 May 1630, 27 May 1638. AT, 1:148, 2:138.

29. On the challenge of skepticism for Descartes, see Richard Popkin, *The History of Scepticism from Erasmus to Spinoza* (Berkeley: University of California Press, 1979), 178-79. For an alternative account of Descartes' relationship to skepticism, see Gaukroger, *Descartes*, 311-15.

30. For a more extensive discussion of this argument in the first *Meditation*, see Harry Frankfurt, *Demons, Dreamers, and Madmen: The Defense of Reason in Descartes' Meditations* (Indianapolis: Bobbs-Merrill, 1970).

31. On the different formulations of this principle and its meaning see my *Nihilism Before Nietzsche* (Chicago: University of Chicago Press, 1995), 1-14, 33-47. For Descartes' account of the differences between his principle and the similar *dubito ergo sum* of Augustine, see Descartes to Colvius, 14 Nov. 1640, AT, 3:247.

32. On this point, see *Passions*, AT, 11:390; CSM, 1:384; and Descartes to Queen Christiana, 20 Nov. 1647, AT, 5:85; CSM, 3:326. See also Jean-Luc Marion, *Sur la Théologie blanche de Descartes: Analogie, création des vérités éternelles et fondement* (Paris: P.U.F., 1981), 427.

33. As Lefèvre puts it, Descartes accommodated the traditional proofs of the schools with a demonstration inspired by the antischolastic spirit. *L'Humanisme*, 226.

34. "The Essential Incoherence of Descartes' Definition of Divinity," in *Essays on Descartes' Meditations*, ed. Amélie Oksenberg Rorty (Berkeley: University of California Press, 1986), 325-27.

35. Marion, *Théologie blanche*, 428; Jean Marie Beyssade, *"Création des verités éternelles et doubte metaphysique,"* *Studia Cartesiana* 2 (1981):93.

36. Marion, *Théologie blanche*, 429.

37. I develop this argument more fully in my *Nihilism Before Nietzsche*, 57-63.

38. J.A. Van Rules, *The Crisis of Causality: Voetius and Descartes on God, Nature and Change* (New York: Leiden, 1995), 258.

39. *Burman,* AT, 5:169.

40. Marion, *Théologie blanche.*

41. *Comments on a Certain Broadsheet,* AT, 8B:353; CSM, 1:300; see also Descartes to Mersenne, 24 Dec. 1640, AT, 3:266; CSM, 3:163.

42. Descartes to Mersenne, 15 Mar. 1630, AT, 1:143-44; Descartes to Hyperaspistis, Aug. 1641, AT, 3:426; CSM 3:191.

43. Descartes to Mersenne, May 1630, AT, 1:150, 53; Descartes to Huygens, 12 May 1647, *Correspondance de Descartes et de Constantin Huygens,* ed. Léon Roth (Oxford: Clarendon, 1926), 251; see also Descartes to Voetius, AT, 8, 2:111.

44. Jean-Luc Marion, "Preface," in *La Querelle d'Utrecht,* ed. and trans. Theo Verbeek (Paris: Les impressions nouvelles, 1988), 9. See also Gaukroger, *Descartes,* 337.

45. Descartes to [Hogelande], Aug. 1638, AT, 2:347.

46. Descartes to Mersenne, 31 Mar. 1641, AT, 3:349; CSM, 3:177.

47. Descartes to Regius, Jan. 1642, AT, 3:501; CSM, 3:207.

48. Descartes to Mersenne, Dec. 1640, AT, 3:259; to [Noël], Oct. 1637, AT, 1:456. While scholars such as Lefèvre may be correct that Descartes supports rational theology, reveres sacred theology, and condemns scholastic theology, we should not conclude that Descartes continues to grant sacred or revealed theology its traditional scope and influence. *L'Humanisme,* 234.

49. Descartes to Mersenne, 30 July 1640, and to Huygens 31 July 1640, AT, 3:124, 152.

50. Descartes to [Vatier], 22 Feb. 1638, AT, 1:564; and to Mesland, 9 Feb. 1645, AT, 4:165-68; CSM, 3:242.

51. Gaukroger, *Descartes,* 357.

52. Nicholas Jolley, "The Reception of Descartes' Philosophy," in *The Cambridge Companion to Descartes,* ed. John Cottingham (Cambridge: Cambridge University Press, 1992), 397; Gaukroger, *Descartes,* 357.

53. AT, 5:53. See also his remarks to Burman, AT, 5:168; CSM, 3:349. The profound depths of this problem for Christianity, however, were only grasped by Pascal who quailed before the infinite dark distances that Cartesian science imagined. *Pensées* 68. On this point, see Alexander Koyré's *From Closed World to Infinite Universe* (Baltimore: Johns Hopkins University Press, 1957).

54. *Burman,* AT, 5:168.

55. This moment of Descartes' thought was the basis for the later charge brought by Revius that in striving for complete certainty, Descartes wanted to make himself God. Verbeek, *Descartes and the Dutch,* 49.

56. Moral certainty like scientific certainty applies only to the realm accessible to natural reason.

57. *Discourse,* AT, 6:24-25; CSM, 1:123. Descartes is so dedicated to the voluntarist position, that he believes our happiness depends upon coming to believe that everything that does not depend on our free will is the result of providence rather than fortune. *Passions,* AT, 11:439; CSM, 1:380. Such a belief helps us to accept our fate without diminishing our sense of freedom. Descartes to Elizabeth, 15 Sept. 1645, AT, 3:291; CSM, 3:265. Indeed, Descartes here affirms the nominalist contention that everything occurs as a result of either divine or human freedom. The unstated implication of this argument is that human beings can master nature to the extent that their knowledge approaches that of God, or to put the matter in other terms, nature ultimately is nothing other than a manifestation of will and thus can finally offer no resistance to will.

58. Descartes to Voetius, AT, 8, 2:26.

59. Descartes' argument here is illustrative of the wide-spread internalization of Christianity that took place during the period of the Reformation, in which a Christian life came to be determined by faith and conviction rather than practice. On this point, see Gaukroger, *Descartes*, 15-37.

60. Descartes to Huygens, 12 May 1647, R, 251; see also Marion, "Preface," in *Querelle*, ed., Verbeek, 14.

61. Descartes to Voetius, AT, 8, 2:48; see also 8, 2:125.

62. The Edict of Nantes allowed Huguenots to worship in their secure cities or, in the case of the greater nobles, in their private homes.

63. *Discourse*, AT, 6:14-15, 25; CSM, 1:118, 123.

64. AT, 6:23; CSM, 1:122. How seriously we should take Descartes' remarks on this question, however, is not entirely clear. He tells Burman, for example, that he formulated his provisional morality when he began calling everything into question in order to protect himself against the charge of subverting religion and morality. AT, 5:178. Etienne Gilson believes that this later claim distorts Descartes' earlier intention, but Gaukroger finds this reading implausible. Gilson, *René Descartes: Discours de la méthode, texte et commentaire*, 4th ed. (Paris: Vrin, 1975), 234; Gaukroger, *Descartes*, 307, 456.

65. AT, 6:24; CSM, 1:123.

66. Descartes to Voetius, AT, 8, 2:14..

67. Ibid.

68. Descartes to Elizabeth, 15 Sept. 1645, AT, 4:295.

69. Descartes to Huygens, 1637, AT, 1:638.

70. Descartes to Voetius, AT, 8, 2:188; see also Descartes to Balzac, 5 May 1631, AT, 1:204.

71. Descartes to Voetius, AT, 8, 2:193: CSM, 3:224; see also AT, 8:110; Descartes to Servien, 12 May 1647, AT, 5:26-27.

72. Descartes to the Curators of the University of Leiden, 4 May 1647, AT, 5:7; Descartes to Voetius, AT, 8, 2:174.

73. Henri Gouhier has made perhaps the strongest argument for the sincerity of Descartes' Christianity. See his *La Pensée Religieuse de Descartes* (Paris: Vrin, 1924).

74. Descartes to Buitendijck, 1643, AT, 4:62-62; CSM, 3:229.

75. To Clerselier, 17 Feb. 1645, AT, 4:188; CSM, 3:248.

76. Descartes to Voetius, AT, 8, 2:180; see also Descartes to Dinet, AT, 7:597.

77. Descartes to Princess Elizabeth, AT, 4:351-352.

78. For Descartes' reflections on these accusations see Descartes to Chanut, 1 Nov. 1646, AT, 4:534.

79. Gaukroger, *Descartes*, 196. Also see, Theo Verbeek, *Descartes and the Dutch: Early Reactions to Cartesian Philosophy, 1637-1650* (Carbondale: Southern Illinois Press, 1992), 17.

80. Verbeek, *Descartes and the Dutch*, 22.

81. On this point, see Martin Versfeld, "The Moral Philosophy of Descartes and the Catholic Doctrine of Grace," *Dominican Studies* 1 (1948):154.

82. For Descartes' defense, see Descartes to Mersenne, Mar. 1642, AT, 3:544: CSM, 3:211; and Descartes to Heerbboord, 19 Apr. 1647, AT, 4:631. On this point, see Verbeek, *Descartes and the Dutch*, 5, 42.

83. Descartes to the Curators of Leiden, 4 May 1647, AT, 5:1-2. See also Descartes to Servien, 12 May 1647, AT, 5:24.

84. The question of Cartesianism was peculiarly important in the Netherlands for somewhat idiosyncratic reasons. The country was an amalgamation of quasi-independent states that were united only by religion and their long struggle against Spanish domination. Within Dutch Protestantism, however, there was a split between the orthodox Calvinists and the followers of Jacobus Arminius, an anti-Calvinist and quasi-Pelagian theologian who believed that virtuous behavior depends on free will rather than grace. His followers, who were known as the Remonstrants, posed a real challenge to the dominant orthodox Calvinism and thus to the religious and political unity of the country. Insofar as Cartesianism moved in the Pelagian direction it threatened Dutch national unity as much as Arminianism and thus from the orthodox point of view was politically dangerous. On this point see Verbeek, *Descartes and the Dutch*.

85. Marion suggests that it was the hatred of Voetius and the affection of Princess Elizabeth that brought Descartes out of the solitude of the ego to social life. "Preface," in *Querelle*, 17.

86. *Passions*, AT, 11:391; CSM, 1:358.
87. *Passions*, AT, 11:388; CSM, 1:356.
88. *Passions*, AT, 11:388; CSM, 1:356.
89. *Passions*, AT, 11:367; CSM, 1:347.
90. *Passions*, AT, 11:368; CSM, 1:347
91. *Passions*, AT, 11:453; CSM, 1:388.
92. AT, 11:446; CSM, 1:384.
93. *Passions*, AT, 11:445; CSM, 1:384.
94. Descartes to Elizabeth, 4 Aug. 1645, AT, 4:264; CSM, 3:257.
95. *Passions*, AT, 11:447-48, 470; CSM, 1:385, 395. Rodis-Lewis points out that if social life is a necessity, there is an obligation to maintain its equilibrium in accordance with liberties which constitute the dignity of each person. *La Moral*, 51.
96. Descartes to Voetius, AT, 8, 2:116; see also Ibid., 49.
97. *Passions*, AT, 11:462; CSM, 1:392.

6

TOLERATION AND THE SKEPTICISM OF RELIGION IN SPINOZA'S *TRACTATUS THEOLOGICA-POLITICUS*

Steven B. Smith

The Enlightenment's Critique of Orthodoxy

The religious issue which was hotly debated at the origins of modernity has once again acquired a new urgency. The rise of religious fundamentalisms which have taken the place of now defunct secular ideologies has created problems that would not have seemed possible even a generation ago. Until recently, secularization theorists confidently averred that religious conflicts, along with their attendant tribal and ethnic wars, would wither away with the advance of modernity. Social and economic modernization would bring the gradual emancipation of society from the dominance of religious symbols and institutions. Similarly, liberal political theory has fared no better in providing the intellectual resources for coming to terms with this problem. Liberals have taken to sheltering themselves behind the famed "wall of separation" between church and state while failing to understand exactly why that wall is under seige. For all of these reasons, it is necessary once more to reconsider the roots of this problem.

Our ability to address the religious issue has not always been so impoverished. The founders of liberal democratic theory were all deeply immersed in an ongoing discussion of what might be called the theologico-political problem.[1] Hobbes, Spinoza, Locke, Hume, and Kant, to name but the most obvious, were all deeply immersed in theological studies and treated them as inseparable from politics. From the outset, these thinkers declared war on biblical orthodoxy or what Hobbes tellingly called "the kingdom of darkness" as the rule of superstition and priestcraft. These thinkers were engaged in more than mere biblical scholarship or research, but with the wholesale project of cultural and political transformation. At issue was nothing short of the replacement of the God of Scripture with unassisted human reason as our "only Star and compass" in Locke's luminous expression.[2]

The Enlightenment provides us with the grounds for the liberal answer to the theologico-political problem. The answer characteristically worked out by the most advanced thinkers of this age was some form of separation of religion and politics. This separation was related to the later liberal distinction between the private and the public in which religion was henceforth to be privatized, deprived of political power, and relegated to the precincts of conscience and intellectual persuasion. The new liberal solution to this age-old problem promised great benefits. It promised an end to the destructive religious wars and crusades that had so ravaged the peace of European communities; by making religion a matter of private belief or conscience, it would abolish the hierarchical and authoritarian features of established churches and religious institutions; and by redefining the scope of religious authority, it would deprive power-hungry clerics of their influence over political life. The result would be a new enlightened era of toleration for religious minorities and other dissenters.

To be sure, the Enlightenment was a vast movement of thought forged by a variety of thinkers working on a variety of problems in a variety of national and theological contexts. The leading representatives of this movement seem to disagree over the most funamental issues of metaphysics, moral psychology, and the meaning of history. Most important for our purposes, Enlightenment liberals were often divided over the best way of combatting religious intolerance. Some favored granting the widest possible liberty to individual freedom of expression within a framework of public legal justice. Others favored the creation of new "rational" theologies that would gradually replace the older revealed dispensations. Yet despite the manifest diversity of philosophical conviction, historical experience, and political belief, there is a sense in which the Enlightenment can be thought of as a common project aimed at the emancipation or liberation of the individual from ecclesiastical tutelage.

Nowhere is the Enlightenment project more strikingly revealed than in Spinoza's *Tractatus Theologico-Politicus*.[3] More boldly than either Hobbes or Locke, Spinoza gave expression to the Enlightenment's critique of orthodoxy with its belief in miracles, prophets, and the revealed character of Scripture.[4] Indeed, so boldly did Spinoza express his views that his writings were universally proscribed throughout the 17th and 18th centuries for their alleged materialism, determinism, and atheism. "Few books occasioned as many refutations, anathemas, insults, and maledictions," Gilles Deleuze has written. "The words 'Spinozism' and 'Spinozist' became insults and threats."[5] This war of words continued throughout the Enlightenment culminating in the debate between Mendelssohn and Jacobi over the alleged Spinozism of Lessing.[6]

The Purpose of the *Tractatus*

Spinoza was particularly well-suited to justify and defend the Enlightenment's answer to the religious question. In 1656 at the age of twenty-four an edict of excommunication or Herem was taken out against Spinoza by the rabbinate of Amsterdam permanently ostracizing him from the Marrano community in which he had been born. The details of this excommunication need not conern us here.[7] What is of interest is that as an excommunicated Jew living on the margins of Dutch society, Spinoza experienced firsthand the sting of religious intolerance. The *Tractatus* (1670) was published in part as a response to his excommunication, but more broadly as an effort to show that freedom of religion and inquiry can be granted without injury to either the state or religion.

The author of the *Tractatus* was scarcely the detached, unworldly spectator of human affairs passed down by the philosophical tradition. Spinoza was rather a passionate and partisan participant-observer in the political struggles of the time in which he lived. The *Tractatus* was not a theoretical study written *sub specie aeternitatis*, but was nothing short of a political tract written to advance the fortunes of a cause. This cause was the republican faction in the Dutch polity headed by Jan de Witt, "the grand pensionary" of Holland.[8] The mainstay of this faction were a variety of dissenting Protestant sects who opposed the Calvinist clergy and the Orangist monarchy. Like the Collegiants and Mennonites with whom he associated, Spinoza was a republican in politics and an advocate of strict toleration in matters of theology.[9] The murder of the de Witts by an angry mob in 1672, an event that Spinoza described as *ultima barbarorum*, merely indicated the extremes to which theologically inspired cruelty can lead.[10]

It was clearly due to his opposition to the established orthodoxies of his day that earned Spinoza not only his excommunication but his reputation as an atheist. As early as 1665, five years before the publication of the *Tractatus*, he wrote to Henry Oldenburg explaining his reasons for intervening in the theologico-political quarrels of his time:

> I am now writing a Treatise about my interpretation of Scripture. This I am driven to do by the following reasons: 1. The prejudice of the theologians; for I know that these are among the chief obstacles which prevent men from directing their minds to philosophy; and to remove them from the minds of the more prudent (*prudentiorum*). 2. The opinion which the common people have of me, who do not cease to accuse me falsely of atheism; I am also obliged to avert this accusation as far as it is possible to do so. 3. The freedom of philosophizing, and of saying what we think; this I desire to vindicate in every way, for here it is always suppressed through the excessive authority and impudence of the preachers.[11]

This statement provides an unusually frank expression of Spinoza's purpose. It tells us that the chief obstacle to toleration is the power of revealed religion or, what comes to the same thing, "the prejudice of the theologians." The fundamental objective of the *Tractatus* is the liberation of the reader from the power of prejudice and superstition. This is not an easy task as the causes of superstition are built into human nature itself. Far from being a simple

Enlightenment rationalist, Spinoza was deeply aware of the power of the passions to cause and maintain superstitious beliefs. Man is above all the superstitious animal or the animal prone to believe in the figments of his own imagination. Superstitions persist because the power of the passions is strong. We are perpetually torn between the competing passions of hope and fear and it is out of this psychological confusion that religion is born *(TTP*, 5 [1]; 6 [7]).

The psychological cause from which the belief in revealed religion arises is the faculty of the imagination (*E*, II, P40 S2). The power of *imaginatio* has none of its later associations with human sympathy and creativity. For Spinoza, it is the cause of both mental chaos and social disorder. The power of the imagination stands in an inverse ratio to the power of reason. It is precisely because reason is a rare achievement that the majority of humankind stands in a perpetual state of bondage to their passions and emotions. It is the faculty of the imagination that has led people to abdicate their reason and cede their right of self-legislation to priests and kings *(TTP*, 7 [10]). Why do we fight so hard to ensure our enslavement and then call it freedom? Why does religion that encourages acts of justice and loving kindness result in persecution and intolerance? These are the questions that the *Tractatus* asks us to consider.

If Spinoza's hope of liberating readers from prejudice and superstition was to bear fruit, the *Tractatus* had to be addressed neither to the multitude who live under the sway of the passions and for whom the book would be useless nor to the philosophers for whom its leading propositions are already well-known and for whom it would be redundant (*TTP*, 12 [33]). Spinoza addresses a third class of readers that he designates the prudent ones who are not philosophers in the strict sense but who resist the authority of the clerics and who have a desire to think and speak freely. The audience for the work seems to be those potential philosophers among those dissident members of the Dutch reformed church who, still under the influence of Scripture, may nevertheless be open to the teachings of the *Tractatus*. Who, then, were these prudent readers to whom Spinoza makes appeal?[12]

The *Tractatus*, I want to suggest, was intended for those "left" leaning dissenting sects who represented a new party in Dutch politics: a party of liberty. Spinoza was not the first to have discerned the emergence of this new party making its appearance on the European scene. One can also see their inklings in the pages of Machiavelli, Descartes, Hobbes, and Montaigne all of whom express admiration for a new and powerful form of individualism. This new kind of individual seeks to be liberated, as far as possible, from dependence on mere authority, wishes to think for himself, seeks to understand and hence master the emotions to which all persons are subject, and is tolerant of others but puts a premium on self-respect. While the idea of the free or autonomous individual had certain classical precedents in the philosophy of Plato and the Stoics, for Spinoza it is based much more radically than in the past on the doctrines of personal independence, self-mastery, and above all, courage.[13]

The Place of the *Tractatus*

In comparison to the major works of Descartes, Hobbes, and Locke, even in comparison to his own *Ethics*, the *Tractatus* is, curiously neglected.[14] The reasons for this neglect have something to do with problems of definition and genre. Is the *Tractatus* chiefly a work of biblical criticism or a work of political theory or a prolegomenon to the *Ethics*? The answer is obviously all the above. Nevertheless, the *Tractatus* has been all but ignored by philosophers who see it as lacking a rigorous and sufficiently deductive manner of presentation and hopelessly mired in biblical and historical minutae. Similarly, political theorists have seen the book as too theological to be of interest and removed from the major currents of European political life. Both of these views are mistaken. The *Tractatus*, is, I believe, a pioneering work of liberal political theory fully meriting inclusion along with Hobbes and Locke and crucially anticipating the ideas of Rousseau and Kant.

The reasons for Spinoza's neglect are due also to the ambiguous reception of his work. He has been both reviled and adored in the history of thought. He has been heralded as one of the great forerunners of modern philosophy, but also a man with one foot still in the medieval world.[15] If he has been seen as a founder of the Enlightenment's critique of religion, he was also subsequently adopted by the romantic counter-Enlightenment as a "God intoxicated man." He has been embraced by both the German idealists and Marxian materialists.[16] He has been denounced as an enemy of Judaism and guilty of an almost incomprehensible betrayal of his own people;[17] at the same time he has been elevated to the status of a founder of political Zionism and a spiritual ancestor of the modern state of Israel.[18] All of these readings can be sustained by something Spinoza says in the text.

As the title of the work implies, the *Tractatus* is devoted both to theology and politics and the relation between them. The first three-quarters of the book's twenty chapters is devoted almost entirely to theological problems. Beginning with a treatment of prophets, prophecy, and divine promises (1-3), Spinoza takes up in succession the themes of the divine and ceremonial law (4-5), miracles (6), and the proper method of scriptural interpretation (7). He proceeds next to a lengthy discussion of the order and composition of the books of the Torah (8-10), the status of the Gospels (11-13), and the proper relation between religion and philosophy (14-15). This section of the *Tractatus* culminates in Spinoza's announcement of a new "catholic" or universal religion (*fides universalis*) that is said to be nothing more than a distillation of the moral teachings of the prophets and apostles and which teaches a theology of charity and justice, interpreted to mean toleration and non-interference with the beliefs of others.

It is only with the last five chapters that Spinoza turns to political theory proper. He introduces his ideas about natural right and social contract (16), elaborates on the history of the ancient Hebrew theocracy and speculates on the reasons for its demise (17-18), and argues that the lessons of the past mandate the subordination of religion to the authority of the sovereign (19). It is only in the final chapter of the *Tractatus* that Spinoza turns to the issue of toleration and freedom of opinion promised in the preface to the book. The title of this chapter alone -- "In a free state everyone is permitted to think what he wishes and to say what he thinks" -- indicates what might be thought of as the highest theme of the work.[19] However, the *Tractatus* does not contain a single defense of toleration. There are several. I want to consider some of these in turn.

Toleration and the Bible

The greatest obstacle to toleration and freedom of thought derives from the power of religion, especially revealed religion, over human life. The greatest single prejudice, the prejudice underlying all prejudice, is the belief in the revealed authority of the Scripture. In order, then, to liberate the reader from this authority, it is necessary to cast a kind of systematic doubt on the credibility of the stories and narratives contained in Scripture. It could be said that Spinoza took Descartes' method of systematic doubt and applied it far more radically than even Descartes had intended to the subject matter of theology. The purpose of the *Tractatus* seems nothing less than an attempt to replace the Bible and its authoritative interpreters with the authority of our natural human reason.

The principle of Spinoza's biblical criticism is that the method of reading Scripture is no different from the method of studying nature (*TTP*, 98 [6]). The "book of nature" and the "book of books" are subject to the same causal laws and processes. The student of the Bible must approach his work in much the same manner as a physicist seeking to understand some natural phenomenon. For Spinoza, this means essentially undertaking a kind of natural history of Scripture. It is an invitation to a type of contextual reasoning about the Bible, understanding it in terms of the time, place, and circumstance in which it was written. It requires the biblical scholar to have a thorough knowledge of the Hebrew language, to note all passages that seem obscure or inconsistent with one another, and to relate the context of each book of the Bible to known facts about the life and character of the author as well as its subsequent reception. Spinoza initiates a method that would today be called "canon formation," showing how the many diverse works that make up the Scripture came to be unified into one body and accepted as sacred texts (*TTP*, 99-101 [15-23]).

Spinoza uses this historical method to show that the Scripture is an eminently human work that contains a host of fallacies and contradictions. Following the examples of Hobbes and La Peyrère, he takes elaborate pains to deny the Mosaic authorship of the Pentateuch.[20] Spinoza makes much of the fact that Moses could not be the sole author of the work for the reason that the last chapters of the book of Deuteronomy record his death and funeral (*TTP*, 121, [17]). He points to repeated references to Moses in the third person as sufficient evidence for him to doubt Mosaic authorship (*TTP*, 121 [15]). Instead, he concludes that the work must have been compiled several centuries after the time of Moses by subsequent redactors, most likely the scribe Ezra.

In addition to the problems of disputed authorship, the Bible is a text that contains outright contradictions. Spinoza's proof text here is Samuel's denial and Jeremiah's affirmation that God repents his decisions (*TTP*, 184 [19]). Spinoza attributes these contradictions not to any properties of God, but to the different psychological states and dispositions of the prophets whose judgments they express. The prophets were not men of powerful intellect but of vivid imagination. The biblical texts provide ample evidence that the prophets were ignorant of the causal mechanisms of physical reality (*TTP*, 23-24, [30]). The power of prophecy implies not "a more perfect mind, but only a more vivid imagination," Spinoza declares at one point, adding later that the power of prophecy is not a gift from God but an unusual human talent something like the ability to compose poetry *ex tempore* (*TTP*, 21[25]) . There is no reason to believe, then, that prophets who claim to speak for God had great speculative powers or were the bearers of profound philosophical truths. Rather their prophecies varied with their individual temperaments and prejudices and expressed "quite ordinary opinions about God" (*TTP*, 37 [31]) .

Spinoza's skepticism about Scripture is clearly intended to diminish its authority in the eyes of its readers. A work that contains so many anachronisms and contradictions cannot be uniformly believed without falling into absurdity. He distinguishes between "hieroglyphic" works like the Bible which require elaborate and painstaking historical reconstruction from "intelligible" works like Euclid's *Elements* whose meaning is self-evident to anyone who can follow a chain of argument from premise to conclusion (*TTP*, 253, note). No one needs to be a profound student of the Greek language or ancient history in order to understand the properties of a triangle. But the content of biblical narrative is something entirely different. Here one needs the skills of the linguist, the social psychologist, and even the archaeologist if one is to make sense of the bizarre and often inexplicable happenings recorded there. When suitably reconstructed, the Bible presents itself as a work of imaginative literature no different from that found among many ancient peoples. He even compares the story of Elijah to the goings-on he claims to recall from the works of Ovid and the tales of Orlando Furioso (*TTP*, 110 [61]).

Spinoza is not, however, a complete skeptic. He is thoroughly skeptical about religion and its ability to arrive at truth claims. He is not skeptical about reason and the possibility of rational truth. In the fifteenth chapter of the *Tractatus,* he distinguishes between the dogmatists who believe that "the meaning of Scripture must be accommodated to reason" and the skeptics who believe that "reason must be accommodated to Scripture" (*TTP*, 180 [1]). The dogmatists, like Maimonides, seek to turn Scripture into a repository of important metaphysical and scientific truths. Those aspects of the Bible that cannot be squared with the claims of reason must be interpreted allegorically until they conform, whereas Spinoza's argument is that this not only does violence to the text but, more importantly, it strains our credulity. A case in point occurs in a biblical passage (Joshua, 10:11) where it appears that the earth stands still in the heavens to which Spinoza rhetorically replies, "are we to believe that Joshua, a soldier, was also skilled in astronomy?" (*TTP*, 36 [27]). The attempt to make Scripture speak the language of reason leads to the creation of a new philosophical clerisy claiming infallibility for itself in matters of textual interpretation. Spinoza adds the stinging rejoinder that the creation of this new scholarly class of priests and pontiffs would more likely lead men to laughter than veneration (*TTP*, 114 [78-79]).

Skepticism remains an even worse alternative than dogmatism. Skepticism, as Spinoza understands it, is not so much skeptical about the claims of Scripture but about the capacity of reason. Overly impressed by an awareness of human fallibility, skepticism leads to an abnegation of reason or at least a subordination of reason to the non-rational claims of the Bible. Spinoza tries to resolve this difference by arguing for a radical separation of reason and revelation, philosophy and Scripture. "Neither ought to be handmaid of the other" (*TTP*, 10 [27]). The result of this separation is that philosophy is assigned the sphere of rational truth whereas religion teaches piety and obedience or, put another way, the Bible is denied any share in the truth.

Toleration and Civil Religion

It is only after the Bible has been subjected to a thoroughgoing critique that Spinoza is able to make the case for toleration on theological grounds. When suitably, that is rationally, reconstructed, Scripture is said to yield a "universal faith" (*fides universalis*) that might serve as a civil theology for the modern democratic state. This universal faith is to be distinguished from two other kinds of religion discussed throughout the *Tractatus*. The first is the religion of the multitude identified with superstition and a belief in a supernatural revelation. This is the religion of the imagination that maintains its adherents in a perpetual state of fear and credulity. The second is the religion of the philosophers circumscribed only by the "natural divine law." This is a religion of pure, unaided reason that requires neither any historical narrative or the performance of any particular ceremonial rites. But the *Tractatus* is not written with the philosopher in mind, but only with readers of the "prudent" sort. Such readers will require a combination of philosophical as well as non-philosophical reasons for the practice of toleration.

The content of Spinoza's universal faith is strikingly minimalist. It is comprised of seven "dogmas" or articles which include such traditional attributes as God's existence, unity, omnipresence and omnipotence, as well as moral qualities like the belief in individual salvation and the forgiveness of sin (*TTP*, 177-78 [25-28]). These dogmas are set forth not so much as a catechism to be believed as a framework for right action. The core of Spinoza's new religion is the command to practice acts of justice and charity which he interprets to mean toleration and the non-persecution of others. The *Tractatus* attempts to provide this unprecedented liberation theology with a sheen of traditional respectability by presenting it as derived from precepts allegedly common to both Judaism and Christianity. Basing this religion on a distillation of the teachings of both the Hebrew prophets and the Christian apostles, Spinoza hoped to use the *fides universalis* to underwrite a new kind of political order that would be tolerant to all religious sects, both Jew and Gentile alike.

Two features of this universal faith are especially worth noting. First, Spinoza maintains that in cases of religious conflict, it is the sovereign that has ultimate authority and right of intepretation. Piety, he remarks, should be "accommodated to the peace and utility of the state" which "must be determined solely by the supreme powers" (*TTP*, 229 [2]). Even still, Spinoza wants to limit the ability of the sovereign to interfere with religious observances and practices only if the common good is threatened or at stake. "The well-being of the people is the supreme law, to which all other laws, both human and divine, must be accommodated" (*TTP*, 232 [24]). The alternative to conceding interpretive rights of Scripture to the sovereign is to concede them to ecclesiastical authorities which can only result in conflict and war. Spinoza further contends that it is only the outward forms of religious practice that remain within the public domain. While speech and ritual have a public dimension that cannot escape the sovereign's notice, the "internal worship" of God and piety itself are within everyone's private rights and over this the individual remains master (*TTP*, 229 [3]).

The second aspect of Spinoza's universal faith is that adherence to it is said in no way to impinge upon or limit one's freedom of mind. The dogmas of his civil faith are precisely that, a matter of faith, not rational belief. Acts of charity and justice are all that the Bible commands, otherwise leaving individuals to think what they like on matters speculative and scientific (*TTP*, 165 [34, 37], 168 [8], 174 [6], 179 [33]). The essence of this religion is that the individual retains "the greatest freedom to philosophize" and to think what he likes "about anything" (*TTP*, 180 [39]). It is said to follow that these dogmas can be avowed for practical purposes without conferring on them any epistemic validity. The *fides universalis* "does not require dogmas which are true as much as it does dogmas which are pious" (*TTP*, 176 [20]). The best faith is not possessed by the person with the best arguments but by who best displays the fruits of toleration. Because Spinoza's universal religion concerns deeds rather than opinions, this religion contains nothing offensive to reason. Thus he avers with confidence that there are no dogmas in the catholic or universal religion to which "honest men" cannot with good conscience subscribe (*TTP*, 177 [22]).

There is a clear connection between Spinoza's universal religion and the prudent reader identified in the letter to Oldenburg. The prudent reader stands between two alternatives, the *vulgus* who are by definition controlled by their passions and imagination and for whom the *Tractatus* would be useless and the philosopher for whom its teaching of toleration and love of neighbor will be redundant. The philosopher needs no civil creed to practice justice and charity as these are intrinsic to the activity of philosophy itself. But the audience for the *Tractatus* is at best comprised of would-be philosophers who are at most imperfectly rational and who require additional support from Scripture or revelation. However Spinoza's defense of the Scriptural case for toleration is not his last word on the subject. For this we must turn to his teaching regarding nature.

Toleration and Natural Right

Spinoza's defense of toleration and freedom of opinion grows out of his teachings on natural right. Natural right, he declares in the *Tractatus*, is that supreme rule or law according to which "each thing strives to preserve itself in its own state, as far as it can by its own power, and does this, not on account of anything else, but only of itself" (*TTP*, 189 [2]). The natural right, then, of every organism derives from an inner-drive or *conatus* which leads it to preserve its own existence. We all have certain biologically implanted powers to preserve and protect our lives and these powers are coextensive with our natural right. Spinoza wants here to deprive natural right of any specific moral or ethical obligations. He denies that natural right is specific to the human species but attaches to all natural kinds. Fish are by nature fit for swimming and the big ones eat the little by virtue of their natural right (*TTP*, 189 [2]).

Spinoza's account of natural right and the state of nature bears a striking resemblance to the work of his greatest contemporary, Thomas Hobbes.[21] Spinoza is generally thought to have borrowed from Hobbes the latter's views on natural right and the state of nature. Certainly, neither man could be accused of under-valuing the role of power and the importance of self-interest as a motive for action. Both made use of the metaphor of the social contract as authorizing the foundations of society and regarded the sovereign as an artificial creation of human agreement. Furthermore, both men were absolutists in the sense that they believed only a powerful national sovereign could protect the liberty of the individual from the organized pressure of mobilized groups armed with doctrine and text. For neither was the sovereign a threat to individual freedom, but a protector of liberty from clerical strongmen and bullies.

Nevertheless, Spinoza departs from Hobbes in at least two important respects. First, Spinoza was the first figure in modern political philosophy to declare democratic government as the *optima Republica*. Only when our natural right is transferred to society in its collective capacity can we be assured that the conditions of the social contract are fair and equal for all. Democratic government can insure against the dangers of arbitrary rule arising from the investiture of absolute power in the hands of one person or body of persons.

Second, unlike the Hobbesian sovereign who exercises extensive censorship rights over what doctrines are fit to be taught, the purpose of Spinoza's sovereign is to guarantee the widest latitude for freedom of expression. Democracy is the kind of regime most compatible with the new type of autonomous or liberated individual. The kind of democracy advocated by Spinoza is a liberal democracy, that is, a regime that extends not just a grudging toleration to human diversity, but regards the freedom of the mind to think what we like and say what we think as the very object of civil association.

It is perhaps difficult to see how a teaching of liberal toleration can be derived from premises that baldly equate right with might. But this is exactly what Spinoza sets out to do. Rather than using the argument from natural right to enlarge the scope of sovereign power, he focuses instead on the limitations of that power. The concluding chapter of the *Tractatus* begins with the following observation: "If it were as easy to command men's minds as it is their tongues, every ruler would govern in safety and no rule would be violent. For everyone would live according to the disposition of the rulers, and only in accordance with their decree would people judge what is true or false, good or evil, right or wrong" (*TTP*, 239 [1]).

Toleration is said to follow from the doctrine of natural right strictly understood. If the right of nature means the liberty to do whatever our power permits, then by the right of nature the sovereign's power is restricted to the control of external behavior. Because no one's mind can lie wholly at the disposition of another, it follows that the sovereign must leave the content of the mind to the discretion of the individual. Spinoza's awareness of the limitations on the scope of sovereign power begins from the recognition that human behavior is easier to control than the mind, for "it cannot happen that a mind should be absolutely subject to the control of someone else" (*TTP*, 239 [2]). The attempt to extend sovereign power to the control of thought and judgment is condemned by the *Tractatus* as tyrannical and violent. Questions of truth and falsity, right and wrong, belong to each person's discretion "which no one can surrender even if he wishes to" (*TTP*, 239 [3]).

At this point Spinoza continues to speak in the language of hard-boiled realism. His arguments so far have been couched solely in terms of the power that the sovereign has at its disposal. The emphasis is not on the rights of the subject, but on the power of the sovereign. Note that Spinoza's judgment about the limitation of sovereign power does not derive from any belief in the sacred or privileged status of the mind but from the definition of what our power permits. Action and behavior can be controlled more easily than thought and opinion. Spinoza does not consider here the possibility that truly tyrannical regimes may and in fact often do control the minds of their subjects to a considerable degree. Presumably, had he known of or contemplated the possibilities for thought control posed by modern propaganda and advertising techniques, he would have seen nothing to prohibit the sovereign from using these tools to enhance his power.

Still, these considerations were not altogether beyond Spinoza's ken. Earlier in the *Tractatus* he remarks that "though hearts cannot be commanded in the same way tongues can, still hearts are *to some extent* under the command of the supreme power" (*TTP*, 202 [9]; emphasis added). Spinoza acknowledges that emotions do not arise at the express command of the sovereign, but "experience abundantly testifies" to the extent to which the authority of the office may influence subjects so that "the great majority of men believe, love, and hate whatever [the sovereign] wills" (*TTP*, 202 [9]). How far Spinoza believed that the thoughts and passions of one's subjects can be shaped by political power is not clear. By the end of the *Tractatus*, however, he is emphasizing less what the sovereign can control than what evades his power. The attempt to control thought is wrong not because it is immoral, but because it is inherently self-defeating.

Toleration and Human Diversity

Spinoza's arguments from natural right do not constitute his only defense of toleration. The *Tractatus* also includes a lively awareness of the place of human diversity in the total economy of human life. Far from producing harmony and consensus, attempts to control thought breed conflict and ultimately revolution. Dangers to society are more likely to come from misplaced efforts to impose unity than from allowing freedom of thought and opinion. He makes this point in the opening paragraphs of the *Tractatus:*

> As for rebellions which are aroused under the pretext of religion, they surely arise only because laws are instituted regarding speculative matters, opinions are regarded as wicked and condemned as crimes, and their defenders and followers sacrificed, not to the public well-being, but only to the hate and barbarism of their opponents. But if, by the law of the state, only deeds were condemned and words went unpunished, such rebellions could not be clothed in any pretext of right, nor controversies turned into rebellions (*TTP*, 7 [11]).

The causes of diversity are woven into the very fabric of human nature. There is, to begin with, the sheer variety of human judgment. Spinoza admits that judgments can be biased in many ways. As he says with brutal candor, what leads one person to piety and religion leads another to laughter and contempt (*TTP*, 11 [28]). This difference of opinion can be carried to "almost incredible lengths." Matters of judgment are like matters of taste; "there are as many differences between men's heads as there are between their palates" (*TTP*, 239 [4]). Spinoza concedes that while sovereigns may wish to brand as criminal ideas that do not accord with their own, "they will never be able to bring it about that men do not make their own judgment about everything, according to their own mentality" (*TTP*, 240 [6]).

It follows from the above that efforts to control speech must fail. Not only are our faculties diverse, but we also have a misplaced confidence in our own opinions. From the "most knowledgeable" to the most feeble, it is a "common vice of men to entrust their plans to others, even if there is need for secrecy" (*TTP*, 240 [9]). Human beings are almost incurable magpies so that any government seeking to limit what people can say would be deemed not only harsh but in violation of a universal tendency of human nature.

It is the very "obstinacy" of human nature that militates against a policy of uniformity. People do not like being told what to do and generally "endure nothing with greater impatience than that opinions they believe to be true should be considered criminal" (*TTP*, 244 [29]). Furthermore, resistance is less likely to come from the greedy, the sycophantic, and the "weak-minded" than from those whose appetite for liberty has been whetted by good education, moral integrity, and virtue. The very constitution of human nature is such that laws made about opinions invariably do less to restrain the wicked than "to aggravate the honorable" and alienate "those who act in a manner worthy of a free man" (*TTP*, 244 [30]). Criminalizing opinions will invariably make it appear honorable to take up the mantle of revolution.

Toleration and Character

Spinoza's defense of toleration begins from an awareness that the mind cannot and therefore should not be controlled. Toleration seems to be deduced from the conditions of his strict naturalism. Even Spinoza's recogition of human diversity as a reason for toleration sounds more like a concession to human weakness than a celebration of freedom. What distinguishes the *Tractatus*, however, is not simply the pragmatic realization that toleration is good policy, but a fully-developed sense that freedom of mind is necessary for the development of a flourishing state of character. The boldness of Spinoza's conception is not that liberty of opinion is useful for securing peace and stability but that liberty is a central component of the human good.

The *Tractatus* is perhaps the first work in Western political theory to defend the proposition that the exercise of free speech is the goal of social policy. Free speech is not, for Spinoza, an end in itself; it is instrumental to the attainment of certain traits of character such as the development of individual judgment and personal autonomy. "The end of the state," Spinoza boldly declares, "is not to change men from rational beings into beasts or automata, but rather that their mind and body should perform all their functions safely and that they should use their reason freely" (*TTP*, 241 [12]). Freedom of speech is desirable because it fosters a certain type of human being with a certain kind of character. We might call this person the autonomous or liberated self.

The type of liberated individual Spinoza helped to create is now a familiar feature of our intellectual landscape, inhabiting many books of moral philosophy and imaginative literature. As we have indicated already, the autonomous self is one who strives to be free from externally imposed authority, who prefers the examined life to dependence on faith or tradition, and who seeks a life of self-mastery and a reliance on the force of reason alone. More than anything else the free individual values the *vita activa* and the means necessary to sustain it. In the *Ethics* Spinoza acknowledges that all human life is subject to the emotions *(affectus)* but that some of these emotions are passive and other are active. The passions control us and we submit to them, but actions contribute to our sense of power and autonomy.

The central life-enhancing virtue Spinoza calls by the comprehensive name of *fortitudo*:

> All actions that follow from affects related to the Mind insofar as it understands I relate to Strength of character [*fortitudo*], which I divide into Tenacity and Nobility. For by Tenacity I understand the desire by which each one strives, solely from the dictate of reason, to preserve his being. By Nobility I understand the Desire by which each one strives, solely from the dictate of reason, to aid other men and join them to him in friendship (*E*, III, P59 S).

Spinoza's model of the *vir fortis* is put forward as the basis for a new ethic of humanitarianism. This humanitarianism which seeks not only the individual's own moral advantage but to aid other men and join them in friendship is used in specific contrast to the older Aristotelian notion of magnanimity or greatness of soul. There is a universal or cosmopolitan character to the virtue of *fortitudo* which Spinoza makes the basis for his vision of a liberal society marked by the free flow of ideas and opinions. The humanitarianism of Spinoza consists in his argument for a harmony of interests between reason and society, or between the class of philosophers and humanity as a whole.

Toleration and the Commercial Republic

Spinoza's ethic of humanitarianism displays his marked preference for universal, cosmopolitan, or "open societies" at the expense of purely local, traditional, or particularistic moralities. The *Tractatus* draws an explicit connection between freedom of speech and intellectual progress. The exchange of ideas and opinions both within and between nations contributes to the intellectual, moral, and material benefits of all. The arts and sciences, he contends, can only be cultivated by those who have a free judgment (*TTP*, 243 [26]). Like Descartes, Spinoza saw the tremendous potential locked inside the emergent sciences of nature, especially medicine, as a tool for increasing the ease and comfort of life. He advises his readers not to "despise" the science of mechanics for the benefits it can confer on society (*TEI*, 9 [15]).

Spinoza also recognized that intellectual and material progress do not take place in a vacuum. The progress of the arts and sciences is linked to issues of trade and commerce. Intellectual freedom is possible only in an environment that encourages commercial freedom. The enlightened republic is necessarily a commercial republic. The *Tractatus* concludes with a ringing praise for the city of Amsterdam which, along with Venice, was regarded by enlightened Europeans of the 17th century as the very model for the commercial or trading society.[22] Amsterdam is a place where the fruits of liberty are available for all to see. Free trade is both a cause and consequence of this liberty. The commercial republic is characterized by freedom in all of its many dimension:

> Take the city of Amsterdam, which knows by experience the fruits of this liberty, among them great growth and the admiration of all nations. For in this most flourishing Republic, this most outstanding city, all men, of whatever nation or sect, live in the greatest harmony. In deciding to entrust their goods to someone, they are concerned to know only whether the person is rich or poor, and whether he is accustomed to acting in good faith or deceptively . . . There is, without exception, no sect so hated that its followers are not protected by the public authority of the magistrates and their forces, provided that they harm no one, give each person his due, and live honorably (*TTP*, 246 [10]).

Spinoza's commercial republic is based on an emphatic rejection of the older classical republicanism theorized in the writings of Plato, and Aristotle and revived by several Renaissance humanists. The ancient republic was a small polis-like body characterized by a high degree of moral and religious homogeneity. The classical polis was furthermore marked by a severity and moral austerity demanding from its citizens a self-sacrificing devotion to the commonweal. Spinoza departs from this tradition above all in his support for individual liberty and toleration of religious and intellectual diversity. In addition to self-government, a cardinal ingredient of liberty is the freedom of property and exchange, something alien to the civic humanist tradition. In Spinoza's republic the urban patriciate is favored over the landed squirearchy. A society in which everyone is engaged in commerce is more likely to promote peace than destructive wars of ambition. A century before the argument for commerce became fashionable, Spinoza understood the attractions of *doux commerce*.[23]

The *Tractatus* indicates its preference for the modern commerical republic in two key respects. First, Spinoza evinces none of the fears of "corruption" by the new commercial classes that exercised many of his contemporaries. For the classical republicans, commerce was thought to bring both economic dependence and moral decay, but for Spinoza it was a source of popular enlightenment and an enlarged sphere of liberty. Second, unlike the civic humanists who often favored harsh sumptuary laws to control for luxury, Spinoza denies that such laws can be effective in controlling forms of private vice. He even encourages the propagation of avarice (*avaritia*) as beneficial to society. Although avarice was strictly prohibited by the ancient moral tradition as *pleonexia*, "the vice of wanting more," and the biblical tradition as *cupiditas* or greed, Spinoza, like Mandeville and Adam Smith, regards it as having beneficial consequences for the welfare of the nation.[24]

Only in the following century would Spinoza's vision of the commercial republic bear fruit in the works of Montesquieu, Hume, Smith, and others. For them increasing trade was offered as something that "polishes" and "refines" manners, fosters peace and toleration, and discourages ferocity and xenophobic zeal. Everywhere the commercial republic was proposed as a more humane alternative to the regimes of civic and Christian virtue that had dominated Europe for centuries. Such a regime would favor commercial over landed interests, the city over the country, the enjoyment of life rather than its mortification, a disposition to cultivate freedom rather than regret it -- these were the ends that Spinoza's commercial republic hoped to make possible.

NOTES:

1. The term is taken from Leo Strauss, *Spinoza's Critique of Religion*, trans. E. M. Sinclair (New York: Schocken, 1965), 1-31; see also Claude Lefort, "The Permanence of the Theologico-Political?" *Democracy and Political Theory*, trans. David Macey (Minneapolis: University of Minnesota Press, 1988), 213-55.

2. John Locke, *First Treatise* in *Two Treatises of Government*, ed. Peter Laslett (Cambridge: Cambridge University Press, 1960), par. 58, 219.

3. Throughout this essay I have used Gebhardt's edition of the *Tractatus* (*TTP*) which appears in volume three of the *Spinoza Opera* (Heidelberg: Carl Winter, 1925); references are to the page number and the Bruder section numbers in brackets. Translations are from Edwin Curley's as yet unpublished edition. All other cited works of Spinoza are from the *Collected Works*, ed. and trans. Edwin Curley (Princeton: Princeton University Press, 1985), vol. 1; references follow the standard pattern.

4. Upon reading the *Tractatus*, Hobbes remarked that the work "had cut through him a barre's length, for he durst not write so boldly;" see John Aubrey, *Brief Lives*, ed. Andrew Clark (Oxford: Clarendon Press, 1898), vol. 1, 357; Locke in his "Second Reply to the Bishop of Worcester" remarked that "I am not so well read in Hobbes and Spinoza" adding a word about "those justly decried names;" see *The Works of John Locke*, (London: Tegg, 1823), vol. 4, 477. Locke's remark may be taken as slightly disingenuous given that he had a copy of Spinoza's *Tractatus* in his library; see Peter Laslett, "Introduction" *Two Treatises*, Appendix B. For English and Dutch intellectual contacts during this period see Rosalie L. Colie, *Light and Enlightenment: A Study of the Cambridge Platonists and the Dutch Arminians* (Cambridge: Cambridge University Press, 1957).

5. Gilles Deleuze, *Spinoza: Practical Philosophy*, trans. Robert Hurley (San Francisco: City Lights, 1988), 10.

6. Gerard Vallée, ed. *The Spinoza Conversations between Lessing and Jacobi*, trans. G. Vallée, J. B. Lawson, and C. G. Chapple (Lanham, MD: University Press of America, 1988); the Spinoza controversy is discussed by David Bell, *Spinoza in Germany from 1670 to the Age of Goethe* (London: Institute of Germanic Studies, 1984); Sylvain Zac, *Spinoza en Allemagne: Mendelssohn, Lessing et Jacobi* (Paris: Meridiens-Klincksieck, 1989); see also Frederick Beiser, *The Fate of Reason: German Philosophy from Kant to Fichte* (Cambridge: Cambridge University Press, 1987).

7. The documents surrounding Spinoza's excommunication have been gathered in I. S. Revah, *Spinoza et le Dr. Juan de Prado* (Paris: Mouton, 1959); for a recent retelling of the story see Yirmiyahu Yovel, *Spinoza and Other Heretics*, vol. 1: *The Marrano of Reason* (Princeton: Princeton University Press, 1989), 40-84; the best account of the Marrano community in Amsterdam at the time of Spinoza is Yosef Kaplan, *From Christianity to Judaism: The Story of Isaac Orobio de Castro*, trans. Raphael Lowe (Oxford: Oxford University Press, 1989).

8. The major work is by Herbert H. Rown, *John de Witt, Grand Pensionary of Holland, 1625-1672* (Princeton: Princeton University Press, 1978).

9. For a comprehensive account of the Dutch theological situation at the time of Spinoza, see Leszek Kolakowski, *Chrétiens sans église: La conscience religieuse et le lien confessional au XVIIe siècle* (Paris: Gallimard, 1969); see also Rosalie Colie, *Light and Enlightenment: A Study of the Cambridge Platonists and the Dutch Arminians* (Cambridge: Cambridge University Press, 1957); Madelaine Frances, *Spinoza dans le pays néerlandais de la seconde moitié du XVIIe siècle* (Paris: Alcan, 1937).

10. For the gruesome details of the murder of the de Witts and Spinoza's response, see Rowen, *John de Witt*, 875-82, 885-86.

11. A. Wolf, ed. *The Correspondence of Spinoza* (New York: Dial Press, 1927), 206.

12. The question of Spinoza's audience and manner of writing has been taken up by me at length in Steven B. Smith, *Spinoza, Liberalism, and the Question of Jewish Identity* (New Haven: Yale University Press, 1997), chap. 2; for other works from which I have benefitted, see Leo Strauss, "How to Study Spinoza's 'Theologico-Political Treatise," *Persecution and the Art of Writing* (Chicago: University of Chicago Press, 1988), 142-201; Edwin Curley, "Homo Audax: Leibniz, Oldenburg, and the *TTP*," *Studia Leibnitiana*, 27 (1990): 277-312; Yovel, *Spinoza and Other Heretics*, 128-52.

13. For the literary construction of the new individualism, see Ian Watt, *Myths of Modern Individualism* (Cambridge: Cambridge University Press, 1996); Spinoza's concept of personal autonomy has lent itself over the years to powerful literary expression, see Isaac Bashevis Singer, *The Spinoza of Market Street* (Philadelphia: Jewish Publication Society of America, 1961).

14. Edwin Curley, "Notes on a Neglected Masterpiece (II): The 'Theologico-Political Treatise' as a Prolegomenon to the 'Ethics," *Central Themes in Early Modern Philosophy*, ed. J. A. Cover and Mark Kulstad (Indianapolis: Hackett, 1990), 109-59.

15. See Harry Wolfson, *The Philosophy of Spinoza* (Cambridge: Harvard University Press, 1934), vol. 1, vii who refers to Spinoza as "the last of the medievals and the first of the moderns." Richard McKeon, *The Philosophy of Spinoza* (New York: Longmans, 1928), 15 remarks that Spinoza "is a contemporary of the first of the philosophers we have come to call modern, but in a significant sense his intellectual fellowship is with the medievals."

16. G. W. F. Hegel, *Lectures on the History of Philosophy*, trans. E. S. Haldane and Frances Simson (London: Routledge, 1968), vol. 3, 283: "Spinoza is made a testing point in modern philosophy, so that it may really be said: you are either a Spinozist or not a philosopher at all." Louis Althusser, *Lire le Capital* (Paris: Maspero, 1973), vol. 1, 128 who calls Spinoza "le seul ancetre direct de Marx."

17. Hermann Cohen, "Spinoza über Staat und Religion, Judentum und Christentum," *Jüdische Schriften*, ed. Bruno Strauss (Berlin: Schwetschke, 1924), vol. 3, 290-372; Emmanuel Levinas, "The Spinoza Case," *Difficult Freedom: Essays in Judaism*, trans. Sean Hand (London: Athlone, 1990), 106-10.

18. See David Ben-Gurion's statement that "Under the conditions of the time and in the place the ban was perhaps justified . . . but as the condemnation of Socrates by an Athenian court did not turn that great Greek philosopher into a non-Greek, so the rabbinical ban in Amsterdam in the seventeenth century cannot deprive the Jewish people of its greatest and most original thinker;" cited in Joseph Dunner, *Baruch Spinoza and Western Democracy* (New York: Philosophical Library, 1955), vii; see also Ze'ev Levy, *Baruch or Benedict: On Some Jewish Aspects of Spinoza's Philosophy* (New York: Peter Lang, 1989).

19. The title of the chapter (in Libera Republica unicuique et senitre, quae velit, et quae sentiat, dicere licere) is taken from Tacitus, *History*, 1, i, 4; the passage is also used by Hume as an epigraph to his *A Treatise of Human Nature*; for the uses of Tacitus during the early modern period, see Arnaldo Momigliano, "Tacitus and the Tacitist Tradition," *The Classical Foundations of Modern Historiography* (Berkeley: University of California Press, 1990), 109-31; see also Chaim Wirszubski, "Spinoza's Debt to Tacitus," *Scripta Hierosolymitana* 2 (1955): 176-86.

20. Smith, *Spinoza, Liberalism, and the Question of Jewish Identity*, 56-58; for the influence of Peyrère on Spinoza, see Richard Popkin, *Isaac La Peyrère (1596-1676): His Life, Work, and Influence* (Leiden: E. J. Brill, 1987); see also Yovel, *Spinoza and Other Heretics*, 80-84; Kaplan, *From Christianity to Judaism*, 132-33.

21. I have treated Spinoza's relation to Hobbes at some length in Steven B. Smith, "Spinoza's Democratic Turn: Chapter 16 of the 'Theologico-Political Treatise," *Review of Metaphysics* 48 (1994): 359-88; for some other works addressing this relation, see Strauss, *Spinoza's Critique of Religion*, 229-38; Robert J. McShea, *The Political Philosophy of Spinoza* (New York: Columbia University Press, 1968), 137-55; Hilail Gilden, "Spinoza and the Political Problem," *Spinoza: A Collection of Critical Essays*, ed. Marjorie Greene (New York: Doubleday, 1973), 377-87; Douglas J. Den Uyl and Stuart D. Warner, "Liberalism and Hobbes and Spinoza," *Studia Spinoziana* 3 (1987): 261-317.

22. See Eco O. G. Haitsma Mulier, *The Myth of Venice and Dutch Republican Thought in the Seventeenth Century* (Assen: Van Gorcum, 1980); see also Hans Blom, "Virtue and Republicanism: Spinoza's Political Philosophy in the Context of the Dutch Republic," *Republiken und Republikanismus im Europa der Frühen Neuzeit*, ed. Halmut G. Koenigsberger (Munich: R. Oldenbourg, 1988), 195-212.

23. For the uses of this term, see Albert O. Hirshman, *The Passions and the Interests: Political Arguments for Capitalism Before its Triumph* (Princeton: Princeton University Press, 1977), 56-63; see also Pierre Manent, *La cité de l'homme* (Paris: Fayard, 1994), 53-72.

24. One of the very few early thinkers to note the importance of commerce for Spinoza was Vico, who disapproved, noting that "Spinoza speaks of the commonwealth as if it were a society of hucksters"; see Giambattista Vico, *The New Science*, trans. T. H. Bergin and M. H. Fisch (Ithaca: Cornell University Press, 1970), par. 335, 54. This association of the commercial society with "hucksterism" finds an important expression in Marx's "On the Jewish Question," *Marx-Engels Reader*, ed. Robert Tucker (New York: Norton, 1978), 47-52; for an interesting comparison between Spinoza's and Marx's views on liberalism see Joel Schwartz, "Liberalism and the Jewish Connection: A Study of Spinoza and the Young Marx," *Political Theory* 13 (1985): 58-89.

7

MONOPOLIZING FAITH: THE LEVELLERS, RIGHTS, AND RELIGIOUS TOLERATION

Alan Craig Houston

I. Introduction

The Levellers were the first modern political movement to organize around the idea of popular sovereignty, call for a scheme of national representation based on frequent elections and a broad franchise, and advocate a written constitution based on a modern conception of rights.[1] They endorsed freedom of conscience, a ban on military conscription, the right against self-incrimination, the right to trial by a jury of one's peers, freedom of trade, and equality before the law.

The Leveller movement was intimately connected with the lives of its three principal leaders: John Lilburne, the younger son of a Durham gentleman and a Civil War veteran; Richard Overton, an occasional actor and former student at Cambridge; and William Walwyn, a successful merchant and—after the Restoration—popular folk physician. Lilburne and Walwyn first met in July 1645; Lilburne and Overton first met in October 1645. For four years these men cooperated in a campaign to reform England's social, political, religious, and economic institutions. By autumn 1649, however, the movement they spearheaded had been crushed by the consolidated power of Oliver Cromwell and the Rump Parliament.

The Levellers drew support from the congregations of the gathered churches of London and its suburbs, and radical soldiers in the New Model Army.[2] They sought influence through petitions and pamphlets. They organized campaigns, funded through subscriptions, to draft and circulate petitions throughout England. They claimed to have obtained thousands of signatures, and once boasted that they could have had 100,000 signatures had their efforts not been impeded by force.[3] They also wrote and published over 100 pamphlets. Their strategy was personal and performative: through dramatic accounts of their own sufferings, they exhorted English men and women to identify with their cause.

The term "Leveller" had been used in the early seventeenth century to describe participants in popular anti-enclosure riots.[4] It was first applied to Lilburne, Overton, Walwyn, and their supporters by Charles I in a declaration of 11

November 1647. Marchamont Nedham, at that time an effective royalist propagandist, quickly seized on the label: it was "a most apt title for such a despicable and desperate knot to be known by, that endeavour to cast down and level the enclosures of nobility, gentry and property, to make us all even, so that every Jack shall view with a gentleman and every gentleman be made a Jack." A Leveller was someone who sought to destroy rank, subvert property, and bring all to an equally low common denominator. The Levellers repeatedly denied this charge. As Lilburne once remarked, they were "Levellers" only insofar as they hoped "that all alike may be Levelled to, and bound by the Law."[5]

The *Agreement of the People* was the official manifesto of the Leveller movement. It was published three times: in November 1647, after the expulsion of conservative Presbyterians from London; in December 1648, after Pride's Purge and the collapse of negotiations between Levellers and Army grandees; and in May 1649, from jail, after the execution of Charles and the declaration of an English republic. In these shifting contexts, the *Agreement* served a variety of purposes: it was a petition of grievances, a declaration of rights, an instrument of public instruction, and a platform for political reform.

Scholarly attention has focused on those clauses of the *Agreement* concerned with the franchise. This is partly a consequence of the practical context within which modern historiographical conventions concerning the English Civil War were developed. As David Wootton has observed, it was "no accident" that the revival of interest in the Levellers coincided with the rise of universal suffrage, the spread of socialism, and the creation of the welfare state.[6] To many scholars—particularly in England—the *Agreement of the People* provided an historical touchstone for modern democratic movements and egalitarian reforms. It is also a reflection of the decisive influence of the Clarke manuscripts, discovered at the end of the nineteenth century and containing an astonishingly complete transcript of the debate of the General Council of the Army assembled at Putney in the fall of 1647 to debate the *Agreement*. In a heated exchange over the franchise, Thomas Rainborough's riveting claim that "the poorest he that is in England, hath a life to live, as the greatest he" was pitted against Henry Ireton's no less commanding assertion that only those with "a permanent fixed interest in this kingdom" were entitled to vote.[7]

Broadening the franchise was of unquestionable importance to the Levellers. But it is not the only—and, arguably, not the most important—cause they championed. In this paper I seek to begin where the Levellers began, not with the franchise, but with religious toleration. At the heart of each draft of the *Agreement* was a call for toleration:

"That matters of Religion, and the wayes of Gods Worship, are not at all
intrusted by us to any humane power, because therein wee cannot remit or

exceed a tittle of what our Consciences dictate to be the mind of God, without wilfull sinne: nevertheless the publike way of instructing the Nation (so it be not compulsive) is referred to their discretion" (*An Agreement of the People*).

"We do not empower our Representatives to continue in force or make any Laws, Oaths, and covenants, whereby to compel by penalties or otherwise, any person to any thing in or about matters of Faith, Religion or Gods Worship, or to restrain any person from the professing his Faith, or exercise of Religion according to his conscience, in any house or place (except such as are or shall be set apart for the publick Worship): Nevertheless, the instruction or directing of the Nation in a publick way, for the matters of Faith, Worship or Discipline (so it be not compulsive, or expresse Popery) is referred to their discretion" (*Foundations of Freedom*).

"That we do not impower or entrust our said representatives to continue in force, or to make any Lawes, Oaths, or Covenants, whereby to compell by penalties or otherwise any person to any thing in or about matters of faith, Religion or Gods worship or to restrain any person from the profession of his faith, or exercise of Religion according to his Conscience, nothing having caused more distractions, and heart burnings in all ages, then persecution and molestation for matters of Conscience in and about Religion" (*An Agreement of the Free People of England*).[8]

The primary aim of these clauses was to deny Parliament the authority to create a uniform and compulsory national church. In the words of the third *Agreement*, "we do not impower or entrust our said representatives" to compel persons in "matters of Faith, Religion or Gods worship." This was the practical meaning of the claim that the right to religious liberty was inalienable.

Despite the Levellers' commitment to religious liberty, they were not opposed to the creation of a national church. In the words of the first *Agreement*, "the publike way of instructing the Nation (so it be not compulsive) is" properly within Parliament's "discretion." In contemporary terms, they sought "negative" toleration, or freedom from interference.[9] The practice of intolerance involved the application of penalties or sanctions to thoughts, words, or deeds. The national church envisioned by the Levellers was incapable of practicing intolerance. It could not compel men and women to worship; it could not compel men and women to tithe; it could not compel a parish to accept an unsuitable minister. The Levellers may have been the first to embrace that sly British strategy of encouraging liberal religious attitudes by establishing a church that no one must take seriously.[10]

Why should a nation tolerate religious diversity? To this question the Levellers presented two distinct answers. In the first *Agreement* they appealed to the sanctity of an individual's conscience: "wee cannot remit or exceed a tittle of what our Consciences dictate to be the mind of God, without wilful sinne." In the third *Agreement*, on the other hand, they appealed to the relationship between toleration and peace: "nothing having caused more distractions, and heart burnings in all ages, then persecution and molestation for matters of Conscience in and about Religion." The argument from conscience, in turn, has two distinct formulations. As a secular argument, it can appeal to the sanctity of conscience, the autonomy of the will, and respect for persons. As a religious argument, it can appeal to the individual's freedom to submit to God's will, and not to the will of another. Religious liberty existed within the bosom of a church whose members voluntarily submitted themselves to the authority of God. The argument from peace, by contrast, was straightforwardly *politique* in its formulation. Religious disagreement was the single greatest cause of civic disorder. Toleration was the precondition of peace.

Each of these positions is represented in scholarly traditions surrounding the Levellers. Whig and radical historians have argued that the Levellers based their arguments for toleration on the autonomy of the conscience. According to Theodore Pease, the Levellers based their "democratic ideals on their faith in the dignity and worth of the individual"; according to H.N. Brailsford, they stood for "a humane and secular republic."[11] More recently, revisionist historians have argued that the Levellers equated religious liberty with the freedom to submit to the will of God. In the words of J.C. Davis, "we should not automatically assume that liberty and authority are antithetical...we should not automatically identify liberty with personal autonomy or individual self-expression, self-realization." Indeed, "the claim of liberty of conscience had virtually nothing to do with a claim to direct or manage ourselves. It was a claim to be free to submit to the governance of God rather than to any other authority...The central argument for liberty of conscience was related to man's incapacity, rather than to his capacity for governing it."[12]

The argument from peace has been identified by post-revisionist historians of political thought. The clearest expression of this interpretation can be found in Richard Tuck's important study *Philosophy and Government 1572-1651*. According to Tuck, modern natural law theory originates in the political and intellectual crises of the late sixteenth century, particularly in the wars of religion. Skepticism and relativism—the lack of common ethical standards by which to judge governments and adjudicate controversies—was met through the language of natural jurisprudence and the principle of self-preservation. All just governments originate in the consent of the governed, and a nation cannot consent to its own destruction. A government that is destructive of the nation is, *ipso facto*, illegitimate. In this framework, political forms were evaluated according to pragmatic considerations. The basic test of an institution was instrumental: its capacity to advance the public interest. The boundaries of toleration were determined by practical necessities, and in particular by the grim lessons learned from religious civil war. Thus William Walwyn once asserted that "every man ought to have Liberty of Conscience of what Opinion soever...unless it be dangerous to the State."[13]

Each of these positions is also associated with a set of claims concerning the relationship between past and present. Historians who emphasize the role of the autonomy of the will in Leveller thought seek to identify, in a teleological fashion, ideals and aspirations that unite us with the past. To such scholars, the Levellers were the seventeenth-century vanguard of a more decent and humane future. They anticipated the U.S. Bill of Rights, the French Declaration of the Rights of Man and of the Citizen, and the U.N. Declaration of Human Rights. Historians who draw attention to the link between liberty and submission to God's will, on the other hand, seek in a resolutely anti-teleological fashion to identify ideas and arguments that separate us from the past. The Levellers were part of a world that has either been lost or forgotten. In the modern, constitutional, and secular world, we have lost sight of the relationship between religious liberty and "the freedom of God Almighty."[14] The sensibility motivating Leveller calls for religious toleration no longer exists. Scholars focusing on the relationship between toleration and peace, finally, seek to identify the core constituents of a world we have inherited and that continues to threaten us. It was in the seventeenth century that political writers first charted the moral and political contours of the modern state.[15]

Each of these interpretive positions excludes—and is meant to exclude—the others. Unfortunately, each also captures an important dimension of Leveller arguments. It is, of course, possible that the Levellers were simply inconsistent. But that ought to be an interpretive strategy of the last resort. The problem lies not in the thought of the Levellers, but in an extremely powerful but frustratingly intractable series of dichotomies that run throughout these interpretations. The alternatives are stark: the politics of conscience vs. the politics of peace; arguments that are conceptually rigorous vs. arguments that are causally plausible; arguments that are a priori and inflexible vs. arguments that are a posteriori and flexible; claims of right vs. the dictates of prudence; principles vs. pragmatism. These dichotomies are not simply an artifact of seventeenth-century historiography. They also inform contemporary moral and political thinking. As John Dunn has recently observed, arguments from autonomy—as in the writings of John Rawls and Ronald Dworkin—are morally strong, but causally implausible. Arguments from social utility, on the other hand, are causally plausible but morally weak, particularly in the face of contentious modern politics. What is needed, for both historiographical and contemporary purposes, is a framework of analysis that combines moral valuation with causal analysis.[16]

If we are to understand Leveller arguments concerning religious toleration, then we must move away from interpretive frameworks based on a sharp distinction between the claims of conscience and the prerequisites of peace. A tolerant society is not just one that embraces a set of ideals, but also one that exhibits a set of social practices. The claims of conscience are not just about the inner movements of the soul, but also about the external actions of believers. In this paper I seek to provide a new foundation for thinking about the religious clauses of the *Agreements of the People* by focusing on the intersection of conscience and peace in a language of monopolies. My aims are three-fold: to reconstruct Leveller arguments concerning religious toleration; to exhibit the structure of a set of arguments that remained powerful well into the twentieth century, particularly in America; and to help illuminate contemporary debates over the nature and limits of religious toleration.

II. The Language of Monopoly

Monopolies give individuals or groups the exclusive possession, control, or exercise of a right or opportunity that could be made available to all. According to one influential definition, "monopoly is a kinde of Commerce, in buying, selling, changing or bartering, usurped by a few, and sometimes but by one person, and fore-stalled from all others, to the Gaine of the Monopolist, and to the Detriment of other men."[17] The paradigmatic forms of a monopoly in early modern England were the commercial and industrial patents and charters granted by Elizabeth and James I. These monopolies were granted by the crown to encourage innovation, regulate the economy, and raise desperately needed cash. An important instrument of fiscal and economic policy, they were repeatedly attacked as inflationary, destructive of trade, and inequitable. Despite repeated efforts to eliminate them, at the outbreak of the Civil War key commodities like soap and salt remained in the control of a handful of men. In the memorable words of Sir John Culpepper,

> like the frogs of Egypt, [monopolists] have gotten possession of our dwellings, and we have scarce a room free from them: they sipp in our cups, they dip in our dishes, they sit by our fires, we find them in our die-fatt, wash-bowle, and powdering tubb; they share with the butler in his boxe, they have marked and sealed us from head to foote.[18]

As David Sacks has recently argued, opposition to monopolies was not simply economic. Attention to

> the grievance of [economic] monopolies helped sustain a powerful intellectual connection between the protection of individual rights and the preservation of the commonweal...What was at stake was not the mere regulation of things indifferent...but the ordering of a most fundamental matter, touching man's duty to fulfill his nature and God's law...Monopolies interfered with one's godly duty, with one's calling. Opposition to them...represented resistance to the state on behalf of a commitment, not of a mere opportunity...[Liberty] came to be associated with the idea of personal autonomy, not because man was to be free to do just as he pleased, but just the reverse.[19]

Elizabethan and Jacobean debates over the legitimacy of monopolies focused attention on the powers of the state, and compelled Englishmen to clarify, refine, and revise basic conceptions of politics, economics, and morality.

Against this background, it is not surprising to find an attack on monopolies contained in John Lilburne's influential 1645 pamphlet, *Englands Birth-Right Justified*. What *is* surprising is that the first monopoly condemned by Lilburne was not economic but religious: "the Patent of ingrossing the Preaching of the Word only to such men as weare Black and rough garments." These "grand Monopolizers" had robbed "the Free-men of England of their birth-right and inheritance."[20]

The Levellers were not the only Englishmen to argue for "free trading of truth." Arguments against monopolies were easily grafted onto stock anti-clerical arguments. In *Areopagitica*, for example, Milton argued that "truth and understanding are not such wares as are to be monopolized and traded in by tickets and statutes and standards."[21] But unlike most of their contemporaries, the Levellers pressed home this argument with abandon. In the summer of 1644, William Walwyn complained that the Presbyterian clergy had "engrossed the trade" of preaching by insisting that Scripture could be understood only by an elite schooled in Greek and Hebrew; in 1645 Richard Overton argued that "the inhancing and ingrossing all Interpretations, Preachings, and Discipline" in the hands of the clergy was "a meere Monopole of the Spirit, worse than the Monopole of Soap"; and in autumn 1646 Lilburne suggested that "the greatest bondage of this land ariseth from the monopolizing patentee-Clergy."[22] More than rhetorical window-dressing was at stake in these claims. To see this point, it is necessary to explore a complex set of causal and conceptual claims concerning the structure of the conscience and the consequences of intolerance.

Tudor and Stuart Englishmen commonly assumed that religious unity was part of the purpose of Creation. It gave expression to God's majesty, and contributed to good order in church and state. Division and disagreement were signs of corruption and a falling away from Christ. Compulsion was necessary to combat error and encourage true belief. Religious unity, moreover, was essential to a good society. Bishop Whitgift once said to Elizabeth that "religion is the foundation and cement of human societies." Bishop Bramhall, attacking Hobbes, repeated this claim: "without religion, societies are but like soapy bubbles, quickly dissolved." In the words of John Maxwell, "religion and the fear of God, and nothing else, preserves all societies amongst men." The Leveller argument for toleration sought to rebut both of these claims: the conscience cannot be coerced; and the attempt to impose religious uniformity creates disorder, not order.

III. Conscience, Sin, and Sincerity

The foundation for Leveller arguments concerning the conscience was laid in the first *Agreement*: "wee cannot remit or exceed a tittle of what our Consciences dictate to be the mind of God, without wilfull sinne." This argument was pressed with great subtlety by Walwyn. "The conscience being subject only to reason...[it] can only be convinced or persuaded thereby." True faith was the fruit of a free, active, and rational mind. It required inner light, not outward conformity. The significance of creeds and rites lay in the sincerity with which they were held. "Though the thing may be in it selfe good, yet if it doe not appear to be so to my conscience, the practice thereof in me is sinfull."[23] Compulsion bred hypocrisy, not sincerity and faith.

This argument was sometimes pitched in terms of a mind/body distinction. Conscience is a matter of mind, while compulsion can only reach the body. "Can it in reason be judged the meetest way to draw a man out of his error, by imprisonment, bonds, or other punishment? You may as well be angry, and molest a man that has an imperfection or dimnesse in his eyes, and thinke by stripes or bonds to recover his sight: how preposterous would this bee?"[24] Religious persecution involved a kind of category mistake, in that judgments of conscience were confused for weaknesses of the body.

The advocates of a uniform and compulsory national church were not unaware of these arguments, and responded with delicacy and skill. If mind and body, conscience and conduct, are truly distinct, then persecution can do no more than test faith. It cannot destroy it. As Henry Hammond argued in *Of Resisting the Lawful Magistrate under colour of Religion* (1643), if it is true that religion is "an act of the soule, which cannot be forced or constrained by outward violence," then "I may confesse Christ in the den of Lyons, in the furnace, on the racke, on the gridiron, and when my tongue is cut out, by patient, constant suffering in that cause. Religion is not so truly professed by endeavouring to kill others, as by being killed patiently our selves rather than we will renounce it."[25]

Mind and body are not, of course, distinct; and as daily experience proves, discipline is inseparable from growth and development.[26] This argument could be made philosophically: "the intent of Government" is not "to make men hypocrites, but by Discipline to bring wicked and wanton wits to a sight of their Errours." Men cannot be compelled to accept the truth, but through discipline and instruction they can be put in the right frame of mind to receive it. This argument was also made poetically, through the force of metaphors and similitudes that struck deep chords in the English moral imagination. "Shall not a Parent compel an obstinate childe to hear, for fear of making him an hypocrite?...A wandering sheep forced at first by Discipline, may at last blesse God for that violence; but being left to it self, and to its own fancies and desires, may for ever curse the Authors of such a Liberty."[27]

The Levellers responded to these arguments with an astutely skeptical combination of cognitive and psychological claims. Cognitively, they drew attention to the limits of human reason. "No condition of men in our dayes have an infallibility of judgment."[28] Human nature had been corrupted by the Fall. In a post-lapsarian world, men and women were liable to confuse truth for error, and error for truth.[29] Indeed, confrontation with others was the only reliable method for "testing" beliefs. "No man knoweth but in part, and what wee know, we receive it by degrees, now a little, and then a little; he that knowes the most, was once as ignorant as he that knowes the least; nay, is it not frequent amongst us, that the thing that we judged heresie we now believe is orthodox?"[30]

From a psychological point of view, the Levellers argued that persecution was irrational because the conscience is unstable and unpredictable. Change and experimentation—not stability and continuity—were typical of the life-histories of most men and women. As John Price remonstrated with the persecuting Presbyterian John Bellamy:

> This is that I would you, all others, should observe in you, how you have made a personal experiment of all those waies; have been for Bishops & against Bishops: for Anabaptists and against Anabaptists: for Separates and against Separates: for Bishops again, and against Bishops: for Common prayer book and against Common prayer book, for conformity & against conformity, and now…you are for Presbytery.[31]

As the soul of each human is unstable, so no man could predict the beliefs of his children. As Richard Overton once argued, "if you would not think upon us, think upon your posterities, for I cannot suppose that any one of you would have your children hang'd in case they should prove Independents, Anabaptists, Brownists."[32] Parents might compel obstinate children to hear, but it was unlikely they would wish their destruction in the process.

Despite the instability of the conscience, men and women adhered to their beliefs with extraordinary tenacity. According to Overton, "nothing is more neere and dear" to a man than his conscience, and "*a wounded Conscience (saith Solomon,) who is able to bear it? Wee had rather loose our lives then deny our Faith; and what will not men doe for their lives?*"[33] Persecution simply confirmed strong-willed men and women in their unorthodox beliefs. It stiffened their resolve and strengthened their faith. One need only look at the behavior of John Lilburne for proof of this observation. In 1638 Lilburne was charged with the crime of distributing unlicensed religious pamphlets. He was sentenced to the Fleet, ordered to pay £500 in damages, and whipped through the streets of London from the prison of the Fleet to the pillory—a distance of approximately one mile. While tied to the cart, dragged through the streets, and being whipped with "a terrible Corded-whip," he delivered "many bold Speeches against the Tyranny of Bishops." In the pillory, he called on the assembled crowd of onlookers to take pamphlets out of his pockets. Gagged, he "stamped with his Feet" as if to indicate that he would speak if he could. In response to these actions Star Chamber ordered that all future prisoners sentenced to corporal punishment must have their garments searched, their hands bound, and their mouths gagged![34] Lilburne, by contrast, counted his day of punishment as "my wedding day in which I was married to the Lord IesusChrist."[35]

Ironically, the possession of a tender conscience—the trait that led to tenacious resistance to religious coercion—was a virtue which could not be done without. As Walwyn argued in *The Compassionate Samaritane,*

> if it be instanced, that some there were that turned with the wind, and were terrified by feare of punishment into a compliance, I answer, that such men are so farre from being examples to be followed, that they may more justly be condemned for weather-cokes (to be set up for men to know which way blowes the wind) of favour, delicacy, ease, and preferment.[36]

Tenacity and truth were inextricably linked. The measure of a good conscience was sincerity of belief, not obedience to rules and forms.

IV. Toleration and Social Order

The second major strand of anti-tolerationist arguments focused on the links between religious diversity and social disorder. To many seventeenth-century Englishmen it was self-evident that a common religion was "the glew and soder that cements a Kingdom or church together."[37] Shared beliefs and practices were essential to the harmony of a well-integrated society.[38] According to the Levellers, this inverted the truth. A uniform and compulsory national church divided nations and inclined them to war.[39] This argument was presented with particular deftness in Overton's allegory, *The Arrangement of Mr. Persecution.* Persecution, hailing from "the Towne of Tyranny, in the County of Martyrdom," was indicted as "an enemy to God and all goodness, a Traytor to Kings and...Kingdomes," and the cause of "the warre and the bloodshed at present in this land." In the inquest, each member of the grand jury represented one facet of the public interest. According to Mr. Power of Parliaments, "Persecution for conscience is Inconsistent with the *Sovereignty of Kingdomes,* for it divideth their *Powers* one against another." Mr. Setled-Peace argued that Persecution "so poysoneth all Nationall Pacifications, Leagues, and Covenants, that their peace changeth with their Religion." Mr. Humaine-Society concurred, observing that Persecution pitted "father against son, and son against father." As the testimony of Mr. Desolate Germany confirmed, the civic consequences of persecution were devastating. "Those that doubt of the truth of this Byll [of indictment] let them but looke upon the Germaine desolations, depopulations, warre, famine, and pestilence." Death and devastation, not peace and order, were the fruits of persecution. In the words of Mr. Nationall-Wealth, "this *Persecution* for Conscience...throweth all into a *Wildernesse*."

While persecution divided nations, religious liberty actually strengthened the bonds of citizenship. The Levellers frequently cited the experience of the Low Countries to verify this claim. In peacetime the Dutch "are well and peaceably governed." But when threatened by war "they unite sufficiently in the defence of the common liberties and opposition of their common enemies."[40] Citizens united with each other, and were more loyal to their government, when their consciences were protected. "Where the government equally respecteth the good and peace of all sorts of virtuous men, without respect of their different judgments in matters of Religion: there all sorts of judgements cannot but love the government, and esteem nothing too pretious to spend in defence thereof."[41]

The Levellers summarized their arguments for toleration in terms that suggest sharp distinctions between private belief and public action, a private sphere of religion and a public sphere of politics. According to Walwyn, "things supernaturall" must be distinguished from "things naturall." Only the latter were "properly subject unto government." "Matters of opinion" are "not properly to be taken into congnisance any farther, then they break out into some disturbance, or disquiet to the State."[42] As Overton crisply put the point, "the inward man is God's prerogative, the outward man is man's prerogative...the limits of Magistracy extend no further then humanity, or humane subsistence, not to spirituality, or spirituall being."[43]

Neither of these dichotomies—public vs. private; belief vs. action—accurately captures Leveller arguments. Consider Richard Overton's response to a slanderous attack on his character by London Independents in 1649:

> As I am in my self in respect to my own personall sins and transgressions; so I am to my self and to God, and so I must give an account; the just must stand by his own faith: But as I am in relation to the Commonwealth, that all men have cognizance of, because it concerns their own particular lives, livelihoods, and beings, as well as my own; and my failings and evils in that respect I yeeld up to the cognizance of all men, to be righteously used against me. So that the businesse is, not how great a sinner I am, but how faithfull and reall to the Common-wealth; that's the matter concerneth my neighbour, and whereof my neighbour is only in this publick Controversie to take notice; for my personall sins that are not of Civill cognizance or wrong unto him, to leave them to God.[44]

Overton rejected any sharp distinction between beliefs and actions, words and deeds, thoughts and practices. "Faith without Workes is dead," and "if [the magistrate] hath power over my body, he hath power to keep me at home when I should go abroad to serve God."[45] Instead, he focused on different *kinds* of actions, particularly on the distinction between "sin" and "crime."[46] His "personall failings"—his sins—were private matters, of no concern to the public; only his "relation to the Commonwealth"—his crimes—deserved notice by others.

To say that faith was private was to say that it constituted a distinct sphere of life, differentiated from the realm of politics.[47] Toleration, by separating religion and politics, rendered impotent the idiosyncratic and parochial beliefs that divided men and women while preserving the shared ("secular") aims and interests that united them.

To say that we are stewards of our own souls is not to say that we are free to believe as we please, nor is it to say that our beliefs are irrelevant to others. Each individual has a responsibility to pursue truth and understanding. According to Walwyn, "you are advised by the Apostle to try all things, and to hold fast that which is good…'tis your selfe must doe it, you are not to trust to the authority of any man, or to any mans relation: you will finde upon tryall that scarcely any opinion hath been reported truly to you." Lilburne concurred. Few things were as dangerous as "living upon other mens light, takeing all for Gospel which Learned men say without tryall."[48] Each individual, moreover, is obligated to assist others in their pursuit of truth and understanding. "No man is born for himself."[49]

These arguments make a mockery of contemporary arguments that liberal rights are inherently privatizing and atomizing. Consider two frequently-asserted claims concerning liberalism: that it assumes that "human beings are atomistic, rational agents whose existence and interests are ontologically prior to society," and that it "conceives of the needs and capacities of individuals as being independent of any immediate social or political condition."[50] The rights advocated by the Levellers neither sought nor presumed a society of atomistic individuals. Instead, they were designed to frustrate some modes of action, and facilitate others. It is important to note in this context that Leveller assertions of self-ownership were made in quite specific contexts. In an ordinance proposed on 10 September 1646, Presbyterians in Parliament sought to brand Independents, Baptists, and Brownists with a "B" on their cheek. This punishment was intended to permanently identify the state of a person's soul, and to publicly proclaim their sins. "Self-ownership" was asserted by the Levellers in an attempt to frustrate this campaign to fix and make visible the consciences of men.

V. Persecution

Despite these powerful arguments for toleration, the fact of persecution remained. To make sense of this situation, the Levellers employed a skeptical strategy that would be popularized in the eighteenth century by freethinkers like Toland, Tindal, and Mandeville. Doctrinal differences, they argued, were frequently a mask for worldly interests. Religious uniformity was pursued for the fruits of office that it produced. According to Lilburne, with a uniform and compulsory national church came "the strict payment of *Tythes*," and "the clergy are such greedy dogges…that they can never have enough." Without having to "labour for it with their hands, nor earne it with the sweat of their browes," the clergy—who comprised less than 1/1000th of the population—extracted one-tenth the nation's wealth.[51]

Religious uniformity also brought status and standing. Walwyn, in an open letter to Thomas Edwards—a particularly zealous Presbyterian minister—argued that Edwards feared toleration because it would "spoile you not onely of your gaine, but of your glory and domination, things dearer to you then your life."[52]

The clergy pursued their aims through a monopoly of religious knowledge. The Levellers frequently explained an individual's failure to pursue his interest in terms of his ignorance. As they argued in the preface to the first *Agreement*, "it cannot be imagined that so many of our Country-men would have opposed us in this quarrel, if they had understood their owne good." The truths of religion are accessible to all. Truth is simple and unadorned. "Plaine truth will prove all." Give truth "but due and patient audience" and "her perswasions are ten thousand times more powerfull to worke upon the most dull refractory minde, then all the adulterate allurements and deceivings of art."[53]

Continued public support for a uniform and compulsory national church was possible only because the truth had not been permitted to speak. This was the fruit of a deliberate campaign by the clergy. The cornerstone of Anglican ecclesiology was the claim that Scripture could be understood and interpreted only within the confines of an authoritative church. Most laymen could not read the Bible in its original languages, and all laymen lacked the divine gift of understanding granted the clergy through Apostolic succession. Presbyterians did not place the same emphasis on ordination, but they, too, insisted that learning, professional expertise, and participation in a well-ordered church were preconditions to the successful interpretation of Scripture. "And thus they keep all in a mystery, that they only may bee the Oracles to dispence what, & how they please."[54]

The clerical monopoly of religious knowledge was reinforced through the political power of censorship. In 1586 a Star Chamber decree vested the Archbishop of Canterbury and the Bishop of London with the right to license books for publication. It also required that all books be registered with the Stationers Company. This decree fell into disuse during the early years of the Long Parliament, but it was revived in 1643. Though "intended by the Parliament for a good & necessary end (namely) the prohibition of all Bookes dangerous or scandalous to the State," the ordinance was used by "the Licencers (who are Divines and intend their owne interest)" for "the stopping of honest mens writings, that nothing may come to the Worlds view but what they please."[55]

Walwyn taunted the clergy for the insecurity these practices reflected. "I should rather thinke that they who are assured of [the truth] should desire that all mens mouthes should be open, that so errour may discover its foulness, and truth become more glorious by a victorious conquest after a fight in open field; they shunne the battel that doubt their strength." Lilburne replaced irony and sarcasm with a frontal assault: "if you had not been men that had been affraid of your cause, you would have been willing to have fought and contended with us upon even ground and equall termes, namely, that the Presse might be as open for us as for you."[56] The Levellers repeatedly challenged their opponents to debate before a jury of their peers on questions in dispute. Their strategy was partly rationalist, predicated on the belief that partial truths and private interests could not survive the harsh light of public hearing. But it was also performative, transferring an aristocratic language of battle to religious disputes. Knights in service to the truth, they sought "a fight in open field," to be "fought and contended...upon even ground and equall terms." The honor of an English man demanded nothing less.

VI. Conclusion

The Levellers linked the language of rights, religious toleration, and the elimination of clerical monopolies. Their arguments were moral, psychological, religious, and political. They crossed boundaries that are normally used to identify and evaluate seventeenth-century political thought: rights and duties, virtues and interests, public and private, liberal and republican.

Liberal arguments linking liberty and the elimination of monopolies remained vital until well into the twentieth century. This was particularly the case in America. The following examples demonstrate the breadth and depth of this current of ideas:

--James Wilson

-- "Lectures on Law" (1790-91): "The contracted and debasing spirit of monopoly has not been peculiar to commerce; it has raged, with equal violence, and with equal mischief, in law and politicks."

-- "Man, As An Individual": "Monopoly and exclusive privilege are the bane of every thing—of science as well as of commerce. The sceptical philosophers claim and exercise the privilege of assuming, without proof, the very first principles of their philosophy; and yet they require, from others, a proof of every thing by reasoning. They are unreasonable in both points."

--Thomas Jefferson

-- "Bill for Establishing Religious Freedom in Virginia" (1785): religious tests for public office "corrupt the principles of that very religion it is meant to encourage, by bribing with a monopoly of worldly honours and emoluments, those who will externally profess and conform to it."

--William Leggett

-- *New York Evening Post* (1834): "the privilege of self-government is one which the people will never be permitted to enjoy unmolested. Power and wealth are continually stealing from the many to the few. There is a class continually gaining ground in the community who desire to monopolize the advantage of the Government, to hedge themselves round with exclusive privileges and elevate themselves at the expense of the great body of the people."

--Walt Whitman

-- "Preface," *Leaves of Grass* (1855): "The American bards shall be marked for generosity and affection and for encouraging competitors... They shall be kosmos...without monopoly or secrecy... glad to pass any thing to any one...hungry for equals night and day."

The language of monopoly provides a complex window on the moral and conceptual, as well as causal and sociological, bases of liberal arguments for religious toleration. It provides unique insights not just into the history of liberalism, but also into the ambiguities of contemporary political discourse.[57]

NOTES:

1. David Wootton, "The Levellers," in John Dunn, ed., *Democracy: The Unfinished Journey* (Oxford, Oxford University Press, 1992), 71.

2. Murray Tolmie, *The Triumph of the Saints* (Cambridge, 1977); Ian Gentles, *The New Model Army* (Oxford, 1992).

3. Lilburne, *An Impeachment of High Treason* (1649), 20-22.

4. David Underdown, *Revel, Riot, and Rebellion* (Oxford, 1985), 114-15.

5. Marchamont Nedham, *Mercurius Pragmaticus* (9-16 November 1647); Lilburne, *A Whip for the Present House of Lords* (1648), 3.

6. David Wootton, "Leveller Democracy and the Puritan Revolution," in *The Cambridge History of Political Thought, 1450-1700*, ed. J.H. Burns (Cambridge, 1991), 416.

7. A.S.P. Woodhouse, ed., *Puritanism and Liberty* (Chicago, 1951), 53-54.

8. *An Agreement of the People For A firme and present Peace, upon grounds of common-right and freedom* (3 November 1647), in David Wolfe ed., *Leveller Manifestoes of the Puritan Revolution* (New York, 1994), 227; *Foundations of Freedom; Or An Agreement of the People, Proposed as a Rule for future Government in the Establishment of a firm and lasting Peace* (15 December 1648), in Wolfe, *300; An Agreement of the Free People of England. Tendered as a Peace-Offering to this distressed Nation* (1 May 1649), in Wolfe, 405.

9. "An individual negatively tolerates x-ing when she does not seek coercively to prevent or inhibit it: she positively tolerates it when she gives some aid or encouragement. The State negatively tolerates x-ing when it does not prevent or intentionally inhibit it by law. It positively tolerates x-ing when it intentionally encourages x-ing, or intentionally avoids discouraging x-ing: that is, it safeguards the opportunity to x" (Deborah Fitzmaurice, "Autonomy as a Good: Liberalism, Autonomy and Toleration," *Journal of Political Philosophy* [1993]: 1).

10. Alan Ryan, in Knud Haakonssen, ed., *A Culture of Rights* (Oxford, Oxford University Press, 1991), 373.

11. Theodore Calvin Pease, *The Leveller Movement* (Washington, DC: 1916), 153; H.N. Brailsford, *The Levellers and the English Revolution* (Stanford, 1961), 151.

12. J.C. Davis, "Religion and the Struggle for Liberty," *Historical Journal* 35 (1992): 513, 515. See also: Blair Worden, "Toleration and the Cromwellian Protectorate," *Studies in Church History* 21 (1984): 209-10.

13. Walwyn, *The Compassionate Samaritane* (1644), in William Haller, ed., *Tracts on Liberty in the Puritan Revolution*, 3 vols. (New York, 1934), 2:67. *Politique* arguments need not yield toleration. As Richard Tuck has argued, "it remains true that strong beliefs are potentially dangerous things, and that the wise relativist may find himself defending intellectual repression on pragmatic grounds" ("Scepticism and Toleration in the Seventeenth Century," in Susan Mendus, ed., *Justifying Toleration*, [Cambridge, 1988], 36).

14. Davis, "Religion and the Struggle for Freedom," 530.

15. "Hobbes saw deeper into the issues of relativism than any philosophy of his time, and perhaps even than any philosopher since. For that reason he must remain the foundational philosopher of our political institutions: the state structures which came into being in his time persist down to our time, and his summation of the political arguments about their emergence is still a textbook for us." "The basic character of modern politics was in place [by 1651]...The description of modern politics we find both in the *ragion di stato*

writers and in Grotius and Hobbes, with standing armies paid for out of taxation, with self-protective and potentially expansionist states, and with citizens very unsure of the moral principles they should live by, looks like an accurate description of a world still recognizable to us" (Richard Tuck, *Philosophy and Government 1572-1651*, [Cambridge 1993], xvii, 348).

16. John Dunn, "The Claim to Freedom of Conscience," in *From Persecution to Toleration*, eds. Ole Grell, Jonathan Israel, Nicholas Tyacke (Oxford, 1991), 172, 192.

17. Edward Misselden, *Free Trade, Or, the Meanes to Make Trade Flourish* (London, 1622), 57.

18. Quoted in Conrad Russell, *The Fall of the British Monarchies* (Oxford, 1991), 219.

19. David Harris Sacks, "Parliament, Liberty, and the Commonweal," in *Parliament and Liberty from the Reign of Elizabeth to the English Civil War* (Stanford, 1992), 86, 100-01.

20. John Lilburne, *Englands Birth-Right Justified* (1645), 8-9, in Haller, 3:266-67.

21. Milton, *Areopagitica*, in K.M. Burton, ed., *Milton's Prose Writings* (London, 1958), 168.

22. Walwyn, *Compassionate Samaritane*, in *The Writtings of William Walwyn, ed.*, Jack McMichael and Barbra Taft (Athens, GA, 1989), 110; Overton, *Sacred Decretal* (1645), 5; Lilburne, *Londons Liberty* (1646), 36.

23. Walwyn, *Compassionate Samaritane*, 14, 43, in *Writings*, 105, 114.

24. Walwyn, *Tolleration Justified*, 8-9, in *Writings*, 164.

25. Hammond, *Of Resisting the Lawful Magistrate Under colour of Religion* (1643), 4, 5.

26. Mark Goldie, "The Theory of Religious Intolerance in Restoration England." in *From Persecution to Toleration*, 331-68.

27. *Anti-Toleration* (1646), 8, 13-14.

28. Walwyn, *Helpe to the Right Understanding*, 4, in *Writings*, 136.

29. Walwyn, *Vanitie of the Present Churches*, in William Haller and Godfrey Davies, eds., *The Leveller Tracts 1647- 1553* (New York, 1944), 255.

30. Overton, *Arraignment*, 24, in Haller, 3:234. This argument is sometimes associated with a "progressive" theory of truth, in which it is claimed that the domain of truth gradually but steadily grows through conversation and disagreement. Versions of this argument can be found from Milton's *Areopagitica* to Mill's *On Liberty*. The relationship between disagreement and progress is, however, contingent.

31. John Price, *The City Remonstrance Remonstrated* (1646), 19.

32. Overton, *An Arrow against all Tyrants* (1646), 14.

33. Overton, *Divine Observations* (1646), 10.

34. John Rushworth, *Historical Collections of Private Passages of State*, 8 vols. (London, 1682-1701), 2:466-69.

35. Lilburne, *Worke of the Beast*, 8, in Haller, 2:10.

36. Walwyn, *Compassionaate Samaritane*, 13-14, in *Writings*, 105.

37. Samuel Clarke, quoted in J.F. McGregor and B. Reay, *Radical Religion in the English Revolution* (Oxford, 1984), 3.

38. With religious diversity came the inversion of social roles. In the words of the satiric poem *Lucifers Lacky* (1641), "When Women Preach, and Cobblers Pray / The Fiends in Hell, make holiday."

39. "In that family strife and heart-burnings are commonly multiplied, where one son is more cockered and indulg'd then another; the way to foster love and amity, as well in a family, as in a State, being an equall respect from those that are in authority" (William

Walwyn, *Tolleration Justified*, 10, in *Writings*, 166).

40. Overton, *Arraignement*, 31, in Haller, 3:241. "Do but tame that old spirit of domination, of trampling upon your brethren, and giving law, and the like [and all may be well]. Witness the country next from us, that hath all the markes of a flourishing state upon it—I mean the Low Countries: they are not so against, or afraid of, this toleration" ("Whitehall Debates," in Woodhouse, *Puritanism and Liberty*, 138).

41. Walwyn, *Helpe to the Right Understanding*, 7, in *Writings*, 140. "There is like to be a concurrence, and joynt assistance in the protection of the Common-wealth, which affords a joynt protection and encouragement to the People" (Walwyn, *Tolleration Justified*, 13, in *Writings*, 169).

42. Walwyn, *Prediction*, 203, in *Writings*, 229; Walwyn, *Tolleration Justified*, 8, in *Writings*, 164.

43. Overton, *Appeal*, in Wolfe, 180-81.

44. Overton, *Picture of the Council of State*, 44, in Haller and Davies, 231.

45. Overton, *Divine Observations*, 4-5; Overton, "Whitehall Debates," in Woodhouse, 139.

46. Wootton, "The Levellers."

47. Don Herzog, *Happy Slaves* (Chicago, 1989), 148-81.

48. Walwyn, *Power of Love*, in *Writings*, 81; Lilburne, *Answer to Nine Arguments*, 1645.

49. Overton, *Defiance*, 2.

50. Mary Dietz, "Context is All: Feminism and Theories of Citizenship," in *Dimensions of Radical Democracy*, ed. Chantal Mouffe (London, 1992), 64. Working from a quite different starting-point, C.B. Macpherson reached a similar conclusion about the Levellers in his justly-classic study *The Political Theory of Possessive Individualism* (Oxford, 1962): the Levellers "grounded all their claims for specific rights, civil, religious, economic, and political," on the "concept of man's essence as freedom, and freedom as the active proprietorship of one's person and capacities" (142).

51. Lilburne, *Englands Birth-Right*, 13, in Haller, 3:271.

52. Walwyn, *Whisper in the Eare*, 2, in *Writings*, 174.

53. Walwyn, *Power of Love*, in *Writings*, 81.

54. Walwyn, *Compassionate Samaritane*, 32, in *Writings*, 110.

55. Walwyn, *Compassionate Samaritane*, 39-40, in *Writings*, 112-13.

56. Walwyn, *Compassionate Samaritane*, 60, in *Writings*, 118; Lilburne, *A Copie of a Letter to Prinne*, 2, in Haller, 3:182.

57. Earlier Versions of this essay were presented at conferences at the University of Chicago ("Ideologies of Toleration and Repression in the Early Modern Period") and the University of California, Riverside ("Early Theories of Toleration in Comparative Perspective"). I would like to thank Steve Pincus and Chris Laurson, and the participants in these conferences, for their comments and suggestions.

8

SKEPTICISM AND TOLERATION IN HOBBES' POLITICAL THOUGHT

Shirley Letwin[1]

We cannot say of Thomas Hobbes, as he did of the physician, William Harvey, that he was a man who lived to see his doctrine established in his lifetime. Three hundred years after Hobbes's death, there is nothing like agreement even on the contents of his doctrine. The only thing that seems to be established is that he had a bad opinion of the human species and proclaimed it with an arrogant assurance. Some praise him for it, and others condemn him. But it is agreed that such grim certainty is out of keeping with the temperance of a good Englishman, and Hobbes has accordingly been described as a kindred spirit of sharp-tongued foreigners like Pascal. Though he has nevertheless been acclaimed as the greatest philosopher produced by England, the title of the most distinctively English philosopher has been reserved for that renegade Scotsman, David Hume.

But if we consider how the temperance, or the lack of it, in these two philosophers is related to their religious belief, we discover some interesting anomalies: Hume is most often described as a sceptic because he is supposed to have denied that men can know anything for certain. There is disagreement about whether he was a deist or an atheist, but he has never been charged with being a Christian. His lack of Christian faith is usually associated with his scepticism, and his scepticism is supposed to account for his temperance. Hobbes is usually described as dogmatic, but he has also been accused not only of lacking Christian

---

[1] *Editor's Note:* This paper was presented by Shirley Letwin at the political theory workshop at Yale University. Unfortunately, Mrs. Letwin died before its publication. Confronted with the erudition and complexity of her scholarship, we have decided not to edit the text but to present it as it originally appeared, i.e., without footnotes (references are alluded to in the text), having only Americanized some spelling. Many thanks to her estate for permission to publish this essay.

faith, but of being so scandalous an enemy of it that, as Clarendon said, a 'good Christian can hardly hear Hobbes's name without saying of his prayers' in order to exorcize the evil of Hobbes's 'loose and licentious reflections upon piety and religion'. Non-Christians have supported Clarendon's opinion: they have agreed with Leslie Stephen that 'Hobbes's system would clearly be more consistent and intelligible if he simply omitted the theology altogether'. But today, only a very brave man, or a very ignorant one, would repeat Stephen's remark. It has become widely acknowledged that, as Hobbes devoted more than a third of his writings to discussing religion and wrote several polemics to combat the charge of atheism and insisted throughout that he was a sound Anglican, there is reason to suppose that he was not wholly indifferent to questions about religion. By now, it has become respectable to suggest even that there is a necessary connection between what Hobbes said about the human world and what he said about God and Scripture.

Many different things have probably contributed to this change, but one reason is obvious. Current defenders of traditional Christianity maintain that being Christian means believing in the rottenness of the human species. A philosopher who painted the human condition in dark colors would then have an undeniable claim to being considered a Christian. But it also follows that religious belief brings gloom, that whilst sceptics like Hume can take a cheerful view, Christians must expect the worst. What then are we to think of the belief in the consolations of religion?

It might, of course, be nonsense. Certainly, many Christians have prided themselves on their misery. A visitor to England during the Commonwealth reported that, whereas he had earlier perceived that 'the people, both poore and rich did looke cheerfully,' when he saw them again under the rule of the saints, their countenances were 'all changed, melancholy, spightfull, as if bewitched'. Was Hobbes such a Christian? His denunciations of the pious rebels who imposed the rule of the saints on England hardly make that plausible. He was not liked by Puritans such as Milton, who declared an antipathy to Hobbes because 'their interests and tenets did run counter to each other'. And what we know of the attitude displayed by Hobbes in his own life suggests anything but a dour Puritan.

Aubrey describes him as full of joy in living, indeed very like the man with the twinkling eyes portrayed in paint. We are told that Mr. Hobbes was distinguished for his cheerful humor, merry wit, pleasant discourse, good nature, lack of rancor, dislike of gravity (which made him averse to wearing a full beard), and a 'harmonical soul', with which it was not consistent to abhor either women or good wine, both of which, Aubrey assures us, Hobbes enjoyed, though always temperately. Hobbes preferred the company of worldly men, like Sir William Petty with whom he could have 'the ingenoise conversation' that he loved. In the witty love poem which he wrote not long before he died, when he was past ninety, there is no trace of either Calvinist gloom or of Dr. Johnson's fear of death, or of any senile forgetfulness of death. Nor was this worldliness of Hobbes's qualified by piety. He could be brisk with clergymen. When he was ill in France, and Roman,

Anglican and Calvinist divines came to torment him, he dismissed them energetically: 'Let me alone or else I will detect all your Cheates from Aaron to yourselves'. But despite all this, Aubrey says firmly that Hobbes was a true believer: 'that he was a Christian 'tis cleare, for he received the Sacrament of Dr. Pierson and in his confession to Dr. John Cosons, on his (as he thought) death-bed, declared that he liked the religion of the Church of England best of all other'.

If we try to assemble these characteristics into something like a whole picture, the result is puzzling. Hobbes appears to be someone who believed that men are not born virtuous nor easily made so; that the human world is full of danger; and yet he went through life in great good humor, making jokes about his fearfulness but in fact showing none. He denied that any man could know the will of God, but firmly declared that his own conclusions about the human world were true. He did not hesitate to scoff at clergymen and churches and insisted on the supremacy of secular over ecclesiastical authority, but nevertheless he steadlly affirmed that he was a true Christian and Anglican and died as such a man should. Can one man consistently think all these things? The commentators have replied, "No," if not directly, at least implicitly, by subtracting one or the other of Hobbes's traits in order to make the sum look more believable. And so we are told on the one hand that Hobbes was a rancorous materialist and atheist, and on the other hand that he was hardly distinguishable from St. Thomas Aquinas.

What makes it so difficult to accept the whole of Hobbes? It is the combination of scepticism and faith displayed both in his writing and his life. It is a combination that few people find thinkable, and therefore some have tried to save Hobbes's religion by denying his scepticism, while others have denied his religion. Both efforts have travestied Hobbes's outlook.

The difficulty disappears once we recognize that scepticism and faith, far from being at war with one another, are not only compatible but complementary, indeed essential to one another. But we must take care not to mistake the meaning of scepticism. In the most general sense, a sceptic is someone who doubts what others take for granted. But this general meaning covers two quite specific ones. A sceptic may doubt that there can be knowledge of any kind. But this sort of scepticism can only be maintained by someone who never says anything and just wags his finger. Anyone who writes treatises advocating this sort of scepticism is indulging in a monstrous self-contradiction and might be called a 'vulgar sceptic'. The other kind of sceptic denies only that human beings have access to non-human, ultimate, necessary truth; and that does not prevent him from acknowledging that human beings can and should distinguish between true and false, good and bad, ugly and beautiful. He might be described as a 'metaphysical sceptic' because he is sceptical only about the ultimate foundations of human thought. He insists that if we try to discover the final grounds of our thought, we must acknowledge that it rests on taking for granted something which we cannot demonstrate to be necessarily and eternally true. All our knowledge rests on an act of faith: we cannot justify our civilization by finding an indisputable foundation for it, but still we are obliged to accept the truths that constitute our civilization. That is the position of a metaphysical sceptic, and it is the position that Hobbes tried to defend.

His psychology was designed to show that man has not within him something of God, no spark of divinity, inner voice, innate illumination, conscience or intuition which gives human beings indubitable knowledge of what is true and good. In Hobbes's account, men can observe themselves and reflect on their observations, and if they reason correctly, arrive at conclusions which they are justified in defending staunchly. When these conclusions describe the fundamental character of the world that God created, they might be said to constitute knowledge of God's commands. That is what Hobbes meant when he described his laws of nature as commands of God. And it means that they are nothing like the universal certainties directly given by a bit of divinity in man, which have long been regarded as the foundation of Christian morality. Hobbes's laws of nature are human inventions, describing experience exclusively of this world. As the belief in certainties given to man by what Locke called 'the Candle of the Lord' within has traditionally been, and still is, associated with religion, Hobbes's rejection of this belief has earned him the reputation of an atheist.

About the kind of certainty with which men may believe in their inventions, Hobbes has encouraged much confusion and he has had considerable assistance from other philosophers. The confusion arises because it is difficult, to say the least, to explain how one can insist that one's opinions are true and should be accepted by others, while denying that human beings can arrive at indisputable truth. Nevertheless it is not an impossible combination because dogmatism is compatible with scepticism. But to explain that now would be a digression.

What matters here is what Hobbes repudiated, and that is clear enough. He denied that men can know what ultimately governs their lives or the destiny that awaits them. In other words, Hobbes rejected any qualification on the incomprehensibility of God. Even revelation, he insisted, does not bring indubitable knowledge of detailed commands because it is transmitted by men in human words and suffers from the same ambiguity as all human utterances--it can be interpreted in more than one way.

Hobbes granted that a man might receive a direct personal communication from God. What he denied was that the claim to have had such a communication gave anyone the right to impose his views on others, because others had no way of knowing that he was correctly or genuinely reporting God's instructions. They might choose to believe him; they might accept him as a true prophet; but their faith in God does not oblige them to do so. A man's refusal to believe those who say that they have spoken to God casts no doubt on his faith. In the Hobbesian picture, the relation between man and God is a mystery mitigated solely by the will to believe.

This is a wholly sceptical view of religion. It is sceptical in the sense that it denies any possibility of knowing with certainty that any doctrine is the true one. It does not prevent anyone from thinking that he has such knowledge. But it does prevent him from supposing that others must acknowledge his possession of the

Truth. This uncertainty about doctrine and church is not, however, a qualification on faith--it is required by faith, because any claim to certain knowledge of God's will denies the incomprehensibility of God. It is tantamount to denying that God is a creator who made man out of nothing, because between a creator and his creatures there is nothing in common, and if we have nothing in common with God we cannot hope to understand him.

Hobbes was not alone in holding this view of the Christian God. Even those Christians who insisted that some things could be known with certainty have acknowledged that the incomprehensibility of God is fundamental to Christianity. But they have rejected the scepticism which this acknowledgment entails. And they have rejected it partly out of fear that such scepticism would destroy religious faith, and it has accordingly become a commonplace that religious belief is identical with taking certain truths to be beyond doubt.

This is what Hobbes denied. In his view, true Christian faith is inseparable from scepticism. He was teaching the same lesson as Hume did later--that the great civilization of Europe rests on accepting that doubt is inescapable without ceasing to believe and to obey. Hume devoted himself to explaining how a combination of scepticism and faith operates with regard to secular knowledge and institutions. Hobbes tackled what is even now a more delicate task--to show how scepticism complements faith in religion. And he has been rewarded with denunciations from both opponents and defenders of Christianity.

It remains to consider just how a man can accept such a sceptical view of his religion and still be a staunch Christian who abides by the discipline of his church. On this, Hobbes said very little explicitly. He addressed himself to explaining the proper relation between church and state. I shall be drawing the implications of what he said for the relation between the church and its members. My attempt would not, I think, offend Hobbes because it is in keeping with his injunction in *Leviathan*: 'It is not the bare Words, but the Scope of the Writer that giveth the true light by which any writing is to be interpreted.'

The most surprising aspect of Hobbes's sceptical religion is probably its conception of original sin. According to the common view, the doctrine of original sin means that all men are tainted by inborn evil, and that a Christian life consists of a constant struggle against it, a struggle which can never wholly succeed. This view rests on understanding men to be compounds of a spiritual self which draws them to God and a base material self which draws them to damnation. Hobbes denied that men are compounds of spirit and matter. Though there is a great deal wanting in his account of human nature, it is perfectly clear that he did not take men to be part spirit and part matter, and that for him the bodily existence of men is intrinsically neither good nor bad. To say that all men are sinners cannot then mean that there is an evil force within human beings thwarting their better spiritual selves. It cannot mean that enjoyment of life on earth is wicked or that whenever a man rejoices in being alive he has succumbed to sin. Instead, original sin means that however good some men are, and however well they may avoid acts said to be sinful, their superiority to other men, by comparison with their distance from the perfection of God, is as nothing.

Men must not even aspire to emulate the perfection of God because in doing so they forget that they are mortals. All men are sinners because all men are mortals. Because mortals live in a world of constant change, in a contingent world, they can never have more than limited knowledge. However good their intentions, men cannot know all that they would need to know in order to discern perfectly what they ought to do. For one thing, every human action is a response to other human responses; these cannot be either predicted or understood perfectly, and may in turn evoke responses that take an unexpected shape. Consequently, men can neither foresee all the consequences of their choices nor even say for certain which outcome would have been best. Secondly, whatever goods mortals choose, nothing can ever be more than partially desirable. Because men cannot do all things at once, they must choose this or that, and in choosing they must necessarily fail to satisfy some desire or some obligation whose claims they acknowledge. Every good chosen necessarily excludes another. And thirdly, though men have precepts, examples and rules to guide them, none of these can guarantee that what is chosen is the one and only right choice, or even the best possible one; there is no knowing 'the right way'. None of this makes it impossible to distinguish between good and bad conduct, nor absolves us from trying to do what is right. But it does oblige us to acknowledge that there is no such thing as a perfectly good human choice; it obliges us to acknowledge that every human choice, however good the intentions and however great the knowledge, is necessarily, inescapably, irremediably defective.

In this picture, what keeps men from perfection is nothing so grand as an evil disposition or dark irrational forces. All men are sinners because they interpret and respond to their experience from different standpoints, in a contingent world, without being able to see or do everything at once. Such imperfection was absent in the Garden of Eden because that was not a human world, not a life among other men, interpreting and responding to one another. In short, the Christian belief that 'we are all sinners' encapsulates the truth that men cannot escape from the limits imposed by a human condition. It is a doctrine not about inborn evil but about the implications of being rational mortals.

The obligation to believe in original sin thus becomes an obligation to recognize that in the best of all possible worlds there will still be much amiss, and to remember that dissatisfaction is inseparable from a human condition. It does not mean that human beings are rubbish, or that it is a duty to abhor what is pleasant on earth. It is rather a warning against presumption, a ground for resignation, an injunction to keep our expectations modest.

How then are we to understand the promise of salvation? It is usually taken to mean that within their mortal clay, men house immortal souls. In those who are saved, it is said, the spiritual part, when separated from the matter that pollutes it, will come into its own and enjoy eternal bliss. This was explicitly and emphatically denied by Hobbes. The promise of salvation can only mean, he insisted, that after dying the death of mortals, men may be offered 'eternal life' or be sentenced to a second, eternal death. But what 'eternal life' is like we cannot know; we can only believe that it is perfect bliss. And Hobbes's emphasis falls on the impropriety of attempting to forecast God's will or of making blueprints of the heavenly city. No man may feel certain that he will be saved or that another will be damned. One mortal may not talk of another as a soul eternally lost because, in doing so, he is speaking as a superior judging an inferior being; he is pretending to be able to judge as God does; he is forgetting that he is just one human being judging another. He is forgetting besides that sinners can repent and that the promise to forgive repentant sinners is at the heart of Christianity.

It does not follow that men should never identify sin or that the sinner should be considered to be no worse for his sin. Something more subtle is required: a readiness to distinguish a human judgment from that of God, to recognize that on the day of judgment God may find an excuse that is not evident to human beings. In short, the Christian injunction, 'Do not judge,' is a corollary to the Christian doctrine that 'all men are sinners'. It reminds men that God will judge them and that they cannot know how God will judge. It commands human beings to recognize that they must judge as best they can, but that they must not identify their mortal judgments, suitable to life on earth, with the eternal judgment of God.

There is still another implication of believing that all men have to answer for their sins before God and that sinners can repent and be saved. They can do so only if each is responsible for his destiny, which means that human beings are what they learn to be. Or, in other words, the belief in eternal punishment or salvation and in the possibility of repentance is inseparable from a belief in human individuality. It implies not only that each human being is distinct from every other and that individuality is of the essence of humanity, but that individuality is not a fixed identity given at birth but something made by men over the course of their lives. The differences among men do not keep them from being equally important in the eyes of God. Nor does that make it sinful for human beings to venerate or reward or obey some of their fellows more than others. Indeed, for men to refuse to make such mortal distinctions is a presumptuous attempt to play God. It does follow from believing that every man has a soul to make--and save--that human beings must not use or manipulate one another as if some were born to be masters and others slaves, that they must not reduce men to parts in a superior whole, that they must, as Hobbes says, honor the Golden Rule.

But if one consequence of believing that God will judge is that human life is inseparable from responsibility for how it is conducted, another consequence is that there is a measure of relief from responsibility. Faith in repentance and salvation allows men to believe that those who fall may right themselves and that despite the wrong done by themselves or others, there is still ground for hope. Men may therefore allow themselves to forgive transgressions, their own as well as those of others, without denying the idea of sin or inviting the chaos of amorality. It is not incumbent on men to punish every sin to keep chaos at bay. For it is God, not men, who keeps the universe in order. Though a believer's prayers may be tinged with a protest against everything in his life, he will recognize an obligation not to try to assign a blame for every wrong or attempt to set everything right, but rather to bear his burdens without attempting to justify them.

But how are men to know what constitutes sin? Can sin be avoided by obeying the rules of one's church? Can there be disagreement about these rules? Is it ever right to resist the commands of the recognized pastors?

Everything that Hobbes says makes it clear that in religions, as in civil matters, what men accept as right rests on what they choose to accept. When they believe what the church tells them, they have chosen to oblige themselves to obey its commands. The church is to be understood as a human institution which is endowed by its followers with the right to decide certain questions for them. Priests are human beings interpreting God's word as they have received it from other human beings whom they have chosen to regard as true prophets. And the same condition that produces the need for a civil sovereign gives rise to the need for a church. Both needs follow from the fact that men can always disagree about whom and what to obey and can agree only by acknowledging someone's right to decide. The sovereign must have a final say in religious as well as civil disputes in order to avoid the war of each against all. In a similar fashion, the church enables men to agree on how to worship and how to obey God. But there is a fundamental difference.

The rules of law constitute civil society. The rules of the church do not constitute Christianity. They are no more than a guide, and a guide to something much more profound and important. They are an abridgement of what a Christian should consider in deciding how to conduct himself. And if the rules of the church are an abridgement, it is not inconceivable that a sensitive moral judgment might not coincide with the simple conclusions drawn from ordinary interpretations of established rules. In unusual circumstances, the ordinary rules may even be altogether inappropriate. Christians who correctly understand the purpose of their church's rules will recognize that sin cannot be avoided just by obeying a set of rules, and that, conversely, not all those who infringe on the rules are necessarily sinners.

Because the church is not an armory from which God's thunderbolts issue forth to strike down sinners, but a human institution that helps to give men a mode of living and a mode of dying, piety is not of the essence of religion. Piety may even be a sign that true religious understanding is lacking. Of course men must make rules and try to enforce them; but they must not pretend, as self-appointed saints do, to possess more than human insight, to know the destiny of men, to speak with the voice of God.

All of this gives ecclesiastical practice a complicated character. Disagreements over doctrines and ceremonies among truly believing Christians have to be accepted. In religion, as elsewhere, there is no ground for eliminating the variety by discovering a universal and necessary superiority of one set of observances. There is no saying that more or less austerity is required by true faith, that three services and three sermons on Sunday are essential, or that a letter dated 'St. John's Eve' is indisputable evidence of idolatry. There is nothing intrinsically holy in a simple black cloth waistcoat and nothing intrinsically evil in a high silken one. And different churches may serve equally well to teach the same Christian truth. For some men, a church that offers grand ceremonies and pomp, August feasts and solemn fasts, and rules so strict that they cannot be broken without producing an unmistakable noise of sin may be more effective than a more austere or more lax church. Arguments about chanted services and intoned prayers, about genuflection, lecterns, candles, incense and credence tables are not to be taken seriously. Perhaps the bell, book and candle are a lesser evil than the severities of the dour low church, but only because such gaudy trappings are signs of a readiness to remember the human character of ecclesiastical institutions. High churchmen may be preferable because they take their addiction to ceremonies and rituals less seriously than their opponents pursue their antipathies, and do not suppose that men should aspire to be spirits. What matters is the lack of presumption, the recognition that no mortal knows the one sure path to salvation.

Even within any given church, however much its adherents may seem to be in agreement, there is unlikely to be a real absence of dissension. Acceptance of Scripture as a revelation of God's will does not eliminate the difficulty of deciding what the words mean nor give men access to non-human guarantees of human conclusions. There is no way to bridge the gap between the revealed Word of God and human interpretations of it. And therefore men may believe in Jesus the Savior and will to obey God but nevertheless disagree about the manner of doing so. They can resolve their disputes only by agreeing to regard a communal interpretation of God's will as authoritative. But that does not guarantee that what the church says is identical to God's will. And nothing necessarily follows about the character of a man's faith from the church that he attends.

None of this, however, should prevent a sensible Christian from thinking of the church into which he is born as the one true church. To try to think through for oneself all the dogmas of a religion and what they require in the way of ecclesiastical practice is an ambition that a thoughtful man might well entertain. But few can realize it. Therefore a good working rule is to honour God according to the established practices of one's community, to regard religion as a thing to believe in, something that is simply there, with all its pastors, rules and rituals.

This does not mean that men must never question the practices of the church to which they subscribe. There is even something to be said for such questioning. Not only might it call attention to religion and teach men to be aware of their faith. In the church, as in any other human institution, injustices accumulate and so it might be useful from time to time to inquire into ecclesiastical practices. Of course, when questions are raised, parties will be formed and entrenched interests will defend themselves. But a true Christian will recognize that good men are apt to be found on both sides, that his enemies in ecclesiastical quarrels may be no less useful to the church than he, and that the battle does not free him from an obligation to abide by his church.

If we attempt to sum up the attitude of a good Hobbesian Christian, it will seem to be paradoxical. He may criticize or even ridicule established forms of worship, and yet strongly resist attempts to overthrow them. He may declare that the truths mouthed by clergymen are no more certain than other truths, and yet expect a clergyman to discharge his priestly duties with complete earnestness. He may point out difficulties in the dogma of his church, and yet preach and practice utter submission to its creed. He may insist that no man can know the truth and yet be fierce against infidels.

These anomalies are of the same sort that have long made the combination of formality, episcopacy and establishment with laxity in the Anglican Church such an incomprehensible curiosity. Halifax tried to explain it by describing the Church of England as a 'Trimmer, between the frenzy of fanatic visions and the lethargic ignorance of Popish dreams'. Newman talked about it as the Church of the 'Via Media, the middle way between Protestant and Roman views of Private Judgments'.

In Canon Hertford's *Prayer Book Dictionary* of 1912, the Via Media of Anglicanism was identified with the 'Prayer Book conception of the Christian Religion,' and described as 'the carefully surveyed road, avoiding the dangerous detours of superstition on the one hand and the seductive short cuts of fanaticism on the other'. And the Hobbesian Christian will as easily fit the description of the normal Englishman's attitude to his church given by Dr. Martineau: The Englishman 'looks on the clerical eagerness about dogma,' Martineau said, 'as he does on his wife's gossip and voluminous correspondence—as inherent in the genius of the class, and somehow related to the nice perception and voluble enthusiasm of which he himself feels the fascination . . . He leaves these things to ecclesiastics, and with so free an indulgence that there is scarcely any intensity of bigotry that may not have its way, provided he and his church are not positively committed to them . . . The decisions of the Articles may be stringent, the pretensions of the ordination service arrogant, and the imprecations of the creed unflinching, but while they are not pressed into any visible form of ecclesiastical action, the persons of a few mild and charitable bishops suffice to counteract their effect, and to persuade men, fresh from the very sound of her anathemas, that they belong to the most liberal of churches.'

There is no real contradiction in these attitudes. What reconciles and explains them is a simple idea--that it is possible to question the infallibility of the teachers without entertaining any doubt about the thing being taught. Whether there is incense or sermons, more or less corruption, does not affect the truthfulness of what the human teachers are supposed to be conveying.

The upshot is a kind of religious tolerance. But it is far removed from what goes by that name today. For it is tolerance that emphasizes, instead of denying, that the church stands against the world. Religion, in this view of it, is divorced from both good works and piety. It is an attitude to the human condition. It consists in understanding oneself as a being who can wonder why and how he has come to be, who can feel sure that he, as every other man, has a destiny for which he is responsible, but who cannot expect to understand why he or anything else ever came to be or what purpose his existence serves.

The religious attitude includes what is commonly said to distinguish a man of 'Christian conscience' from a heathen--a 'voice within him' which he feels obliged to heed. To a Hobbesian Christian that is only a way of saying that he lives with an awareness that something more is required of him than surviving as effortlessly and pleasantly as he can manage, that he is obliged to consider the consequences of his actions and the quality of his life. Without such an awareness, a man can but drift or rush from one satisfaction to the next; he is reduced to little more than a bundle of desires or interests; and such a life is empty of substance and shape. It is from this kind of emptiness, which Hobbes called 'felicity,' that religious faith can save men. And there is no inconsistency. In what he says about religion as in what he says about 'felicity,' Hobbes insists that no end or pattern for a human life is given to men. And denying that there is a given end or pattern is entirely compatible with saying that a man's awareness of having to answer to his Maker for how he has conducted his life can spur him on to care about living decently.

Is it possible to maintain such a religious attitude without believing in the Incarnation and other supernatural aspects of Christian doctrine? In principle, the answer is yes. But on the other hand, the line that separates the religious attitude, without formal Christianity, from atheism, even in the weak form of agnosticism, is sharp and strong. Atheism puts man at the centre of the universe and dismisses supernatural events like the life and death of Jesus as meaningless. The non-doctrinal religious attitude does neither. What distinguishes it from Christianity is its indifference to the communal life and dogmas of a church and its readiness to do without a definite hope of eternal bliss or a personal sense of God's presence. The line that divides such an attitude from Pelagianism, from an arrogant reliance on one's own strength, is certainly very fine. But it is nevertheless clear. In non-doctrinal religion, there is no suggestion that salvation can be achieved by unaided human effort. Even the idea of salvation remains a mystery beyond understanding. Whether the religious attitude can be maintained in practice without the aid of formal religion is, however, another question. For most men that is probably impossible. Moreover, the emphasis on the importance of Grace in Christian doctrine would seem to require Christians to believe that it is impossible. But on the other hand, given its emphasis on the impossibility of knowing God's will or the interior of another man's soul, a sceptical Christianity also implies that faith may appear in various and unknown forms.

The upshot is an even more complicated conception of the distinctiveness of Christianity than of the distinctiveness of any Christian church. Hobbes's sceptical religion does not absolve a Christian from believing in the Incarnation, and all the doctrines about the supernatural associated with this belief. He is not given permission to regard all religions as equally good. But he is required to distinguish between those who do not share all his beliefs and those who are enemies of Christianity. Indeed he is required to recognize that this enemy might as easily appear in the garb of a pious member of his own church as in the character of an atheist.

Although Hobbes directed his barbs at a variety of enemies--pagan philosophy, scholastic theology, Roman Catholicism, Calvinism, the object of his enmity is always the same. And this object is pantheism. Today, pantheism flourishes in forms that were unknown to Hobbes--in Humanism, Marxism, Jungianism, Oriental Mysticism, Scientism, and Rationalism. But in all its forms, pantheism is the belief that human reason is a participation in the shaping principle of the universe, that human beings can divine the ruling principle of the universe and achieve undeniable knowledge of the given pattern which governs their lives and of the destiny that awaits them.

What may have annoyed Hobbes worst of all in pantheism is the blatant self-contradiction in its secular prescriptions. On the other hand, pantheism teaches that every man has innate knowledge of how to live, but on the other hand, pantheist doctrines have regularly demanded that men submit their lives to management by a leader, whether in the form of a philosopher king, the 'rule of the saints,' submission to a 'guru' or 'the dictatorship of the proletariat'. This self-contradiction arises from the pantheist conviction that there is a given, final perfection which can be achieved by human beings when this perfection eludes them pantheists cannot resist the offer of a 'sure path' to achieve what they take to be possible. And so they become the dupes of any 'leader' who comes their way. Hobbes nowhere talks of the need for 'leadership,' not even in connection with religion. There he speaks of 'pastors'. In civil life, he speaks of the need for a sovereign authorized to make rules for preserving peace. And that follows from the sceptical religion for which Hobbes gives us the postulates. Sceptical religion teaches that any man who claims to know the pattern for perfection is to be shunned as the devil. Sceptical religion prohibits talk of absolute targets, indisputable commands or inevitabilities. The signs of faith are not a conviction that one knows the truth but the opposite--a determination to acknowledge the perils and responsibilities of an existence embedded in mystery, and a readiness to deal with these perils and responsibilities without seeking final solutions. True believers are those who can decide what is true and do what is right with firmness, while remaining aware that all their convictions and actions are questionable. In short, the essence of Hobbes's sceptical religion is what Keats described as 'a negative capability' of living with 'uncertainties, mysteries, doubts, without any irritable reaching after fact and reason,' coupled with the courage to do what one can.

Sceptical religion offers no escape from the tribulations of human life. Its teaching is summed up in Hobbes's remark that 'the estate of man can never be without some incommodity or other.' But these tribulations lose the sensational character of either deviations from a natural perfection or a natural evil. They acquire the banal character of being just the stuff out of which mortals have to make their lives. That this stuff should in some respects be poor or good is simply part of the mystery that surrounds human existence. But this mystery has its compensations. As nothing is eternal in human life, as nothing is just what it seems to be and the consequences of our actions are never just what we intended, then today's evils, like today's blessings, may not seem quite so bad or good tomorrow. They certainly cannot last forever. As there can be no certainty about how God will judge, God may forgive and reward what men cannot; what seems all important here and now may be trivial in His eyes; there may be a reason for things beyond the comprehension of any man. Therefore hopefulness is not only reasonable but obligatory. Despair is a sin because it betrays an arrogant pretension to foresee the future and to know more than a human being may aspire to know. Thus, if sceptical religion rules out the certainties of pantheism, it saves men from the greatest danger faced by a self-conscious being, the danger of destroying the balance of his mind by too searching an awareness. The ability to avoid the abyss of bitterness, dread and despair is the consolation offered by sceptical religion. For three centuries, Hobbes has been celebrated for his acerbity. We might now begin to celebrate him for teaching us to reconcile ourselves to our human condition.

9

JOHN LOCKE AND THE FOUNDATIONS OF TOLERATION

Nathan Tarcov

In thinking about John Locke and the foundations of toleration, it is useful to start with a few caveats or qualifications. Depending on exactly what one means by toleration, the term may not capture the character of Locke's position and its foundations.

First, some might challenge Locke's right to be called an advocate of toleration on the grounds that he is not an advocate of absolute or unqualified toleration. William Popple in his Preface to his English translation of Locke's *Letter Concerning Toleration* declares that "Absolute Liberty, Just and True Liberty, Equal and Impartial Liberty is the thing that we stand in need of."[1] But Locke himself in the *Essay Concerning Human Understanding* declares that "No Government allows Absolute Liberty: The *Idea* of Government being the establishment of Society upon certain Rules or Laws, which require conformity to them; and the *Idea* of absolute liberty being for any one to do whatever he pleases."[2] More to the point, in the *Letter Concerning Toleration* itself, Locke's position is that "No Opinions contrary to human society, or to those moral Rules which are necessary to the preservation of Civil Society, are to be tolerated by the Magistrate."[3] In addition he argues there that sects that "arrogate to themselves . . some peculiar Prerogative . . . in effect opposite to the Civil Right of the Community . . . . have no right to be tolerated by the Magistrate."[4] He gives as examples sects that teach the doctrines that "Princes may be dethroned by those that differ from them in Religion; or that the Dominion of all things belongs only to themselves" presented under the specious guise that "Faith is not to be kept with Heretics," that "Kings excommunicated forfeit their Crowns and Kingdoms," and that "Dominion is founded in Grace." Indeed he says more generally that "those that will not own and teach the Duty of tolerating all men in matters of mere Religion" have no right to be tolerated by the magistrate. He also denies the right of toleration to any church that delivers itself up to "the Service of another Prince." Together these exceptions to the right of toleration would perhaps have excluded from its benefits almost all the churches of Locke's day except the Quakers; in contrast, practically all the major religious groups in America today have come to qualify under Locke's principles. Finally, he concludes that "Those are not at all to be tolerated who deny the Being of a God" since "Promises, Covenants, and Oaths, which are the Bonds of Humane Society, can have no hold upon an Atheist."

In addition to these limitations on the toleration of religious *opinions,* Locke also limits the toleration of religious *practices,* excluding those practices that do any injury to anyone or prejudice to another man's goods, such as human sacrifice or even animal sacrifice in circumstances of extreme scarcity; similarly the magistrate may impose a practice serving civil purposes, for example one useful for curing or preventing any disease children are subject to, even if their parents find it religiously objectionable.[5] Put positively, Locke insists that all Churches be "obliged to lay down Toleration as the Foundation of their own Liberty . . . equally belonging to dissenters as to themselves; and that no body ought to be compelled in matters of Religion, either by Law or Force."[6] Far from being an advocate of absolute unqualified toleration, then, Locke is for the "Establishment of this one thing," the paradoxical establishment of a sort of civil religion of toleration -- an established religion albeit one potentially shared by many otherwise diverse churches.

Locke might therefore be viewed by some as an advocate for something *less* than toleration, although the exceptions to absolute toleration he advises are meant to secure the principle of toleration and to rest on the same foundations as the rule they are exceptions to.

The second caveat, in contrast, is that Locke is an advocate of something *more* than toleration, if toleration is taken to mean only a grudging endurance or gracious allowance of something that one has the right not to tolerate. On the contrary, Locke emphasizes that toleration is a *duty* for magistrates and churches and a *right* for dissenters. He would have agreed with the spirit of George Washington's remark in his letter of August 1790 to the Jewish congregation of Newport, Rhode Island, that "It is now no more that *toleration* is spoken of as if it were the indulgence of one class of people that another enjoyed the exercise of their inherent natural rights."[7]

There is another sense in which Locke is an advocate for more than toleration, which forms my third caveat. If toleration is taken, as it is historically with reference to the controversies of the seventeenth and eighteenth centuries, as meaning specifically *religious* toleration (toleration *of* religious opinions and practices, and perhaps also toleration justified *by* religious opinions), then Locke is properly seen as an advocate of something broader than toleration, something that has come to be called liberalism. It is not only diverse *religious* opinions and practices that have a right to be tolerated. The argument in the *Second Treatise* for the protection of the rights of life, liberty, and property as the end of government is made without reference to specifically religious rights (they are mentioned only once in passing in connection with the exercise of the right of resistance[8]) and is much broader in its extent. Similarly, the argument for liberty or toleration in the *Essay Concerning Human Understanding* is about the pursuit of truth including not only religious truth but other kinds of truth as well. And even some, though not all, of the arguments for specifically *religious* toleration in the *Letter Concerning Toleration* provide foundations that are not specifically religious for a liberty that is in turn much broader than religious toleration.

Finally, Locke is an advocate for something *more* than toleration in yet another sense. He is concerned not only with trying to get the possessors of authority not to use that authority to impose their opinions on others, though that is a very important objective for him. But in itself that would perhaps ultimately not matter very much for him unless he could accomplish a more fundamental objective. That deeper objective is to get what we might call the subjects of authority to question authority, not to accept opinions on authority, but to examine their opinions and think for themselves. Without that intellectual freedom, that mental liberation (which is hardly captured by the term toleration), toleration would amount only to a group that accepts its opinions out of subjection to one authority allowing another group to accept different opinions on another authority. All the individual members of those groups would remain "enslaved in that which should be the freest part of Man, their Understandings," just as they are in places where people are "*cooped in* close, *by the Laws* of their Countries."[9] It is this liberty which is the special subject of the *Essay Concerning Human Understanding*.

Despite all these caveats about the propriety of describing Locke's position as toleration, I will go on to use that term, only occasionally speaking of liberty or liberalism to indicate the greater breadth and depth of Locke's position, since he himself uses the term in the *Letter Concerning Toleration* and since that is the term chosen to denominate the theme of this volume.

The arguments for religious toleration Locke presents in the *Letter Concerning Toleration* are remarkably diverse, especially in their stance toward truth and our ability to know it, both religious truth particularly and truth more generally. Before examining them, however, it is necessary to sketch the situation that Locke presents his doctrine of toleration as intended to rectify. It is one of people who "persecute, torment, destroy, and kill other Men upon pretence of Religion," who "deprive them of their estates, maim them with corporal Punishments, starve and torment them in noisom Prisons, and in the end even take away their Lives" supposedly "to make Men Christians, and procure their Salvation". It is a case of what Locke calls "burning Zeal for God, for the Church, and for the Salvation of Souls; burning, I say, literally with Fire and Faggot."[10] The problem is that of those who profess to be "sincerely solicitous about the Kingdom of God" and think it their duty "to endeavor the Enlargement of it amongst Men," and who therefore "maintain that Men ought to be compelled by Fire and Sword to profess certain Doctrines, and conform to this or that exterior Worship".[11] This was for Locke, of course, primarily a matter of persecution carried out in the name of Christianity, making it seem to be not the religion of love and peace it should be, but "the worst of all Religions," so productive did it then seem of factions, tumults, and civil wars as well as of persecution and struggles for ecclesiastical dominion.[12] Although Locke indicates his doctrine is meant also to justify the toleration of Christians in non-Christian India or Turkey,[13] his immediate priority is to justify toleration *by* Christians, to persuade those who profess Christianity to profess and practice toleration. The problem was primarily that of the existence of diverse and mutually intolerant sects each claiming to be the true Christian Church.

The first kind of argument for toleration Locke presents is that toleration is itself the chief characteristic mark of "the True Church."[14] Locke argues elsewhere in the *Letter* for toleration not only *of* Christians but of adherents of other religions, specifically mentioning Jews, Muslims, and Pagans, including American Indians, and for toleration *by* non-Christians as well.[15] Nonetheless his initial argument is presented as an argument from a proper understanding of Christianity as "the True Church" and "true Religion". According to this understanding, Christianity requires "Charity, Meekness, and Good-will in general towards all Mankind, even to those that are not Christians," "Holiness of Life, Purity of Manners, and Benignity and Meekness of Spirit." Locke declares that "If the Gospel and the Apostles may be credited, no Man can be a Christian without *Charity*, and without *that Faith which works*, not by Force, but by *Love*."[16] "Christian Warfare," Locke insists, requires the imitation of "the Captain of our Salvation . . . . the perfect Example of that Prince of Peace, who sent out his Soldiers to the subduing of Nations, and gathering them into his Church, not armed with the Sword, or other Instruments of Force, but prepared with the Gospel of Peace, and with the Exemplary Holiness of their Conversation".[17]

This kind of argument seems far from sceptical. On the contrary, it seems to presume that we know the truth, that we know Christianity is the true religion, and that we know Locke's interpretation of it as requiring the profession and practice of toleration to be the true interpretation of Christianity. Alternatively, this argument may be construed to depend on the articulation of a rational or natural theology that requires toleration so that teaching and practicing toleration becomes not the byproduct of a determination on other grounds of the true religion and its correct interpretation, but the criterion for such determination and interpretation.

The advantage of this kind of argument is that it is supposed to appeal on their own terms to the Christian believers who seem to be causing the problem Locke addresses. If the problem of persecution that toleration is meant to remedy is caused by Christian believers, then what good would arguments for toleration do that do not accept the truth of Christianity?

The disadvantage of this kind of argument is precisely that it presupposes the possibility of doing away with the diversity of Christian sects and interpretations of Christianity, rather than the necessity of living with it. If it were that easy to get people to agree on the truth and meaning of Christianity, then toleration would hardly be necessary. Furthermore, this kind of argument would not extend Locke's position to toleration by non-Christians, which it is meant to include. Perhaps if it were necessary, Locke would have attempted to produce a *Reasonableness of Islam*, a *Reasonableness of Judaism*, a *Reasonableness of Hinduism*, or a *Reasonableness of Paganism*, to show that toleration was the mark of true adherents of those religions as well. Undoubtedly the practice of toleration would be more universal if such efforts had been successfully made by counterparts of Locke elsewhere. In any case, this kind of argument for toleration encounters the difficulty that recognition of the true religion is understood by many Christians and other adherents of revealed religions to be a matter of faith rather than knowledge or reason.[18] Perhaps for this reason Locke does not rest with this kind of argument. Immediately after this opening argument for toleration as the mark of true religion, he suggests that toleration is agreeable not only to the Gospel of Jesus Christ, but "to the genuine Reason of Mankind."[19]

A second kind of argument for toleration that Locke employs or at least suggests is that truth generally or true religion in particular would win out if only toleration were to replace persecution. He says "Truth certainly would do well enough, if she were once left to shift for her self."[20] This may remind us of the later view that truth will win out in the marketplace of ideas.[21] Instead of arguing that we already know the true religion and that it requires toleration, or alternatively that we can know which is the true religion by seeing whether it preaches and practices toleration, as Locke seems to do in the first kind of argument, this second kind of argument suggests that we cannot know the truth until we have toleration, that toleration is a *necessary* prerequisite for the truth to win out. This kind of argument is zetetic rather than sceptical: truth is knowable though not yet known under present (intolerant) political circumstances. This argument would be much too sanguine if it claimed that toleration were a *sufficient* prerequisite for truth to win out. Locke explains most fully in *Of the Conduct of the Understanding* that the pursuit of truth is a most strenuous activity requiring great effort at self-examination as well as freedom from imposition by others.[22] This argument also derives support from the Christian doctrine that true religion is a matter of freely accepted faith rather than merely external worship, with the result that it may share some of the difficulties of the first kind of argument. In any case, the passage making this suggestion stresses less the certain success of truth under toleration than its likely failure under persecution, which brings us to the third kind of argument.

The third kind of argument for toleration Locke employs is basically that persecution does not work, that it does not succeed in propagating the truth. Locke explains that "such is the nature of the Understanding, that it cannot be compell'd to the belief of any thing by outward force. Confiscation of Estate, Imprisonment, Torments, nothing of that nature can have any such Efficacy as to make Men change the inward Judgment that they have framed of things."[23] This argument also derives support from the Christian doctrine that religion consists in inward faith more than outward worship: "Faith is not Faith without believing" and "true and saving Religion consists in the inward perswasion of the Mind."[24] The problem with this argument is unfortunately that it is not simply true. We have learned that systems of persecution can have effects on beliefs. Even where torture does not change the beliefs of the tortured, it may prevent those beliefs from even reaching other people. We should not go so far in the opposite direction as those theorists of totalitarianism who thought persecution could totally compel belief. For we have also learned that beliefs can resist systems of persecution. It would be an extremely interesting question for students of comparative politics to investigate empirically where the truth lies between this claim of Locke's and that opposite claim, or perhaps rather where it drifts along that speçtrum under varying circumstances.

Locke himself knew that this claim that persecution cannot compel belief is not simply true, as we can see most simply by looking again at his presentation of the second argument. On closer inspection it proves to claim less that truth will necessarily win out under toleration than that "*Errors indeed prevail by the assistance of foreign and borrowed Succours.*"[25] Toleration would not matter so much, if there were not *some* truth in the second kind of argument, that truth has a better chance under toleration and is indeed obstructed though not obliterated by persecution. Indeed the thrust of this passage is partly that persecution will not succeed in propagating truth not so much because of the inefficacy of force as because of the unlikelihood that the wielders of force possess the truth: truth "will never receive much Assistance from the Power of Great men, to whom she is but rarely known, and more rarely welcome."

This leads us to the fourth kind of argument for toleration Locke makes, that even if persecution could change people's minds, it would not serve the cause of salvation but simply subject people to "the Religion, which either Ignorance, Ambition, or Superstition had chanced to establish in the Countries where they were born."[26] This argument is far from accepting every religion as a valid way to salvation or denying that we have any way of knowing which if any of them is true. It explicitly presumes, like the first kind of argument, that there is "but one Truth, one way to Heaven," so that if princes could dictate their subjects' religion then "one Country alone would be in the right, and all the rest of the World put under an obligation of following their Princes in the ways that lead to Destruction," and people would absurdly "owe their eternal Happiness or Misery to the places of their Nativity." This argument does not imply that we now know which is the true religion; on the contrary, it might even be taken to imply that we do not (or we might specify that only rulers who adhere to that religion can dictate it to their subjects). It sidesteps the question of which is the true religion and emphasizes instead the empirical "variety and contradiction of Opinions in Religion, wherein the Princes of the World are as much divided as in their Secular Interests." (It thereby might even suggest that this religious diversity reflects the diversity of secular interests among rulers.)

The fifth kind of argument that Locke seems to make and the one that appears in contrast most radically sceptical is that there is no judge of the truth, especially of religious truth. "Every one is Orthodox to himself" and "The Decision of that question [the controversy between churches about the truth of their doctrines] belongs only to the Supreme Judge of all men," God.[27] This most sceptical argument seems the opposite of the first, least sceptical argument: instead of claiming we know the true religion and it requires toleration, it seems to claim no one can know which is the true religion and such ignorance requires toleration. The two arguments would converge if *all* we knew about the true religion were that it preaches and practices toleration. In any case, this argument may not be as sceptical as it seems. It may be not a denial of any objective religious truth or falsehood, but merely an invocation of the empirical facts of the existence of diverse churches with incompatible claims to religious truth and their failure to recognize any common judge of such truth: "every Church is orthodox to it self; to others, Erroneous or Heretical. For whatsoever any Church believes, it believes to be true; and the contrary unto those things, it pronounces to be Error. So that the Controversie between these Churches about the Truth of their Doctrines, and the Purity of their Worship, is on both sides equal; nor is there any Judge . . . upon Earth, by whose Sentence it can be determined."[28] This would represent only a further specification of the situation to which toleration is a response, rather than a radical form of religious scepticism.

In the sixth kind of argument Locke offers for toleration, the one he most emphasizes, toleration rests on the knowledge of the truth, not the true religion, however, but the truth about civil society and its relation to religion -- and that truth is that civil society is *not* concerned with truth, religious or otherwise. Locke describes the political community as a society of people constituted only for preserving and advancing their civil goods, which he defines as comprising life, liberty, bodily health and freedom from pain, and possession of external things such as land, money, houses, furniture, etc. Government acts by depriving its subjects of those goods only in order to punish them for depriving others of those goods, only to preserve those civil goods.[29] In the *Letter Concerning Toleration* Locke emphasizes the contrast not made explicit in the *Two Treatises of Government:* "that all Civil Power, Right and Dominion, is bounded and confined to the only care of promoting these things [civil goods]; and that it neither can nor ought in any manner to be extended to the Salvation of Souls." On the contrary, "the Care therefore of every man's Soul belongs unto himself, and is to be left unto himself."[30] According to Locke, the purpose of government is limited not only to protecting civil goods rather than the care of the soul, but also to protecting those civil goods from harm by others rather from self-inflicted harm: "Laws provide, as much as is possible, that the Goods and Health of Subjects be not injured by the Fraud or Violence of others; they do not guard them from the Negligence or Ill-husbandry of the Possessors themselves."[31]

These limitations on government rest on Locke's claims that whereas individual pursuit of salvation neither interferes with its pursuit by others nor can be interfered with by the violence of others, individual pursuit of the property required for bodily preservation can affect its pursuit by others and can be interfered with by the violence of others. Similarly, the physical force wielded by government can prevent interference with the pursuit of the property required for bodily preservation in a way that it cannot facilitate the pursuit of salvation.[32] These limitations rest therefore not on scepticism about or denial of the goods of the soul or the means of achieving them, but these particular claims about the differing natures of the pursuits of the goods of the soul and those of the body.

This liberal restriction on the purpose of government excludes not only religious concern by government with the salvation of our souls, but also moral concern by government with the improvement or perfection of our souls. Locke argues in the *Letter* that "Covetousness, Uncharitableness, Idleness, and many other things are sins, by the consent of all men, which yet no man ever said were to be punished by the Magistrate. The reason is, because they are not prejudicial to other mens Rights, nor do they break the publick Peace of Societies."[33] In Locke's earlier so-called "Essay Concerning Toleration," not published until the twentieth century, he makes this point more emphatic: "however strange it may seeme, that the lawmaker hath nothing to doe with morall vertues and vices . . . otherwise than barely as they are subservient to the good and preservation of mankind under government." Indeed Locke says there that the lawmaker "is not bound to punish all, i.e. he may tolerate some vices."[34] Just as Locke denies that government ought to be concerned with the religious salvation or moral perfection of our souls, so similarly, he makes clear in the *Letter* that "laws are not concerned with the truth of opinions, but with the security and safety of the commonwealth and of each man's goods." The aim of government, according to Locke, therefore is, contrary to Plato, Aristotle or Aquinas, not the salvation or perfection of the soul, not cultivation of a particular kind of human being, not the inculcation of a set of moral virtues, nor the establishment of a body of truths or right opinions, but the security of civil goods, of rights or liberty.

Locke does not, however, rule out a kind of moral concern by government. Even the statement quoted above from the so-called "Essay Concerning Toleration," that the lawmaker has nothing to do with moral virtues and vices, does not end there: it continues "otherwise than barely as they are subservient to the good and preservation of mankind under government." That is to say the lawmaker *does* have to do with moral virtues and vices insofar as their promotion or curtailment *is* subservient to the good and preservation of mankind under government. Similarly although civil society is not concerned with the truth of opinions as such, it must establish the opinion of toleration itself. The *Two Treatises* aim to disestablish Sir Robert Filmer's doctrines of absolute monarchy by divine right and establish Locke's doctrines of natural liberty and government by consent, though this is a matter of private publication rather than government action. Liberal politics require a liberal public opinion in favor of liberty.

The last kind of argument for toleration Locke makes that I will deal with relates to the question of truth on a different level or from another angle. It involves a redescription of the situation to which toleration is Locke's response. Instead of saying that the intolerant sincerely believe in truth and therefore persecute those whom they regard as in error, Locke unmasks the motives of the persecutors as desire for power and greed for the property of others. He shifts the issue from one of rival claims to truth to one of motives manifest in conduct toward others. Boasts of orthodoxy are not marks of the true church but rather "Marks of Men striving for Power and Empire over one another"; persecutors aim not at the advancement of the kingdom of God but at "another Kingdom." At one point early in the *Letter,* Locke presents himself as a mediator between those who persecute under pretence of care for the public weal and those who seek "Impunity for their Libertinism and Licentiousness" under pretence of religion, one side seeking to color their pride and ambition, the other their passion and uncharitable zeal, all of which are "Faults from which Humane Affairs can perhaps scarce ever be perfectly freed."[35] But it becomes clear that persecutors are as likely to invoke the good of the church as that of the civil commonwealth, and that religious zeal is at least as likely to be used to persecute harmless sects as to plead for immunity for harmful ones. Locke's diagnosis wavers as to whether religious zeal mixes with or simply conceals other motives: speaking of the violent expropriation of the territory of innocent pagan American Indians by greedy Christian Europeans, he says "Then at last it appears what Zeal for the Church, joyned with the desire of Dominion, is capable to produce; and how easily the pretence of Religion, and of the care of Souls, serves for a Cloak to Covetousness, Rapine, and Ambition."[36] More precisely, Locke suggests that religious strife is produced not by Christianity itself ("which carries the greatest opposition to Covetousness, Ambition, Discord, Contention, and all manner of inordinate Desires; and is the most modest and peaceable Religion that ever was") or by the diversity of (especially Christian religious) opinions ("which cannot be avoided"), but rather by the refusal to tolerate different opinions based on the mixed motives of an unholy alliance: "The Heads and Leaders of the Church, moved by Avarice and insatiable desire of Dominion, making use of the immoderate Ambition of Magistrates, and the credulous Superstition of the giddy Multitude, have incensed and animated them against those that dissent from themselves."[37] Civil rulers, he explains, are invited by these incendiary preachers to share in the spoil and in turn use them as ministers of their own government; these preachers flatter the ambition and favor the dominion of princes to promote that tyranny in the commonwealth needed to establish the tyranny in the church they aim at. Ambition and avarice seem to motivate both civil and ecclesiastical tyrants; superstition seems to move only the multitude they exploit.

In opposition to the persecutors' ambition and desire for dominion, Locke appeals to the opposite motive, the desire to be free or to think of oneself as free. This powerful human desire is the foundation not only of toleration but of that more important objective, freedom of the mind, without which toleration itself hardly matters. We are not left in a situation of utter scepticism unable to judge between the claims to truth of the persecutors and the persecuted; resolution is more readily found on the level of motivation, where the claims to truth of the intolerant are discredited by their motives in contrast to the superior motives of the tolerant.

To appreciate these psychological foundations of toleration, it is necessary to look at Locke's fundamental political psychology, his view of human nature as it supports the liberal politics argued in the *Two Treatises*. Locke clearly emphasizes that the fundamental premise or hypothesis of those liberal politics is what he calls natural freedom, the claim that all human beings are by nature free and equal. This is equivalent to the negative statement that no human being has by nature a right to rule others, to exercise political power over them otherwise than as they reciprocally have the same power over him. Locke explains in the *First Treatise* that "all that share in the same common Nature, Faculties and Powers, are in Nature equal, and ought to partake in the same common Rights and Priviledges."[38] It is tempting simply to identify the common human nature, the common human faculty whose possession is the foundation of the natural freedom and equality of mankind, as rationality. Locke explains that it is reason which teaches human beings their equality and to respect its moral and political implications.[39] In his chapter on paternal or rather parental power, Locke explains that a child is subject to his parents, but becomes free when he becomes an adult because he then is capable "to provide for his own Support and Preservation, and govern his Actions according to the Dictates of the Law of Reason," whereas previously he was "without the use of *Reason*."[40] Locke concludes there that "The *Freedom* then of Man and Liberty of acting according to his own Will, is *grounded on* his having *Reason*."[41] Thus one might well conclude that the possession of reason is simply *the* reason why human beings are by nature free and equal, that it is because human beings are capable of directing themselves to the means of their own preservation[42] that they are not naturally subject to the will of others.

But if human beings were simply rational then freedom and equality might be possible but would hardly be necessary. Simply rational human beings could safely be subject to other simply rational creatures. This objection is partially obviated by the observation that the rationality identified here as the relevant common human faculty is an ability to direct oneself to the means to one's *own* preservation. Subjection to another human being, rationally directed to the means to *his* preservation, would not therefore necessarily secure one's *own* preservation. Nevertheless reason is supposed by Locke to dictate the preservation of all mankind or at least the negative prohibition against harming another in his life, health, liberty, or possessions.[43] Reason, however, retains a powerful primary element of self-concern: even the dictate to preserve the rest of mankind is limited by the proviso "when one's own Preservation comes not in competition."[44] In addition, reason is unreliable: its dictates on behalf of the preservation of all mankind (which Locke calls the Law of Nature) are supposed to be "plain and intelligible to all rational Creatures," but human beings, being "biassed by their Interest, as well as ignorant for want of study of it," are not apt to follow it consistently.[45]

It would still be too simple to say that the common human faculty of reason, even thus understood to be primarily self-concerned and unreliable, explains natural freedom and equality. After all, in the passages where Locke explains natural equality he does not single out reason but writes in the plural of unspecified "faculties."[46] What both differentiates human beings from irrational creatures and makes their freedom from one another natural for Locke is not merely their guidance by reason, but the presence of alternative sources of guidance. In a key passage in the *First Treatise,* Locke says that "the busie mind of Man [can] carry him to a Brutality [far] below the level of Beasts, when he quits his reason." Locke explains there that man's "fancy and passion must needs run him into strange courses, if reason, which is his only Star and compass, be not that he steers by. The imagination is always restless and suggests variety of thoughts, and the will, reason being laid aside, is ready for every extravagant project."[47] Thus, according to Locke, whereas the irrational animals "keep right by following nature" through their instincts, human beings are free either to follow their reason or to surpass the beasts in brutality through following imagination and passion. It is the co-presence in human nature of imagination and passion together with reason that makes equality a natural necessity and rules out natural subjection. Whereas one simply rational creature might naturally be ruled securely by another simply rational creature, a creature torn by reason, imagination, and passion is not naturally ruled securely by another such creature. The point of natural as well as civil liberty is not freedom from direction by the *reason* of others, but rather freedom from being subject to "the *in*constant, *un*certain, *un*known, *arbitrary* Will of another Man."[48]

The rivalry between fancy or imagination and reason is exacerbated in politically crucial ways when considered not within a single abstract individual but within historical societies. There both the interpersonal and the temporal dimensions magnify the power of fancy: when reason is laid aside, Locke continues in the key passage from the *First Treatise* quoted above:

> "he that goes farthest out of the way, is thought fittest to lead, and is sure of most followers: And when Fashion hath once Established, what Folly or craft began, Custom makes it Sacred . . . . He that will impartially survey the Nations of the World, will find so much of their Governments, Religions, and Manners brought in and continued amongst them by these means, that he will have but little Reverence for the Practices which are in use and credit amongst Men."[49]

Imagination is closely tied to the human tendency toward imitation so the imagination of one person can easily guide the conduct of another. Crafty men (both priests and rulers) are able to take advantage of this vulnerability, and the passage of time gives authority and even sacredness to custom.[50]

Fancy and passion play largely negative roles in the political psychology or pathology of the *Two Treatises*. Locke characterizes Filmer's theory of divine right patriarchal monarchy, against which his work is directed, as a product of Filmer's fancy.[51] More generally, Locke presents ideas of perfect government or "Eutopia" generated by the fancy as the enemies of political order.[52] Indeed, according to Locke, a great part of the positive laws are "the Phansies and intricate Contrivances of Men, following contrary and hidden interests" rather than reason or the law of nature.[53] Similarly, Locke's famous teaching on property is based in part on the opposition between "the Fancy or Covetousness of the Quarrelsom and Contentious" and the labor of "the Industrious and Rational," and on the distinction between value derived from fancy and "real Use, and the necessary Support of Life."[54]

Passion plays a similarly negative role in Locke's argument against absolute monarchy, which requires submission to whatever one man does "whether led by Reason, Mistake or Passion."[55] Locke distinguishes tyranny from lawful government by the ruler's directing his actions not to the preservation of the property of his people, but to "the satisfaction of his own Ambition, Revenge, Covetousness, or any other irregular Passion."[56]

Ambition is the passion that plays the greatest role in the political pathology Locke's liberal politics are designed to cure. Doctrines like Filmer's, which dress up power "with all the Splendor and Temptation Absoluteness can add to it," flatter and give a greater edge to the natural ambition of man, only too apt of itself to grow and increase with the possession of any power.[57] Ambition seems to be the passion that makes it most necessary for human beings not to be naturally subject to one another, not to be subject without their consent, not to be subject to absolute power, but to be naturally free and equal. Locke says it is the ambition or insolence of empire that teaches people to beware of absolute power.[58] It is also ambition and luxury that corrupt people's minds into misunderstanding true power and honor and that teach princes to have distinct interests from their peoples.[59] It is ambition that fills the world with disorders, war, and conquest.[60] The pride and ambition of private persons and rulers have caused great disorders in commonwealths.[61]

Yet human pride of a certain kind also plays a more positive role complementary to that of reason as a natural ground of Locke's liberal politics. The *First Treatise* opens with the following sentence: "Slavery is so vile and miserable an Estate of Man, and so directly opposite to the generous Temper and Courage of our Nation; that 'tis hardly to be conceived, that an *Englishman,* much less a *Gentleman*, should plead for't."[62] The pride Locke ultimately appeals to, however, is less a national or class pride than a species pride, a pride in human rationality and superiority to the irrational animals. This pride affirms natural human equality and rejects natural subordination "as if we were made for one anothers uses, as the inferior ranks of Creatures are for ours."[63] This pride expresses indignation at those rulers who would treat their peoples like herds of cattle and those political theorists who justify their doing so; indeed this pride treats those who would treat their fellow human beings as cattle themselves as wild beasts fit to be destroyed.[64] The subject of an absolute prince is treated, Locke complains, "as if he were degraded from the common state of Rational Creatures."[65] Conversely, people can consent only to political power that is to be used for their common good since "a Rational Creature cannot be supposed when free, to put himself into Subjection to another, for his own harm."[66] It is our pride or sense of what is due to us as rational creatures that makes us potential partisans of liberalism and toleration.

It is indeed difficult to distinguish Locke's grounding natural freedom, liberalism, and toleration on human rationality from his grounding them also on human *pride* in human rationality, in our sense of "what may be suitable to the dignity and excellency of a rational creature."[67] Indeed we can see in Locke's *Thoughts* that granting liberty constitutes the most prudent as well as the most rightful way of governing human beings, above all because of their desire to "be thought rational creatures, and have our freedom," "to show that they are free, that their own good actions come from themselves, that they are absolute and independent."[68] The sense of my own *rationality*, my own ability to direct myself to the means to my preservation, seems inseparable from a proud desire for *liberty* and resistance to those who would deprive me of it or treat me as if I were not a rational creature.

This pride is not itself entirely rational. Others might well try to deprive me of my liberty or even destroy me without denying that I have an ability to determine the means to my preservation -- they may simply prefer their comfort to my preservation. Perhaps for the possession of rationality to rationally justify this pride, rationality must be conceived as more than the ability to determine the means to one's preservation -- it may have to be a sense that one is created in the image of God.[69]

The argument on behalf of toleration or liberalism in the *Essay Concerning Human Understanding* has a similar character. The *Essay* argues on behalf of toleration or liberalism not as a set of political institutions or doctrines, but as a set of moral dispositions supportive of such institutions or doctrines. Locke complains in the *Essay* that people are deprived of "the Liberty and Opportunities of a fair Enquiry" in places "where men are forced . . . to be of the Religion of the Country."[70] Following the opinions of others has the same consequence as being obligated to follow the legally established religion: it would give people "Reason to be Heathens in Japan, Mahumetans in Turkey, Papists in Spain, Protestants in England, and Lutherans in Sueden."[71] The *Essay* urges its readers not to be "content to live lazily on scraps of begg'd Opinions," and neither to assume an authority of dictating their opinions to others nor to accept the opinions of those church or party leaders who would impose them by authority.[72]

Locke's argument for toleration or liberalism in the *Essay* attempts to unite the duty to examine one's own opinions insofar as one can and the duty to let others do so too.[73] He tries to unite these two by claiming that "those, who have not throughly examined to the bottom all their own Tenets, must confess, they are unfit to prescribe to others" and "those who have fairly and truly examined . . . are so few in number, and find so little reason to be magisterial in their opinions, that nothing insolent and imperious is to be expected from them." Conversely, Locke argues, "assuming an Authority of Dictating to others, and a forwardness to prescribe their opinions" is a constant concomitant of being one who does violence to his own faculties and "tyrannizes over his own mind."[74] It is therefore above all to our desire to believe that our own minds are free that Locke appeals to restrain us from trying to enslave the minds of others.

The *Essay* affirms human rationality, the capacity of human reason to find measures whereby a rational creature ought to govern his opinions and actions.[75] But it does not support toleration or liberalism simply on the basis of the power of human rationality, as if each human being were fully capable of finding out the truth unassisted, likely to do so if left unhindered, and therefore entitled to liberty. For the *Essay* is only in part an affirmation of human rationality; it is also an elaborate catalog of the obstacles and limits to human rationality. Yet neither does the *Essay* make its argument for toleration simply on the basis of the impotence of human rationality, as if every human being were incapable of finding out the truth and therefore not entitled to impose his opinions on others but obligated instead to respect their liberty. On the contrary, the *Essay* like the *Two Treatises*, makes its argument for liberty on the basis of a view of human nature that emphasizes both rationality and the obstacles to it, and even what might be called the rationality of the limits of human rationality.

This paradoxical character of the *Essay*'s case for liberty can perhaps be seen most clearly in an argument Locke makes introducing his consideration of the degrees of assent based on probability.[76] He starts by pointing out that people often firmly stick to opinions without remembering the reasons that first made them embrace that side of the question, thus becoming obstinate in error. The fault is not, however, that we rely on our memories and forget the good reasons we once knew, but rather that we judged wrong in the first place, or more likely that we never questioned or examined the grounds of our opinions. We therefore cannot be sure that there is not more evidence that would change our minds. Locke asks "Who almost is there, that hath the leisure, patience, and means, to collect together all the Proofs concerning most of the Opinions he has" so as to safely conclude there is no more to be alleged that might change his mind? "And yet," Locke notes, "we are forced to determine our selves on the one side or other. The conduct of our Lives, and the management of our great Concerns, will not bear delay." Not only is it therefore "unavoidable to the greatest part of Men, if not all, to have several *Opinions,* without certain and undubitable proofs of their Truth," but they cannot reasonably be expected "to quit and renounce their former Tenets, presently upon the offer of an Argument which they cannot immediately answer." Locke's liberal and tolerant conclusion is that it would "become all men to maintain *Peace,* and the common Offices of Humanity, *and Friendship, in the diversity of Opinions*, since we cannot reasonably expect that anyone should readily and obsequiously quit his own Opinion, and embrace ours with a blind resignation to an Authority which the Understanding of Man acknowledges not." If others do not think our arguments weighty enough to be worth going over all the evidence again, we should not take it amiss. The necessity of believing without knowledge should make us more concerned to inform ourselves than to constrain others. It is unreasonable to expect people to be open to every reason they encounter because it is reasonable of them to limit their pursuit of truth. Locke avoids the danger that precisely his call for self-examination might lead an enlightened few to lose patience with the dogmatic many. He urges his readers to embark on the struggle for their own intellectual liberation, the struggle that ultimately justifies toleration, but he recognizes the practical limits on that quest and thereby guarantees toleration even for all those who shirk that call.

NOTES:

1. John Locke, *A Letter Concerning Toleration.* ed. James H. Tully (Indianapolis: Hackett, 1983), 21.
2. John Locke, *An Essay Concerning Human Understanding,* ed. Peter H. Nidditch (Oxford: Oxford University Press, 1975), 550 (IV 3.18).
3. Locke, *Letter* 49-50.
4. Locke, *Letter* 49-50.
5. Locke, *Letter* 40-42.
6. Locke, *Letter* 51. I omit the phrase "that Liberty of Conscience is every mans natural Right," inserted by Popple; see John Locke, *Epistola de Tolerantia/A Letter on Toleration,* ed. & trans. Raymond Klibansky and J.W. Gough, 134-37, 161 n. 58.
7. *George Washington: A Collection,* (Oxford: Oxford University Press, 1968), ed. W.B. Allen (Indianapolis: Liberty Classics, 1988), 548.
8. Locke, *Two Treatises of Government,* ed. Peter Laslett (Cambridge: Cambridge University Press, 1988), 404-405 (II 209): if the majority of the people "are persuaded in their Consciences, that their Laws, and with them their Estates, Liberties, and Lives are in danger, and perhaps their Religion too, how they will be hindered from resisting illegal force, used against them. I cannot tell."
9. Locke, *Essay* 708-709 (IV 20.4).
10. Locke, *Letter* 23-24.
11. Locke, *Letter* 24-25.
12. Locke, *Letter* 54.
13. Locke, *Letter* 32, 43.
14. Locke, *Letter* 23.
15. Locke, *Letter* 32, 40, 43, 54, 93.
16. Locke, *Letter* 23.
17. Locke, *Letter* 25.
18. For Locke, however, it is reason that must determine whether what purports to be revelation is genuine, *Essay* 691-95 (IV 18.5-.6, .8).
19. Locke, *Letter* 25.
20. Locke, *Letter* 46.
21. Cf. Oliver Wendell Holmes, Jr., "the best test of truth is the power of the thought to get itself accepted in the competition of the market," *Abrams v. United States,* 250 U.S. 630 [1919].
22. John Locke, *Some Thoughts Concerning Education and Of the Conduct of the Understanding,* ed. Ruth W. Grant and Nathan Tarcov (Indianapolis/Cambridge: Hackett Publishing Co., 1996), stet.
23. Locke, *Letter* 27.
24. Locke, *Letter* 26-27.
25. Locke, *Letter* 46 (emphasis added). See also *Essay* 708-709 (IV 20.4).
26. Locke, *Letter* 27-28.
27. Locke, *Letter* 23, 32.
28. Locke, *Letter* 32.
29. Locke, *Letter* 26.
30. Locke, *Letter* 26, 35.
31. Locke, *Letter* 34-35.
32. Locke, *Letter* 47-48.

33. Locke, *Letter* 44.

34. John Locke, *Scritti Editi e Inediti Sulla Tolleranza*, ed. Carlo Augusto Viano (Turin: Taylor Turino, 1961) 90-91.

35. Locke, *Letter* 23, 25.

36. Locke, *Letter* 43.

37. Locke, *Letter* 54-55.

38. Locke, *Two Treatises* 190 (I 67); see also 269 (II 4).

39. Locke, *Two Treatises* 271 (II 6).

40. Locke, *Two Treatises* 305-306 (II 56-57).

41. Locke, *Two Treatises* 309 (II 63, emphases in the original).

42. Locke, *Two Treatises* 205 (I 86).

43. Locke, *Two Treatises* 270-71 (II 6-7).

44. Locke, *Two Treatises* 271 (II 6).

45. Locke, *Two Treatises* 351 (II 124).

46. Locke, *Two Treatises* 190, 269 (I 67, II 4).

47. Locke, *Two Treatises* 182-83 (I 58).

48. Locke, *Two Treatises* 284 (II 22); see also 305-308, 359-60 (II 57-60, 137).

49. Locke, *Two Treatises* 182-83 (I 58).

50. Locke, *Two Treatises* 329 (II 94).

51. Locke, *Two Treatises* 146 (IT 7).

52. Locke, *Two Treatises* 202-203, 249-50 (I 81, 147).

53. Locke, *Two Treatises* 275 (II 12).

54. Locke, *Two Treatises* 291, 300 (II 34, 46).

55. Locke, *Two Treatises* 276 (II 13).

56. Locke, *Two Treatises* 398-99 (II 199).

57. Locke, *Two Treatises* 148, 219 (I 10, 106); see also 363 (II 143).

58. Locke, *Two Treatises* 338 (II 107).

59. Locke, *Two Treatises* 342-43 (II 111).

60. Locke, *Two Treatises* 384-85 (II 175).

61. Locke, *Two Treatises* 418 (II 230).

62. Locke, *Two Treatises* 141 (I 1).

63. Locke, *Two Treatises* 271 (II 6).

64. Locke, *Two Treatises* 181, 256, 273, 274, 279, 328, 377, 382-83, 389, 390 (I 56, 156, II 10, 11, 16, 93, 163, 172 and n., 181, 182).

65. Locke, *Two Treatises* 327 (II 91).

66. Locke, *Two Treatises* 377 (II 164); see also 353 (II 131).

67. Locke, *Thoughts* 25 (#31).

68. Locke, *Thoughts* 31, 51 (#41, #73).

69. Locke, *Two Treatises* 162, 168 (I 30, 40).

70. Locke, *Essay* 708-709 (IV 20.4).

71. Locke, *Essay* 657 (IV 15.6); compare Locke, *Letter* 27-28.

72. Locke, *Essay* 6-7, 657, 698, 718-19 (Epistle to the Reader, IV 15.6, 19.2, 20.17-18).

73. Locke, *Essay* 99-100, 559-61 (I 4.22, IV 16.4).

74. Locke, *Essay* 698 (IV 19.2).

75. Locke, *Essay* 46 (I 1.6).

76. Locke, *Essay* 657-61 (IV 16.1-4).

10

PIERRE BAYLE'S ATHEIST POLITICS

Kenneth R. Weinstein

Pierre Bayle's long-neglected *Miscellaneous Thoughts on the Comet* (1682) is perhaps the boldest work of early modern political philosophy. The *Thoughts* start with an indirect attack upon the historical veracity of the New Testament before becoming the first work of political philosophy to openly argue that a society of atheists can exist and prosper. Bayle sees the society without religion as the most stable solution to the violence endemic to political life in the 17th century. Ultimately, however, Bayle doubted that such a society could be established in western Europe. Instead, Bayle sought to promote a second-best solution to the political crisis of Christendom: rule by elites indifferent in matters of religion. Bayle's third-best political solution is a wise policy of toleration within Christendom. Toleration circumscribes the political role of religion, thereby approximating the stability achieved by the society of atheists or the state ruled by an atheist elite.

Bayle's Free-Thinking Attack on Christian Tradition Via the Pagans

Before one can interpret Bayle's political philosophy, we must determine how his vast oeuvre is to be read. Bayle's writing style contains an admixture of pious declarations and infrequent impieties. Until the 1960s, almost all scholars understood Bayle's piety as feigned, seeing him as an irreligious skeptic whose attacks on tradition, priestcraft, and Christian practice consciously paved the way to the era of Voltaire and Didérot.[1] In recent years, however, following the lead of Elisabeth Labrousse, most scholars see Bayle's pious declarations as the essence of his thought – and as proof that he was a pious albeit heterodox product of the Huguenot exile milieu in the 17th century Holland in which he lived. Such studies portray Bayle as an idiosyncratic Calvinist whose attacks on Catholic assent to tradition, priestcraft and "idolatry" were mistaken by Enlightenment thinkers for attacks on Christianity itself.[2] According to Labrousse, Bayle remained Calvinist until he suffered a spiritual crisis in 1685. After that, she argues, pessimistic passages in his writings on the origin of evil, skepticism of divine providence and apparent support for the possibility that the universe was generated by material forces lacking guidance from God make it impossible to ascertain Bayle's precise religious views.[3]

Though Labrousse's opinion had been scholarly orthodoxy for a quarter century, an important study of a 1679 manuscript by Bayle points to the need for reassessment. Analyzing *The Objections to Pierre Poiret,* Gianluca Mori demonstrates that by 1679, Bayle elaborated on all the "pessimistic" themes that Labrousse associated with the post-1685 Bayle: arguments against divine providence and in favor of material naturalism, and discussions of the impossibility of reconciling divine omnipotence with the presence of evil in the world. Furthermore, Mori shows that Bayle even argued against Cartesian body-mind dualism, and against Descartes' proofs of the existence of God and of the immortality of the soul, in the same manner as he would two decades later in the most skeptical passages of the *Historical and Critical Dictionary.*[4]

Three years after writing the *Objections*, Bayle speaks in the *Thoughts* of those – unmistakably like himself – who spend their time pondering "if Descartes, in his metaphysics, did a good job of demonstrating the existence of God and the immortality of the soul and if he responded well to objections."[5] Bayle calls such thinkers the "strong spirits," the same term he applies to a variety of irreligious skeptics, ranging from François de La Mothe Le Vayer to Gabriel Naudé to the Latin Averroist Pierre Oriol.[6] These strong spirits are the "enemies of religion...[who]...believe nothing;" they spend their time "clarifying the objections raised against Providence," as Bayle himself did in the *Objections.*[7]

Bayle's unmistakable if subtle self-advertisement as an enemy of Christianity provides justification for seeking a strong thinker's attack in the *Thoughts.* The *Thoughts* is a complex work, one in which Bayle, nominally a Calvinist, takes the guise of a Catholic theologian to explain why the great comet of 1680 could not have been a sign sent from God to bring mankind to repent. The first part of the work, which serves as the preface to the discussion of the possibility of an atheist society, attacks tradition in general and astrology in particular. This attack, I believe, is nothing short of an indirect criticism of the veracity of the New Testament, focusing on its Achilles' heel – its account of miracles with astronomical origins, namely the Star of Bethlehem and the eclipse at the time of the Crucifixion.[8]

To calm the fears generated by the comet, Bayle rejects the notion that comets "are like heralds" sent by God to bring men to repent. Bayle offers what he terms a "theological argument" to prove that it is against God's wisdom to use such "vague and confusing" signs as comets and eclipses at all. Such express miracles would have the "terrible consequence" of leading hordes of pagans to perform rituals to honor their gods.[9] Were God to send comets as signs to mankind, they would have the "terrible consequence" that He made express miracles that led pagans to perform bloody rituals to honor His sham imposters.[10] Were God to have formed comets by miracles, He would have concurred with the Devil to lead men deeper and deeper into pagan superstition, "which is something that cannot either be said or thought without impiety."[11] "Signs that are so general and obscure," such as "new heavenly bodies" are "undignified of the wisdom and holiness of God."

Such vague signs would only "arouse false alarm" – something more appropriate for Pan and Apollo.[12]

In the midst of his brief against miracles that would increase pagan devotion, there is a peculiar contradiction. Bayle feigns to overlook this theological argument when "defending" the eclipse that occurred at the Crucifixion. Bayle argues that if God wanted to send clear signals to rational beings, He would perform miracles that could not be confused for natural phenomena, as "when He wanted the sun to serve as a witness by its darkness to the profound mysteries of the passion of Jesus Christ." To work this miracle, God chose to darken the heavens "at a time when darkness could not be natural."[13]

Yet Bayle's defense of the New Testament raises severe doubts about this miracle.[14] For just after denying that such darkness was natural, Bayle points to the need for philosophy to ascertain the extraordinary character of this eclipse: without philosophy, "the people…would be carried to error and superstition in seeing uncommon natural effects."[15] The devil would immediately profit from such error.

Since miracles are "particular wills of God," they must yield information "so clearly and so distinctly as to reveal the real God, so there is no reason to doubt whether Jupiter is acting or the creator of all things."[16] When "God chooses to interrupt the order He establishes in nature," as He does in performing miracles such as the eclipse at the Crucifixion,[17] "our reason cannot conceive that He should do that which…[would]…bring men into the trap of Idolatry."[18] The omnipotent and omniscient creator could not possibly imagine that by shining a comet over the heads of idolaters He could convince them that He is the true God.[19]

To highlight this problem, Bayle draws our attention to the shoddy method of those who appropriated heavenly phenomena for their accounts of the lives of heroes. Bayle attacks those responsible for spreading tales that later became popular – the poets and historians -- for embellishing their otherwise bland stories with supernatural phenomena. Although Bayle does not attack the authors of the Gospel by name, the implicit parallels he draws to the Star of Bethlehem and the solar eclipse at the Crucifixion – common themes for the strong thinkers – leave little doubt that the New Testament is his target. He repeatedly scoffs at pagan miracles, such as the stars alleged to have appeared at the birth of the emperors Honorius (384-428 A.D.) and Mithridates (171-138 B.C.), or the unnatural changes in the sun occurring at the death of Caesar (44 B.C.).[20] Bayle laughs at the foolishness of the mythmakers who suggest that eclipses can presage or cause catastrophes, such as the "death of a king."[21] Bayle also attacks the panegyrists for seizing upon comets that "appear at the birth of a Prince who became strong and victorious."[22]

Moreover, Bayle focuses at length on the question of whether the sun went into hiding at the time of Caesar's death. This problem is paralleled by the question of the differing chronologies in the New Testament's account of the eclipse of the Crucifixion.[23] The Gospel of John tells us that Christ was condemned at noon, while, according to Mark, Christ died on the cross three hours earlier.[24] Likewise,

Bayle criticizes the poets at Augustus' court for not coordinating the stories they told about Caesar's death. Horace claimed that the Tyber overflowed; Suetonius claimed that Caesar's soul became a comet that ascended to heaven.[25] Virgil somehow overlooked the comet; if he had common sense, he would "have accommodated himself to the others." Virgil, however, did claim that the "sun covered itself with darkness at Caesar's death." Ovid, who spoke of the comet, claimed that the sun became pale, but before Caesar's death.[26] Bayle notes that there is one "true way" to decipher the difficulties in these differing accounts: "for if it is said that the sun went down before the death of Caesar or if one says that it went down after, it is the same thing for the glory of his successor." Virgil, Ovid, Horace and Suetonius had only one aim: "to court, with the strength of incense, the Emperor Augustus."[27]

Bayle's repeated references to writers and poets who associated stars, eclipses, ghosts and earthquakes with the births and deaths of their heroes indicate an agenda that goes beyond the Calvinist critique of Catholicism.[28] Using the example of astrology, "the most absurd thing in the world" to make his case against the veracity of the New Testament, Bayle calls for the extermination of all popular errors in the section of the *Thoughts* that serves as the preface to the discussion of the atheist state.

Popular Error and the Rise of the Priestly Control of the Soul

Popular errors such as astrology, which for Bayle contaminated Christianity from the outset, arise because man's natural laziness combines with his credulousness to popularize the misguided tales concocted by a few. Rather than "examining…with great care" such accounts, men accept hearsay, incorrectly assuming that "two or three persons…[who originated an opinion]…examined what they taught." The fact that traditions rest solely on the word of those who originate them becomes buried under the stampede of popular consent.[29] Although the popularity of a belief makes it seem venerable, the more venerable an opinion is, the less likely it is to be properly examined. Fearing ostracism, men come to feel "the necessity to believe that which all the world believes." Educated individuals, whom Bayle notes should serve as a "light" unto others, get swept up in this "torrent." They ignore experience and common sense, and come to accept "dogmas that perturb public tranquility."[30]

Bayle suggests an antidote to harmful popular doctrines: to examine "things well on the principles of philosophy."[31] Rather than accepting "authority," Bayle argues for a thorough, impartial evaluation of the facts: "the testimony of a man should only have force in proportion to the degree of certitude he has accrued in fully learning the facts."[32] "No man," he declares, "has the right to ask that his own sentiment be heard," no matter how popular his opinion may be, unless he has "examined the heart of the matter."[33]

Since 'the people' do not examine the heart of the matter, it is easy to understand how rare natural events strike terror in their hearts. Sensing the utility of this fear, politicians first sought to exploit it, by frightening their subjects into obedience through the menace of ever-vigilant gods. In addition, politicians fomented religious zeal to tie their subjects to the fatherland: promising divine rewards against "enemies seeking to profane these hallowed grounds," magistrates worked to fill their citizens with "fear...veneration and...respect" and arouse their courage against enemy peoples.[34]

The priests who managed these sacred ceremonies also sought to maintain popular superstitions. The fear and respect kindled by ritual soon engendered fear and respect of those ministering these rites. Using artifice to capitalize on popular alarm, priests gave themselves new prominence through elaborate ceremonies by which they asserted their indispensability. Indeed, though magistrates once used religion to keep subjects in check, eventually ambitious priests made their positions seem so important that even magistrates and members of prominent families sought priestly reward from their new posts. These men "worked harder and harder to establish an empire over souls;" they imposed new burdens upon the people and scared them into believing that all uncommon events were signs from the gods requiring expiation.[35] This 'empire over souls' presented a direct challenge to the political domain.

As ambitious priests placed themselves above rulers, they made themselves appear to be "mediators between gods and men."[36] The people saw priests as capable only of understanding divine will and also redressing divine wrath: "it became believed that they had the key to the heavens, that they could repulse the evils which faced the state, in a word, that in them resided the public good."[37]

Thus, through ignorance and fraud, fear triumphed over common sense and the priests profited from popular superstition to establish an 'empire over souls.' This 'empire over souls' soon took precedence over the realm of politics, leading politicians to grievous errors that could easily have been avoided. Nicias, the Athenian general at the battle of Sicily in the Peloponnesian War, was "so seized by a superstitious panic" at a lunar eclipse, that, rather than profiting from an occasion to retreat, he waited for the lunar cycle to pass, thereby bringing doom to his soldiers and himself.[38] Bayle notes that philosophers could help politicians like Nicias avoid such disasters; however, the threat of persecution prevents them from assisting.[39]

Bayle suggests that philosophers enlighten statesmen in the way that Anaxagoras enlightened Pericles, saving him from the "vain apprehension" that Nicias faced. Pericles, Bayle notes, was able to bring a frightened captain to realize that a solar eclipse at the outset of a voyage posed no threat to the Athenian flotilla.[40] Noting that anyone can follow Pericles' example, Bayle points to the political implications of correcting popular errors. Politicians will no longer be prey to superstition or priestly blackmail once they are freed from fears that result from the mistaken association of independent phenomena. The autonomy of the political realm can be maintained more effectively; those insurrections that result from taking rare natural events as signs that "those who do not perform their duties well in the eyes of God" will be prevented.[41]

Religion's Failure to Produce Good Behavior: Toward the Atheist State

The purpose of Bayle's discussion of comets and eclipses was to raise doubts about the evidence for religious belief, including Christian belief. Having made the case against the sloppy historical method he sees at the root of religion, Bayle shifts his emphasis from comets and eclipses. He uses his method of careful examination to eliminate popular myths about the relation of religious belief to morality, of the civil law to the ecclesiastic, and of atheism to politics. Having subtly debunked miracles associated with Christ, Bayle goes on to prove that the cardinal virtues ascribed to religious belief can arise in men devoid of faith.[42] Because religion cannot accomplish anything to enhance morals that cannot be accomplished otherwise with less danger, Bayle argues that the dangers posed by religion should be mitigated or, indeed, avoided.

To convince politicians that religion is not politically necessary, Bayle continues his battle against popular errors; in particular, he needs to crush the mistaken association of religious belief with virtue and atheism with vice. By proving that one can believe in God and behave abhorrently or be an atheist and behave reasonably, Bayle shows that religious belief does not cause virtue and that disbelief does not cause vice. In this way, Bayle seeks both to dissipate the horror associated with atheism, and to strengthen awareness of the civil turmoil that religious belief has engendered. In explaining that religious belief is not a source of virtue, Bayle lays down the principles that guide his secularized explanation of man's behavior. The more we understand that dangerous behavior arises despite or indeed perhaps because of religious belief, the more our tendency to attribute good behavior to religious motives will be reduced.

At Bayle unmasks the flattering lies men tell themselves to present their behavior in the most pious light, he unmasks the impact of religion on human behavior. Because the flames of hell do not keep men in check, the earthly fires of zealotry ought not to be stoked. If man can be shown to be governable by manipulation of the passions in accordance with earthly psychology, then wise politicians will no longer perceive a need to rely upon religious sanctions for stability. Religion can thereby be taken out of the public realm. Neither sovereigns nor peoples will feel the need to force their beliefs upon others.

Bayle starts from common opinion, noting that the man who does not acknowledge the existence of God is generally considered to be the most malevolent of all beasts. Tradition holds the atheist ruler to be the most dangerous of the mockers of convention and truth, unfettered as he is by both civil and divine law. Having no moral principles to guide him, "if he is in a position that places him above the human laws, just as he already put himself above the remorse of conscience [by his atheism], there is no crime that cannot be expected from him."[43] "Neither held back by the fear of any divine punishment nor moved by the hope of any heavenly reward," the atheist ruler would be led to commit the most heinous crimes.[44]

Contrary to this violent glutton seeking only utility and sensual pleasure, one would expect those who believe that a providential God governs the universe always to behave virtuously. Fearing the omniscient and omnipotent God who "gives infinite happiness to those who love virtue, and punished with eternal penalties those who give into vice," pious men could be expected to be truthful and deny earthly desires.[45] Believers ought to follow the principles they take as established by God and imbued in their conscience, preferring heavenly felicity to fleeting pleasure. Heeding the conscience, man's moral guide, which "knows in general the beauty of virtue," pious men could be expected to act in accord with equity.[46]

According to Bayle, however, this view, that man follows his conscience, heeding the moral law established by a providential God, is merely a "metaphysical abstraction," incompatible with the facts.[47] Just like astrological miracles, this belief cannot withstand careful examination. We fail to live in accord with our duty because our behavior has far more immediate causes than our "general opinions."[48] Our behavior is utterly contingent: "man does not decide one course of action instead of another because of general knowledge of what he ought to do, but instead makes a particular judgment about each thing, when he is about to take action."[49]

Instead of following conscience, "man consults the passions alone and decides that he must act here and now against the general idea…of duty." Man is moved by his character, the result of both nature and nurture, a potpourri of "the passion that dominates his heart, the proclivity of his temperament…the force of acquired habits and the taste or sensibility he has for certain objects." Given the strength of this mix of passion, temperament, habits and taste, Bayle argues that "there is nothing more subject to illusion than to judge the ways of a man by the general opinions he holds."[50]

In the *Thoughts*, Bayle regrets the lack of reliable records of atheist nations to compare to other nations; however, he notes that atheists would certainly not be worse behaved than other men, (excepting, in a bow to convention, those blessed with the grace of the Holy Spirit). As god-fearing pagans committed every crime imaginable, from avarice to hatred to cruelty, men deprived of belief could hardly do worse.[51] Moreover, the great criminals of history, men such as Tarquin, Catiline and Nero, were not atheists.[52]

For Bayle, religion fails to serve as a brake on the passions; instead, religious belief may lead men to commit greater crimes than their nature itself recommends. If the pagans had no religion, Bayle claims that they would not have unleashed so much cruelty against the early Christians. The pagans would not have seen Christians as the "cause of public calamities" in the Empire, nor would they have been so attached to their gods as to be threatened by Christianity's anti-pagan sentiments. Had Julian the Apostate been an atheist, he would not have persecuted

Christians in the name of religion.[53]

This tendency to persecute those who do not share one's faith is aggravated, Bayle notes, by Catholicism and its strange distinction between doctrinal errors and vices.[54] By focusing its wrath on those who disagree with Church teachings rather than on those with abhorrent morals, the Church makes belief easier for members, and persecution of dissidents far more likely. Rather than leading Catholics to correct their own vices, Bayle argues that Church practice encourages them to persecute others. Catholics are not alone in this tendency toward persecution; "blind adherence to tradition and custom" is as characteristic of the Church as of its pagan predecessors in Rome, but Calvinists are also inclined to ostracize those innovators who disagree with them.[55]

Noting the horrors of persecution, Bayle argues that "there are greater errors than denying" Providence. Rather than disbelief, "nothing can be more heretical than to believe that one can please God in violating the common notions of equity."[56] Bayle declares that it is one thousand times better to be indifferent toward all Christian sects than to be filled with the type of zeal that leads to tyrannicide and civil war. "If the court of France had been atheist," rather than being controlled by the intolerant and deceptive Catherine de Medici, France might have been spared the horrors of civil war.[57] The Catholic missionaries who persuaded magistrates to persecute Huguenots under the pretext of piety are far more criminal than men indifferent in matters of religion.[58]

Mere belief in God is "too weak a barrier to control the passions of men" and therefore cannot change man's inner disposition: all it can do is encourage outward signs of devotion. Religion's effects are "more physical than moral;" it ties men to the fatherland through ceremonies in places held to be of special import to the gods. Religion does not help men combat the corruption of their nature; it merely leads them to combat their enemies more ferociously.[59]

Besides encouraging patriotism through promise of divine reward, religion emboldens men through the "natural aversion one has for the enemies of one's faith." This natural aversion is the root of intolerance, perhaps the most powerful effect that religion has on the souls of believers. In many cases, this attachment is no different from the attachment to one's country. Noting these dangers in his typical understatement, Bayle says that the Italian humanist Giralomo Cardan had "some reason to say that belief in the immortality of the soul caused great disorders in the world by the wars of religion that it had aroused at all times."[60]

Unable to tame the passions, religion excites them, unleashing ferocity and authorizing crimes in the name of God. Belief may not be the ultimate cause of human actions, nevertheless, "religion often gets mixed in...and it gives great force for the things to which our temperament is inclined: for instance, a bilious man is more quickly armed with zeal against those who are not of his sect."[61] This zeal is fortified by the "natural desire and pleasure we take in surpassing our rivals and in avenging ourselves on those who condemn our behavior." Motivated against people of a different faith by an "implacable hatred," violence is justified by piety.[62]

Christianity, too, fails to make its followers virtuous; like societies of pagans, without human laws to establish order, "all Christian societies, too, would quickly collapse."[63] Rather than preventing crimes, fervent religious practice may lessen guilt from crime as believers come to think they can expiate past sins.[64]

"The knowledge of God and of Providence is too weak a barrier to hold back the human passions," except, of course, if men's hearts have been sanctified by the Holy Spirit.[65] Neither pagan superstition nor Christian revelation prevents men from living in disorder.[66] As the fear of God is not enough to control men, those who lack this fear "are not more free of a brake than those who have it."[67] Paris would be destroyed in a couple of weeks if left unbridled by human law and placed under the authority of predicators and confessors.

Human justice is the source of "virtue for the vast majority of the people."[68] If the laws permit a certain sin, few people do not commit it. The invisible constraint of the canon law offers no match for the visible force of the civil law.[69] Part of the ineffectiveness of ecclesiastic law lies in the fact that it makes no distinction in degrees of sin. Highlighting a difficulty that Bayle had already noted in the *Objections*, Bayle argues that "good Theology teaches us that the evilness of an action consists [merely] in that it is banned by God." In the Garden of Eden, Adam's behavior hurt no one, yet "was punished in so terrible a manner" simply because God banned it. Though lying is no worse a sin than murder, it is infinitely more frequent. If certain sins, like murder, occur relatively rarely, they do so not because of fear of God or even of human laws, but because such sins do not suit most people's tastes.[70]

Bayle cites the conduct of women to prove that religion does not guide behavior. Pagan women, whose religion did not prohibit shameful behavior, offer examples of virtue that put Christians to shame. When Christian women avoid lewdness, they do so not so much from fear of God, but from fear of another law to which they are subject: "the harsh law of honor."[71] This visible law exposes women to "infamy when they succumb to the penchant of nature." Had men not "attached the honor and glory of women to chastity," women would be more guilty of carnal pleasures than men. The force of honor is weaker in women than in men: more women of noble origins lose their reputations for their morals than do gentlemen for their cowardice. Fearful of infamy, men prefer to risk death than to face insult.[72]

Honor is central to Bayle's psychology: he notes that "nothing pleases a man more than to see himself as an object of admiration." This fear of "what would be said" causes many to behave virtuously.[73] Honor, however, is a double-edged sword; if not properly channeled, this passion can be destructive. In sixteenth century Paris, thousands of unmarried women, fearful of 'what would be said,' hid their pregnancies, and drowned their newborns at night in the Seine, despite their belief that such behavior would condemn both themselves and their non-baptized babies to eternal damnation. Only a harsh law stopped this travesty.[74] Religion, furthermore, does not control behavior because if we commit heinous crimes, we are unable to believe that God could be anything but all merciful in our own cases. "We persuade ourselves that God pardons everything," but act as if man pardons nothing.[75] Hence, it is not so much virtue as the appearance of virtue that people seek. The fear of humiliation in the visible world is a far stronger force than the fear of eternal punishments in the next.[76]

Bayle catalogues a long list of virtuous atheists – men such as Spinoza, Averroes and Epicurus – to prove that atheism itself is not the cause of an evil life.[77] But Bayle does not claim that disbelief suffices to ensure good behavior. Citing Seneca, Bayle notes how Epicureanism received a bad reputation after Epicurus' death. Dishonest men joined the sect to cover their evil passions under the pretext of philosophy. Voluptuaries with "souls filled with all sorts of vices" became atheists as they "perceived that the fear of the afterlife sometimes troubled their repose."[78] These men were not evil because of disbelief; rather, these Don Juans denied the existence of God to better fulfill their passions.

Bayle has made clear that religious belief does not control human behavior and that the miraculous evidence provided to support Christianity's divine claims is dubious, i.e., that, in his view, Christian belief is no different in principle from pagan belief. If religious belief is false and ineffectual, a society of atheists could exist and prosper, provided that it followed the laws of decorum and honor necessary for all societies. If strict laws were put in place, and honor and infamy assigned their proper roles, a society of atheists "would practice civil and moral actions as well as other societies." Atheists could "deal fairly in commerce and friendship…either from desire of praise or fear of criticism." Ignorance of a "creator and preserver of the world" does not prevent atheists from being subject to the passions that guide other men: the desire for glory and reward, and the avoidance of contempt and punishment. These dispositions, Bayle notes, can be strengthened by reference to the real factors that make men act: education, praise, personal interest, and the instinct of reason and other motives, found in both atheists and other men.[79]

Bayle's Hobbesianism

Having demonstrated that, from at least as early as his *Thoughts* of 1682, Bayle believed a society of atheists to be possible, we will now explore the reasons why he believed it to be desirable. The society of atheists offers the most stable solution to the two foremost political problems in Christianity: intolerance and rebellion. These dangers arise because ecclesiastic authority claims sovereignty distinct from and higher than the state. This distinct sovereignty is especially dangerous because of the paradoxical impact religion has upon behavior. Bayle sees religion as simultaneously almost omnipotent and impotent: almost omnipotent in causing political turmoil, almost impotent in controlling behavior. Accordingly, the society of atheists is Bayle's model of the best that politics has to offer: in such a society, the statesman relies upon the things that lie within his control, particularly strict laws and the sense of honor. But though Bayle believes that an atheist society can best attain stability, he does not believe that all men can be brought to the irreligious skepticism necessary to restore the undivided sovereignty of politics. Seeing superstition to be endemic to the populace, Bayle's best practical hope is rule by religiously indifferent men who will do their utmost to keep religious questions off the political agenda.

Bayle's politics can be seen as a radical fulfillment of Hobbes' absolutist project to diminish the importance of the divine law and to subordinate it to the civil law.[80] Bayle declares that Hobbes' 1640 work *De Cive* "obliged the most far-sighted [judges] to admit that the fundamentals of politics had never before been so well discovered." Hobbes' *De Cive* "destroyed forever the doctrine of the lawfulness of subjects conspiring and rebelling against their sovereigns, and the monstrous opinions of overthrowing and executing princes."[81] Bayle's atheist state is best understood as a Hobbesian attempt to make the fear of the sovereign prevail over the commotion in civil society caused by fear of hellfire. But in arguing that religion was politically unnecessary, Bayle drew out the implication of Hobbes' thought to a degree that Hobbes never did openly. Like Hobbes, Bayle believes that scientific enlightenment must enervate the "fear of powers invisible," a fear that leads to disobedience and revolution.[82] Hobbes' system secures the state from revolution by "restoring to the civil powers those rights of which they had been robbed by Ecclesiastics in the ages of ignorance, and [by] heroically subduing that cruel hydra of the sectarians…the limitless liberty of conscience."[83]

As long as religious belief continues to exercise its present influence on politics, tolerance and obedience cannot be brought about. The sovereignty of civil power must reassert itself over the rival claims of ecclesiastical forces. If not, men will obey their clergymen instead of their princes.[84] Fear of violent death at the hands of the sovereign "cannot bring to peace those moved to fight by an evil worse than death," those divided about the path necessary for salvation.[85] As "no man can serve two masters," the civil sovereign's power necessarily ends where the subject prefers to obey the ecclesiastical forces that threaten men with fear of eternal damnation.[86] This fear of eternal damnation has to be reduced while the fear of the civil sovereign is augmented.

Instead of Christian subjects, torn as they are between the fear of powers temporal and spiritual, Hobbes sought the extraordinary obedience of those living uncorrupted in the days before philosophers and clergymen launched the self-serving doctrines that encouraged civil disobedience.[87] These primitives, Hobbes notes, "revered the supreme power…as a certain visible deity."[88] In Bayle's later writings, he echoes Hobbes' praise and offers it to three different groups: primitive atheists whose existence is eventually confirmed by reports of travelers to Africa, America and Asia; speculative atheists who are not subject to the tension posed by the dual sovereignty of Christianity; and the Christians of the first few centuries, obedient and unarmed, who sought toleration from their magistrates.

Bayle's Hobbesianism is most clearly revealed in his praise of atheist African tribesmen, "who, when asked what their religion was, responded that it consisted in fully obeying their kings and their governors and not bothering with anything else."[89] Bayle asserts that all "well enlightened and well intentioned statesmen" seeking "only security and tranquility for the state" could not wish for better subjects.[90] In addition to primitive tribesmen, Bayle praises the less extreme submission of virtuous atheists like Epicurus, whom Bayle notes "never varied in the zeal he had for the good of the country." Though Epicurus "wished for good sovereigns," he "submitted to those who governed badly as well." This submission, Bayle tells us, "is very necessary to the public good; it is *the foundation* of all states." [91]

Bayle's image of Epicurus as model citizen offers a stark contrast – one not free of irony – to the traditional view of Epicurus, fleeing the ephemera of politics for the pleasure of contemplation. In arguing that Epicurus was politically virtuous, Bayle indicates just what sort of decrease in public spirit he seeks. Political virtue will be reduced to obedience to the law. The ideal Baylian subject will accept the judgement of his rulers in political matters, rather than assuming that his conscience gives him the right to take politics into his own hands. Political matters themselves will be restricted to secular questions. As long as subjects obey the law, they will be free to behave as they wish.[92]

Finally, Bayle cites the passivity of early Christian subjects: in the *Thoughts*, he notes that they were the best subjects in the world, preaching obedience and never opposing force to force.[93] He contrasts the "benign, sweet, [and] patient" submission of early Christians to the violent "path of rebellion" undertaken since the sixteenth century.[94] This comparison of his contemporaries to the early Christians is clearly intended as a rebuke, but his praise of early Christians is severely qualified. Why were the early Christians so obedient and tolerant? According to Bayle, the peaceful ways of the early church can be attributed to the fact that it lacked the force to persecute its enemies. Though the early Christians gently acquiesced to pagan emperors, as soon as Christianity came to the throne it changed abruptly and "only spoke of overthrowing idolatry."[95] Bayle does not expect such acquiescence to return: "the early days [of Christianity] will not come again."[96]

Hence, Bayle considers himself a Hobbesian because he believes that the sovereign must assert his power over the challenges posed by ecclesiastic and civil threats to centralized authority. Bayle's primary focus is upon the results that Hobbes seeks: the restoration of the autonomy of the political realm and the restoration of obedience in subjects. The political realm will be reduced in size because disputes over salvation will not occur in its domain. But Bayle is too skeptical to follow the universal, theoretical method Hobbes has created for a new science of politics.

Bayle, moreover, declares that Hobbes doubtless "carried many things too far," for Hobbes wrote with a "great aversion" to the parliamentarians who were the cause of his exile. In particular, Bayle believes that Hobbes goes too far in giving the sovereign the right to limit the liberty of conscience.[97] He rejects Hobbes' idea that the sovereign may establish an official church to decide what doctrines and rites are to be followed. Bayle likewise denies that the sovereign should decide what doctrines are necessary to salvation in order to prevent civil turmoil.[98] Bayle, like Hobbes, is opposed to the limitless liberty of conscience that leads to civil war; however, Bayle believes that liberty of conscience can be granted as long as citizens do not use it to create civil strife.

Revolution and intolerance are not accidental but essential to the type of politics that is guided by the faulty principles currently in practice in Christianity. These principles create structural problems ensuring that Christian peoples suffer "more troubles and ravages" than others.[99] Christianity is particularly subject to civil wars and revolutions because of its tendency toward schism and sectarian strife.[100] Though certain Christian countries may be less subject to these difficulties than others, this is because of the "differing characters of peoples and diverse constitutions of governments" than the Christian faith.[101] Holland, Bayle notes, in particular, has been able to avoid the most terrible consequences of religious warfare, but only through wise policy that leads her to disregard the theological principles that are the source of this turmoil in Christendom.[102]

In explaining the theoretical origins of the political troubles that have wracked Christian Europe, Bayle places blame squarely upon two widely held doctrines. First at fault, he notes, is the "general doctrine of Roman Catholics and Protestants...that sovereigns should use their power to punish those who rise against the true religion as it is established in their state." This animosity is reinforced by the belief that those who abandon the official religion do so only as a result of evil intent. Thus, "those who raise altar against altar view those who oppose them as terrible beasts."[103] The opponents of the dominant religion are thus branded "enemies of the state," seeking not merely to change its ecclesiastic doctrine, but its government as well.[104] Accordingly, the king, empowered to maintain the established religion, attacks its opponents violently.[105]

Although the belief that the monarch has the right to persecute heretics suffices to "guarantee...disorder," the "confusion is even greater" when those who have abandoned the official religion of their country -- often at great cost to themselves -- resort to force against their oppressors.[106] The foundation of society is shaken.[107] Chaos and anarchy, the greatest of evils, ensue. Rulers are left with no middle ground: they "must either suppress the innovators or place themselves in the condition of being oppressed."[108] Once a third to a quarter of a state comes to follow a new doctrine, the country "will find itself in the most perilous situation possible." The dominant religion will press the sovereign to use force against innovators; the innovators will resist with force, or even with foreign arms and money.[109] Persecuted sects become internal enemies. They openly "rejoice at the progress of an enemy," hoping for prolonged external warfare so that the armed forces cannot return home to be used in civil strife.[110]

If the new sect fights very strongly, the rulers may be left with no choice but to tolerate this religious minority as a political expedient. In this sense, "putting up with" a religion that one detests is highly tenuous. Society will be divided into two or more enemy camps, each merely awaiting the chance to annihilate the other.[111]

Bayle argues that "in all the Christian communions that have made any appearance in the world," kings have been exposed to "continual revolutions." These revolutions arise from the erroneous doctrine -- in no way exclusive to Christianity -- that "the authority of kings is inferior to that of the people" and that kings, therefore, "can be punished in certain cases by the people."[112] As a result of their faulty convictions which give religious beliefs priority over civil needs, individuals believe that they have the right to judge -- and pass sentence on -- the behavior of their monarch: revolutions naturally follow.

The clergy, the shameless instigator of most revolutions, exploits the doctrine that places the authority of kings under that of peoples.[113] Bayle declares that "there is nothing more dangerous in a state" than theologians, who, as "trumpeters of sedition," justify tyrannicide and the overthrow of monarchs they deem heretical.[114] Rather than letting sovereigns "hold their peoples under the yoke of obedience," as some have suggested," religion thus places the sovereign under the thumb of his subjects. Those who claim that the clergy restrains the people are simply wrong; at best, priests have caused three uprisings for every one they have prevented.[115] Peaceful priests cannot undo the damage of corrupt and passionate ones, especially if a large body of avaricious and voluptuous idlers controls a religion. Conspiracies against the state will arise upon any specious pretext: old superstitions, new miracles, oracles and prophecies.[116]

Toleration

The view presented here, that Bayle seeks a fully secular society from the time of his earliest political work, runs counter to the dominant scholarly opinion that his fundamental political aim is the establishment of liberty of conscience.[117] As noted above, those who do see Bayle primarily as a proponent of religious liberty underestimate his emphasis on the political virtues of atheism, both in rulers who do not persecute for religious reasons and in subjects who do not disobey their rulers for reasons of religion. Instead of seeking toleration, we believe that Bayle's primary aim is to weaken the political impact of the 'fear of invisible powers.' Once this political impact has been diminished and civil sovereignty has been reasserted over ecclesiastical claims to sovereignty, toleration can function in Christendom.

The belief that a Christian view of liberty of conscience is the essence of Bayle's political thought places undue emphasis upon appeals to conscience made in his second major political work, the *Philosophic Commentary on These Words of Jesus Christ, "Compel Them to Enter In."*[118] This work seeks to prove that intolerance cannot be the character of Christianity. The *Commentary*, first published in October 1686, attempts to refute Saint Augustine's argument that force should be used to compel heretics to submit to the Church.[119] Examining the parable of the banquet upon which Augustine had based his argument, Bayle contends that the words of the Gospel cannot be taken literally; Jesus could not have called for the horrors of persecution. He would not have risked the possibility that the True Church be persecuted by unwitting heretics heeding the words of Luke 14:23, "compel them to enter in."[120] As Augustine's interpretation of this parable leads to terrible iniquities, it is "contrary to the purest and most distinct ideas of reason," and, therefore, condemned by what Bayle calls natural light -- i.e., "the idea of natural equity."[121] As Christ could not possibly have desired warfare and hatred, Bayle lays down a strategy for all sects to come together to mutually renounce persecution.[122]

Though Bayle's argument begins in the first part of the *Commentary* with an appeal to "natural light," a shift occurs as the work proceeds. Bayle moves from his discussion of equity as our guide to a plea for the rights of conscience.[123] Each person's conscience, he argues, "is the voice and law of God, known and accepted" by him. Disobedience to one's own conscience, thus, is equivalent to the desire to "violate the law of God."[124]

According to this new understanding, rather than seeing adherence to heterodoxy as sinful, "anything done against the dictates of conscience is sin."[125] Whereas the traditional Christian understanding of conscience argued that one had to act in accord with one's own conscience, one's conscience itself had to be in accord with views that were objectively true.[126] Bayle now shifts the criterion of piety. Instead of dogma being sacrosanct, conscience now is. Sincerity, not adherence to correct dogma, now is the judge of orthodoxy. "The first and most indispensable of all our obligations is that of not acting against the conscience."[127]

This new understanding of conscience leads to toleration, not persecution. Forcing someone to accept an opinion that disagrees with his own conscience now becomes the moral equivalent of forcing him to disobey God.[128] Obedience to conscience must therefore be unconditional.[129] The earnestness of belief thus gains respect and constraint is proscribed. Applying criminal procedures for religious reasons thus violates the law of God.[130]

The idea that conscience had to be correct led to forceful imposition of opinions in the name of orthodoxy. By shifting the standard by which religious belief is to be judged, Bayle allows for religious diversity and excludes persecution. Religion comes to be predominantly a personal matter. Rather than placing soul saving foremost on the public's agenda, souls, instead, are saved in private. The public realm is thus reduced while the private realm is expanded. In certain respects, Bayle sets the *Philosophic Commentary* apart from his other works.[131] Its tone and metaphysical doctrine of the conscience understood as the locus of one's personal relationship with God mark a departure from the disbelieving skepticism of the *Objections* and the *Thoughts*. Bayle's argument that God reserves for Himself the domain of conscience stands in sharp contrast to the "strong thinker" who questioned divine providence. In the *Thoughts*, Bayle dismisses appeals to metaphysical principles as mere appeals: the conscience, there presented primarily as the moral judge of our behavior, is unfortunately never heeded.[132] The non-judgmental character with which all individual consciences -- strong-thinking and otherwise -- are treated in the *Commentary* differentiates itself from the *Thoughts*.

These differences might suggest a lack of coherence to Bayle's overall philosophy. Instead, we believe it to be a practical accommodation that seeks to achieve through toleration what Bayle seeks to achieve through the atheist state. If toleration based on respect for the individual conscience could be achieved in Christianity, then toleration and the atheist state might even be understood as alternate means to restore order through the eradication of the disruptive influence of religion on political life.[133] The absence of religion in the atheist state is mimicked in a tolerant state by the brake upon zealous excesses produced by the agreement amongst rulers and ruled that gives the principle of toleration greater importance than any specific religious creed. Whereas dogmatic religious beliefs have no place in the politics of the atheist state, in the tolerant state, sects both work together and check each other to assure that no single religion tyrannizes the others. Bayle points toward this link when he indicates that although "religion is pernicious to the state when schisms arrive," "if the spirit and dogma of toleration" would be embraced, "the diversity of sects would be more useful than detrimental to the temporal good of societies." True toleration would lead each sect to seek to surpass the others in good deeds. Each sect would seek to become reputed for its devotion to country and letters. Though tolerance is the remedy for containing the ills brought by schism, Bayle notes that societies sick with religious warfare refuse to take this medication, thereby making their situation more acute. Indeed, this remedy has been so useless against the evils of schism that "it is as if nobody followed it."[134]

So toleration offers a practical approximation to the stability of the society of atheists. However effective toleration might be, the scheme proposed in the *Commentary* is less stable politically than the atheist state. The tension that marks the difference between equity and conscience as the standard of our behavior indicates the potential weakness of Bayle's case for toleration. This tension was seen in the *Thoughts* as a major source of religious strife; there, Bayle declared that "nothing can be more heretical than to believe that one can please God by violating the common notions of equity."[135] But in adhering to his appeal to the right of conscience in the commentary, Bayle is forced to conclude that if individuals are "persuaded that to obey God, it is necessary to abolish [other] sects," they are "obliged to follow the inclinations of this false conscience." If they do not do so, "they fall into the crime of disobeying God, because they do something that they believe to be disobedience to God." Aside from the sovereign's use of force to prevent such crimes, Bayle argues that men must be educated to believe that toleration takes priority: God could not ask them to act in such an iniquitous way.[136] The danger from the sincere belief that one must be intolerant, however, would be greatest should the sovereign himself decide that he must act iniquitously.

Whatever the theoretical differences that toleration might face, Bayle does praise Holland's policy of toleration which he seems to think is the best example of toleration in Christendom. Holland is a place where secular toleration dominates

-- not an ecclesiastical toleration based on the doctrine of conscience that Bayle offers. The ecclesiastical doctrine of the established church in Holland states that magistrates must use their force not only against criminals but also against heretics.[137] In this regard, the church follows "almost all [Christian] theologians" in arguing that "sovereigns must use their power to punish those who rise up against the true religion."[138] Fortunately for the Catholic and Jewish minorities of Holland, however, a "wise policy" leads the Dutch states to ignore their official ecclesiastical doctrine and to "direct themselves by human reasons (sic) alone." As a result, Holland enjoys tranquility and prosperity.[139] For all Bayle's praise of Holland, he still does not consider it to be the best governed state in the world. Perhaps in accepting the theoretical principle that magistrates may force men against their consciences, Holland indicates the defect of its policy: toleration has not come about as the conscious decision of the rule of an irreligious elite. The best practical example for Bayle is China, the regime that comes closest of all civilized nations to rule by irreligious elites.[140]

China: Atheist Mandarins

Although the societies of atheists that Bayle speaks of in his later writings -- the Mariana Islanders, as well as various North American and African tribes[141] -- can live simply and peacefully in primitive ignorance, an uneducated condition is simply not possible for the educated men of Europe. Whereas primitive atheism is an unrealistic alternative for Europe, the superstitious character of the people makes an educated society of atheists also appear unlikely. Movements of nature will bring natural disasters thus causing superstitious fear in the minds of the people.[142] These prejudices are so inbred that attempting to correct them may just exacerbate them further.[143] Raised with religious practices, filled with these "thousand sentiments of fear," men taught to look toward heaven for consolation cannot be brought fully to forsake religion.[144]

Because an entire society of enlightened atheists seems difficult, Bayle looks to the next most stable alternative: rule by men indifferent in matters of religion. An upright atheist, aware of the dangers of persecution and rebellion, would do his utmost to prevent religious questions from intruding upon politics. Returning to a theme present since the *Thoughts*, Bayle stresses the advantage of rule by irreligious men in his later works. Spinozists, Bayle asserts, would not have persecuted Christians as pagans did; English and French Protestants would be better off as subjects of Spinozistic than of Papist rulers. Bayle compares the conscience of the religious zealot to that of the Spinozist:

> You should consider that the conscience, seized by a false zeal of religion, cannot be stopped by the resources that would stop a Spinozist. Reason, the respect for the public, human honor, the ugliness of injustice, would prevent him frequently enough from doing evil to his fellow man.[145]

In the second edition of the *Dictionary*, Bayle begins to show great interest in the Fo-Kaio sect, a sect of Chinese men of learning that Bayle believes to hold a metaphysical doctrine similar to Spinozistic naturalism:[146]

> [T]hat the first principle of all things, and all the beings that compose the universe, are only a single and same substance, that all things are God, and that God is all things, in such a way that God and all the things that exist make up one and the same being.[147]

This sect, Bayle tells us, has a two part doctrine: an "external" salutary doctrine, "publicly preached and taught to the people," and an "internal" doctrine, "hidden from the vulgar," that is bleak, but "solid and true." For a half-century, the beneficial external doctrine was taught by its founder, Fo, the Chinese Buddha. Fo stressed the distinction between good and evil and spoke of the punishments that awaited evildoers in the afterlife. Claiming divine status, Fo declared himself the savior of mankind, offering salvation and a path to beatitude. Upon his deathbed, however, Fo unmasked himself to his disciples, acknowledging that he alone – not divine inspiration – was the source of the doctrine he taught. He admitted that he was an atheist who truly believed that the principle and end of all things was the vacuum and nothingness from which we all come and to which we all return.[148]

This sect of philosophical atheists – the majority of learned men in China – dominates three other major sects, especially the sect of idolators led by the priests, the ignorant Bonzes.[149] These Chinese atheists come to have central importance for Bayle.[150] They are the bulwark of the Chinese regime: "learned in literature, they alone take part in government." They "are uniquely guided by the public good;" each of them fights his passions and tries to "have perfect conformity of his thought, words and actions with right reason." Though the Emperor of China, the supreme pontiff, is not officially a member of the lettered sect of atheists, his own religion is hollow, arising out of a sentiment of piety and respect for elders.[151]

China is a concrete example of the society that works; not only is China the "wisest and most ingenious nation of the Orient," Bayle declares it to be the best governed nation in the world.[152] In contrast to Christian nations, the Chinese have assured that religion has no force in politics; Chinese subjects are obliged to "be fully submitted to the sovereign and to give him unconditional fidelity."[153] Religious liberty functions in China as the dual problems of intolerance and disobedience are solved: the ruling class is guided by equity and subjects do not believe in doctrines that may lead them to revolt. Though the learned men of China leave the people in their ignorant superstition, they do all that they can to make sure that this superstition has no political impact.[154]

Conclusion
Despite its apparent contradictions, Pierre Bayle's political philosophy offers a coherent whole: a Hobbesian vision of politics that seeks to gradually mitigate the

impact of "powers invisible" from the political arena. The cornerstone of Bayle's philosophy is offered in his first major political work, the *Thoughts*, which argues that a society of atheists can exist and prosper. Since the society of atheists cannot be established, however, Bayle seeks to foster rule by irreligious elites. Such rule is connected to Bayle's cultivation of a "Republic of Letters" or his project of Enlightenment and Biblical criticism presented in the *Thoughts*. Bayle's long-term goal was to foster a new anti-clerical elite aware of the limits of tradition; this elite would seek to check the dangers posed by superstition. The new era of enlightenment that Bayle consciously anticipates is to be marked by a gradual diminution in the power of religion, a diminution whose effect would nonetheless be revolutionary: to replace the divided sovereignty of clergymen and monarchs beholden to superstition by a secular alliance of enlightening philosophers and enlightened rulers. Accordingly, Bayle's plea for tolerance in the *Philosophic Commentary* should not be taken as the essence of his political philosophy; this vision of tolerance within Christendom is a mere pit stop on the path to a post-Christian society.

NOTES:

1. See especially Joseph Fabre, *Les Pères de la Révolution (de Bayle à Condorcet)*, (Geneva: Slatkine, 1970 [reprint]); Jean Delvolvé, *Religion, critique et philosophie positive chez Pierre Bayle*, (Paris: Félix Alcan, 1906); Howard Robinson, *Bayle the Sceptic*, (New York: Columbia University Press, 1931). The most influential contemporary book offering this viewpoint is Gianni Cantelli, *Teologia e ateismo. Saggio sul pensiero filosofico e religioso di Pierre Bayle*, (Florence: La Nuova Italia, 1969).

2. Elisabeth Labrousse, "Reading Pierre Bayle in Paris," in Alan Charles Kors, editor, *Anticipations of the Enlightenment in England, France and Germany*, (Philadelphia: University of Pennsylvania Press, 1987), 11; Walter Rex, *Essays on Pierre Bayle and Religious Controversy*, (The Hague: Martinus Nijhoff, 1965), x-xv.

3. Labrousse believes that one must either accept as sincere or reject as insincere Bayle's fideism, for Bayle "oscillates between two options...between the Christian faith and atheism, between the image of an all-powerful and transcendent God and that of a materialist monism;...hence, the profound seduction that Manichean dualism offered him, [the chance] to simultaneously explain these contrary intuitions." Bayle's pessimism, she argues, leads him away from any optimistic naturalist or deistic solution. See Elisabeth Labrousse, *Bayle*, (Oxford: Oxford University Press, 1983), 31-33; Labrousse, *Pierre Bayle: Hétérodoxie et rigorisme*, (The Hague: Martinus Nijhoff, 1964), Volume II, 603 (henceforth referred to as Labrousse, *II*.)

4. Gianluca Mori, *Tra Descartes e Bayle: Poiret e la Teodicea*, (Bologna: Il Mulino, 1990). Labrousse downplayed the *Objections*, suggesting its materialist themes were incompatible with the body-soul duality Bayle espoused in his lecture classes (Labrousse, *II*, 145-146).

5. *Pensées diverses* (henceforth *P.D.*) § 175; edition cited is Pierre Bayle, *Oeuvres Diverses* (henceforth *O.D.*), (Hildesheim: Georg Olms, 1965 [reprint]), Volume III, 112.

6. On Bayle's method of writing, see "Aureolus," remark C, *Dictionnaire historique et critique* (henceforth all references to the *Dictionary* shall reference the article name and relevant remark of the *Dictionary*'s fifth edition [Pierre Bayle, *Dictionnaire historique et critique*, (Basel: Jean-Louis Bandmuller, 1738)]). On the strong spirits' use of double entendre, "hesitation," and attacks on Biblical history to attack the pagans, see René Pintard, *Le libertinage érudit dans la première moitié du XVIIè siècle*, (Paris: Boivin, 1943), 30, 86-87, 146-148, 323, 437, 514-515, 519, 525-529, 534, 571-576).

7. *P.D.* §175; *O.D. III*, 112. The strong thinkers should not be confused with those such as the anti-Cartesian Pierre-Daniel Huet, Bishop of Avranches (1630-1721), who employ skepticism as a path to faith. Popkin confuses these two categories of skeptics by placing La Mothe Le Vayer and Bayle in the latter category (Richard Popkin, *History of Scepticism from Erasmus to Spinoza*, [Berkeley: University of California Paperbacks, 1979], 87-96).

8. Matthew, 2:1-2:2; 27:45; Mark, 15:33; Luke 23:44-45. Rex claims that Bayle's thought contains "carefully limited ironies" paralleling Catholicism and paganism, but that these ironies remain respectful of Scripture (Rex, *Essays on Pierre Bayle*, 29). He does note how the pagans Bayle criticizes have "pointedly Catholic" features (*Ibid.*, 46);

nevertheless, Rex ignores how the pagan writers Bayle attacks recount natural and supernatural phenomena that pointedly resemble those phenomena recounted about the Nativity and Crucifixion.

9. *P.D.* §53-62; *O.D. III*, 38-42.

10. *P.D.* §60; *O.D. III*, 41.

11. *P.D.* §70; *O.D. III*, 47.

12. *P.D.* §74; *O.D. III*, 49.

13. *P.D.* §56; *O.D. III*, 44; in the *Dictionary*, written a decade and a half later than the *Thoughts*, Bayle openly denies that there was an eclipse at the Crucifixion. Such an eclipse would have been noted by the historian Phlego, "the most avid man [of all times] in compiling supernatural circumstances," "Phlégon," remark E.

14. On backhanded praise, see Douglas H. Gordon and Norman L. Torrey, *The Censoring of Didérot's Encyclopaedie and the Re-Established Text,* (New York: Columbia University Press, 1947), 77-78.

15. *P.D.* §56; *O.D. III*, 44.

16. *P.D.* §232; *O.D. III*, 141-142.

17. *P.D.* §21; *O.D. III*, 44.

18. *P.D.* §232; *O.D. III*, 140.

19. *P.D.* §222; *O.D. III*, 137.

20. *P.D.* §88; *O.D. III*, 54-55.

21. *P.D.* §51; *O.D. III*, 37.

22. *P.D.* §88; *O.D. III*, 54-55.

23. *P.D.* §82; *O.D. III*, 53-54.

24. John 19:14; Matthew, 27:45; Mark, 15:33; Luke, 23:44-45.

25. *P.D.* §82; *O.D. III*, 53.

26. *P.D.* §82; *O.D. III*, 54.

27. *Ibid.*

28. Bayle's indirect attack on these Christian miracles also indicates a complicated relationship to the man whom he calls "one of the greatest philosophers of this century": Father Nicholas Malebranche (1638-1715). Malebranche is generally credited with attempting a synthesis of Cartesian principles and Catholicism in his *Treaty on Nature and Grace,* published in 1681, shortly before the appearance of Bayle's *Thoughts.* Recent scholars claim the Malebranchian foundation of the *Thoughts* proves the work's pious intent (Rex, *Essays on Pierre Bayle*, 38-42; Labrousse, *II*, 351-352; Patrick Riley, *The General Will Before Rousseau: The Transformation of the Divine into the Civic,* [Princeton: Princeton University Press, 1986], 80-85). We follow Devolvé and Landucci, who note that Bayle's use of certain Malebranchian hypotheses is counterbalanced by anti-Malebranchian hypotheses [Delvolvé, *Religion, critique, philosophie positive,* 46; Sergio Landucci, *La teodicea nell'eta Cartesiana,* (Naples: Bibliopolis, 1986), 89-90). Bayle follows Malebranche's rationalist system in placing God, the universal legislator, far above petty concerns with His creation; nonetheless, Bayle counterbalances Malebranche's universal legislator by emphasis on an aspect of

revelation that Malebranche downplays: the arbitrary use of divine power as manifested in that anathema of rationalist theology, the jealous God of the Hebrew Bible (*P.D.* §225; *O.D. III*, 138.) In line with the strong thinkers, Bayle highlights God's capriciousness by focusing on the irrational character of revelation in a way that seems to nullify a strict adherence to Malebranche's philosophy (Delvolvé, *Religion, critique, philosophie positive*, 49-50).

29. *P.D.* §7; *O.D. III*, 12; *P.D.* §47; *O.D. III*, 35. See also Cantelli, *Teologia e ateismo*, 20-24.

30. *P.D.* §7; *O.D. III*, 12.

31. *Ibid.*

32. *P.D.* §8; *O.D. III*, 12.

33. *P.D.* §22; *O.D. III*, 22.

34. *P.D.* §108; *O.D. III*, 73.

35. *P.D.* §109; *O.D. III*, 73.

36. *Ibid.*

37. *P.D.* §50; *O.D. III*, 108.

38. *P.D.* §81; *O.D. III*, 52-53. As the case of Nicias implies, Christianity is not the only threat to the autonomy of the political realm. Bayle cites Quintus Curtius' account of how a lunar eclipse brought unrest to the army of Alexander the Great: "Nothing is as powerful as superstition for keeping a people in check. However unruly and inconstant a people might be, if their minds have been filled with a false image of religion, they will heed their divines better than their (political) chiefs" (*Ibid.*).

39. *P.D.* §50; *O.D. III*, 36-37; on the persecution of Protagoras, Anagoras and Socrates, see *P.D.* §110; §127; *O.D. III*, 74, 81.

40. *P.D.* §52; *O.D. III*, 37-38.

41. *P.D.* §81; *O.D. III*, 53.

42. *P.D.* §178-§179; *O.D. III*, 114-115.

43. *P.D.* §133; *O.D. III*, 86.

44. *P.D.* §129; *O.D. III*, 83.

45. *P.D.* §133; *O.D. III*, 86.

46. *P.D.* §136; *O.D. III*, 87-88.

47. *P.D.* §136; *O.D. III*, 87.

48. *P.D.* §138; *O.D. III*, 89.

49. *P.D.* §135; *O.D. III*, 87.

50. *Ibid.*

51. *P.D.* §129; *O.D. III*, 83.

52. *P.D.* §130; *O.D. III*, 84.

53. *P.D.* §121; *O.D. III*, 79.

54. *P.D.* §199; *O.D. III*, 126-127.

55. *P.D.* §127; *O.D. III*, 81-82.

56. *P.D.* §197; *O.D. III*, 124.

57. *P.D.* §155; *O.D. III*, 100.

58. *P.D.* §127; *O.D. III*, 125.

59. *P.D.* §131; *O.D. III*, 84.

60. *P.D.* §131; *O.D. III*, 84.

61. *P.D.* §181; *O.D. III*, 116.

62. *P.D.* §139; *O.D. III*, 89.

63. *P.D.* §131; *O.D. III*, 84.

64. *P.D.* §137; *O.D. III*, 88.

65. *P.D.* §131; *O.D. III*, 84.

66. *P.D.* §136; *O.D. III*, 87.

67. *P.D.* §145; *O.D. III*, 94.

68. *P.D.* §162; *O.D. III*, 104.

69. *Continuation des pensées diverses* (henceforth *C.P.D.*), §138; *O.D. III*, 386.

70. *P.D.* §167; *O.D. III*, 106.

71. *P.D.* §162; *O.D. III*, 104.

72. *P.D.* §163; *O.D. III*, 104.

73. *P.D.* §164; *O.D. III*, 104.

74. "Patin," remark C.

75. *P.D.* §164; *O.D. III*, 105.

76. *C.P.D.* §138; *O.D. III*, 386.

77. *P.D.* §124; §178-183; *O.D. III*, 110-111; 114-118

78. *P.D.* §174; *O.D. III*, 110-111.

79. *P.D.* §172; *O.D. III*, 109-110.

80. Letter to Jacob Bayle, December 28, 1678; *Nouvelles lettres de Monsieur Bayle*, (The Hague: Jean Van Duren, 1739), volume II, 53-54.

81. "Hobbes," remark E.

82. Leo Strauss, *Natural Right and History*, (Chicago: The University of Chicago Press, 1964), 198-199, note 43.

83. "Hobbes," remark E.

84. *P.D.* §81; *O.D. III*, 52.

85. "Hobbes," remark C.

86. Thomas Hobbes, *De Cive* in *Man and Citizen*, edited by Bernard Gert, (Garden City, N.Y.: Anchor Books, 1972), 179.

87. *Op. cit.,* 248; 370.

88. *Op. cit.,* 97.

89. *Réponse aux questions d'un provincial* (henceforth *R.Q.P.*), III, §20; *O.D. III*, 956; cited in Delvolvé, *Religion critique et philosopie positive*, 387.

90. *R.Q.P.*, III, §20; *O.D.* III, p.956; cited in Delvolvé, *Religion, critique et philosophie positive*, 387.

91. "Epicure," remark O.

92. Harvey C. Mansfield, Jr., *America's Constitutional Soul*, (Baltimore: Johns Hopkins University Press, 1991), 107.

93. *P.D.* §120; *O.D. III,* 78.

94. "Japon," remark E.

95. *R.Q.P.*, IV, §1; *O.D. III,* 1011.

96. "Henri II," remark D.

97. "Hobbes," remark E.

98. *Commentaire philosophique* (henceforth *C.P.*), II, §5; *O.D. II,* 412; cited in Labrousse, *Pierre Bayle*, II, 546-547; Hobbes, *Man and Citizen*, 250, 364-368.

99. *R.Q.P.*, III, §20-21; IV, §1; *O.D. III,* 952-959; 1012.

100. *R.Q.P.*, III, §20; IV, §1; *O.D. III,* 952-953; 1012.

101. *R.Q.P.*, III, §21; *O.D. III,* 957.

102. *R.Q.P.*, IV, §1; *O.D. III,* 1012-1013.

103. *R.Q.P.*, IV, §1; *O.D. III,* 1012.

104. *R.Q.P.*, III, §20; *O.D. III,* 955.

105. *R.Q.P.*, III, §18; *O.D. III,* 950.

106. *R.Q.P.*, IV, §1; *O.D. III,* 1012.

107. *R.Q.P.*, III, §18; *O.D. III,* 950.

108. *R.Q.P.*, IV, §1; *O.D. III,* 1012.

109. *R.Q.P.*, III, §18; *O.D. III,* 950.

110. "Henri II," remark D.

111. *R.Q.P.*, III, §18; *O.D. III,* 949.

112. "Loyola," remark S; "Althusius," remark A; *Nouvelles de la république des lettres* (henceforth *N.R.L.*), September 1684, article VI; *O.D. I,* 127. Bayle shares Hobbes' view of the destructive character of the doctrine that private persons can judge the justice or injustice of sovereign edicts (Hobbes, *Man and Citizen*, 97).

113. "Chrysostome," remark B; "Savanarole;" "Anabaptistes," remarks A, B.

114. "Jacques le Bossu."

115. In yielding this point, Bayle thereby admits that religion could potentially serve the stability of the state. But the calculation is clear: it does far more harm than good.

116. *R.Q.P.*, III, §18; *O.D. III,* 950.

117. Most recent scholarship takes Bayle's plea for toleration in the *Philosophical Commentary* as the essence of his thought and therefore understands his discussion of the atheist state within the context of a plea for toleration. It correspondingly understands Bayle's political views as representative of the tolerationist party among Calvinist exiles in Holland (Elisabeth Labrousse, "The Political Ideas of the Huguenot Diaspora [Bayle and Jurieu]," translated by Mollie Gerard Davis, in Richard M. Golden, editor, *Church, State and Society Under the Bourbon Kings of France,* [Lawrence, KS: Coronado Press, 1982], 222-283; W.J. Stankiewicz, *Politics and Religion in Seventeenth Century France*, [Berkeley and Los Angeles: The University of California Press, 1960],

215-242). Although Bayle argues for toleration, he supports it for political, not theological, reasons: he views it as a means to control the political effect of religion. Seeing Bayle as a Calvinist proponent of toleration, most scholars contrast his position to the intolerant views of Pierre Jurieu, Bayle's former friend and colleague who followed him in exile in Rotterdam. Bayle and Jurieu came to quarrel openly in the aftermath of the *Philosophical Commentary*. In his *Rights of Two Sovereigns in Matters of Religion, the Conscience and the Prince* (1687), Jurieu claimed that the *Commentary*'s denial of the sovereign's right to exercise power in matters of conscience was tantamount to an open apology for religious indifference (Labrousse, "Hugeunot Diaspora," 246; *Supplément du commentaire philosophique* [henceforth *S.C.P.*]; *O.D. II*, 497-504). Jurieu's position was thus closer to both the intolerance of Calvin and the Catholic apologists of persecution in France; rejecting the autonomy of the individual conscience, Jurieu believed that magistrates must uphold the true religion by use of force. The collision between Jurieu and Bayle over liberty of conscience and submission offers merely a faded reflection of Bayle's true position. In the *Thoughts*, written several years before his open clash with Jurieu, Bayle had already laid the groundwork for his secure alternative to the dangers posed by Christianity: the society of atheists.

118. See Labrousse, *II*, 520-591, especially 591-582; Lucien Dubois, *Bayle et la tolérance*, (Paris: A. Chevalier Marescq, 1902), 48, 75-107.

119. *C.P.*, "Préface," III; *O.D. II*, 445.

120. *C.P.*, I, §4; *O.D. II*, 374-375.

121. *C.P.*, I, §1; *O.D. II*, 367-368.

122. *C.P.*, I, §4; *O.D. II*, 361.

123. Rex, *Essays on Pierre Bayle*, 181-185; compare *C.P.*, I, §3; *O.D. II*, 374 with *C.P.*, II, §7; *O.D. II*, 422.

124. *C.P.*, I, §6; *O.D. II*, 384.

125. *C.P.*, II, §7; *O.D. II*, 422.

126. Bayle's position can be most directly contrasted with Aquinas' view that "*Synderesis* is...the law of our mind,, because it is a habit containing the precepts of the natural law..." (Saint Thomas Aquinas, *Summa Theologica*, [Translated by the Fathers of the English Dominican Province], [New York: Benziger Brothers, 1947], I, 1008; cited in Robert Kraynak, "John Locke: From Absolutism to Toleration," *American Political Science Review*, 74 [1980], 61, note 11; Pierre Manent, *Les libéraux*, [Paris: Hachette, 1986], I, 115, note 1).

127. *C.P.*, II, §7; *O.D. II*, 425.

128. *C.P.*, II, §8; *O.D. II*, 426-427.

129. *C.P.*, II, §8; *O.D. II*, 422

130. *C.P.*, I, §6; *O.D. II*, 381.

131. Others have seen difficulties in reconciling the *Philosophical Commentary* with the rest of Bayle's corpus, most notably Jean-Pierre de Crousaz, *L'examen du pyrrhonisme ancien et moderne*, (The Hague: Pierre de Hondt, 1733), 696-698. Moreover at the outset of the *Commentary*, Bayle declares that "our century is full of strong spirits and deists. Some are surprised by this, but...I am surprised that there are not more, seeing the ravages that religion has brought to the world, and the destruction

that it brings by *almost inevitable consequences*...by authorizing all crimes imaginable for her temporal prosperity" ("Préface," *C.P.*; *O.D. II*, 366 [italics added]).

132. *P.D.* §134; *O.D. III*, 87.

133. On the political management of religion, see Robert Kraynak, "John Locke: From Absolutism to Toleration," *American Political Science Review*, 74 (1980), 53-69.

134. *R.Q.P.*, IV, §1; *O.D. III*, 1011.

135. *P.D.* §197; *O.D. III*, 124.

136. *S.C.P.*, §21; *O.D. II*, 539-540.

137. *R.Q.P.*, IV, §1; *O.D. III*, 1012-1013.

138. *R.Q.P.*, IV, §1; *O.D. III*, 1011-1012.

139. *R.Q.P.*, IV, §1; *O.D. III*, 1013.

140. Bayle presents China as a society ruled by an atheist elite beginning with the second edition of the *Dictionary* (1702), after reading Father Charles Le Gobien's *Nouveaux mémoires sur l'état présent de la Chine*, (Paris: J. Anison, 1696-1698), cited in René Etiemble, *L'Europe Chinoise*, (Paris: Flammarion, 1989), volume I, 312. In so doing, Bayle revises his image of China, which he earlier held to be a tolerant albeit idolatrous nation (see *N.R.L.*, February 1685; article X; *O.D. I*, 231-232; *P.D.* §132; *O.D. III*, 85.

141. *C.P.D.* §14; §85-87; *O.D. III*, 207; 312-316; 352.

142. *P.D.* §104; §107; *O.D. III*, 71; 73.

143. "Agar," remark H. Writing twenty years after the *Thoughts*, Bayle notes how astrological superstition had become even more ingrained (*C.P.D.*, §40; *O.D. III*, 242).

144. *P.D.* §104; *O.D. III*, 71.

145. *R.Q.P.*, III, §20; *O.D. III*, 955.

146. "Spinoza," remark A; *R.Q.P.*, III, §24; *O.D. III*, 968. On the importance of China as a model for Bayle, see Willy Berger, *China-Bild und China-Mode im Europa der Aufklärung*, (Cologne: Böhlau, 1990), 59-66; Etiemble, *L'Europe Chinoise*, I, 308-320; Sergio Zoli, "Pierre Bayle e la Cina," *Studi Francesi*, 99 (1989), 467-471.

147. "Japon," remark D.

148. "Spinoza," remark A.

149. *C.P.D.* §113; *O.D. III*, 343.

150. *C.P.D.* §154; *O.D. III*, 413.

151. *C.P.D.* §113; *O.D. III*, 343.

152. *C.P.D.* §18; *O.D. III*, 210; *R.Q.P.*, IV, §4; *O.D. III*, 1044.

153. *R.Q.P.*, III, §20; *O.D. III*, 956.

154. *R.Q.P.*,III, §20-21; *O.D. III*, 956-959. In *What is Wholly Catholic France*, Bayle notes the great danger posed to China by the arrival of Jesuit missionaries in 1685. Bayle warns that Jesuit promises to earthly sovereigns cannot be trusted. Though they begin by "asking only to be put up with, their only aim is make themselves masters" of China, through conversion at knifepoint, if necessary. By using force as a tool of conversion the Jesuits may spread the disease of religious warfare to China (*La France Toute Catholique*, III, *O.D. II*, 350-351). The Emperor, therefore, is "obliged from

principles of conscience, eternal law antecedent to all religions of positive right to banish all Christians from his dominions." Endangering China's toleration, the presence of the Jesuits may bring "disorder, confusion, civil war, sedition and rebellion" (*C.P.,* I, §5; *O.D. II,* 376-380; Basil Guy, *The French Image of China Before and After Voltaire,* Studies on Voltaire and the Enlightenment [35], [Geneva: Institut et Musée Voltaire, 1963], 129-130; see also *R.Q.P.,* III, §20-21; *O.D. III,* 956-959).

11

OF BELIEVERS AND BARBARIANS: MONTESQUIEU'S ENLIGHTENED TOLERATION

Diana Schaub

"The pious man and the atheist always speak of religion; the one speaks of what he loves and the other of what he fears."[1] Montesquieu opens book 25 of *The Spirit of the Laws* with this arresting one-sentence chapter entitled "On the feeling for religion." He leaves it to us to determine which of the two he himself is—or whether, indeed, he is either. Religion, after all, is not Montesquieu's sole topic. According to their titles, only two of the thirty-one books of *The Spirit of the Laws* deal with religion (books 24 and 25). In truth, however, the topic is much more pervasive than that figure indicates. From the discussion of a law-governed divinity in book 1 to the proper articulation of divine and human law, made possible by "the sublimity of human reason," in book 26, religion is often at issue. As to the nature of Montesquieu's "feeling for religion," it seems to partake more of fear, or at least concern, than love. The character of his concern is indicated by the titles of the two books that explicitly treat religion: "On the laws in their relation to the religion established in each country, examined in respect to its practices and within itself" and "On the laws in their relation with the establishment of the religion of each country, and of its external police." In other words, Montesquieu inquires into whether and how religion can be harmonized with the political order. Can religion, and more specifically Christianity, be civilized?

Through an account of the origins of religious zeal—an account remarkable for its anthropological and psychological insights—Montesquieu shows just how difficult this task of civilizing or policing religion is. We learn that religious intolerance and the proselytizing spirit are the products of a certain sort of spiritual and intellectual advance. Religious barbarism (the barbarism of crusades and inquisitions) is paradoxically a product of civilization. Real primitives— nomadic and idolatrous—are naturally tolerant. Those without fixed dwellings for themselves erect no dwellings for God either.[2] And as Montesquieu says: "Peoples who have no temples have little attachment to their religion: this is why the Tartars have always been so tolerant."[3] Similarly, while idolatry may be in accord with "our natural penchant for things that can be felt," nonetheless human beings are "not strongly attached to idolatrous religions."[4] Primitive tolerance, it seems, is largely a function of religious indifference. That very indifference, however, makes savage peoples receptive to new religions. The belief that God might be anywhere, including in other religions, leaves them open to conversion to the more stringent, universalistic, revealed religions. Montesquieu says that "the barbarian peoples who conquered the Roman empire did not hesitate for a moment to embrace Christianity."[5]

Once in the folds of monotheism, one's attitude toward religion is no longer easygoing. Montesquieu explains that "we are scarcely inclined to spiritual ideas, and nevertheless we are very attached to religions that have us worship a spiritual being."[6] His explanation for this paradox hinges on human vanity. Our attachment to a "difficult" religion—one that is mentally and morally demanding—is a form of self-congratulation. Montesquieu refers to "the satisfaction we find in ourselves for having been intelligent enough to have chosen a religion that withdraws divinity from the humiliation in which others had placed it."[7] This pride in our "enlightenment" is complemented by another pride, not in the choice we have made,

> but in that we believe God has made. The Mohammedans would not be such good Muslims if there were not, on the one hand, idolatrous peoples who make them think they are avengers of the unity of god and, on the other, Christians, to make them believe that they are the object of his preferences.[8]

Vis-à-vis idolators, we pride ourselves on our choosiness; vis-à-vis other monotheists, we pride ourselves on our chosenness. This prideful attachment, increased further by the addition of more sensual elements (such as the passionate character of the worship) culminates in zealotry and intolerance.

Montesquieu sketches an interesting dilemma: How can tolerance defend itself against intolerance, especially if tolerance is correlated with primitivism and indifference, while intolerance is associated with political progress and spiritual enlightenment? Or perhaps more to the point, now that intolerance has triumphed, could tolerance be reestablished on a new footing?

In books 24 and 25 Montesquieu reveals the sorts of changes that would need to be made in established religions before tolerance could return. Much of book 25 is concerned with the problem of priests and pontiffs. Priests are another cost of civilization; "peoples without priests are usually barbarians."[9] Once a people has houses, it will have a house of God, and soon a householder (i.e., priests) to look after it, and eventually a pontiff to order the priests. As there is no going back to those pre-agricultural days, wherein "each man could be a pontiff within his family,"[10] it becomes a matter of policing the clergy, seeing to it that this new form of household has certain limits set to it. This is especially important since religious bodies, in their own nature, are perpetual and unlimited: "The clergy is a family which cannot perish; therefore, goods are attached to it forever and cannot pass out of it."[11] Accordingly, Montesquieu recommends that the civil law put an end to the church's "endless acquisitions,"[12] at the same time, however, cautioning that this reform should be carried out indirectly. As another part of his opposition to clerical excesses, Montesquieu is critical of the law of celibacy on which this "family" (or at least the Catholic branch of it) is founded (25.4). Like a miser, the church hoards both men and material, taking them out of productive circulation.

In subsequent chapters, Montesquieu endorses the separation of church and state (25.8), and hints at the possibility of civic tolerance for a plurality of religions (25.9-10). Yet, it is clear that rendering the state tolerant is not the main issue. The real difficulty lies in obliging the various religions to tolerate one another. Indeed, Montesquieu suggests that legislators might want to prevent the entry of new religions into the state, especially since any religion intent on missionary expansion is likely to be itself intolerant ("a religion that can tolerate others scarcely thinks of its propagation"[13]). The principle seems to be the Lockean one of "no tolerance for the intolerant," with the knock on the door taken as a sign of intolerance. We need not—indeed we should not, under this rule—open the door to someone so disrespectful of our views as to seek to change them. However, this closed-door policy is not without its difficulties, for as Montesquieu also says, "every religion which is repressed becomes repressive itself; for as soon as, by some chance, it can shake off oppression, it attacks the religion which repressed it, not as a religion, but as a tyranny."[14] It seems that neither an open door nor a closed door can handle certain sorts of importunate guests. The inability of political laws to meet the political-religious problem is illustrated by the structure of the two chapters explicitly devoted to a consideration of toleration (25.9-10). The first is entitled "On toleration in religious matters" and voices a "principle" in favor of civic tolerance. The second is entitled "Continuation of the same subject" and voices a "principle" in favor of exclusion.

We see the misapplication of both principles in the Japanese empire's response to Christianity. We learn in a footnote that Tartar tolerance did not disappear with Genghis Khan (Montesquieu's surprising exemplar of tolerance). It is still found among the Japanese: "This turn of mind has been transmitted as far as the Japanese, who were originally the Tartars, as is easily proved."[15] Indeed, "[a]ll the eastern peoples, except the Mohammedans, believe all religions are indistinguishable in themselves" and so among the Kalmucks for instance, "they make it a matter of conscience to allow all sorts of religions."[16] In Japan, this tolerance was initially extended to Christianity, which rapidly gained converts. Montesquieu explains the attraction in his chapter "On the motive for attachment to the various religions":

> Men are exceedingly drawn to hope and to fear, and a religion that had neither hell nor paradise would scarcely please them. This is proved by the ease with which foreign religions have been established in Japan and the zeal and love with which they have been received.[17]

When the powers-that-be noticed this zeal, their tolerant indifference towards Christianity instantly changed to proscription and persecution. As a despotism, Japan "by its nature requires tranquility above all."[18] (Note that this brand of tolerance is compatible with, maybe even characteristic of, despotism.) The sudden action against Christianity was not inspired by religious hatred, but rather by fear of civil unrest: "It is only as a change in government that they fear the establishment of another religion."[19] Christianity justifiably gives rise to such fear because of the zealotry of its followers: "The magistrates regarded the firmness inspired by Christianity as very dangerous,"[20] and because of Christianity's tendency to schism: "when debates break out among those who preach, one begins to find distasteful a religion in which those who propose it are not in agreement."[21]

Montesquieu's understanding of the Japanese dilemma does not excuse their resort to the methods of the Inquisition (we learn that "the emperor of Japan had all the Christians in his states burned by a slow fire"[22]). Montesquieu makes very clear his condemnation of forced renunciations and conversions: "Penal laws must be avoided in the matter of religion. They impress fear, it is true, but as religion also has its penal laws which inspire fear, the one is canceled out by the other. Between these two different fears, souls become atrocious."[23] Throughout *The Spirit of the Laws*, Montesquieu is quite consistent in describing both the laws and the souls of the Japanese as "atrocious."[24] But his criticism of Japanese despotism does not absolve Christianity. Despite Montesquieu's footnote (added after his troubles with the religious authorities) asserting that "the Christian religion is the first good,"[25] his presentation suggests something else. Instead of countering despotism, Christianity is itself a form of despotism.[26]

The rhetorical high point of book 25 is chapter 13, Montesquieu's denunciation of the Inquisition, crafted in the form of a "Very humble remonstrance to the inquisitors of Spain and Portugal," ostensibly written by a Jewish witness to the immolation of a young Jewish girl. Here Montesquieu returns to the methods employed in the *Persian Letters*. The argument is a highly reasoned one, not at all ad hominem. Nonetheless, the fictional ruse heightens the impact of the argument on the reader by virtue of the emotional charge it carries. Moreover, by placing himself at one remove from the "remonstrance," Montesquieu is able to protect himself from the heretical implications of certain statements (which he does in one instance by an editor's footnote on "the source for the Jews' blindness"), but also, in introducing the piece, to deliver a stinging insult to the inquisitorial audience: "An eighteen-year-old Jewess, burned in Lisbon at the last auto-da-fe, occasioned this small work, and I believe it is the most useless that has ever been written. When it is a question of proving such clear things, one is sure not to convince."[27] The Christians would seem to be every bit as blind as the Jews.

Montesquieu's Jew is a tolerant man and a respecter of Christianity. Indeed, it is his professed intention "to take away from princes who will not be Christians a plausible pretext for persecuting [Christianity]."[28] That plausible pretext is the behavior of Christians, who have forgotten their own Golden Rule. The emperor of Japan is merely doing to Christians what Christians have done to Jews. Tolerance on the part of political authorities is shown to depend upon Christianity's reformation. To bring about that reformation, Montesquieu makes sophisticated appeals to the vanity of Christian believers. If, as chapter 2 revealed, vanity figured largely in the adoption of Christianity, perhaps it could also figure in its correction. The remonstrance unfavorably compares Christian behavior to that of infidels ("it has to be admitted that you are much more cruel than this [Japanese] emperor"), Jews ("today you take the role of the Diocletians, and you make us take yours"), and Muslims ("You deprive yourselves of the advantage over the Mohammedans given you by the [violent] manner in which their religion was established"). In each case, Montesquieu urges gentleness and moderation by playing upon the desire to hold oneself superior to all others. He calls upon proud believers to be true to the humble example of Christ.

Midway through his remonstrance, however, the Jew changes tack, calling for fidelity to humanity rather than Christ. The source for humane behavior is "natural enlightenment" and concern for the verdict of History.

"But if you do not want to be Christians, at least be men; treat us as you would if, having only the feeble lights of justice that nature gives us, you had no religion to guide you and no revelation to enlighten you.

. . . .

"You live in a century when natural enlightenment is more alive than it has ever been, when philosophy has enlightened spirits, when the morality of your gospel has been better known, when the respective rights of men over each other, the empire that one conscience has over another conscience, are better established. Therefore, if you do not give up your old prejudices, which, if you do not take care, are your passions, it must be admitted that you are incorrigible, incapable of all enlightenment and of all instruction; and a nation is very unhappy that gives authority to men like you.

. . . .

"We must warn you of one thing; it is that, if someone in the future ever dares to say that the peoples of Europe had a police in the century in which we live, you will be cited to prove that they were barbarians, and the idea one will have about you will be such that it will stigmatize your century and bring hatred on all your contemporaries."[29]

Using the concern for reputation, Montesquieu has attempted to realign the meaning of both barbarism and enlightenment. In the beginning of book 25 (chapters 3 and 4), the "barbarians" were those peoples without houses or priests; by the end, the "barbarians" are the leaders of Christianity. Early on, "enlightenment" was associated with the worship of a spiritual being (chapter 1); now, "enlightenment" is separated from religion ("treat us as you would if . . . you had no religion to guide you and no revelation to enlighten you") and attached instead to nature and philosophy.

This project of redefinition began in 25.7 when Montesquieu cited Plato approvingly as the fountain of "natural enlightenment." The point of that chapter was to deplete the Church's coffers, repress "the luxury of superstition," and induce the ministers of religion to leave the people their property: "Religion must not, with gifts as the pretext, exact from the peoples what the necessities of the state have left over for them."[30] Branding magnificence in the externals of worship as "impious" (an attempt to bribe the divinity) is far from being merely a matter of externals. As Montesquieu understands it, the criticism of religious extravagance, if successful, would contribute to tolerance. We learned back in 25.2 that:

When the externals of worship are very magnificent, we are flattered and we become very attached to the religion. Wealth in the temples and the clergy affects us greatly. Thus, the very poverty of peoples is a motive attaching them to that religion, which has served as a pretext for those who have caused their poverty.[31]

If the magnificence of the houses of God could be rendered suspect, to the point even of suggesting that the priestly householders achieved such magnificence by deliberately impoverishing the people, the result would be both greater prosperity for the people and a more impecunious church—a result that would in turn lessen the attachment to Christianity. Montesquieu believes that the reform of externals cuts to the heart. Eventually, a church that has lost its hold over the parishioners' pocketbooks will lose a measure of its hold over their souls as well.[32]

Barbarian tolerance, on the model of the Japanese, has been a failure. That was a tolerance based on ignorance which either gave way in the face of missionary zeal or turned to atrocious persecutions in order to resist conversion. Montesquieu wants to show that there is a third way other than either beating them or joining them—namely, seducing them. In the course of criticizing the use of state power to compel disbelief, Montesquieu gives a remarkably forthright description of his alternative:

> Therefore, one does not succeed in detaching the soul from religion by filling it with this great object [fear of death], by bringing it closer to the moment when it should find religion of greater importance; a more certain way to attack religion is by favor, by the comforts of life, by the hope of fortune, not by what reminds one of it, but by what makes one forget it; not by what makes one indignant, but by what leads one to indifference when other passions act on our souls and when those that religion inspires are silent. General rule: in the matter of changing religion, invitations are stronger than penalties.[33]

In place of the old, pre-Christian tolerance, which was based on ignorance and compatible with despotism, there must be a new post-Christian tolerance, secure and sophisticated, grounded in economic prosperity, and abstracted from the fear of death. The "feeling for religion" with which book 25 began might become a matter of "indifference." Forgetfulness is not necessarily a bad thing.[34]

This passage on the benefits of forgetfulness should perhaps be linked to the concluding lines of the first chapter of the first book, where Montesquieu seems to bemoan mankind's tendency toward forgetfulness:

> As a feeling creature, he falls subject to a thousand passions. Such a being could at any moment forget his creator; god has called him back to him by the laws of religion. Such a being could at any moment forget himself; philosophers have

reminded him of himself by the laws of morality. Made for living in society, he could forget his fellows; legislators have returned him to his duties by political and civil laws.[35]

However, already in book 1, the possibility of conflict between these different sorts of laws and lawgivers can be glimpsed. Montesquieu says that "if one intelligent being had created another intelligent being, the created one ought to remain in its original dependency"; yet, at the same time he informs us that "it is in their nature [the nature of intelligent beings] to act by themselves."[36] Book 1 offers considerable evidence that Montesquieu himself does not disapprove of this independent streak. He redefines law, for instance, in a way clearly favorable to human pretensions. The opening chapter defines law as "the necessary relations deriving from the nature of things" and elucidates that by saying: "There is, then, a primitive reason; and laws are both the relations that exist between it and the different beings [included among those beings is "the divinity"], and the relations of these various beings to each other." Very quickly, however, we find out that human beings "do not consistently follow their primitive laws," unlike the creator whose act of creation "presupposes rules as invariable as the fate claimed by atheists."[37] By the close of book 1, Montesquieu has abandoned fixity for free will and we are proffered a new definition of law: "Law in general is human reason insofar as it governs all the peoples of the earth."[38] Book 1 is remarkable for the concision with which it drops the whole question of the divine.[39] Montesquieu gives a lesson in how philosophers, by reminding man of himself, might cause him to forget his creator. Witness in particular Montesquieu's treatment of the laws of nature in 1.2: after a preliminary obeisance to the Thomistic inclination toward God, Montesquieu neglects to include anything related to religion in his enumeration of the four natural laws. (Note also that these four natural laws, which "derive uniquely from the constitution of our being"[40] replace the four apriori "relations of fairness" which assume the existence of God and which we "constantly violate."[41]) Given the multiplicity of human passions, perhaps one might learn how to guide the passions by heightening some and downplaying others.

By the time the readers, and particularly the potential legislators among them, get to Part 5, books 24-26, the groundwork has been laid for a purely civic assessment of religion. Montesquieu begins his this-worldly considerations with humble self-deprecation:

As in this work I am not a theologian but one who writes about politics, there may be things that would be wholly true only in a human way of thinking, for they have not been at all considered in relation to the more sublime truths.[42]

Two books later, after completing his consideration of religion, "sublimity" is now ascribed to "human reason,"[43] which is able to discern the different orders of laws and what belongs to them. Divine law comes under the disposition of the human legislator; and, if Montesquieu's guidelines are followed, its scope will be severely constricted. A sampling of the chapter titles is sufficient to indicate Montesquieu's intention: "That one must not decide by the precepts of religion when those of natural law are in question" (26.7); "That things ruled by the principles of civil right must not be ruled by the principles of what is called canonical right" (26.8); "The things that should be ruled by the principles of civil right can rarely be ruled by principles of the laws of religion" (26.9); "In what case one must follow the civil law that permits and not the religious law that forbids" (26.10); "That human tribunals must not be ruled by the maxims of the tribunals that regard the next life" (26.11).

The *Esprits Forts* and the *Esprit Doux* of Montesquieu

Montesquieu's irreligion, however, must be distinguished from that of his precursors (Hobbes, Bayle, the *esprits forts*) and his contemporaries (Voltaire, Diderot, the *Encyclopedists*). While Montesquieu joins his fellows in regarding Christianity as a danger to sound politics, Christianity is not the only threat he sees. He is concerned to ward off despotism of all varieties. Accordingly, he seeks to reform Christianity and solve the theological-political problem, but to do so without augmenting the power of earthly sovereigns. Montesquieu is not a political centralizer. (Unlike Bayle and Voltaire, for instance, Montesquieu saw China as a despotic state.) With Montesquieu, the link between liberalism and absolutism is severed.

While he strives to constrict the sphere of universalistic religion, Montesquieu does not aim, as Hobbes does, to subject matters of belief to political determination; nor does he recommend, as Bayle does, a society of atheists (or alternatively, rule by irreligious elites over superstitious but politically inert masses). Montesquieu directly takes on both Hobbes and Bayle in *The Spirit of the Laws*. In book 1, he quarrels with Hobbes about the laws of nature and "the constitution of our being,"[44] dissenting from Hobbes's psychology, and by implication its political consequence (the great Leviathan) as well. Montesquieu's thematic consideration of religion in books 24 and 25 is launched with an attack on

Bayle ("Bayle's paradox" [24.2] and "Another of Bayle's paradoxes" [24.6]). With respect to both Hobbes and Bayle, what is at issue is the extent and efficacy of various types of fear. Bayle does not find religious fear to be a restraint on human wrongdoing, indeed quite the opposite, the fear of God is often the motive for violence toward others. While recognizing its potential dangers, Montesquieu is less ready to dispense entirely with the fear of powers invisible. According to him, "Even if it were useless for subjects to have a religion, it would not be useless for princes to have one and to whiten with foam the only bridle that can hold those who fear no human laws."[45] In a despotic regime, religion (even false religion) may be the only available check upon absolute power. This point is made elsewhere in *The Spirit of the Laws* as well: "There is, however, one thing with which one can sometimes counter the prince's will: that is religion. . . . The laws of religion are part of a higher precept, because they apply to the prince as well as to the subjects. But it is not the same for natural rights; the prince is not assumed to be a man."[46] Rather, as the continuation of the passage in book 24 reveals, the prince is "a lion":

> A prince who loves and fears religion is a lion who yields to the hand that caresses him or to the voice that pacifies him; the one who fears and hates religion is like the wild beasts who gnaw the chain that keeps them from throwing themselves on passers-by; he who has no religion at all is that terrible animal that feels its liberty only when it claws and devours.[47]

Religion may be a mode of lion-taming, yet Montesquieu hints that there is another mode by which princes may be not simply tamed, but actually humanized. Natural right teaches that even princes are men. Religion, to the extent that it fosters a belief in divinely ordained rulers, may stand in the way of the teaching of natural right. As Montesquieu points out elsewhere: "In these [despotic] states, religion has more influence than in any other; it is a fear added to fear. In Mohammedan empires the peoples derive from religion a part of the astonishing respect they have for their prince."[48] When we link Montesquieu's chapter-contra-Bayle, which seems to express such a strong endorsement of the utility of religion, to these related passages throughout *The Spirit of the Laws*, the force of his endorsement is greatly weakened. While religion is indeed something of a restraint, it is at the same time a very real prop for despotism. Because the principle of despotic government "is corrupt by its nature," Montesquieu says that despotism "can maintain itself only when circumstances, which arise from the climate, the religion, and the situation or the genius of the people, force it to follow some order and to suffer some rule. These things force its nature without changing it; its ferocity remains; it is, for a while, tractable."[49] Putting all these passages together, one might conclude that to the extent any given nation can move from despotic to moderate government, there would have to be a simultaneous dismantling of the chains of religion—chains that both bind and support despotic government.

Montesquieu's initial dispute with Bayle is crafted as a defense of "idolatry" against atheism. Yet, in seeming to reject atheism (but without fully denying that atheism might "be better for a certain man or a certain people"[50]), Montesquieu adopts an almost equally heretical position, namely, that the truth or falsity of religion is not what matters, but rather its civic value, its contribution to constitutional liberty. Judging by that standard, he goes on to offer an appreciation of Christianity, particularly the Protestant branch (and within that, seeming to prefer Calvinism to Lutheranism). As compared to Islam, Christianity's salutary features include the "gentleness so recommended in the gospel"[51] and the establishment of monogamy (which has the political effect of equalizing the prince and his subjects). Further, in comparison to the blood-soaked ancient and Oriental world, "we shall see that we owe to Christianity both a certain political right in government and a certain right of nations in war, for which human nature can never be sufficiently grateful."[52]

This praise of the humanitarian character of Christianity—"it is much more evident to us that a religion should soften the mores of men than it is that a religion is true"[53]—culminates in Montesquieu's second disagreement with Bayle. Chapter 6, "Another of Bayle's paradoxes," begins: "Bayle, after insulting all religion, stigmatizes the Christian religion; he dares propose that a state formed by true Christians would not continue to exist." Montesquieu claims that Bayle has made two fundamental mistakes: he has confused Christianity "itself" with the church (which Montesquieu calls "the orders for the establishment of Christianity"), and he has not distinguished properly "the precepts of the gospel from their counsels" ("precepts" are laws; "counsels" are highminded suggestions). Montesquieu's ostensible defense of Christianity as much as admits that the church is politically problematic and that the principles of Christianity, drawn from the New Testament, cannot be the basis for either the laws or the spirit of the laws. Montesquieu suggests that Jesus himself did not intend for his counsels of perfection to pertain to politics: "When the legislator, instead of giving laws, has given counsels, it is because he has seen that his counsels, if they were ordained like laws, would be contrary to the spirit of the laws."[54] Montesquieu can rescue Christianity from Bayle's charge only by radically limiting Christianity's purview, allowing it to address the individual heart, but not "men or things universally."[55]

It seems that Montesquieu has adeptly made use of the animus against Bayle to further an aim he shares with Bayle. Montesquieu's handling of the religious question is less provocative, but not for that reason less successful. In this chapter, Montesquieu calls Bayle a "great man" in the course of noting how "astounding" it is "that one can impute to this great man a misunderstanding of the spirit of his own religion."[56] Perhaps it is too astounding for us to find the imputation credible, particularly when we remember that the Preface to *The Spirit of the Laws* ends with a paragraph in which Montesquieu considers his relation to the "great men" who have preceded him:

> If this work meets with success, I shall owe much of it to the majesty of my subject; still, I do not believe that I have totally lacked genius. When I have seen what so many great men in France, England, and Germany have written before me, I have been filled with wonder, but I have not lost courage. "And I too am a painter," have I said with Correggio.[57]

The passage should alert us to Montesquieu's admiration for Bayle, but also to Montesquieu's very real conviction that his own canvas, and the techniques used to create it, might rival Bayle's.

By turning to non-Christian examples, Montesquieu next shows how religion can be transmuted into socially useful morality. He gives examples of two peoples, one barbarian (the Peguans in 24.8), one Jewish (the Essenes in 24.9), whose religious injunctions were reducible to what Montesquieu calls in the *Persian Letters* "the obligations of charity and humanity."[58] In that work, Usbek (in this instance speaking for Montesquieu) applies the lesson to Christianity, arguing that if God loves mankind, then the way for us to please God is by emulating his philanthropy. The imitation of God ought to redirect human sight earthward, toward "obedience to the law, love of fellow man, and reverence for one's parents."[59] By the time he gets to 24.14, Montesquieu is bold enough to say that "religion and the civil laws should aim principally to make good citizens of men."

Just as he recasts religion as morality, in the process stripping away any conception of duties toward God (or "god," to use Montesquieu's preferred typography), so too Montesquieu dissolves the distinction between philosophy and religion, claiming that "[t]he various sects of philosophy among the ancients could be considered as kinds of religion."[60] The best of these sects is Stoicism, for "it alone knew how to make citizens; . . . it alone made great emperors."[61] Montesquieu does not allow the reader to lose sight of the fact that his praise of the Stoics implies reservations about the desirability of Christianity's advent. The following hypothetical reminds us of the trade-off: "*if I could for a moment [un moment] cease to think that I am a Christian*, I would not be able to keep myself from numbering the destruction of Zeno's sect among the misfortunes of human kind"[62] [emphasis added]. Three paragraphs later, the "moment" arrives, emphatically, rather than conditionally:

> Let us momentarily [*pour un moment*] lay aside the revealed truths; seek in all of nature and you will find no greater object than the Antonines; Julian even, Julian (a vote thus wrenched from me will not make me an accomplice to his apostasy); no, since him there has been no prince more worthy of governing men.[63]

Just in case our knowledge of imperial Rome is a little sketchy, Montesquieu indicates that this is Julian "the Apostate" he is extolling—Julian who sought to undermine an already established Christianity by instituting toleration for all religions and reviving the pagan worship. Constantine, who had earlier prepared the way for Christianity's establishment by the Edict of Milan (decreeing toleration for Christianity) and by his own conversion, is pointedly not considered a great emperor by Montesquieu. Indeed, in chapter 13, Constantine is mentioned only to have aspersions cast, via the writings of Julian, upon the motive of his conversion. (Constantine had murdered his eldest son, a crime which the God of the Bible could forgive—after all, filiacide figures in God's own plan from the binding of Isaac to the crucifixion of His only begotten son—but which paganism could not.) The implied contrast between Julian and Constantine, both of whom issued edicts of toleration, reveals once again that toleration is not recommended in and of itself. It is valued, instead, as a post-Christian strategy for diffusing religious fervor and calming theological disputes that eventuate in civic strife.[64]

Like the religions of the Peguans and the Essenes, the Stoic sect is celebrated by Montesquieu for its public-spiritedness, its inculcation of active benevolence, its attention to "the duties of society."[65] This subset of chapters (24.8-10) on admirable heathens and infidels provides the ground for Montesquieu's subsequent criticism of certain key dogmas of Christianity. Often, Christianity is not mentioned directly; instead, religions with similarities to Christianity are singled out. So, for instance, the chapter following that on the happily busy Stoics criticizes Islam for its extreme other-worldliness—an attitude ingrained by the practice of prayer. Montesquieu states as a general rule that "[m]en, being made to preserve, feed and clothe themselves, and to do all the things done in society, religion should not give them an overly contemplative life."[66] When the doctrine of predestination (attributed once again to the Muslims) is superadded to this abstraction from life, the result is politically disastrous: "Men who believe in the certainty of rewards in the next life will escape the legislator; they will have too much scorn for death.

How can one constrain by the laws a man who believes himself sure that the greatest penalty the magistrates can inflict on him will end in a moment only to begin his happiness?"[67] Certainty of salvation is a recipe for martyrdom. The passage confirms that stronger measures on the part of the secular authorities will only produce more martyrs, since divine hopes outweigh earthly fears. The dilemma of the law's powerlessness might be addressed in a variety of ways: 1) keep hell in contention—divine hopes are not quite so dangerous when kept in check by divine fears; 2) increase skepticism about the afterlife altogether, thereby weakening both divine hopes and fears; 3) tempt believers with the joys associated with this life—in essence, use more tangible earthly hopes as the antidote to divine hopes. Once one entertains hopes from life, fear of the law is restored, and with it, the force of the law as well.

The first of these strategies would require meeting "the elect" on their own ground by entering into theologically-based dispute with them. It is not a contest Montesquieu wants any part of. He seems to prefer some mix of the second and third strategies. The second could be pursued by means of straightforwardly anti-theological argument, but Montesquieu never appears openly irreligious. Indeed, he criticizes those (Hobbes, Bayle, Spinoza) who have reputations for atheism. Given the continuing virulence of Christianity, open irreligion, instead of inoculating men against fanaticism, risks another bout of it. Montesquieu seeks to alter Christian sensibilities without needlessly antagonizing them. He is even willing to play to the prejudices of his audience, as when he criticizes Islam, in order to gain a hearing that will eventually lead the audience to indict its own beliefs as much as those of Islam. Self-knowledge is attained gradually and by circuitous routes. By deferring to the reigning opinions in an attempt to reshape those opinions, Montesquieu leaves belief with its sense of independence intact. Montesquieu's willingness to do this is a sign of his view that religion, once properly pruned, can be an aid to good government. According to Montesquieu "religion, even a false one, is the best warrant men can have of the integrity of men,"[68] perhaps because the content of natural equity, simple though it is, remains abstruse and, even when promulgated, too abstract to oblige ordinary men.[69] Thus, instead of arguing directly for religious skepticism by taking up "foundational" questions about the status of revelation and the knowability of miracles, Montesquieu skirts the whole issue of whether the teachings of religion are true or false.[70] He asks instead whether they are useful. This very stance, however, since it implies the priority of politics over religion, might be said to convict its author of irreligion. Nonetheless, Montesquieu's "antifoundationalism" consists less in his demolition of foundations than in his deliberate neglect of them. He is not a "root and branch" revolutionary. As a vintner, Montesquieu was familiar with the technique of grafting—completely new vines might be grown upon old stock; it is not always necessary or advisable to disturb the roots. Thus, in the main, Montesquieu favors the third approach: the creation of substitute satisfactions. This helps to account for the prominent place he accords economic considerations. For Montesquieu, economics is not "the dismal science." It is the art by which human life is redeemed.

In chapter 19, which bears the title "That it is less the truth or falsity of a dogma that makes it useful or pernicious to men in the civil state than the use or abuse made of it," Montesquieu enters into the most delicate territory, discussing the twin teachings of the immortality of the soul and the resurrection of the body. Neither Stoicism nor Confucianism believes in an immortal soul. "From their bad principles," according to Montesquieu, "these two sects drew consequences that were not just, but were admirable for society."[71] By contrast, those religions that do believe in "such a saintly dogma" (Taoism, Buddhism, and Hinduism among others are mentioned) have drawn "frightful consequences" from it: "Almost everywhere in the world, and in all times, the opinion that the soul is immortal, wrongly taken, has engaged women, slaves, subjects, and friends to kill themselves in order to go to the next world and serve the object of their respect or their love."[72]

No mention is made of Christianity until the final paragraph where it is said that Christianity has directed these dogmas "remarkably well" by giving such a "spiritual" cast even to the dogma of bodily resurrection. As a result, a Christian king is not followed to the grave by the whole of his household retinue. Yet Christianity is not completely exonerated. Montesquieu appends a footnote in which he gives the response of a Confucian ("[a] Chinese philosopher") to "the doctrine of Foë" (a version of Chinese Buddhism). I believe it would not be amiss to read this footnote as expressing, as well, the response of a Western philosopher to Western Christianity. Here it is:

> It is said in a book of this sect that our body is our house and the soul, the immortal host living in it [the parallel biblical passage would be 1 Corinthians 3:16-17, 6:19]; but if the body of our parents is only a dwelling, it is natural to consider it with the same disdain that one has for a pile of mud and dirt. Does this not intend to uproot from the heart the virtue of loving one's parents? This also leads to neglecting the care of the body and refusing to it the compassion and affection so necessary for its preservation; thus the disciples of Foë kill themselves by the thousands.[73]

In lieu of this sort of (Christian) asceticism and martyrdom, Montesquieu endorses an alternative view of saintliness. In chapter 20, which bears the odd title "Continuation of the same subject"—a title much favored by Montesquieu[74]— he recommends the "useful" dogma of the Zoroastrians: "'If you want to be a saint, instruct your children, because all the good acts they do will be attributed to you.'"[75] The message seems to be that men and women should think less about "the resurrection of the body" and more about the generation of new bodies. Immortality needs to be reconceived in this-worldly, biologically-based, and socially-responsible terms. These same ancient Persians "counseled early marriage," unlike the Christians, for whom "[c]elibacy was a counsel."[76] Montesquieu wants a political order that values prosperity and procreation rather than poverty and celibacy.

This attention to the here and now culminates in Montesquieu's application of his climate theories to religion in the concluding chapters (23-26) of book 24. Religious doctrines and practices ought to be in line with a people's way of life, as that way of life is shaped by natural forces. So, for instance, in more northerly climes, where the opportunity for leisure is less—and, importantly, in other places, whether northerly or not, that "maintain themselves by commerce"[77]—the frequency of worship and the number of religious festivals must be dramatically scaled back. Montesquieu says that "When a religion orders that work come to an end, it should have more regard for the needs of men than for the greatness of the being that it honors."[78] In other words, human contracts have precedence over divine covenants, including that of the Sabbath. When Montesquieu relates various religious opinions to a country's climate, he doesn't quite say that the climate is the cause of the opinion, but he does stress the importance of fitness or suitability. "The opinion of metempsychosis is," according to Montesquieu, "made for the climate of the Indies."[79] Similarly, the religious prohibition on pork is medically justified in Arabia, but "could not be good for other countries."[80] Listen to the scientific rationale:

> Santorio has observed that when one eats pork it transpires little and that this food even greatly prevents the transpiration of other foods; he has found that the decrease was as much as a third; one knows, besides, that the lack of transpiration forms or sharpens diseases of the skin: therefore, eating pork should be forbidden in climates where one is subject to these diseases, as in Palestine, Arabia, Egypt, and Libya.[81]

This medicalization of religious practices has become popular. Americans today routinely defend or account for such things as the incest taboo, the laws of kashrut, and the covenant of circumcision on the (reductionist) grounds of health. One hears that prohibiting incest is a genetically sound rule, since inbreeding leads to retardation; or that the prohibition of pork made sense in times when trichinosis was a danger; or that circumcision lessens the chance of infections. Rarely does one hear the more profound spiritual, moral, or political reasons for these injunctions.

By linking climate and religion and by offering essentially materialistic explanations of religious matters, Montesquieu chastens those religions with universalistic aspirations, primarily Christianity and Islam. Accordingly, the title of book 24's penultimate chapter speaks of "The drawback in transferring a religion from one country to another." In a footnote, Montesquieu issues a disclaimer —"The Christian religion is not spoken of here because, as was said in bk. 24, chap. 1 at the end, the Christian religion is the first good."[82] Nonetheless, he pretty clearly ignores his own disclaimer in the final chapter, "Continuation of the same subject," when he says "it seems that climate has prescribed limits to the Christian religion."[83] Moreoever, he earlier spoke well of Montezuma's relativistic rationale for resisting conversion to Christianity: "And when Montezuma persisted in saying that the religion of the Spaniards was good for their country and that of Mexico for his own, he was not saying an absurd thing, because, indeed, legislators could not have kept from having regard for what nature had established before them."[84] The reference to legislators—of the human not divine variety—is interesting, since it suggests that religion is a terrestrial construction, a compound of nature and human reason.

Although Montesquieu deploys the climate argument here to defend religious particularity against universalistic pretensions, it is not the case that legislators must simply bow to the force of the climate. In Part III of *The Spirit of the Laws* (books 14 through 19), which deals specifically with the ways in which climate and terrain shape human character and laws, Montesquieu shows that nature's influence is neither simple nor irresistible. Indeed, the message that emerges is not one of climatic determinism, but of the need for wise legislators adept in countering the potential despotism of nature. Montesquieu holds out the possibility that proper laws and institutions, together with the liberating potential of technology, could overcome the despotic tendency of even the worst climates. A key chapter bears the title: "That bad legislators are those who have favored the vices of the climate and good ones are those who have opposed them."[85] The example Montesquieu gives of a bad legislator is Foë: "Foë, legislator of the Indies, followed his feelings when he put men in an extremely passive state; but his doctrine, born of idleness of the climate, favoring it in turn, has caused a thousand ills."[86] Revealingly, this is the very same Foë who is mentioned at two other points in *The Spirit of the Laws*: namely, at 24.11, entitled "On contemplation," where his doctrine is criticized for prescribing "an overly contemplative life"; and at 24.19, entitled "That it is less the truth or falsity of a dogma that makes it useful or pernicious to men in the civil state than the use or abuse made of it," where the religion of Foë is criticized for the "frightful consequences" of its teaching on the immortality of the soul. If, as I suggested earlier, the religion of Foë may be taken as a stand-in for Christianity, Montesquieu's point is not simply that Christianity is "a religion founded on a climate,"[87] but rather that it is founded on an objectionable acquiescence to the vices of a particular climate, namely an excessively hot Middle Eastern climate. It may be expected that when Christianity is transplanted to more northerly climes, it will either fail to take hold or will undergo certain salutary modifications, such as are visible in Protestantism. But it would be desirable if, even in its native habitat (or other climatically congenial habitats like southern Europe), Christianity were fundamentally refashioned. Montesquieu sketches the alternative to Foë when he describes those "sensible" legislators who "considered men not in terms of the peaceful state in which they will one day be but in terms of the action proper to making them fulfill the duties of life," and accordingly, "made their religion, philosophy, and laws all practical."[88] The guideline Montesquieu suggests is that "[t]he more the physical causes incline men to rest, the more the moral causes should divert them from it."[89] We see Montesquieu practicing such diversion in books 24 and 25. In book 24, he assesses theological dogmas in the light of political interests; in book 25, he examines, by the same light, the structure and practices of the church.

Montesquieu uses climate in a somewhat disingenuous way. In the books on religion, climate serves as a rationale for toleration. One must respect religious differences because they are rooted in cultural differences which are in turn rooted in environmental differences. Nature—which is to say nature's diversity— is deployed to discourage Christianity's missionary zeal. Yet while Montesquieu is certainly serious about the attention he gives to physical factors, his position is not that temperature determines temperament. Nor could he himself be said to be tolerant in the sense that whatever is, is okay. His is not a position of thoroughgoing cultural relativism. Such a position is too conservative for Montesquieu, since Montesquieu is an opponent of despotism, whether of the political, religious, or climatic variety. That opposition to despotism indicates his subscription to a kind of universalism—albeit a moderate, liberal universalism. There is available to human beings a principled ground from which one can render judgments. There is, as Montesquieu states in the Preface, "the nature of things" and man's "own nature," both of which man is "capable of knowing." Indeed, Montesquieu already knows them. "[A]midst the infinite diversity of laws and mores" Montesquieu claims to have found "the principles." Further, he claims to have seen beyond man's "flexible being"—inasmuch as our adaptability to society conceals us from ourselves—to genuine self-awareness. In the manner of the philosophers described in 1.1, Montesquieu has "reminded him of himself by the laws of morality."

While Montesquieu is rightly known for his attention to and appreciation of diversity of many sorts, from the variety of nature to the variety of regimes, it is nonetheless important to note both the boundaries of his toleration and its instrumental or ancillary character. In our own age, toleration has become a new kind of absolute. Indeed, under the banner of "multiculturalism," we are urged not simply to tolerate diversity but to "celebrate" it. In view of the extent to which despotic arrangements (whether domestic, political, or religious) exist throughout the world, past and present, such a demand would strike Montesquieu as ill-conceived and illiberal. Contemporary tolerance has become like the barbarian tolerance that Montesquieu faulted. It is openness to the point of mindlessness (or spiritlessness), offering no resistance to the spread of fanaticism and extremism. By contrast, Montesquieu's enlightened tolerance depends on enlightenment—of others, as well as oneself. For Montesquieu, more fundamental than toleration is moderation. In book 29, "On the way to compose the laws," he declares "I say it, and it seems to me that I have written this work only to prove it: the spirit of moderation should be that of the legislator; the political good, like the moral good, is always found between two limits."[90] Through the instruction he offers in the art of legislation—an art in which the understanding of a nation's general spirit becomes the fulcrum for reform—Montesquieu shows how the extremes might be brought within measure. By returning to Montesquieu, perhaps one might garner insights into how contemporary liberalism could fortify itself for the struggle against new extremisms, on both left and right, both religious and anti-religious (including those that have internally beset liberalism). What we need to recover is Montesquieu's intransigent moderation.

NOTES:

1. *The Spirit of the Laws*, translated and edited by Anne M. Cohler, Basia Carolyn Miller, and Harold Samuel Stone (NY: Cambridge University Press, 1989), 25.1. All citations will be to this edition.

2. Montesquieu would not have been surprised at the invention of drive-in churches in that land of almost nomadic mobility: Los Angeles.

3. 25.3

4. 25.2.

5. 25.3.

6. 25.2.

7. 25.2.

8. 25.2.

9. 25.4.

10. 25.4.

11. 25.5.

12. 25.5.

13. 25.10.

14. 25.9.

15. 25.3.

16. 25.15.

17. 25.2.

18. 25.15.

19. 25.15.

20. 25.14.

21. 25.15.

22. 25.13.

23. 25.12.

24. See 6.13, 14.15, 25.14, also 12.13, 13.11, 19.4, 20.14, 24.14.

25. 25.10.

26. Montesquieu uses similar language in describing the Japanese and the Christians. In rebuking the Spanish Inquisitors he says: "The character of truth is in its triumph over hearts and spirits and not in this powerlessness (*impuissance*) you avow when you want to make it accepted by punishments" (25.13). Earlier, he had devoted a whole chapter to the "Powerlessness (*Impuissance*) of Japanese laws" (6.13), wherein he discussed the Japanese attempt to destroy Christianity.

27. 25.13.

28. 25.13.

29. 25.13.

30. 25.7.

31. 25.2.

32. Consider the fate of tithing in mainstream denominations today.

33. 25.12.

34. As residents of a world awash in creature comforts, but largely indifferent to reflection on the theological and moral implications of our creaturehood, we might wonder whether Montesquieu is right. Without becoming apologists for the Inquisition, we might ask whether the constricted horizon of modernity can satisfy the human soul.

35. 1.1.

36. 1.1.

37. 1.1.

38. 1.3.

39. For an analysis of book 1 see David Lowenthal, "Book One of the *Spirit of the Laws*," *American Political Science Review* 53 (1959).

40. 1.2.

41. 1.1.

42. 24.1. Montesquieu adopts a similar strategem with respect to "virtue." He claims (both in the footnote to 3.5 and in the Author's foreword added in 1757) that his usage is purely political, and that it does not encompass moral or Christian virtue. According to his emphatic declaration "I speak . . . not at all about that virtue which relates to revealed truths" (3.5.n9). And he continues: "This will be seen in book 5, chap. 2." But the proof text he offers is an odd one, for in the course of defining what he means by political virtue, he cites as *the* example of political virtue "monks" and the "love" they bear their order—an extraordinary, supernatural, general love that turns out to be a product of the rigorous suppression of all ordinary, mundane, particular loves. This is but one of many instances in which Montesquieu in fact assimilates Christian virtue to ancient "political" virtue and calls into question the extremism of both. Montesquieu's critique of virtue throughout Part I is the opening gambit in his recasting of Christianity's role in European political life. Although he tells us that there should be no cause for consternation at his assertion "That virtue is not the principle of monarchical government" (3.5), since that does not mean Christian virtue is absent from monarchies, in point of fact, it may be the presence of Christian virtue (or Christian teaching) that is problematic, since it runs contrary to the monarchic mainspring of "honor." In 4.4, Montesquieu laments the "opposing educations" modern men receive—divided as they are between "the ties of religion and those of the world."

43. 26.1.

44. 1.2.

45. 24.2.

46. 3.10. See also 2.4 on "the power that alone checks arbitrary power."

47. 24.2.

48. 5.14.

49. 8.10.

50. 24.2.

51. 24.3.

52. 24.3. One might add to this list what Montesquieu says earlier about Christianity's role in the abolition of slavery. In 15.7-8 he credits Christianity with abolishing civil servitude in Europe. There is another side to the story however, for the quest for converts to Christianity was also used to justify slavery outside of Europe: "It was this way of thinking," Montesquieu points out "that encouraged the destroyers of America in their crimes" (15.4). Once African slavery had been established, those souls-to-be-saved were eventually declared soulless. In his supremely ironic chapter, "On the slavery of Negroes," Montesquieu mocks the rationalizations of Christian racists: "It is impossible for us to assume that these people are men because if we assumed they were men one would begin to believe that we ourselves were not Christians" (15.5). Slavery is at odds with the Christian teaching of universal human brotherhood. One response to the contradiction between principle and practice is to ruthlessly resolve it by denying the slave's humanity. Montesquieu's remark points up the contrast between ancient and modern attitudes toward slavery. The ancients at least included the slave within the family of man, and sought to justify slavery, however erroneously or hypocritically, on charitable grounds. The modern defenders of slavery are driven to deny a common creation. The force of the contradiction between principle and practice is part of the reason for the greater viciousness of modern race-based chattel slavery, but also (we might add) what made possible its eventual abolition. The American struggle over the slavery question, in all its glory and all its sordidness, would be unimaginable in the ancient world.

53. 24.4.

54. 24.6.

55. 24.7.

56. 24.6.

57. The only other author Montesquieu specifically names as a "great man" is Machiavelli, a contemporary of Correggio (VI.5).

58. *The Persian Letters*, translated by George R. Healy (Indianapolis: Bobbs-Merrill, Library of Liberal Arts, 1964), #46.

59. #46.

60. 24.10.

61. 24.10.

62. 24.10.

63. 24.10.

64. Montesquieu also compares the two emperors in chapter 17 of his *Considerations on the Causes of the Greatness of the Romans and Their Decline*. For an insightful analysis of the comparison, see Douglas Kires, "The Displacement of Christian Historiography in Montesquieu's Book on the Romans," in *Piety and Humanity: Essays on Religion and Early Modern Political Philosophy*, ed. Douglas Kries (Lanham, MD: Rowman & Littlefield, 1997), 234-238.

65. 24.10.

66. 24.11.

67. 24.14.

68. 24.8.

69. One is reminded of Thomas Jefferson's famous query in his *Notes on the State of Virginia*: "can the liberties of a nation be thought secure when we have removed their only firm basis, a conviction in the minds of the people that these liberties are of the gift of God?" (*The Portable Jefferson*, edited by Merrill D. Peterson [NY: Penguin, 1975], 215.

70. *The Persian Letters* is directed somewhat more at the claim of miraculous revelation, although there also Montesquieu does not proceed by forthright argumentation, but rather by satire. For a discussion of Montesquieu's use of ridicule as a mode of criticism, see my *Erotic Liberalism: Women and Revolution in Montesquieu's "Persian Letters"* (Lanham, MD: Rowman & Littlefield, 1995), particularly pp. 101-103.

71. 24.19.

72. 24.19.

73. 24.19n.25. Montesquieu is quoting from the "Dialogue d'un philosophe Chinois," found in the collection by Father du Halde.

74. Fifty-five out of 605 chapters have this title, including the very last chapter of the last book.

75. 24.20.

76. 24.7.

77. 24.23.

78. 24.23.

79. 24.24.

80. 24.25.

81. 24.25.

82. 24.25n.38.

83. 24.26.

84. 24.24.

85. 14.5.

86. 14.5.

87. 24.26.

88. 14.5.

89. 14.5.

90. 29.1.

12

THE TOLERANT SKEPTICISM OF VOLTAIRE AND DIDEROT: AGAINST LEIBNIZIAN OPTIMISM AND "WISE CHARITY"

Patrick Riley

I

One can approach Voltaire's tolerant skepticism from several directions; one might, for example, consider his humorously deflationary treatment of salvific "grace" in the *Dictionnaire philosophique:*

> Why would the absolute Master of all have been more concerned to direct the interior of a single man [through particular grace] than to conduct the rest of entire nature? Through what *bizarrerie* would he change something in the heart of a Courlander or a Biscayan, while he changes nothing in the laws that he has imposed on the stars?[1]

And one could then show that, had Voltaire been heeded, France might have been spared the uncharitable quarrels which set the Jansenists and the Jesuits intolerantly at each other's throats as late as the 1760's -- as they had been at each other's throats in the days of Pascal's *Provincial Letters* a century earlier.[2]

Surely, however the most natural and convenient way to illuminate Voltaire's tolerant skepticism, while saving Diderot for later, is to focus on the one work of Voltaire which is still widely read -- *Candide, or Optimism* -- then to show that Voltairean skepticism is best brought out through a contrast with Leibnizian optimism: the notion that the present, actual world is the "best" [optimum] of all logically possible ones, that God had a "sufficient reason" for creating it, and that it is justifiable as the best choice of a "wisely charitable" and "universally benevolent" *être infiniment parfait*.[3] And after showing that Voltaire's deep suspicion of rationalist metaphysics and theology (as far back as the *Traité de métaphysique* of 1734) made him unavoidably *anti-Leibnitzien* -- to quote his own phrase from a letter to the President of the Leibniz-founded Berlin Academy of Sciences[4] -- it will remain to point out that, ironically, Voltaire shared with Leibniz a devotion to enlightened, tolerant and generous political leadership which might alleviate poverty and misery, establish scientific and educational institutions, spurn religious superstition and persecution, and prefer prosperity and felicity to war and violence.[5] The practical aims of Leibniz and Voltaire are not so far apart, even if their views about "finding" principles of universal justice which are as valid for God as for men in all possible worlds diverge radically and wholly. If their "first philosophies" were as far apart as they could very well be -- since Leibniz was an anti-skeptical, Christian-Platonic, neo-Augustinian rationalist who thought that "English" empiricism was wrong in countless ways, while Voltaire drew together the French Pyrrhonist skepticism of Montaigne, Charron, Pascal and Bayle and the Lockean/Newtonian empiricism which he found during his English years[6] -- their shared political insistence on enlightenment, toleration and social improvement linked them profoundly. Both of them could share the celebrated motto, *Écraser l'infame*[7] -- even if they wouldn't agree at every point about what counts as "infamous" and is worthy of being crushed.

A final introductory remark: in the post-*Candide* article, "Bien, tout est bien" from the 1770 edition of the *Dictionnaire philosophique*, Voltaire traces the notion that "all is well" to Plato's *Timaeus* and then to Leibniz' *Theodicée*: "Leibniz ... took Plato's part .... But after having read both more than once, we avow our ignorance, according to our custom; and since the Gospel has revealed nothing to us on this point, we shall remain without remorse in the shadows"[8] -- that is, in Plato's cave without any ascent toward the sun.[9]

But Leibniz never says that all is well (or good); he says that the world is best (optimal). "Best," however, is not good; God alone is (perfectly) good, simply. Bestness is (and must be) congruent with the real existence of Caligula and of Dr. Goebbels; the Leibnizian world is best despite being riddled with "physical," "metaphysical" and "moral" evil.[10] And so Voltaire's horrendously funny inventory of earthly disasters in *Candide* -- murder, rape, beating, hanging, vivisection, slavery, cannibalism, bestiality, syphilis, sodomy, incest, mutilation, drowning, the Lisbon earthquake and the Spanish Inquisition (not to mention ordinary injustice and garden-variety cruelty) -- cannot damage mere "bestness" in the way that it would be fatal to straightforward *goodness*. In Chapter 28, when Candide is reunited with the supposedly long-dead Dr. Pangloss -- who has now lost his nose to tertiary syphilis -- the following conversation ensues:

> --Well, my dear Pangloss, Candide said to him, now that you have been hanged, dissected, beaten to a pulp, and sentenced to the galleys, do you still think that everything is for the best in this world?
> --I am still of my first opinion, replied Pangloss; for after all I am a philosopher, and it would not be right for me to recant since Leibniz could not possibly be wrong.[11]

But Leibniz would not say that everything (taken individually) is "for the best in this world"; he would say that the world as a totality, as a whole, is best overall. Not that that distinction would matter much to Voltaire: what he despises is any effort to rationalize evil, to make it comprehensible and acceptable within a so-called "universal jurisprudence." No doubt, for Voltaire, we must endure evil (since it is inescapable for finite, sentient beings); but we need not (and indeed cannot) find a "sufficient reason" for it. "One must at least grant," Voltaire says, "that this puny animal [man] has the right to cry out humbly, and to seek to understand, while crying out, why these eternal laws [of the "best" world] are not made for the well-being of each individual."[12] (On this last point, almost without knowing it, Voltaire puts his finger on a grave difficulty in Leibnizian optimism -- as will be seen.)

So if Leibniz never says that *tout est bien*, he does assuredly say that the world is and must be best. But Voltaire never touches the most appalling difficulty in Leibniz' thought: why would a wisely charitable and universally benevolent *être infiniment parfait* create in time (when he need not) any "world" at all -- a world which is (at best) "best," but not good? Would not a wise, loving, benevolent perfect Being simply contemplate his own perfection *ad infinitum* -- in the manner of Aristotle's divinities at 1178b in the *Nicomachean Ethics* -- and not "translate into existence" a (merely) best world in which the admission of evil is the *condition sine qua non* of the creation of any finite world? Leibniz himself poses the radical question, "why is there something rather than nothing?," in the *Principles of Nature and Grace*[13]; and if, as Leibniz thinks, the Anselmian ontological proof demonstrates the necessity of God's existence, it doesn't (and can't) show that anything finite (imperfect or "metaphysically evil") exists *ex necessitatis*. Voltaire, in a sense, didn't appreciate what is worst in the Leibnizian "best": how to get from God's perfection to the mere bestness of an actual, created world.

II

To understand Voltaire's critique (or rather ridicule) of Leibnizian "optimism," one must first understand what Leibniz meant by a *jurisprudence universelle* of "wise charity" which is as valid for God as for men.

The central idea of Leibniz' "universal jurisprudence," which aims to find quasi-geometrical eternal moral verities equally valid for all rational beings, human or divine, is that justice is "the charity of the wise (*caritas sapientis*)"[14] -- that it is not mere conformity to sovereign-ordained "positive" law given *ex plenitudo potestatis* (in the manner of Hobbes), nor mere "refraining from harm or even "rendering what is due" (the *neminem laedere* and *suum cuique tribuere* of Roman law). Now the equal stress on "charity" and on "wisdom" suggests that Leibniz' practical thought is a kind of fusing of Platonism -- in which the "wise" know the eternal truths such as "absolute" goodness (*Phaedo* 75d) which the gods themselves also know and love (*Euthyphro* 9e-10) and therefore deserve to rule (*Republic* 443 d-e) -- and of Pauline Christianity, whose key moral idea is that charity or love is the first of the virtues ("though I speak with the tongues of men and of angels and have not charity, I am become as sounding brass or a tinkling cymbal")[15]. There is, historically, nothing remarkable in trying to fuse Platonism and Christianity; for Augustine's thought (particularly the early *De Libero Arbitrio*) is just such a fusion.[16] But Leibniz was the last of the great Christian Platonists, and left the world just as Hume, Rousseau and Kant were about to transform and "secularize" it: Hume by converting morality into psychology ("sentiments" of approval and disapproval disjointed from "reason"[17]), Rousseau by reverting to pre-Christian antiquity (the "Spartan mother" with a radically civic "general will"[18]), and Kant by rethinking Aristotelian *telos* (in order to respect persons as "ends" who ought never to be treated merely as "means," and in order to define morality as "pure practical teleology"[19]).

But if justice rightly understood is "wise charity" (or universal benevolence), three main questions arise: (1) Where does Leibniz find this novel notion of justice? (2) Can an infinite Being be said to be restricted by timeless moral ideas which he finds "imbedded" in his own understanding and does not create in time (ideas which he then follows in fashioning a fully justifiable "best" of all possible worlds from a range of logically possible ones)? And (3) Can finite beings, for example human beings in the "human forum," actually act with greater wise charity, if their sheer finitude and limitation -- what Leibniz calls their "metaphysical evil"[20] -- keep them from knowing and therefore willing the right and the good?

The first question is mainly historical: if one decomposes *caritas sapientis* into its parts, charity and wisdom, the provenance of both elements is clear enough -- charity or love is the very heart of Christian ethics (St. Paul's "the greatest of these is charity" or St. John's "a new commandment I give unto you, that you love one another"[21]); and the notion that justice requires the rule of the wise is famously Platonic. How charity and wisdom relate, how they might modify each other, is not just an historical but a philosophical problem -- since love is "affective," wisdom "cognitive;" but the really grave difficulties in Leibniz' universal jurisprudence relate to questions (2) and (3). For it is not clear that a wisely charitable God would create a world which, though it may be "best," is not simply good; and *être infiniment parfait* might sooner contemplate his own perfection, *ad infinitum*. And whether Judas or Pontius Pilate "could have" acted better, been more benevolent, is notoriously problematical given Leibniz' ideas of "substance" (or monad) and of pre-established harmony.[22] (Since, however, Leibniz is a supremely architectonic thinker who wants to relate everything to "first philosophy," one cannot just cordon off his moral and political thought from his metaphysics and theology: that is precisely what he himself did not do.)

The essential thing, then, in a philosopher of Leibniz' stature, is to relate his central moral and political ideas to the structural principles of his first philosophy. The celebrated *Monadology*, for example, is Leibniz' theory of "substance" -- but for him a (rational) substance or monad is a person, a mind, a "citizen" of the City of God governed by "eternal moral verities" and by moral memory; in short the *Monadology* is a theory of personality on which all further Leibnizian convictions about morality and justice are based.[23] And the *Theodicy* is a theory of the perfect justice of a divine "person" or mind who brings about what is "best," and who "justifies himself against complaints."[24] Leibniz is always a moralist thinking of what is justifiable, even when he seems to be a metaphysician or a theologian: "theology is the highest point in knowledge of those things which concern the mind, and includes in some way good morals and good politics."[25] (That statement about what is "highest" should give pause to those who view Leibniz mainly as a mathematician and logician.[26])

What is crucial, then, is to see how Leibniz' central moral-political convictions flow reasonably, and possibly irresistibly, from his "pure philosophy." The radically fundamental question in Leibniz is indeed, "Why is there something rather than nothing?"; but to that he also returns a moral-political answer, or set of answers: God is there, *ex necessitatis*, because "perfection" (which includes moral perfection above all) entails automatic existence, and then that necessary Being creates everything and everyone else in time by the moral principle of what is "best."[27] The whole of Leibnizianism is one huge "theodicy," one vast "universal jurisprudence" -- but theodicy is an account of what ought to be, what deserves to be, what has "sufficient reason" for being. To state it another way, it hardly matters whether one calls Leibniz a "theodist" or a "monadologist," because God as creator of the "best" world is the just "monarch" of substances or persons or monads. At bottom Leibniz, like all the greatest philosophers, is a moralist.

Leibniz will remain incomprehensibly strange, will perhaps even be thought guilty of "category mistakes," if one fails to see that for him theory and practice, God and men, theology and justice, are welded together by "perfection": the perfect Being, who exists *ex necessitatis*, must govern his created world as well as is possible (in the "best" way), and we (finite) beings must recognize and indeed feel that perfection (which leads to love as a "feeling of perfection"), and that love or *caritas* spreads from the perfect Being to those finite creatures whom he had "sufficient reason" to translate into existence. This incredibly ambitious universal jurisprudence, valid for any "mind" in any logically possible "world," must seem extravagant in our present moral-political world -- in which a Rorty argues that political principles have (and can have) no metaphysical-theological "foundations,"[28] and in which a Rawls wants to use only "thin" and widely-shared assumptions to underpin his theory of justice.[29] Leibniz' universal jurisprudence is, by contrast, "thick": it aims to deduce moral-political perfectionism from metaphysical-theological perfectionism. It aims to present earthly justice as an outgrowth of universal justice, as the limb of a tree is the outgrowth of the trunk.

Leibniz' final object in his universal jurisprudence, is to show that a just or wisely charitable perfect Being ("God is not only charitable, but charity itself "[30]) has actually chosen the "best" world from a range of logically possible ones. "It follows from the supreme perfection of God," he insists in *Principles of Nature and Grace*, "that in producing the universe he has chosen the best possible plan, in which there is ... the most power, knowledge, happiness, and goodness in created things that the universe allowed ... the most perfect actual world that is possible."[31] And Leibniz explicitly stresses that "one must seek the reason for the existence of the world, which is the whole assemblage of contingent things ... in the substance which carries with it the reason for its existence, and which in consequence is necessary and eternal."[32] For even if, as Leibniz often says, finite creatures "tend" toward existence in proportion to their "degree" of perfection (*Monadology*, prop. 54), that tendency cannot amount to a self-translation into existence. Anselm's "ontological" proof is valid only for the perfect Being, not for creatures who merely approach perfection. "All existences, except for the existence of God, are contingent [*Omnes existentiae excepte solius Dei Existentia sunt contingentes*]."[33]

Leibniz does not want to make matters easy for himself, however, by minimizing the objections which could be raised against God's having created a "best" contingent universe through *caritas sapientis*: on the contrary, he magnifies the difficulties, and the opening sections of Book 1 of the *Theodicy* constitute a *catalogue raisonnée* of the charges that can be brought against God--by fideistic skeptics such as Bayle, but above all by those who use harsh Calvinist notions of unmeritable grace and salvation in a way that makes God guilty of an arbitrary "acceptation of persons."

Surely Leibniz knew that he was taking a great moral risk in calling the world "best" and in ascribing "wise charity" to God; for an opponent could say that it is precisely in virtue of *caritas sapientis* that a perfect being would refrain from giving existence to "metaphysically evil" substances. If one just stresses God's power, in the manner of the Book of Job or Hobbes' *Leviathan*, or of St. Paul's *Romans* ("hath not the potter power over the clay?"), the problem disappears: then it is only a matter of what God can do--everything--not of what he "ought" to do. But Leibniz gives himself no avenue of escape.

It is not just the case, Leibniz begins, that some critics allege that God is the cause of sin or moral evil (since "all creatures and their actions derive from him the reality which they have"); it is not just that some say that, "conservation being a perpetual creation...man is perpetually created corrupt and erring"; it is not just that "man is exposed to a temptation to which it is known that he will succumb, thereby causing an infinitude of frightful evils," so that "wickedness will hold sway and virtue will be oppressed on earth." Those charges might be thought to raise doubts about the charity and perfection of God; "but it is much worse when one considers the life to come, since but a small number of men will be saved and since the rest will perish eternally"[34]--at least on a late Augustinian or Calvinist or Jansenist view.

> Furthermore these men destined for salvation will have been withdrawn from the corrupt mass through an unreasoning election, whether it be said that God in choosing them has had regard to their future actions, to their faith or to their works....One must return to the same conclusion that God is the final reason of salvation, of grace, of faith and of election in Jesus Christ...[and] that he gives faith or salvation to whom he pleases, without any discernible reason for his choice.[35]

So it is a "terrible judgment," Leibniz goes on to say (in *Theodicy* I, 5), that

God, "giving his only son for the whole human race and being the sole author and master of the salvation of men," nonetheless "saves so few of them" and "abandons all the others to the devil his enemy," who "torments them eternally and makes them curse their creator," even though "they have all been created to diffuse and show forth his goodness, his justice and his other perfections." And this outcome "inspires all the more horror" since the "sole cause why these men are wretched to all eternity" comes from "God's having exposed their parents to a temptation that he knew they would not resist"--so that these men "are condemned to be forever rebellious against God and plunged in the most horrible miseries," even though "some of them have perchance been less guilty than some of that little number of the elect, who were saved by a grace without reason."[36]

Heightening rather than damping down the difficulties for a "wisely charitable" God which are found in an "Augustinian" position, Leibniz finally says that one can see how some "theodicies" represent God "as an absolute prince employing a despotic power, unfitted to be loved and unworthy of being loved"--a despot who plunges men into an "abyss of sin" even if they have "never heard" of Jesus Christ.[37] If, despite these "horrible miseries," Leibniz can persuasively urge that the world is "best," and created in time through the justice or *caritas sapientis* of a perfect being, then his philosophical triumph is enormous.

God is perfect in every way, and therefore perfectly just (inter alia); if he endowed the "best" world with real existence in time--which he plainly did, since finite substances do not exist *ex necessitatis*--he must have had a morally praiseworthy "sufficient reason" for doing so. (This reason may be beyond our reason, Leibniz urges, but it cannot be contrary to it; for now we see through a glass, darkly, but then...) In short, Leibniz insists, there are no conclusive "reasons at all" which can overcome "the assurance or confidence in God wherewith we can and ought to say that God has done all things well." The objections of skeptics such as Bayle are therefore only "prejudices and probabilities" which are "overthrown by reasons incomparably stronger."[38]

III

Such, in outline, is Leibniz' "universal jurisprudence," in which a fully defensible "best" world is made and governed by a wisely charitable and universally benevolent *être infiniment parfait*. Obviously Leibnizian "optimism"-- in which, so to speak, "bestness" is good enough--was a perfect object of ridicule for the Voltaire who fused French skepticism and English empiricism: the very things which Leibniz strove to combat (but *from* a deep understanding of both).

As is well-known, Voltaire's first serious encounter with Leibniz came in 1740, when his lover Mme du Chatelet was converted to Leibnizianism, and when Voltaire could not resist reacting to this domestic embarrassment--by writing *La Métaphysique de Newton, ou Parallèle des sentiments de Newton et de Leibniz*. In this early work Voltaire is skeptical indeed, but not yet morally outraged by optimism: "Even if it were possible that God had done everything that Leibniz imagines, must one believe it on the basis of simple possibility?...Do you not feel how much such a system is purely imaginary? Is not the admission of human ignorance superior to so vain a science? What a use of logic and geometry, when one...walks toward error with the very torch which is destined to enlighten us!"[39]

That is comparatively mild, and indeed throughout the 1740s Voltaire's skeptical anti-Leibnizianism (grounded in "human ignorance") is mocking rather than indignant: the Leibnizians, Voltaire wrote to Maupertuis in 1741, "spread about in Germany all the horrors of Scholasticism, surcharged with sufficient reasons, with monads, with indiscernibles, and with all the scientific absurdities which Leibniz brought into the world through vanity, and which the Germans study because they are Germans."[40] (Here, to be sure, there is a provisionally humorous intimation of what will later become grimly angry: Leibniz' Scholastic "horrors" are [in effect] Gothic, and the equally Gothic Roman Catholic Church intolerantly countenanced the killing of Calas and the Chevalier de La Barre. Things equal to the same [Gothic] thing are equal to each other; *ergo*....)

But in the celebrated 1755 poem on the Lisbon earthquake--the poem that so distressed Rousseau--mere Voltairean mocking skepticism gives way to furious indignation against those (Pope-disciples as well as the Leibnizians) who imagine that they can find a divinely sufficient reason for

> Cent mille infortunés que la terre dévore,
> Qui, sanglants, déchirés, et palpitants encore
> Enterrés sous leurs toits, terminent sans secours
> Dans l'horreur des tourments leurs lamentables jours![41]

And Voltaire goes on to say: "You cry, 'all is well,' in a lamenting voice / The universe denies you, and your own heart has refuted the error of your mind a hundred times." This leads him to the dark end of the Lisbon poem which he (at first) thought of using:

> Mortels, il faut souffrir,
> Se soumettre en silence, adorer, et mourir.

But this was simply too dark, and so in the definitive version of the poem Voltaire brought himself to say,

> Un jour tout sera bien, voilà notre espérance;
> Tout est bien aujourd'hui, voilà l'illusion.
> Les sages me trompaient, et Dieu seul a raison.[42]

If one read just *Candide* (1758) and the poem on the Lisbon earthquake (1755), one might think that Voltaire's considered view is that the justice of God (governing a best world) is *refuted* by piling up the bloody corpses of crushed women and babies -- here mere "intolerance" pales in comparison -- and especially that Leibniz' *jurisprudence universelle* of "charity" and "benevolence" is overturned. Strictly speaking, however, Voltaire's early insistence on "human ignorance" (in the 1740 *Métaphysique de Newton*) is still in place in the 1750's: we cannot *know* the justice or the injustice of God or the cosmos, and should therefore have the skeptical decency to stop declaring dogmatically that "all is good" or "all is evil" -- especially because dogma is nothing but rationalized "imagination." This is clear in the very important article, "Du bien et du mal, physique et moral," from Voltaire's *Dictionnaire philosophique:*

> We here treat of a question of the greatest difficulty and importance. It relates to the whole of human life. It would be of much greater consequence to find a *remedy* for our evils; but no remedy is to be discovered, and we are reduced to the sad necessity of tracing out their origin. With respect to this origin, men have disputed ever since the days of Zoroaster, and in all probability they disputed on the same subject long before him. It was to explain the mixture of good and evil that they conceived the idea of two principles - Oromazes, the author of light, and Arimanes, the author of darkness; the box of Pandora; the two vessels of Jupiter; the apple eaten by Eve; and a variety of other systems. The first of dialecticians, although not the first of philosophers, the illustrious Bayle, has clearly shown how difficult it is for Christians who admit only one God, perfectly good and just, to reply to the objections of the Manichaeans who acknowledge two Gods - one good, and the other evil.[43]

Having audaciously lumped apple-eating Eve with Pandora and the Manicheans -- all useless in accounting for evil -- Voltaire now adds sarcastically that "the Christian doctors (independently of revelation, which makes everything credible) explain the origin of good and evil no better than the partner-gods of Zoroaster."[44] And the main "Christian doctor" in his philosophical sights is almost certainly Leibniz.

> When they say God is a tender father, God is a just king; when they add the idea of infinity to that of love, that kindness, that justice which they observe in the best of their own species, they soon fall into the most palpable and dreadful contradictions. How could this sovereign, who possessed in infinite fulness the principle or quality of human justice, how could this father, entertaining an infinite affection for his children; how could this being, infinitely powerful, have formed creatures in His own likeness, to have them immediately afterwards tempted by a malignant demon, to make them yield to that temptation to inflict death on those whom He had created immortal, and to overwhelm their posterity with calamities and crimes![45]

And Voltaire goes on to say, in a way that ridicules (rather than refutes) the Leibnizian notion of God as a "just" monarch of a "best" universe, that

> A father who kills his children is a monster; a king who conducts his subjects into a snare, in order to obtain a pretext for delivering them up to punishment and

torture, is an execrable tyrant. If you conceive God to possess the same kindness which you require in a father, the same justice that you require in a king, no possible resource exists by which, if we may use the expression, God can be exculpated; and by allowing Him to possess infinite wisdom and infinite goodness you, in fact, render Him infinitely odious; you excite a wish that He had no existence; you furnish arms to the atheist, who will ever be justified in triumphantly remarking to you: Better by far is it to deny a God altogether, than impute to Him such conduct as you would punish, to the extremity of the law, in men.

We begin then with observing, that it is unbecoming in us to ascribe to God human attributes. It is not for us to make God after our own likeness. Human justice, human kindness, and human wisdom can never be applied or made suitable to Him. We may extend these attributes in our imagination as far as we are able, to infinity; they will never be other than human qualities with boundaries perpetually or indefinitely removed; it would be equally rational to attribute to Him infinite solidity, infinite motion, infinite roundness, or infinite divisibility. These attributes can never be His.[46]

This had been Voltaire's general view since the 1734 *Traité de métaphysique:* "We have no other ideas of justice than those which we formed for ourselves from [considering] all action which is useful to society, and in conformity to laws established by us for the common good; now, this idea being only an idea of relations between men, it can have no analogy whatever to God. It is as absurd to say ... that God is just or unjust, as to say that God is blue or square."[47]

Philosophy informs us that this universe must have been arranged by a Being incomprehensible, eternal, and existing by His own nature; but, once again, we must observe that philosophy gives us no information on the subject of the attributes of that nature. We know what He is not, and not what He is.
With respect to God, there is neither good nor evil, physically or morally.[48]

And finally Voltaire says (in the *Dictionnaire philosophique*), in a way that makes it clear that we know human injustices perfectly, even if we know nothing about divine or cosmic justice and injustice, that

Man, you say, offends God by killing his neighbor; if this be the case, the directors of nations must indeed be tremendous criminals; for, while even invoking God to their assistance, they urge on to slaughter immense multitudes of their fellow-beings, for contemptible interests which it would show infinitely more policy, as well as humanity, to abandon. But how--to reason merely as philosophers--how do they offend God? Just as much as tigers and crocodiles offend him. It is, surely, not God whom they harass and torment, but their neighbor. It is only against man that man can be guilty. A highway robber can commit no robbery on God. What can it signify to the eternal Deity, whether a few pieces of yellow metal are in the hands of Jerome, or of Bonaventure? We have necessary desires, necessary passions, and necessary laws for the restraint of both; and while on this our anthill, during the little day of our existence, we are engaged in eager and destructive contest about a straw, the universe moves on in its majestic course, directed by eternal and unalterable laws, which comprehend in their operation the atom that we call the earth.[49]

This is aimed at Leibniz as much as at anyone else: Leibniz hoped that from charity and benevolence (as outgrowths of universal jurisprudence) a man might avoid "killing his neighbor" -- and that is because, for Leibniz, the "essence" of Christianity is Pauline charity. For Voltaire the "essence" of Christianity was (almost) two millennia of intolerant cruelty and institutional oppression; Voltaire thought of what the Church had often done, while Leibniz thought that the Church ought to live up to its own highest principle, *caritas*. For Voltaire, "human ignorance" of divine justice should skeptically keep us from judicially murdering "heterodox" people; for Leibniz, *wise* charity should achieve the same effect. And this means that there is no necessary connection between skepticism and toleration, even if these (historically) go together in certain cases, e.g., that of Pierre Bayle.[50] One can be as morally certain as Leibniz, and nonetheless urge toleration grounded in *caritas sapientis*; one can be as skeptical as Hobbes ("to know truth is to remember that it was made by ourselves" [*De Cive* XVIII]) and nonetheless try to impose artificial certainty through sovereign "authority."[51] Similar practical results can be arrived at from radically different paths: if one is a skeptic who also thinks that "the passion to be reckoned upon is fear," one may less-than-tolerantly impose an official religion as an antidote to civil war -- while a belief in "wise charity" may lead one to tolerantly accept any religion which (in turn) makes love and benevolence ethically central. Radically different (and utterly incompatible) theoretical bases may lead to nearly-converging practical conclusions: both Kant and Bentham, after all, wrote treatises called *Eternal Peace*.[52] So if skeptical Voltairean "ignorance" and confident Leibnizian *caritas sapientis* both lead to toleration, that should not be an occasion for astonishment.

IV

What then must Voltaire's conclusion be? That we know nothing about the justice or injustice of the universe or of God -- since, to know what is "best," one would have to know what might be absolutely good or perfect, and that is hidden from us. And therefore the calamities of *Candide* prove nothing universally. (For Voltaire we don't even know, with Kant in the second *Critique*, that God *would* be just -- crowning virtue with deserved happiness, realizing the *summum bonum* -- if he turns out to exist.[53]) Thus *Candide* cannot "refute" Leibniz (though it can effectively mock him) -- since no one can demonstrate the justice or injustice of the cosmos. The all-too-real injustices, cruelties and horrors of the human world prove nothing *beyond* themselves -- except, perhaps, that if we stay quietly at home, "work without reasoning," and cultivate our gardens, we will be less likely to be hanged, drowned, beaten, cannibalized, raped, or mutilated. The "garden" at the end of *Candide* -- a very limited post-Eden -- is another anti-Leibnizian joke: for at the end of the *Theodicée* Leibniz says that we can (as a logical possibility) imagine a slightly different Sextus Tarquinius (the last king of Rome) who does not rape Lucretia (and thereby bring about the Roman Republic) -- a Sextus Tarquinius with different "predicates" who buys a house with a *garden* in a "city between two seas" (Constantinople, where Candide also winds up), and who lives happily ever after.[54] But that (logically possible) Sextus is not the one whom God "translates into existence" as the *conditio sine qua non* of the "best" world. (*Candide*, of course, is full of anti-Leibnizian jokes: Mademoiselle Cunégonde is given her name, almost certainly, because Leibniz *als Historiker* prided himself on having discovered that Cunégonde was an 11th century founder of the (Guelph) House of d'Este in Northern Italy, and that the House of d'Este was the forerunner of the House of Brunswick-Lüneburg -- the ruling house of Hannover, which Leibniz served for forty years. If Cunégonde was, in effect, a proto-Hannoverian, what better joke at Leibniz' expense than to make her the heroine of *Candide* but to ruin her and make her horribly ugly? Voltaire the scholar would have known all of this information about Leibniz/Cunégonde from the 1724 Paris publication of the *Oeuvres posthumes* of Mabillon -- the antiquarian with whom Leibniz had an historical *Briefwechsel* in the 1690s.[55]

We know, of course, that Voltaire did not always stay quietly in his "garden" at Ferney, in imitation of Candide at the end of that *conte*: Voltaire's skeptical conviction that divine or "universal" justice (or injustice) is unknowable never led him to give up the fight against particular earthly injustices, against tyranny, war and superstition -- against known, visible, sensible evils which are not "imaginary." When he might have "worked without reasoning" he instead defended Calas and the Chevalier de La Barre against judicial murder by intolerant ecclesiastical courts and superstitious *parlements*. (Or rather, *hélas*, he worked for their posthumous rehabilitation.) He courageously faced down what Judith Shklar has called "the faces of injustice."[56] But here, in the realm of practice, he and Leibniz were not so far apart: Leibniz' favorite modern Christian writer, after all, was the Jesuit Father Friedrich Spee -- who had managed to abolish witchcraft trials in Mainz by a judicious appeal to "charity."[57] If Voltaire would have preferred to rest his toleration on "ignorance" and "weakness" sooner than on *caritas*, that is simply because he could not break up and separate the parts of St. Paul's I *Corinthians* as successfully as Leibniz -- who underscored "the greatest of these is charity" (I *Corinthians* xiii) while minimizing the "body" of the Church (I *Corinthians* xii). Leibniz' selective Christianity let him raise Christian morality (*caritas*) above Christian historical institutions in a way that Voltaire could not follow. "The most absurd of all despotisms," Voltaire wrote, "the most humiliating for human nature, the most contradictory and lethal, is that of priests; and of all the priestly empires, that of the priests of the Christian religion is without a doubt the most criminal. It is an affront to our Gospels, for Jesus said in twenty places: 'But many that are first shall be last; my kingdom is not of this world; the son of man came not to be served, but to serve etc.'"[58] After all, when Diderot wrote to Voltaire in the 1760s to praise him for his "heroic" defense of widows and orphans, above all in the Calas case, he styled Voltaire "sublime, honorable and dear *antéChrist*"[59] -- and that is not merely ironic. For Diderot, as for Voltaire, letting what is "best" in Christianity (*caritas*) triumph over what is worst (centuries of intolerant oppression) simply won't do; a Leibnizian talent for finding and stressing "the best" did not find its way into French skepticism.

To be sure, the Voltaire of the *Dictionnaire philosophique* knew that Christian charity -- really, consistently *followed* -- *should* bring about toleration: "of all religions, the Christian ought doubtless to inspire the most toleration, although hitherto [i.e. historically] the Christian have been the most intolerant of all men." Why, Voltaire lamentingly asks, "do the same men who in private admit charity, beneficence and justice [in effect Leibnizian' universal jurisprudence] oppose themselves in public so furiously against those virtues?" In the article "Theism," he adds: "we are all brethren; if one of my brothers, inspired by the most fraternal charity... does not salute our common Father with the same ceremonies as I do, ought I to cut his throat and tear out his heart?"[60] And in the article "Virtue," Voltaire makes "the honest man" say: "as to charity, is it not that which the Greeks and Romans understood by humanity -- love of your neighbor? This love is nothing, if it does not act; beneficence therefore is the only true virtue." (In other words, even *before* St. Paul and St. John, Plato in the *Symposium* and Cicero in *De Amicitia* had glorified sublimated love and *caritas*. Cicero indeed, had asked, "Is there no natural charity [*caritas naturalis*] between the good?") But Voltaire has "the honest man" answered by "the theologian" who says merely, "What a fool!"[61]

In his late essay, *Un Chrétien contre six juifs* (1776), Voltaire says: "The great Fénelon embraced all men in his spirit of *toleration*, in his zeal and in his love."[62] There was *caritas*. But what happened? Fénelon was crushed by the tyrannical theocrat, Bossuet, who had Fénelon condemned at Rome and then internally banished by Louis XIV.[63] For Voltaire the practices of the Church always overwhelm its ideals. And therefore it's not safe to ground toleration in charity: for even Bossuet (theoretically) appealed to that virtue.

Leibniz' determination to save everything "best" in the Western tradition, to have a truly synthetic (not merely syncretistic) philosophy, finds no echo in French skepticism. For Voltaire the history of Christianity simply contained too much that was "infamous," worthy of being crushed. Leibniz was more selective, and perhaps more charitable, in his view of the past.

V

At first sight one might think that Diderot's version of "tolerant skepticism" -- which is more light-hearted, free and fanciful than Voltaire's, though finally more radical -- would be tolerant of Leibnizian optimism. And at that same first sight Diderot does indeed shower praise on Leibniz:

"When one considers oneself and compares one's talents with those of a Leibniz," Diderot wrote in the *Encyclopédie* (that Leibnizian project par excellence), "one is tempted to throw books away and seek some hidden corner of the world where one may die in peace. This man's mind was the foe of disorder: the most entangled things fell into order when they entered it. He combined two great qualities which are almost incompatible with each other--the spirit of discovery and that of method; and the most determined and varied study, through which he accumulated knowledge of the most widely differing kinds, weakened neither the one quality nor the other: In the fullest meaning these words can bear, he was a philosopher and a mathematician."[64]

What one notices in this encomium, however, is that it is Leibniz the mathematician and discoverer who is praised, not Leibniz the theologian-jurisconsult who had insisted on "wise charity" in God's governance of a "best" universe (and in human conduct as well). Nor is this surprising, given Diderot's general view of theologians in the *Additions aux penseés philosophiques*: "Lost in an immense forest at night, I have only a little light to show me the way. Along comes a stranger who says to me: 'Friend, blow out your candle, the better to find your way.' This stranger is a theologian."[65]

In that passage, characteristically, Diderot's makes his case in a "novelistic" way -- not unexpectedly, given that his greatest accomplishments are precisely philosophical novels: *Rameau's Nephew, D'Alembert's Dream, Jacques the Fatalist and his Master*. And it is in the last named work that Diderot reveals that it is not just theologians of whom one should be skeptical (and not too tolerant), but even those who try to insist on Christian charity and benevolence as something (supposedly) separable from Christian history and institutions -- in the manner of Leibniz in the *Theodicée*.

In the brilliantly invertebrate *Jacques the Fatalist and his Master* (which is in some sense "parallel" to *Candide*, and probably inspired by it), Diderot has Jacques perform a notable act of charity -- giving the last of his money to an impoverished widow whose children will otherwise go hungry. And what then happens? He is beaten senseless by highway robbers who are furious that there is nothing left to steal; and when the Master hears this story he indignantly draws his sword to "defend" charitable Jacques, whom a just God has not protected.

> Master: I'm avenging you. Tell me how it is that whoever wrote out the great scroll [in the heavens] could have decreed that such [violent robbery] would be the reward of a noble act? Why should I, who am merely a miserable compound of faults, take your defense, while He calmly watched you being attacked, knocked down, manhandled and trampled underfoot, He who is supposed to be the embodiment of all perfection?
> Jacques: Master, be quiet; what you are saying stinks to high heaven of heresy.[66]

But Jacques himself later adds, with skeptical resignation, that "we travel in darkness underneath whatever it is that is written up above."[67]

Why should Diderot, like Voltaire, have been so reluctant to "save" *caritas sapientis* as a basis for toleration (and for morality more generally) -- a basis which is arguably more "positive" and obligation-imposing than skepticism and "ignorance"? To see that, one must turn to the little-treated *Entretien d'un philosophe avec la Maréchale de* *** (1765). In the *Entretien*, the *philosophe*, Crudeli, begins by asking Mme la Maréchale whether "the terrible ravages" which religion "has caused in past times, and which it will cause in times to come," are "compensated" by the *petits biens* which religion is alleged to provide. For religion, Crudeli urges, has "created and perpetuated the most violent antipathy between the nations," so that there is not a single Moslem "who does not imagine that he is performing an action which is pleasing to God and to the Holy Prophet in exterminating all the Christians -- who, for their part, are scarcely more tolerant." And the *philosophe* goes on to say that religion "has perpetrated in society, between citizens, and in the family, the strongest and the most lasting hatreds." To this la Maréchale, who wants *(à la* Leibniz) to rescue Christian morality from Christian historical practices, says: "There are abuses, indeed; but it is not the thing itself [*ce n'est pas la chose*]." But the *philosophe* Crudeli retorts that, "It is the thing itself, if the abuses are inseparable from it."[68]

> La Maréchale: And how will you show me that the abuses of religion are inseparable from religion?
> Crudeli: Very easily: tell me, if a misanthrope had decided to cause the unhappiness of the human race, what better thing could he have invented than the belief in an incomprehensible Being about whom men could never agree, and to whom they would attach more importance than to their life? Now, is it possible to separate the notion of a divinity from the deepest incomprehensibility and the greatest importance?
> La Maréchale: No.
> Crudeli: Draw conclusions, then.
> La Maréchale: I conclude that it is an idea which is not without consequences in the heads of fools.
> Crudeli: And add that the fools have always been and will always be the greatest number; and that the most dangerous [of them] are those fashioned by religion.[69]

To make it even clearer that religion is "inseparable" from historical "abuses" -- so that one cannot precipitate out *caritas* and leave behind a mere historical residue -- Diderot wrote the first version of the article *Philosophe* (for the *Encyclopédie*) in such a way that "reason" is privileged against *central* Christian "things," not just against historically peripheral ones: reason is privileged against "grace" and St. Augustine, not just against the Crusades or Pope Alexander VI:

> Reason is to a philosopher what grace is to a Christian in the system of Saint Augustine....
> The philosopher, then, is an honest man who acts in all things according to reason, and who combines good morals [*moeurs*] and sociable qualities with a mind disposed toward reflection and preciseness.

...Civil society is, as it were, the only divinity that he recognizes on earth; he worships it, and honors it by probity, by an exact attention to his duties, and by a sincere desire not to be a useless or troublesome member of it....[70]

(The last clause is almost certainly a deliberate inversion of the *pensée* in which Pascal, paraphrasing I *Corinthians* xii, complains of "useless" members who, out of egomania, decline to submit their self-loving *volonté particulière* to the *bien général* of the Church's body.[71])

Having (literally) deified "civil society," Diderot then goes on to "secularize" *caritas* or neighbor-love by finding a tolerant, non-religious version of charity in the "pagan" Roman playwright, Terence. "Our philosopher ... is full of humanity. He is the Chremes of Terence, who feels himself a man and who interests himself in the good or bad fortune of his neighbor out of humanity alone. *Homo sum, humani a me nihil alienum puto.*"[72] This purely naturalized humanitarianism -- which would of course be tolerant, *inter alia* -- has no religious component (let alone foundation); but that is in no way astonishing, given the naturalism of Diderot's theory of justice as revealed in the *Réfutation d'Helvétius* (1762): "It is possible to find in our natural needs, in our life, in our existence, in the way we are [physically] organized, and in the sensitivity which exposes us to pain, an eternal basis for justice and injustice."[73] (Here "eternal" physiology and psychology displace an eternal Being and Platonic "eternal moral verities" of the sort cherished by Leibniz.) Diderot adds, in the *Réfutation*, that it is "very difficult" to be "a good moralist" without being "an anatomist, naturalist, physiologist, and doctor." In that utterance there is no place for "doctors" of theology, who in any case would find heretical the "eternity" of "natural" needs -- which amounts to the eternity of (uncreated) matter. And all of this leads (naturally) to Diderot's insistence, in the *Supplément au voyage de Bougainville*, that "in basing morality on the eternal relations which exist between men, religious law perhaps becomes superfluous, and the civil law should only be the enunciation of the law of nature."[74] In that sentence the word "perhaps" is itself superfluous; it's only there as a small "hedge," easily jumped over.

In a Diderotian state fully governed by (purely natural) "humanity" and "justice," in which religious law is "superfluous," generous toleration would prevail, grounded in an (eminently reasonable) skepticism about everything supposedly "beyond" nature (metaphysical). By contrast, for Diderot, "intolerance" and religion always ("inseparably") accompany each other in unjust states: "In an intolerant state," Diderot urges in the *Lettre à mon frère* (1760), "the prince would only be an executioner in the pay of priests." And even if the prince were an "infidel," one still might not escape religious cruelty and persecution: "If an unbelieving prince asked the missionaries of an intolerant religion how it would treat those who don't believe at all, they would either have to admit something odious, or lie, or maintain a shameful silence."[75] (Almost certainly, for Diderot, they would choose to remain silent -- for "if an intolerant person explained clearly what he really is, what corner of the earth would not be closed to him?")

For Diderot it was out of (purely natural) "humanity" and "justice" that Voltaire, forsaking his garden, had posthumously rehabilitated the most celebrated victims of intolerance and religious superstition -- above all Calas. In a provocative letter (1763), Diderot half-hopes for a Christianity which would "save" the virtuous Voltaire:

> Oh! my friend, what a fine employment of genius. This man [Voltaire] must have soul, sensitivity, that injustice revolts him and that he feels the attractiveness of virtue. For what are the Calas to him? what can interest him in them? what reason has he for interrupting the work that he loves, in order to occupy himself with their defense? If there were a Christ, I assure you that Voltaire would be saved.[76]

And in *Rameau's Nephew*, Diderot makes one of his characters say, "I know of certain deeds which I would give all I possess to have done. [Voltaire's] *Mahomet* is a sublime work, but I would rather have rehabilitated the Calas family."[77] In that *cause celèbre*, for Diderot, Voltaire's "love" turned from his own "great works" to altruistic "good works" -- a Christian phrase, to be sure, but one now endowed with a purely "natural" significance. The "inseparability" of Christian doctrine from "abuses" means that what one now needs is Ciceronian *caritas naturalis* -- not something supposedly supernatural or metaphysical. What one now needs is something (or someone) Roman, not Roman Catholic. And that is why, in naturalizing "humanity," Diderot quotes Terence rather than any thinker in the Christian tradition. The Pauline *caritas* celebrated by Leibniz yields to the *caritas naturalis* of Cicero, Terence and Seneca; it is no accident that one of Diderot's last works dealt with Senecan morality.[78] For Seneca lived in a Rome without a Vatican.

VI
CONCLUSION

If Voltaire, and sometimes even Diderot, could occasionally bring themselves to countenance a "naturalized" charity which is to be found in Cicero or Terence rather than in Paul or Augustine -- a tolerant, naturalistic humanism which denies Pascal's insistence that charity is "supernatural" and "of another order" made possible by "grace" (*Penseé* 792 [Br.]) -- this was not their typical or characteristic way of shoring up toleration. Especially for Diderot (but often for Voltaire as well), one cannot "separate" a Christian theology of charity/love from horrific "Christian" historical practices; and for Voltaire as much as for Diderot one cannot put *enough* space between "theologians" and "executioners." For Voltaire in *The ABC*, it is a lamentable fact of Christian history that gradually

> ...it was generally established that all men are born possessed by the Devil and damned: without doubt a strange idea, an abominable idea, a horrible insult to the Divinity to imagine that the Divinity continually creates sensitive, rational beings just to be tortured forever by other beings, who are themselves eternally engulfed in torment. If the executioner in Carlisle, who in one day tore the hearts from eighteen supporters of Prince Charles-Edward, had been given the responsibility of founding a dogma, this is the one that he would have chosen. Moreover, it would have been necessary for him to have been drunk on brandy, for unless he had both the soul of an executioner and that of a theologian, he would never have been able to invent in cold blood a system by which so many thousands of infants still at the breast are delivered up to eternal executioners.[79]

It is the last phrase which is revelatory: even St. Augustine, the principal "Father" of the Church, in insisting on the eternal damnation of unbaptized infants, was the mere agent of "eternal executioners." And who can "eternal" executioners be, if not the "persons" of the Trinity?.

Leibniz, of course, in the *New Essays concerning Human Understanding*, urged that one should not attribute anything to God which would be detrimental to a "universal justice" of wise charity and benevolence, and that St. Augustine sometimes (in his harsh proto-Jansenist vein) "rushed to the other extreme... in spite of his intelligence and insight ... and damned children who die unbaptized."[80] Since one cannot *know* the distribution or operation of grace, for Leibniz, one should suggest nothing which would be incongruent with *caritas sapientis* as the governing principle of a "best" world.

For Leibniz, indeed, toleration (and generosity and enlightenment) flow out of wise charity and universal benevolence more reliably than out of skepticism and "human ignorance": for every Pierre Bayle who thinks that skepticism should lead to tolerated diversity (including the acceptance of "virtuous" atheists), there is a Thomas Hobbes whose skepticism is so colored by fear of fatally clashing "appetites" that he imposes authoritarian "sovereignty" -- so that life will not be "solitary, poor, nasty, brutish, and short."[81] (For Leibniz, Hobbes' "initial step was false, namely to seek the origins of justice in the fear of the evil rather than in concern for the good, as if men had to be wicked in order to be able to be just."[82])

It is at least arguable that toleration is better defended by something like Leibnizian "wise charity" or Kantian respect for persons as "objective ends" in themselves -- both of which make toleration a *duty*, a "moral necessity" -- than by a skepticism which may lead equally in the direction of Bayle *or* Hobbes. Here Kantianism might be presently more eligible than Leibnizianism, since the Kingdom of Ends has no theological foundations; that might help sever the connection between "theologians" and "executioners" which Voltaire and Diderot could not help seeing. But they saw it because -- in the cases of Calas and de La Barre -- it was really there; perhaps it was in virtue of their theological skepticism that something like Leibniz' version of tolerant *caritas* has finally been able to make itself persuasive in our times.

It may be that the good effects of 200 years of Enlightenment religious skepticism have, ironically, finally made Leibniz' effort to "save" *caritas* from historical Christianity both plausible and (above all) *safe*. For the 18th century Church still had the fresh blood of Calas and de La Barre on its hands -- not to mention the dried blood of Giordano Bruno and the spiritual blood of Galileo. Christianity may owe its moral "salvation" to the very Voltaire and Diderot who thought it "infamous."

NOTES:

1. Voltaire, *The Works of Voltaire*, trans. and ed. Tobias Smollett, et. al., modernized by J. Morley (London and Paris: Dumont et Cie, 1901), Vol. IX, *Dictionnaire philosophique*, article "grâce," 340 ff.

2. See Philippe Sellier, *Pascal et Saint Augustin* (Paris: A. Colin, 1970), Ch. 3.

3. See Leibniz, *Théodicée*, Amsterdam 1710, passim. See also André Robinet, *G.W. Leibniz: Le meilleur des mondes* (Paris: Presses Universitaires de France, 1994), Ch. 3.

4. Voltaire, letter to Maupertuis (October 1741), in *Voltaire: Correspondence and Related Documents*, ed. Theodore Besterman, in *Complete Works of Voltaire* (Geneva and Oxford: Voltaire Foundation, 1968-77), Best. 3756.

5. For this point in Leibniz' thought, see Patrick Riley, *Leibniz' Universal Jurisprudence: Justice as the Charity of the Wise* (Cambridge, Mass.: Harvard University Press, 1996), Ch. 5.

6. See "Introduction" to *Voltaire: Political Writings*, ed. David Williams (Cambridge: Cambridge University Press, 1994), xiii ff.

7. Williams, *Voltaire: Political Writings*, xiii ff.

8. Voltaire, *Dictionnaire philosophique*, op. cit., article "Bien, tout est bien," 90 ff.

9. Plato, *Republic*, Book VII (Jowett ed. Vol. IV, 401 ff.)

10. For Leibniz' use of three kinds of evil, see *Théodicée*, op. cit., Preliminary Dissertation.

11. Voltaire, *Candide*, trans. and ed. Robert M. Adams (New York: Norton, 1991) (2nd ed.), Ch. 28, 69-70.

12. Voltaire, *Dictionnaire philosophique*, op. cit., "Bien," 93.

13. Leibniz, *Principles of Nature and Grace*, in *Monadology*, ed. R. Latta, (Oxford: Oxford University Press, 1898), 412 ff.

14. Leibniz, *Codex Iuris Gentium*, xi, in *Political Writings*, ed. Patrick Riley (Cambridge: Cambridge University Press, 1988) (enlarged ed.), 171.

15. St. Paul, I *Corinthians* xiii (King James version).

16. St. Augustine, *De Libero Arbitrio* (c. 395-396), Book I.

17. Hume, *Treatise of Human Nature* (1740), Book III, Ch.1 ("Moral Distinctions not Derived from Reason").

18. Rousseau, *Émile*, trans. B. Foxley (London: Everyman, 1910), 7 ff.

19. Kant, *Über den Gebrauch Teleologischer Prinzipien in der Philosophie* in *Werke*, ed. E. Cassirer (Berlin: Bruno Cassirer Verlag, 1922), Vol. V, 322.

20. Leibniz, *Théodicée*, op.cit., passim.

21. St. John, *Gospel*, 17:34 (King James version)

22. See Giles Deleuze, *The Fold* (Minneapolis: University of Minnesota Press, 1992), Ch. 3.

23. On this point see Riley, *Leibniz' Universal Jurisprudence*, op. cit., Ch.1, "Foundations."

24. Leibniz, *Théodicée*, op. cit., partic. Book III.

25. Leibniz, letter to Joachim Bouvet (1697), in *Sämtliche Schriften und Briefe* (Academy Edition), (Berlin: Akademic Verlag, 1922), Series I, Vol. 14, 831.

26. Especially Bertrand Russell in *A Critical Exposition of the Philosophy of Leibniz* (Cambridge: Cambridge University Press, 1900), passim.

27. See Robinet, *Le meilleur des mondes*, op. cit., 98 ff.

28. Richard Rorty, "Pragmatism, Relativism, Irrationalism," in *Consequences of Pragmatism* (Minneapolis: University of Minnesota Press, 1982), 160 ff.

29. John Rawls, *A Theory of Justice* (Cambridge, Mass.: Belknap Press of Harvard University Press, 1971), 39 ff.

30. Leibniz, "Unvorgreiffliches Bedencken," in *Textes Inédits*, ed. G. Grua (Paris: Presses Universitaires de France, 1948), Vol. I, 430.

31. Leibniz, *Nature and Grace*, in Latta, op. cit., 417.

32. Leibniz, *Théodicée*, op. cit., I,7.

33. Leibniz, *De Libertate* (c. 1680), in *Textes Inédits*, op. cit., Vol. I, 288.

34. Leibniz, *Théodicée*, op. cit., "Preface."

35. Leibniz, *Théodicée*, I, 5.

36. Leibniz, *Théodicée*, I, 3-5.

37. Leibniz, *Théodicée*, I, 4.

38. Leibniz, *Théodicée*, I, 5.

39. Voltaire, *La métaphysique de Newton*, in *The Works of Voltaire*, Smollett-Morley ed., op. cit., Vol. II.

40. Same as note 4 (supra).

41. Voltaire, poem on the Lisbon earthquake, in *The Works of Voltaire*, Smollett-Morley ed., op. cit., Vol. II.

42. Voltaire, *The Works of Voltaire*, Vol. II. See also Ernst Cassirer, *Philosophy of the Enlightenment* (Princeton: Princeton University Press, 1951), 141 ff.

43. Voltaire, *Dictionnaire philosophique* (Smollett-Morley, op. cit.,) 264 ff.

44. Voltaire, *Dictionnaire philosophique,* 264 ff.

45. Voltaire, *Dictionnaire philosophique,* 265-66.

46. Voltaire, *Dictionnaire philosophique*, 267.

47. Voltaire, *Traité de métaphysique*, in *Works of Voltaire*, op. cit., Vol. 1, 87 ff.

48. Voltaire, *Dictionnaire philosophique*, op. cit., 267-268.

49. Voltaire, *Dictionnaire philosophique*, 267-268.

50. On this point see the many articles by Dr. Sally Jenkinson, as well as the Introduction to her edition of Bayle's *Political Writings* (Cambridge: Cambridge University Press, 1998).

51. See Michael Oakeshott, Introduction to *Leviathan*, in *Hobbes on Civil Association*, (Oxford: Basil Blackwell, 1975), Ch. 1.

52. Kant, *Eternal Peace*, in *Political Writings*, ed. H. Reiss, (Cambridge: Cambridge University Press, 1973).

53. Kant, *Critique of Practical Reason*, trans. L.W. Beck, (Chicago: University of Chicago Press, 1955), 108.

54. Leibniz, *Théodicée*, op. cit., sec. 413 ff.

55. André Robinet, *Iter Italicum* (Florence: Olschki Editore, 1988), Ch. 3.

56. Judith N. Shklar, *The Faces of Injustice* (New Haven: Yale University Press, 1990), passim.

57. See Riley, *Leibniz' Universal Jurisprudence*, op. cit., 153-54.

58. Voltaire, "Republican Ideas," no. V, in *Political Writings*, op. cit., 196.

59. Diderot, letter to Voltaire (1766), cited in Yvon Relaval, "*Diderot, lecteur de Leibniz?*," in *Revue des sciences humaines*, fasc. 112, October-December 1963, 244 ff.

60. Voltaire, *Dictionnaire philosophique*, op. cit., Vol. V.

61. Voltaire, *Dictionnaire philosophique*, article "Virtue," Vol. X.

62. Voltaire, *Un Chrétien contre six juifs*, in *Oeuvres complètes*, ed. Condorcet et. al. (Paris: 1784-89), Vol. 37, 156 ff.

63. See "Introduction" to Fénelon's *Telemachus*, ed. Patrick Riley (Cambridge: Cambridge University Press, 1994), vii ff.

64. Diderot, "Leibniz," in *Encyclopédie*, ed. Assezat (Paris: Didot Frères, 1875), Vol. XV, 440.

65. Cited in Belaval, "*Diderot, lecteur de Leibniz?*" op. cit., 248.

66. Diderot, *Jacques the Fatalist and His Master*, Penguin ed., London 1965, 202.

67. Diderot, *Jacques the Fatalist and His Master*, 203.

68. Diderot, *Oeuvres complètes*, Pléiade edition, Paris 1951, 897 ff.

69. Diderot, *Oeuvres complètes*, 897 ff.

70. Diderot, "Philosophe," in *Encyclopédie*, op. cit., Vol. XIX.

71. Pascal, *Pensées*, ed. L. Prunschvicg, in *Oeuvres de Pascal* (Paris: Les Grands Écrivain, 1914), Vol. XIV, nos. 483 ff.

72. Diderot, "Philosophe," in *Encyclopédie*, op. cit., Vol. XIX.

73. Diderot, *Réfutation d'Helvétius*, in *Oeuvres complètes*, op. cit., 763 ff.

74. Diderot, *Supplément,* in *Oeuvres complètes*, op. cit., 645 ff.

75. Diderot, *Lettre à mon frère*, in *Oeuvres complètes*, op. cit., 789.

76. Diderot, letter to Voltaire, cited in A.O. Wilson, *Diderot* (Princeton: Princeton University Press, 1973).

77. Diderot, *Le neveu de Rameau*, in *Oeuvres complètes*, op. cit., 1146 ff.

78. See A.O. Wilson, *Diderot*, op. cit., "Conclusion."

79. Voltaire, *The ABC*, in *Political Writings*, op. cit., 111-112.

80. Leibniz, *New Essays concerning Human Understanding* (Cambridge: Cambridge University Press, 1982), Book IV, Ch. 18.

81. Hobbes, *Leviathan*, ed. M. Oakeshott (Oxford: Basil Blackwell, 1946), Ch. 13, 82.

82. Leibniz, letter to Thomas Smith (1695), in *Textes Inédits*, op. cit., I, 407.

Index

About the Contributors

Michael Gillespie is Professor of Political Science and Philosophy at Duke University. He is the author of *Hegel, Heidegger and the Ground of History* (1986) and *Nihilism Before Nietzsche* (1995), and many other essays and articles in the history of political philosophy.

Maryanne Cline Horowitz is Professor of History and Title IX Officer, Occidental College, and Associate, Center for Medieval and Renaissance Studies, University of California, Los Angeles. A Consulting Editor of the *Journal of the History of Ideas*, she is the editor of *Race, Gender and Rank: Early Modern Ideas of Humanity* and *Race* (1992), *Class, and Gender in Nineteenth-Century Culture* (1991); she is the author of *Seeds of Virtue and Knowledge* (1998) and numerous articles.

Alan Craig Houston is Associate Professor of Political Science, University of California, San Diego. The author of *Algernon Sidney and the Republican Heritage in England and America* (1991), he is currently writing a book on the Levellers and co-editing a volume of essays on politics and culture in England after the Restoration.

Shirley Letwin died in June, 1993 in London. She had taught at numerous universities and authored *The Pursuit of Certainty: David Hume, Jeremy Bentham, John Stuart Mill, Beatrice Webb* (1965), *The Gentleman in Trollope* (1982), and *The Anatomy of Thatcherism* (1993).

Alan Levine is Assistant Professor of Government in The School of Public Affairs at American University. He has published articles on Montaigne and Chinua Achebe and is completing a book on Montaigne's Political Thought.

Joshua Mitchell is Associate Professor of Government at Georgetown University. He is the author of *Not By Reason Alone: Religion, History and Identity in Early Modern Political Thought* (1993) and *The Fragility of Freedom: Tocqueville on Religion, Democracy, and the American Future* (1995).

Patrick Riley is Oakeshott Professor of Political and Moral Philosophy at the University of Wisconsin (Madison). His publications include *Will and Political Legitimacy* (1982), *Kant's Political Philosophy* (1983), *The General Will Before Rousseau* (1986), *Leibniz' Universal Jurisprudence: Justice as the Charity of the Wise* (1996), and more than twenty book chapters and 150 articles.

Diana J. Schaub is Associate Professor of Political Science at Loyola College in Maryland. She is the author of *Erotic Liberalism: Women and Revolution in Montesquieu's "Persian Letters"* (1995).

Steven B. Smith is Professor of Political Science and Master of Branford College at Yale University. His most recent book, *Spinoza, Liberalism, and the Question of Jewish Identity,* was awarded the Ralph Waldo Emerson Prize in 1997.

Nathan Tarcov is a Professor in the Committee on Social Thought, the Department of Political Science, and the College of the University of Chicago. He is the author of *Locke's Education for Liberty* (1984) and numerous articles, translator (with Harvey C. Mansfield, Jr.) of Machiavelli's *Discourses on Livy* (1996), and editor (with Clifford Orwin) of *The Legacy of Rousseau* (1997) and (with Ruth Grant) of Locke's *Some Thoughts Concerning Education* and *Of the Conduct of the Understanding* (1996).

Kenneth R. Weinstein is Deputy Director of the Shalem Center, a research institution for Israeli public policy and Jewish social thought. His doctoral dissertation from the Department of Government at Harvard University is entitled *Atheism and Enlightenment in the Political Philosophy of Pierre Bayle* (1992).